BEAST
AND
MAN

BEAST AND MAN

THE ROOTS OF HUMAN NATURE

MARY MIDGLEY

A MERIDIAN BOOK

NEW AMERICAN LIBRARY

TIMES MIRROR

NEW YORK AND SCARBOROUGH, ONTARIO

NAL BOOKS ARE AVAILABLE AT QUANTITY DISCOUNTS
WHEN USED TO PROMOTE PRODUCTS OR SERVICES. FOR
INFORMATION PLEASE WRITE TO PREMIUM MARKETING DIVISION,
THE NEW AMERICAN LIBRARY, INC., 1633 BROADWAY,
NEW YORK, NEW YORK 10019.

MERIDIAN TRADEMARK REG. U.S. PAT. OFF. AND FOREIGN COUNTRIES
REGISTERED TRADEMARK—MARCA REGISTRADA
HECHO EN FORGE VILLAGE, MASS., U.S.A.

SIGNET, SIGNET CLASSICS, MENTOR, PLUME, MERIDIAN and
NAL BOOKS are published in the United States by
The New American Library, Inc.,
1633 Broadway, New York, New York 10019,
in Canada by the New American Library of Canada Limited,
81 Mack Avenue, Scarborough, Ontario M1L 1MB

First Meridian Printing, March, 1980

1 2 3 4 5 6 7 8 9

PRINTED IN THE UNITED STATES OF AMERICA

Library of Congress Cataloging in Publication Data

Midgley, Mary, 1919–
Beast and man.

Bibliography: p.
Includes index.
1. Man.   I. Title.
BD450.M496   1980   128'.3   79–26813
ISBN 0–452–00529–9

TO MY SONS,

with many thanks for making
it so clear to me that the
human infant is not blank paper

Contents

Acknowledgments

Much of the work for this book was done in 1976 at Cornell University, which I visited at the invitation of Max Black, a member of the Program on Science, Technology, and Society, to introduce some discussions on Man and Beast at interdisciplinary seminars. I am most grateful to everybody there for the endless help and encouragement they offered in my confused attempts to organize a subject so interdisciplinary as to be nearly impossible to sort out. As so many people were kind, I can name here only the two who probably made me think hardest, Professor Black himself and William Wimsatt. The paper I later wrote for their program is the basis for Chapter 11 of this book.

Colleagues at Newcastle University have been more than generous with their assistance. In particular, Alec Panchen and Alan Ibbotson read the middle part of the book and saved me from many howlers, recommended much reading, and in general oversaw the book's zoological aspects. Jane Heal kindly looked through Chapter 10 and helped me with problems about language. Renford Bambrough and Julius Kovesi generously vetted Chapter 9, including a great deal that has finally been crowded out for lack of room. I thank each of them warmly for their time and attention. Errors that remain are entirely my contribution.

I thank my family and friends for putting up with a lot, and for much help with the argument. I am especially grateful to colleagues in my university's Adult Education Department, who originally gave me the chance to get this confusing subject off the ground by inviting me to teach an adult class on it—a method I vigorously recommend to anyone who wants to get an impossible bundle of questions under control. I am indebted to the students in that class, who refused to allow me to get away with easy answers.

I am grateful to the editor and proprietors of *Philosophy* for allowing me to draw on a paper called "The Concept of Beastliness," published in *Philosophy*, 48 (1973). This forms the basis for the first three chapters.

I thank the following for permission to include quotations: Harvard University Press for those from *Sociobiology* by Edward O. Wilson, copyright © 1975 by the President and Fellows of Harvard College; Faber and Faber Ltd. and Harcourt Brace Jovanovich, Inc., for lines from T. S. Eliot's *The Hippopotamus* and *The Waste Land*; Anthony Powell and his publishers, William Heinemann Ltd. and Little, Brown, Inc., for those from his novels *The Acceptance World* and *Books Do Furnish a Room*; Michael Frayn and Wildwood House Ltd. for those from *Constructions*; Mrs. Hodgson and Macmillan (London and Basingstoke) for "Reason Has Moons," from *Collected Poems*, by Ralph Hodgson; Chatto and Windus Ltd. and Random House, Inc., for the extract from *Within a Budding Grove*, copyright 1924 and renewed 1952 by Random House, Inc., and reprinted from *Remembrance of Things Past*, Volume 1, by Marcel Proust, translated by C. K. Scott Moncrieff; and the Society of Authors, literary representative of the Estate of A. E. Housman, and Jonathan Cape Ltd., publishers of Housman's *Collected Poems*, for lines from *A Shropshire Lad*.

MARY MIDGLEY

Newcastle upon Tyne

Introduction

We are not just rather like animals; we *are* animals. Our difference from other species may be striking, but comparisons with them have always been, and must be, crucial to our view of ourselves. This is a general book about how such comparisons work and why they are important. The gap between man and other animals comes, I believe, in a slightly different place from the one where tradition puts it, as well as being rather narrower. The traditional view has certainly distorted argument in ethics and may have caused mistakes about the possibilities open to humanity.

Many people dislike using concepts evolved for talking about animal behavior to describe the human scene. The first use of such concepts, however, is the uncontroversial one of telling us more about animals themselves. This knowledge alone directly alters our idea of man, because that idea has been framed, traditionally, by contrast with a profoundly ignorant and confused idea of other species. We can now do something to correct this ignorance and confusion. The kind of animal that careful observation shows us does not seem by any means so obviously incomparable with men as the travesty we are used to.

Still, people have a lot of obvious and important things that other species do not—speech, rationality, culture, and the rest. Comparison must deal with these. I have tried to discuss some of the most important of them, not attempting at all to deny their uniqueness, but merely to grasp how they can occur in what is, after all, a primate species, not a brand of machine or a type of disembodied spirit. I have tried to show these capabilities as continuous with our animal nature, connected with our basic structure of motives.

Obviously, this attempt must invade the territory of a dozen subjects. But the project still belongs to philosophy, because finding how the basic concepts of *any* inquiry work is a philosophical problem. Of course this does not mean that a philosopher must always be brought in to do it. Scientists of the caliber of Newton or Darwin do their own philosophizing. And we all, in our thinking, work out to some extent our own system of concepts. Philosophy, like speaking prose, is something we have to do all our lives, well or badly, whether we notice it or not. What usually forces us to notice it is conflict. And on the matter of our animal nature a pretty mess of conflicts has arisen— between different elements in the common-sense tradition, between common sense and various learned studies, among those learned studies themselves, and between all these and the remarkable facts turned up by those who, in the last few decades, have taken the trouble to observe dispassionately the behavior of other species.

I first entered this jungle myself some time ago, by slipping out over the wall of the tiny arid garden cultivated at that time under the name of British Moral Philosophy. I did so in an attempt to think about human nature and the problem of evil. The evils in the world, I thought, are real. That they are so is neither a fancy imposed on us by our own culture, nor one created by our will and imposed on the world. Such suggestions are bad faith. What we shall abominate is not optional. Culture certainly varies the details, but then we can criticize our culture. What standard do we use for this? What is the underlying structure of human nature which culture is designed to complete and express? In this tangle of questions I found some clearings being worked by Freudian and Jungian psychologists, on principles that seemed to offer hope but were not quite clear to me. Other areas were being mapped by anthropologists, who seemed to have some interest in my problem, but who were inclined (at that time) to say that what human beings had in common was not in the end very important; that the key to all the mysteries did lie in culture. This seemed to me shallow. It is because our culture is changing so fast, because it does *not* settle everything, that we need to go into these questions. What shapes, and what ought to shape, culture? I then came upon another clearing, this time an expansion of the borders of traditional zoology, made by people studying the natures of other species. They had done much work on the question of what such *a nature* was—recent work in the tradition of Darwin, and indeed of Aristotle, bearing directly on problems in which Aristotle was already interested, but which have become peculiarly pressing today. What I found here seemed to me, and still seems, enormously important, though there are great difficulties in connecting it neatly with other things we know, without being slick and oversimple. This book is an attempt to work out some of these connections.

I have tried to write without technical terms. Because so many disciplines border the topic, I think it must necessarily be discussed in plain language. This is not at all a piece of condescension, a translation of learned matter into rougher and less suitable terms. Each subject evolves technical language to suit its own assumptions. These may well be good enough to use within that subject, and still serve badly for relating it to its neighbors. On very general questions of method, therefore, it is important to force oneself to write and speak plain English. As everyone used to the academic scene knows, the boundaries between subjects, recognized at any time have grown up partly by chance—they commemorate strong pioneering personalities, bits of teaching convenience, even the flow of research money, as well as real principles of investigation. The true structure of the problems may cut right across them.

But besides this general consideration there is a special one about discussions of motives. Like many areas of moral philosophy, this is ground already familiar to common sense. Making up a terminology here is not at all like making one up for biochemistry or nuclear physics. The facts are not new. People have been trying to understand their own and other people's motives for thousands of years. They have thrashed out quite a sophisticated terminology, namely, the one we use every day. Of course it needs refining and expanding, but to by-pass it and start again as if it were all ignorant babble is arrogant and wasteful. B. F. Skinner has demanded a brand-new technical language for psychology, on the ground that "the vernacular is clumsy and obese."[1] What elegant slimness technical language may possess, however, is bought at the price of reinforcing prejudice. Jargon always tends to make unwelcome facts unstatable. We can all see this when we look at other people's jargon. It is just as true of our own. In this book, I have used a few technical terms in ethology[2] because I am talking *about* them; they stand for concepts that are useful to all of us, but new, and they need explaining. Some of them are, in any case, entering common language. Apart from them, I try to stick to ordinary speech.

Consideration of motives brings up the matter of free will. I had better say at once, that my project of taking animal comparisons seriously does not involve a slick mechanistic or deterministic view of freedom. Animals are not machines; one of my main concerns is to combat this notion. Actually only machines are machines. Nothing else is made by human beings from parts and for purposes entirely supplied by themselves. Nothing else therefore can be understood simply by reading off those parts and purposes from the specifications. The model of comparison with machines is useful enough in some simple animal contexts, notably for explaining insect behavior. At any higher level it is an incubus. The motivation of the more advanced creatures is enormously more complex than the tradition supposes. That is why it can, as I am suggesting, throw light on human motives. But understanding and explaining motives does not compromise freedom; nor does even predicting acts necessarily do so. A person seriously committed to a political cause may vote predictably, and intelligibly, in an election. He does not vote less

---

1. See *The Behavior of Organisms* (New York, 1938), p. 7.
2. The term *ethology*, first coined by Konrad Lorenz and his followers to describe their own studies of animal behavior, and disowned by some who disagreed with him, is now quite generally used for all systematic animal behavior studies. The convenience of having this single word, together with some progress in settling disputes, make this use helpful, and I shall follow it.

freely than someone who flips a coin at the last minute. So if we find comparison with animals any help in understanding motives, it will not mean that conduct is not free. And since animals are not (as Descartes supposed) automata, the issue of freedom does not make comparing man with other species a degrading irrelevance.

Man has his own nature, not that of any other species. He cannot, therefore, be degraded by comparison, if it is careful and honest, because it will bring out his peculiarities, it will show what is unique about him as well as what is not.[3] Certainly he is *more* free than other species. But that extra freedom flows from something natural to him—his special kind of intelligence and the character traits that go with it. It is not, and does not have to be, unlimited. (In fact, unlimited freedom is an incoherent notion.) It is not something added by his own will after birth, or by some external force called culture.

A very recent controversy closely related to this theme has changed the scope and balance of my book. I had completed the first draft before I came across Edward O. Wilson's remarkable tome, *Sociobiology*,[4] and the suggestion arose that I should add some comments on it.

What Wilson says on many points rounds out and completes admirably what I want to say. On others I differ from him sharply. Both the agreement and the difference light up my theme. His book is an immensely comprehensive survey of social life throughout the animal kingdom. The determined combination of breadth with scholarly thoroughness is most impressive. Because it is so encyclopedic, because it bears hallmarks of academic respectability unmistakable to the most obtuse, it has got through even to many of those who still persisted in believing that the study of social behavior in animals was something

3. For further criticism and a line on the controversies now current, see R. A. Hinde's works listed in the bibliography. Opposition to Lorenz's line may be found there, also in T. C. Schneirla's paper "Some Conceptual Trends in Comparative Psychology" (*Psychological Bulletin*, Nov. 1952), and at a popular level in Ashley Montagu's works. But I think we should probably trade off Montagu against Robert Ardrey, stop squabbling, and take it that we are all trying to discuss the same world.

4. *Sociobiology: The New Synthesis* (Cambridge, Mass., 1975).

thought up on a Saturday afternoon by Robert Ardrey. On the other hand, the book has run into opposition of a political kind from people who believe that any notion of inborn active and social tendencies, if extended to man, threatens human freedom.

I take this opposition extremely seriously; I believe it to be thoroughly misconceived, and very dangerous to human freedom itself. The notion that we "have a nature," far from threatening the concept of freedom, is absolutely essential to it. If we were genuinely plastic and indeterminate at birth, there could be no reason why society should not stamp us into any shape that might suit it. The reason people view suggestions about inborn tendencies with such indiscriminate horror seems to be that they think exclusively of one particular way in which the idea of such tendencies has been misused, namely, that where conservative theorists invoke them uncritically to resist reform. But liberal theorists who combat such resistance need them just as much, and indeed usually more. The early architects of our current notion of freedom made human nature their cornerstone. Rousseau's trumpet call, "Man is born free, but everywhere he is in chains,"[5] makes sense only as a description of our innate constitution as something positive, already determined, and conflicting with what society does to us. Kant and Mill took similar positions. And Marx, though he officially dropped the notion of human nature and often attacked the term, relied on the idea as much as anybody else for his crucial notion of Dehumanization.

People have been strangely determined to take genetic and social explanations as *alternatives* instead of using them to complete each other. Combining them without talking nonsense is therefore by now fearfully hard work. But there is no future in refusing to try, and no value in starting a game of cops-and-robbers whenever anybody else does. Wilson works from the zoologist's angle, and is often naive in his use of general concepts. The cure for this shortcoming is not to abuse him for trying, but to do the job better. He speaks not just for himself,

5. *Social Contract*. Bk. 1, chap. 1.

but for a multitude of scientifically trained people who want to extend the methods they know over a wider territory. Where these methods help, others should accept them; where they do not, people should show why. No dogfights are called for. As far as academic territory is concerned, it has to be admitted that Wilson asks for trouble by offering to take over ethics and psychology as part of his subject on his way to putting the "bio" into sociology. ("Having cannibalized psychology, the new neurobiology will yield an enduring set of first principles for sociology"—p. 575.) But then, those concerned with all these subjects have for some time asked for trouble themselves by grossly neglecting the genetic angle. They cannot really complain if somebody tries to fill the vacuum they leave.

Where politics is concerned, however, Wilson offers no grievance at all. For every political purpose, but particularly for reforming and revolutionary ones, we need to understand our genetic constitution.[6] The notion that reformers can do without this understanding is a bizarre tactical aberration, closely comparable to that of the Christian church in the nineteenth century when it rejected the theory of evolution—and indeed rather like its similar rejection of Galileo in the seventeenth. In both these cases, the church exhausted, distorted, and discredited itself in order to combat a quite imaginary danger. Most Christians today readily accept that the earth does not have to be in the middle of the universe, and that God, if he could create life at all, could do it just as well through evolution as by instant fiat. Many would add that this more complex and organic performance is the greater miracle. They have not for some time needed to retain, as a literal statement of fact, the story in Genesis 1 and 2, which, besides contradicting itself, contradicts many other things that clearly have to be believed. Neither do reformers and revolutionaries now need to retain the dogma that man is indeterminate. In fact, they need it like a hole in the head. That dogma, in its sociological form, where it says that man is entirely the product of his society, must, as I have suggested, destroy all the

6. A point admirably and sympathetically made by Theodosius Dobzhansky in discussing the ambiguities of *inherit* (*Mankind Evolving* [New Haven, 1962], chap. 2).

central arguments for freedom. In its Existentialist form, where it says that we create ourselves *out of nothing*, it does not make sense.

These somewhat sweeping remarks merely sketch in tele-graphic form points I shall be discussing at length in this book. I am taking both Wilson's position and the arguments brought against him seriously. As to the opposition, I admit to some personal concern. Like most people who have spent time and caught colds on plenty of leftwing demonstrations, I am un-happy when I see the comrades tearing off down a useless blind alley. There are real things in the world that require their atten-tion. What should trouble everybody, however, is the waste and distraction caused by such futile contentiousness. The strange habit of misrepresenting one's opponent's statements in order to prove that he does indeed belong to the dreaded opposition has been carried to extraordinary lengths against Wilson.[7] There is plenty wrong with his book, and what is wrong can be answered—although answering it does involve some hard think-ing. There is also plenty right. Wilson, originally an expert on insect populations, does have a bias toward noticing inherited tendencies and ignoring causes that operate after birth. But that bias is overdue as a counter to its opposite. And he repeatedly explains that he does recognize the importance of social condi-tioning in man. Indeed he even tries to explain it, and that gets him into even more trouble.

Every attack on him I have seen protests strongly at his saying that "human beings are absurdly easy to indoctrinate; they *seek* it," and "men would rather believe than know" (*Sociobiology*, p. 562). Now this seems simply to be an explicit statement of the force of social conditioning, which is the very fact he is accused of neglecting. People are indeed very easily indoctrinated by their societies. That is what makes their nature so much harder to study than that of other species. But anyone who holds that we really *have no nature* is surely forced to believe that we are, not just absurdly, but *infinitely* easy to indoctrinate, since we can have

---

7. Those interested in this melancholy subject can find some of the material in question in *BioScience*, 26 (1976), no. 3 ("Sociobiology—Another Biological De-terminism"), and in the letters column of *The New York Review of Books*, November 13, 1976.

no inborn tendencies that either deflect or resist the process. No doubt the word *indoctrinate* sounds harsh. For the normal business of cultural acclimatization we might choose a milder one, keeping *indoctrinate* for the instilling of false opinions. But then—as everyone not wholly satisfied with the present state of the world must surely agree—people do very often hold false opinions. There are many iniquitous and confused societies around, kept going by the fact that people do absorb without criticism the beliefs of those around them. They would not do so if they did not feel the need for some sort of belief, or if they did not mind disagreeing with everyone in sight, or if they insisted on clear proof before they ever accepted a suggestion. Wilson simply points out that there is a general human tendency to pick up any belief that is current. He does not say that it is irresistible. But it certainly is one thing that has to be assumed to explain social conditioning. And it becomes especially relevant when people are perpetuating a *bad* society, one which fails to "reward" them with anything more palpable than the sense that they are agreeing with their neighbors and are supporting the honored status quo. Yet (as Wilson says) this same openness and suggestibility in us is a necessary condition of our building up any sort of culture. It is natural and useful. Acknowledging this does not commit us to saying that it is irresistible, or that it ought never to be resisted, or that it is the only tendency we have in relation to culture, or that it is always a good thing. Just what it does commit us to is the kind of question I shall be asking in this book.

In Part One I shall look at the suggestion that man is so different from other species as not to have a nature at all. I shall ask what this can mean. I shall try to size up the difficulties of thinking straight about the species barrier, and to clean up awkward concepts like Instinct, Purpose, and Nature itself. I conclude that, if we understand it properly, the acknowledgment that we have a nature does not harm human dignity.

In Part Two I ask how this nature ought to be studied. Here we have to consider the generous offer of Wilson and other biologists to take over the job. Many people share his suspicion that any decent inquiry is a part of some physical science, and ought to be conducted as such. I shall point out how much hard background thinking we need here which is not part of science itself, though it is necessary if science is to be properly done, and is itself "scientific" in the sense of being disciplined, methodical, and appropriate. I then demonstrate this point practically by clearing up a tangle of concepts, among them "the selfish gene" and "inclusive genetic fitness," which spoil Wilson's useful book and retard the general understanding of evolution.

In Part Three, I turn to the practical consequences. Can our understanding of our nature affect our lives? I look at the puzzling but deep-rooted notion of a fixed Upward direction in evolution. Social Darwinists and "evolutionary moralists" have hoped to use this as a direct practical guide. But the facts of evolution cannot guide us directly. They matter only insofar as they can help us to understand our nature, our emotional and rational constitution. Yet our understanding of that *does* give us practical guidance. Facts about it are directly relevant to values. Values register needs. It is a mistake to suppose that there is some logical barrier, convicting such thinking of a "naturalistic fallacy" (Chapter 9). We are not, and do not need to be, disembodied intellects. We are creatures of a definite species on this planet, and this shapes our values.

Part Four is really the core of the book. There I take it for granted that the general notion of our having a nature has been vindicated, and consider the relation of its various parts. I look at the traditional marks of man, such as speech, rationality, and culture, and try to show how we might view them, not as alien or hostile to the underlying emotional structure in which we so much resemble other species, but as growing out of and completing it. Reason and Emotion are not antagonists.

Part Five is a brief conclusion, pointing the way to further work. There I bulldoze, somewhat hastily, some more of the fences that have been held to prevent our seeing ourselves as in any serious sense a part of the biosphere in which we find ourselves, with the idea of showing how fatal—to our real dignity as well as to our survival—must be any insistence on radical isolation. I conclude that man can neither be understood nor saved alone.

Part One

CONCEPTUAL PROBLEMS
OF AN UNUSUAL SPECIES

The broad-backed hippopotamus
Rests on his belly in the mud;
Though he seems so firm to us,
He is merely flesh and blood.

Flesh and blood is weak and frail,
Susceptible to nervous shock;
While the True Church can never fail,
For it is based upon a rock.

—T. S. Eliot, *The Hippopotamus*

CHAPTER 1

Have We a Nature?

Understanding Our Motives

Every age has its pet contradictions. Thirty years ago, we used to accept Marx and Freud together, and then wonder, like the chameleon on the turkey carpet, why life was so confusing. Today there is similar trouble over the question whether there is, or is not, something called Human Nature. On the one hand, there has been an explosion of animal behavior studies, and comparisons between animals and men have become immensely popular. People use evidence from animals to decide whether man is naturally aggressive, or naturally territorial; even whether he has an aggressive or territorial instinct. Moreover, we are still much influenced by Freudian psychology, which depends on the notion of instinct.[1] On the other hand, many sociologists and psychologists still hold what may be called the Blank Paper view, that man is a creature entirely without instincts. So do Existentialist philosophers. If man has no instincts, all comparison with animals must be irrelevant. (Both these simple party lines have been somewhat eroded over time, but both are still extremely influential.)

---

1. For Freud's own discussion of this term, see his paper "Instincts and Their Vicissitudes," 1915, *Complete Psychological Works,* Tr. and ed. James Strachey et al. (London, 1948–1974), Vol. 14. For a good modern revision of Freudian views in relation to ethology, see Anthony Storr, *Human Aggression* (New York, 1968). I discuss instincts further myself in Chap. 3.

According to the Blank Paper view, man is entirely the product of his culture. He starts off infinitely plastic, and is formed completely by the society in which he grows up. There is then no end to the possible variations among cultures; what we take to be human instincts are just the deep-dug prejudices of our own society. Forming families, fearing the dark, and jumping at the sight of a spider are just results of our conditioning. Existentialism at first appears a very different standpoint, because the Existentialist asserts man's freedom and will not let him call himself a product of anything. But Existentialism too denies that man has a nature; if he had, his freedom would not be complete. Thus Sartre insisted that "there is no human nature. . . . Man first of all exists, encounters himself, surges up in the world, and defines himself afterwards. If man as the Existentialist sees him is not definable, it is because to begin with he is nothing. He will not be anything until later, and then he will be what he makes himself."[2] For Existentialism there is only the human condition, which is what happens to man and not what he is born like. If we are afraid of the dark, it is because we choose to be cowards; if we care more for our own children than for other people's, it is because we choose to be partial. We must never talk about human nature or human instincts. This implicit moral notion is still very influential, not at all confined to those who use the metaphysic of essence and existence. So I shall sometimes speak of it, not as Existentialist, but as Libertarian—meaning that those holding it do not just (like all of us) think liberty important, but think it supremely important and believe that our having a nature would infringe it.

Philosophers have not yet made much use of informed comparison with other species as a help in the understanding of man. One reason they have not is undoubtedly the fear of fatalism. Another is the appalling way terms such as *instinct* and *human nature* have been misused in the past. A third is the absurdity of some ethological propaganda.

About the fear of fatalism I shall not say much, because it seems to me quite misplaced here. The genetic causes of human

2. *Existentialism and Humanism,* tr. Philip Mairet (London, 1958), p. 28.

behavior need not be seen as overwhelming any more than the social causes. Either set would be alarming if treated as predestined to prevail. But no one is committed to doing that by admitting that both sets exist. Knowing that I have a naturally bad temper does not make me lose it. On the contrary, it should help me to keep it, by forcing me to distinguish my normal peevishness from moral indignation. My freedom, therefore, does not seem to be particularly threatened by the admission, nor by any light cast on the meaning of my bad temper by comparison with animals.

As for words such as *instinct, drive* and the *nature* of a species, ethologists have done a great deal of work here toward cleaning up what was certainly a messy corner of language. Much more is needed, and I shall try to do a little of it. Such words must somehow be reorganized, not just thrown away. They are necessary if we are to talk either about other species or about our own.

As for the bizarre uses that have sometimes been made of ethology, if we were to veto every science that has some lunatic exponents, we could quickly empty the libraries. What we must do in such cases is sort out the wheat from the chaff, and particularly observe just what sort of argument each point belongs to, what job it is doing. R. A. Hinde, a particularly fair and patient ethologist, remarks that in the present state of his science, "Superficial generalizations of wide validity and precise ones of limited scope are complementary to each other, and both are necessary".[3] He can say that again, and (as he obviously intends) without any offensive flavor to the word "superficial." Ethology is still being *mapped.* It is at the "descriptive phase." Whatever we are studying, it is universally agreed, we have to describe it sufficiently before we can usefully experiment on it. And the "descriptive phase" of any science is not something to be hurried through by blindly "collecting facts," ready-made, as a matchbox collector gathers matchboxes. It is more a time for hard thinking—for inventing concepts. *What counts as a fact depends on the concepts you use, on the questions you ask.* If someone buys stamps, what is going on can be described as "buying stamps," or

3. *Animal Behavior* (New York, 1966), p. 8.

as the pushing of a coin across a board and the receiving of paper in return—or as a set of muscular contractions—or one of stimulus-response reactions—or a social interaction involving role-playing—or a piece of dynamics, the mere movement of physical masses—or an economic exchange—or a piece of prudence, typical of the buyer. None of these is *the* description. There is no neutral terminology. So there are no wholly neutral facts. All describing is classifying according to some conceptual scheme or other. We need concepts in order to pick out what matters for our present purpose from the jumble of experience, and to relate it to the other things that matter in the world. There is no single set of all-purpose "scientific" concepts which can be used for every job. Different inquiries make different selections from the world. So they need different concepts.

People may still wonder, however, why we should need, for understanding human life, concepts developed to describe animal behavior. Perhaps I can best bring out the reason by glancing at a problem we often have when we try to understand human motivation—the shortage of suitable conceptual schemes.

Consider the case of someone (call him Paul) who buys a house with an acre of land, though he can scarcely afford it, instead of one without. How should we describe this "scientifically"? What should we say he is doing? Plenty of economic descriptions are available. He might be meaning to grow turnips to sell or to supply his household; he might be speculating for resale, or buying as an investment or as a hedge against inflation. It is interesting that even at this stage, where all the alternatives are economic, we already need to know his motive in order to decide among them. The "facts" of the particular transaction are not enough to classify it, or explain it, even economically, unless they include motives.[4] (Motives, of course, are not just his private states of mind, but patterns in his life, many of which are directly observable to other people.) We cannot say *what* he is doing until we know *why* he does it.

---

4. The question what "facts" are is not so simple as it might look. See pp. 110, 178 (note).

Now, what happens if the motives are not economic? Paul, it turns out, is not trying to make money out of the land at all. When asked, he says that he bought it to secure his privacy. He hates being overlooked by strangers. As his whole conduct is consistent with this, we believe him. Besides believing, however, we still need to *understand* this motive. That is, we want to see how it fits into the background of his life, and of human life generally.

Shall we accept a simple Marxist interpretation, that he is showing off his riches to establish his class status? This will not get us far. Of course people do show off for that reason. But merely saying so does not account for the particular forms showing off takes. The ostentatious rich buy big cars, because those are what most people would like to have if they could. They do not usually display their status by burning themselves to death on piles of paper money in the streets. And it is the basic taste that we are trying to understand. Explaining motives by ostentation is always producing a box with another box inside it. We must ask next; why display *that*? This was the weakness of Thorstein Veblen's view of art as conspicuous expenditure to impress the populace. As later and more subtle Marxists have pointed out, if art is to be worth displaying, it has to have a real point in the first place.[5] Of course a particular ostentatious person can display things he sees no point in. Whole groups within a society may do it; many Romans thus collected Greek art. But this is still parasitical. It depends on acknowledging the authority of people who do see the point, and treating them as the norm. It needs too, I think, an explicit doctrine that the thing itself actually is valuable, with reasons given. Thus, the more people explicitly praise pictures, or horses, or yachts, or abbeys to pray for one's soul, the more likely other people with no genuine taste for these things are to want them. But this wanting is a *by-product* of the praise. It is not what the praise itself is about. Ostentation, in fact, is just one of the cure-all political explanations which people produce for motives and which turn out circular. The

5. For example, Ernst Fischer in *The Necessity of Art*, tr. Anna Bostock (Penguin, 1963).

most central case is power. The desire for power is necessarily secondary to other desires, because power is *power to do* certain things, and valuing those things has to come first. Those who really pursue power just for its own sake are neurotics, entangled in confusion by habit and destroying their own lives. Hobbes realized this:

> So that in the first place, I put for a general inclination of all mankind, a perpetual and restless desire of power after power, that ceaseth only in Déath. And the cause of this is not always that a man hopes for a more intensive delight than he has already attained to; or that he cannot be content with a moderate power: but because he cannot assure the power and means to live well, which he hath present, without the acquisition of more.[6]

This puts power in its place as an insurance. But Hobbes still made it central and probably never realized how much this circular psychology limited the value of his political theory. I suspect that Marx's position was similar. Nietzsche, when he made the Will to Power a primary motive, did try to give it a more direct meaning. He thought of power as straightforward dominance over other people—indeed, more specifically still, delight in tormenting them[7]—which is certainly clearer, but happens to be false, except of psychopaths.

Now Paul certainly might be just being ostentatious, buying land he did not want, solely because he saw other rich men doing so. But if so, his case would be a parasitical one, and we should need to shift our attention, if we wanted to understand the motive, to some rich man who actually did want the stuff. This same consideration works even more strongly against another equally fashionable, and more respected, shortcut, the notion of con-

---

6. *Leviathan*, Pt. 1, chap. 11. The character of Widmerpool in Anthony Powell's series *The Music of Time* is a splendid study of someone who "cannot be content with a moderate power," having really decided, as Powell says, to "live by the will." The philosopher who is most reliably clear on the point that power is only a waiting room for actuality is Aristotle.

7. See, for example, *The Genealogy of Morals*, tr. Walter Kaufmann, Essay 2, sec. 6, end, where he makes the totally false claim that "apes . . . in devising bizarre cruelties anticipate man and are, as it were, his prelude." Also *Beyond Good and Evil*, sec. 229. Nietzsche always regarded the fascination with power as a sign of strength, though it seems quite as plausible to say, with Hobbes, that it is a sign of weakness.

formity. He bought it, some say, because his society had conditioned him to value it. Now (again) some people certainly are
so distractedly conventional that they will do almost anything to
be like the neighbors. But their existence depends on having
neighbors who are not like them, who make positive suggestions.
If the neighbors too did not care what they did apart from
conforming, there would be nobody to generate the standards
that everybody conforms to. Society is not a subsistent Being, a
creative divinity. Not everybody can always be at the receiving
end of culture.

Paul, we will say, knows what he is doing, to the extent that
what moves him actually is the motive he mentions, not his class
or society. Indeed, both may disapprove of what he does, and he
himself may even be rather puzzled by his motive, in the sense
that its strength surprises him, and that it is not explicitly linked
to his value system.[8] In this sense, he does *not* quite know what
he is doing. He needs further understanding of what his motive
means or amounts to. We all have motives sometimes that put us
in this quandary, which is why we badly need to understand our
motives better.

His motive then really is the wish for privacy. He "hates being
overlooked by strangers."

I have picked this motive because it is one on which all the
main traditional theories of motive are particularly unhelpful—a
fact that may well leave Paul, if he is an educated fellow, puzzled,
defensive, and even somewhat ashamed of its force. Freud does
supply us with the notions of voyeurism and exhibitionism. But
these are positive tastes. How will they explain anybody's *dislike*
of being looked at? Certainly there could be an inversion here, a
horror of sex. If someone has a morbid and excessive fear of
being looked at, we might suspect that it linked up with a disturbance of his sexual life, and there would be ways to check this
suspicion. But perfectly normal people want privacy; indeed,
everybody sometimes does so unless he is a gravely deranged
exhibitionist. And since we do not need (as Freud did) to balance
a contemporary concealment of sex by dragging it forcibly into

---

8. Such a situation can be seen in the U.S.S.R., where the demand for country
houses, though ideologically incorrect, is still strong.

every explanation, we can ask dispassionately whether there is evidence for a sexual motive of any explanatory value. This must be something more than the mere sexual *aspect* which (as Freudians rightly point out) most motivation can be found to have if you really look for it. All the main strands of human motivation—affection, fear, aggression, dominance, sex, laziness—pervade our lives and have some influence in shaping all our actions. Sexual behavior itself can obviously have its aggressive, frightened, or domineering aspect. But sexual motivation does not seem to help us in understanding the notion of privacy.

Freud's weakness here can be seen in his startlingly perverse and insensitive way of interpreting the nightmare of his patient the Wolf Man.[9] As a child of five or less, this man had dreamed that, as he lay in bed, his window fell open of its own accord, and he saw six or seven white wolves standing in the walnut tree outside and staring at him intently. Freud ruled that this dream was not a dream about being stared at at all, but about staring, and that it stood for a (hypothetical) occasion when the child must have watched his parents making love. It does not matter much here that Freud's preferred view was probably wrong, since the Wolf Man, as a Russian aristocrat, not a middle-class Viennese, would not have been sharing his parents' bedroom. What matters is Freud's overlooking the distinct and primitive horror of *being stared at*. The patient emphasized two things about his dream, which, he said, "made the greatest impression on him, first, the perfect stillness and immobility of the wolves, and secondly, the strained attention with which they looked at him."[10] Both these things Freud simply transmuted into their opposites. The stillness, he said, must be regarded as standing, contrariwise, for "the most violent motion," namely that of the copulating parents, and the attention had to be that of the child himself staring at them. By these principles of interpretation, anything can, quite literally, mean anything.

In citing Freud at his least helpful I do not mean to travesty

9. See *The Wolf-Man and Sigmund Freud*, ed. Muriel Gardiner (Penguin, 1973).
10. Ibid., pp. 196–198.

him. Of course he was often more sensible than this. But on many puzzling topics, many whole areas of life, he had really nothing helpful to say, because he was not interested in them for themselves at all, only in using them to round out a particular view of sex. And in considering many of these, parallels with other species can be helpful. Staring is one such case. It might seem a small matter, but it is part of a most important complex.[11]

Being stared at produces horror widely, not only in man, but in a great range of animal species. In most social creatures, a direct stare constitutes an open threat. Normal social approaches to those one does not know well always proceed somewhat indirectly, with various forms of greeting to show one's friendly intentions, interspersed with intervals of turning away and appearing occupied with something else. And eye contact in particular is at first limited to brief glances, often broken off and renewed. To stare steadily while you approach someone, or to stand still staring after he has seen you, is as direct a threat as can be made. *Why* this should be so is an interesting field for inquiry. It may well have something to do with the fact that predators naturally stare fixedly at prospective prey before jumping on it. And they are of course regarding it as an object, not as a possible friend—which is just the effect a direct stare conveys to a human being. Whatever the cause, so strong and so general is this tendency that a number of species have been able to exploit it by developing eyelike spots on their bodies, with which they frighten off their enemies. Many species of butterfly have separately developed detailed and lifelike eye-spots on their wings. Displaying these effectively frightens off predators, some of which never attack such a butterfly again. And this effect has been shown to vary according to how closely the spots actually resemble eyes.[12] Human beings, of course, deliberately produce a similar device by painting eyes on things. "Staring eyes have a threatening effect, and spellbinding eye-spots are therefore widely used as protective devices on uniforms, ships, houses and

11. Claustrophobia and agoraphobia are other examples. They, too, seem to be primarily disorders of our spatial orientation.
12. See Niko Tinbergen, *Curious Naturalists* (New York, 1968), pp. 157–171.

the like."[13] Also in advertisements. But because pictures stay still, we are not so much upset by their staring. When a live human being does it, it is most unnerving. Those stared at often feel as much attacked as if they had been actually abused or hit. This is not a cultural matter. I have seen a cheerful baby eight months old burst into tears and remain inconsolable for some time on being stared fixedly at by strange aunts, although the aunts were only vaguely curious and absentminded. Dogs too, as is well known, can be "stared down." People sometimes take this as evidence that they recognize men as their superiors, but all it actually shows is that, if you exhibit hostility to someone smaller than yourself, he will dislike it and probably go away. Dogs do not stare at each other except in the challenge to a fight, when the stare appears, along with the obligatory slow, steady approach, the growl, and the bristling hair, as a natural expression of hostility. And the primates seem to avoid the direct stare strongly.

Thus it would be little comfort, if one were overlooked by staring neighbors, to know that they were merely curious. The stare is not just a threat. It constitutes an actual intrusion.

Are we any further on with understanding what is worrying Paul? I certainly think so. If people, like other creatures, quite directly and naturally mind being stared at, this in part explains his touchiness on the subject. But what, you may wonder, about the numerous people who live at close quarters, overlooked, and do not mind it?

We should notice that it is primarily *strangers* who cause alarm. People in small primitive societies know everybody around them well. So do people in stable modern neighborhoods like villages, or indeed old-fashioned slums. They do not always like the closeness, and may move out. But at least they have had time to settle into a more or less tolerable relation with those around them, and there is likely to be some mutually accepted code about not doing irritating things like staring. Moreover they

13. Irenäus Eibl-Eibesfeldt, *Love and Hate*, tr. Geoffrey Strachan (London, 1971), p. 24. The very widespread fear of magical "overlooking" by the evil eye is another example.

know a great deal about each other already, so curiosity will not be so much of a problem. All the same, some privacy usually is provided. And where communities grow bigger, more of it is at once needed. Chinese and Indian cities have long been large and confusing, full of strangers. For that reason, the houses became highly defensive—usually closed in by solid outer walls. More clothes are worn; women are locked up; manners, too, become defensive.

And everywhere, not just in our society, rich people who have made good in crowded cities move out and make space round themselves.[14]

This matter of what is called personal space is just one part of the complex set of patterns now discussed under the general heading of territorial instincts. I shall say more about it later, though not as much as I should like.[15] All I am concerned to do at the moment is to point out that there really is a range of phenomena here which needs describing, and that animal comparisons help because concepts for describing similar behavior already exist in that area, and turn out, on the whole, quite applicable. Earlier theories of instinct ignored the matter, without actually denying it. They could leave it alone because, for one thing, nobody was trying to change people's lives radically in this respect. But so drastic have social changes been in this century that it becomes necessary to state all kinds of facts about our animal nature which used to be taken for granted—for instance, that we cannot live properly in infinite crowds or in conditions of ceaseless change.

14. See further development of this point at the end of Chap. 3.

15. I am fairly baffled about fitting adequate examples into this book, because the explanatory power of such notions depends on following through the whole system of concepts. Merely naming an impulse as territorial may tell you quite a lot about it, just as naming it as sexual may. But you will understand much more if you have an adequate idea of how territory works generally, and still more if you know how it works in a given species, how it relates there to other motives like dominance, affection and aggression. All these general motives are *groupings* of particular impulses. Personal space is only one aspect of territory. But it is one that matters greatly to all advanced social creatures, including those with no fixed home. And staring is only one form of intrusion.

What We Can Ask of Our Concepts

I am suggesting that we badly need new and more suitable concepts for describing human motivation.

The alarming truth is, of course, that it is not only animal behavior studies that are still in the descriptive phase. Certainly, a particularly deep snowfall of virgin ignorance has till lately been observable there. People in general never knew very much about animals; they had various motives for distorting what they did know, and when in the last two centuries we in the West mainly moved into towns, we cut ourselves off from what little we might ever have discovered. (That is why the recent renaissance of this subject interests us so much.) It might seem, on the other hand, that we know plenty about that much-described matter, human conduct. So we might, if we had always asked the right questions and had not been more anxious to deceive ourselves than to learn the truth. But we can always do with new questions. People like Nietzsche, Freud, and Marx, by asking new questions, have taught us much, and it is yet further questions, and a more intelligent connecting of questions, that we still need.

Freud should never be dismissed as "unscientific" on the simple grounds that he did not make detailed predictions that could be falsified in experiment. What he was providing was concepts. His general question: what is the structure of human instinct? was a perfectly sensible one. His answer was oversimple and overconfident, but his suggestions still make excellent indicators of where inquiry can start—of what, for instance, must be wrong, but points the way to what is right. He made "good mistakes"—a most useful habit, the value of which is perhaps more familiar to philosophers than to scientists. He made possible the making of concepts.

A good concept-maker has to be a man of great general intelligence and wide interests, or he cannot make connections with other fields and is liable to produce a scheme that some other study will shatter. But he needs also, and quite as much, to be more or less soaked in, committed to, involved with, and generally crazy about his subject. A long phase of fairly omnivorous observation, of deep receptiveness and genuine wonder, is needed to appreciate the formal peculiarities of the thing one is dealing with, to see *what* about it should be laid hold on for description. That background of experience is the strength of Konrad Lorenz, Niko Tinbergen and their school. They have been animal people all their lives. Their involvement in the concrete has, as Hinde justly says, "ensured that explanatory concepts have been chosen to suit the phenomena studied, rather than vice versa"[16]—an advantage that is rarer than it ought to be.

But we still have the problem of relating the study of animal behavior to other ways of studying man. *Homo sapiens* is an animal. (At least he is not a machine, or an angel, or a fairy, or even something from Vulcan.[17]) So it would really be odd, would need a lot of accounting for, if comparative methods that make good sense over the wide range of other terrestrial species suddenly simply had no application to him at all. But *Homo sapiens* is already marked out as the property of the social sciences. And they are because of their early history to some extent committed to the view that he has no nature, or none that can be important, that his behavior (apart from a few simple physical needs) must be understood entirely in terms of his culture.

The thing we must keep in mind here is that there is room for all methods. As my small example of stamp-buying shows, no one way of studying mankind has a monopoly or needs one. Innate factors can be ignored for some purposes because they are taken for granted, without therefore vanishing from the scene.

What each method has to do is to establish its usefulness. It must fill a need. It seems obvious to me that we do need to understand human motives better, both what they are and how they connect. There is a load of common-sense lore about them, some of it excellent, some confusing, some worthless. But the

16. "Ethological Models and the Concept of Drive," *British Journal for the Philosophy of Science*, 6 (1956), 321.

17. The common use of the word *animal* which contrasts it with *man* is obscure. I have so used it for convenience sometimes, even in this book, but it must never be forgotten that we do not have a clear basis for it, as we do if we oppose *animals* to vegetables, minerals, or machines. Drawing analogies "between people and animals" is, on the face of it, rather like drawing them "between foreigners and people" or "between people and intelligent beings."

intellectual systems that have tried to organize it work mostly by
reducing many motives to one or a few basic ones—sex, self-
preservation, power. They tidy one province, but then they distort themselves in an effort to take over the whole. Human life
simply contains more motives, even more separate groups of
motives, than they allow for. We have to work out their natural
relations, not hack or wrench them to fit Procrustes' bed. Comparison with other species shows possible groupings more subtle
and more helpful than these flat reductions. Certainly this comparison itself must not be used reductively. We must not say
"university departments are really only territories." "Only" is an
exaggeration. But with that word removed, the remark can still
be useful. Similarly, a reviewer put the question: "on Desmond
Morris's own principles, should not his book *The Naked Ape* be
seen as the dominance display of a rising male, eager to gain
followers and compete for leadership of the troop?" Well, *among
other things*, yes. And so should *Eminent Victorians, Language,
Truth and Logic, Les Demoiselles d'Avignon*, [18] and half the papers
in periodicals. Human contentiousness is a fact. We could
never keep our heads in the babble of controversy if we did not
know how to allow for it. Indeed it is just those readers least
aware of the deliberately polemical, challenging element in
works such as these who are most likely to be drawn in by it, to
involve themselves in the amusing but irrelevant game of cops-
and-robbers that the authors want to play, rather than sticking to
the central questions about the value of what is being said or
done.

Still, we say, these motives belong to human beings. Why
should we need to look outside the human scene to understand
them?

Because, (as I have just suggested), our cultures limit so subtly
the questions that we can ask and reinforce so strongly our
natural gift for self-deception. When we ask why something that
is normal in our culture is being done, official answers are always

18. For Picasso's polemical intention in this picture, and its success, see E.
Gombrich, "Psycho-Analysis and the History of Art," in his *Meditations on a Hobby
Horse* (London, 1963). This whole essay is of enormous interest for my theme.

prompt. Spaniards tend not to be short of reasons for bullfighting, Romans for gladiatorial games, totalitarians for torture, Erewhonians for punishing illness. To break this circle, to make our local presuppositions stand out, fabulists have long used animals. They rely on the shock of a different context to make a familiar pattern visible at last. It often works. But of course its value depends on the power of the fabulist's own imagination, on his being able himself to take a new point of view. The device has a different kind of force when facts are used rather than fiction. When other human cultures are found acting at cross-purposes to ours or caricaturing it by pushing its vices to startling excess, we are impressed, and quite rightly. Here, in fact, we already accept the value of looking *away* from the familiar scene in order to understand it. Many notions first evolved for the study of primitive peoples have been found useful for the study of more complex ones like ourselves, who did not know they had these things because they never thought to ask, but had already half-formed puzzles to which these notions provide the answer. (Examples are initiation rites and crisis rites generally, competitive giving, conspicuous expenditure.) And many half-formed suspicions about our own society have been shaken up and clarified into valuable insights by comparison with strange cultures.

What happens with patterns first spotted in animals is very similar. Someone first detects a pattern in animal behavior—he finds, that is, a notion that unifies and makes sense of a common sequence of behavior, say, displacement activity, or dominance displays, or redirected aggression. He then looks at the human scene and sees something similar. So much is traditional. The further things which are needed, and which are now being vigorously developed, are a careful, thorough, disciplined procedure for making the original observations of animals precise and a subtler technique for comparison for checking the different sorts of variation in different species and linking them to their different sorts of causes.

The value of animal comparisons here depends on a simple point about what understanding is, which I think has come home to the public much more quickly than it has to the theorists. *Understanding is relating*; it is fitting things into a context. Nothing can be understood on its own. Had we known no other animate life-form than our own, we should have been utterly mysterious to ourselves as a species. And that would have made it immensely harder for us to understand ourselves as individuals too. Anything that puts us in context, that shows us as part of a continuum, an example of a type that varies on intelligible principles, is a great help. People welcome seeing how animals behave, either directly or on film, in just the same way in which a man who had begun to practice, say, mathematics or dancing on his own would welcome seeing others who were already doing it, though differently. There has been an arbitrary principle, laid down for a variety of reasons in European thought, that only human activities can concern us in this sort of way.[19] It is false. It comes out entertainingly when people deeply involved with owls, otters, and whatnot are interviewed for television. Toward the end of the proceedings the animal person is asked, rather solemnly, "And what do you think is the point of (or the *justification* for) spending time on these creatures?" Far from replying, "Just what brought you here, chum—I like them. They have a life akin to mine, but different—they make me feel more at home in the world—they fill the gap between me and the dead things I have to manipulate—they help me to understand myself," he usually answers that they are educational for children (but why? except on the grounds just mentioned) or—and this passes as a perfectly respectable reason—that nobody has succeeded in breeding them in these latitudes before. The really monstrous thing about Existentialism too is its proceeding as if the world contained only dead matter (things) on the one hand and fully rational, educated, adult human beings on the other—as if there were no other life-forms. The impres-

19. Just because this *is* our tradition, many people think of it as obvious common sense. It became the tradition, however, as a result of a deliberate and sustained campaign by Christian thinkers, using some very strange material gathered from Rationalist philosophers, to crush a natural respect for animals, and for nature generally, which they saw as superstitious. John Passmore in his book *Man's Responsibility for Nature* (London, 1971) gives a careful and fascinating account of this strange process, which explained to me many things I had always found incomprehensible.

sion of *desertion* or *abandonment* which Existentialists have is due, I am sure, not to the removal of God, but to this contemptuous dismissal of almost the whole biosphere—plants, animals, and children. Life shrinks to a few urban rooms; no wonder it becomes absurd.

Could People Be Blank Paper?

I am sure then that the contribution of ethology is useful and that it can be fitted in without damaging anything worth keeping in the social sciences—though it certainly conflicts with the still influential Blank Paper theory. This theory, though first popularized by Locke, was brought to its extreme form by John B. Watson, the founding father of behaviorism, and was a cornerstone of the original version of that doctrine. Locke himself had meant by it merely that we are born without *knowledge*: "Let us then suppose the mind to be, as we say, white paper, void of all characters, without any ideas; how comes it to be furnished? . . . To this I answer in one word, from EXPERIENCE; in that all our knowledge is founded."[20] He had never doubted that we had *instincts*—that we were born adapted to act and feel in specific ways. However, Locke did supply the language for this further step, and Watson went on to take it. Man, he declared, had no instincts. This mysterious news was remarkably well publicized; there seems to be nobody who studied any sort of social science in English-speaking countries between the wars who was not taught it as gospel. Its obscurity, however, has made it increasingly a nuisance and no sort of a help to inquiry. Not only do people evidently and constantly act and feel in ways to which they have never been conditioned, but the very idea that anything so complex as a human being could be totally plastic and structureless is unintelligible. Even if—which is absurd—people had no tendencies but the general ones to be docile, imitative, and mercenary, those would still have to be innate, and there would have to be a structure governing the relations among them.

20. *Essay Concerning Human Understanding*, Bk. 2.1.2.

Sensible psychologists have accordingly tended more and more to admit that people do have some genetically fixed tendencies. What makes this admission hard, however, is the very strong impression still prevalent that we have to *choose* between considering these tendencies and considering outside conditions, that we must be either loyal innatists or faithful environmentalists. This polarization seems much like holding that the quality of food is determined *either* by what it is like when you buy it *or* by how you cook it, but not both. Thus Skinner, who in his early work simply ignored innate determining factors,[21] has now for some time admitted that they exist, but still doesn't want them studied, on the ground that they cannot be altered. Knowledge of them, he says, "is of little value in an experimental analysis because such a condition cannot be manipulated after the individual has been conceived. The most that can be said is that knowledge of the genetic factor may enable us to make better use of other causes." And again, "since we cannot change the species of an organism, this variable [species-status] is of no importance in extending our control, but information about species-status enables us to predict characteristic behavior, and, in turn, to make more successful use of other techniques of control."[22]

How would our inability to effect changes be received as a reason for not studying the weather, or indeed the laws of chemistry? Of course there is nothing wrong with wanting one's knowledge to be useful. But from that very angle, knowing what one *cannot* change matters as much as knowing what one can. Skinner appears to admit this so fully at the end of these two quotations that one expects him to move on to saying that psychology will have to study both. But he never does. In *Beyond*

---

21. The index to *The Behavior of Organisms* (1938) has no entries under *instinct, innate, inherited, genetic,* or any similar term, and though the book has a section on Drive, the concept is reduced to the ideas of frequency and intensity. Yet the behavior discussed in that book was almost entirely that of rats, so arguments against applying such notions to humans were not in any case relevant. Watson's simple and popular doctrine had deflected attention from the topic entirely. Halcyon days.

22. *Science and Human Behavior* (New York, 1953), pp. 26 and 157.

Freedom and Dignity (1971) he may still be seen apparently hold-ing himself bound, even after recognizing the two complemen-tary aspects, to make an agonizing, and indeed unintelligible, choice between them:

The ethologists have emphasized contingencies of survival which would contribute these features [aggressive instincts] to the genetic endow-ment of the species, but the contingencies of reinforcement in the lifetime of the individual are *also* significant, since anyone who acts aggressively to harm others is likely to be reinforced in other ways—for example, by taking possession of goods. The contingencies explain the behavior *quite apart from* any state or feeling of aggression or any initiat-ing act by autonomous man. [pp. 185-186, my italics]

An explanation that quite patently can work only for *repetitions* of aggressive acts, and then only for those that were rewarded in the first place, is placidly extended to account for *all* such acts, including the unrepeated originals. More generally, the formula of smooth transition from "*x* as well as *y*" to "therefore not *y*" reappears constantly, as where he says: "For 'instinct' read 'habit.' The cigarette habit is presumably something more than the behavior said to show that a person possesses it; but the only other information we have concerns the reinforcers and the schedules of reinforcement which make a person smoke a great deal" (p. 196). More information obviously does exist—for in-stance, on the one hand, about the effect of nicotine on the human organism, and on the other, about people's innate ten-dency to suck things. That information, however, is not sup-posed to concern psychologists. Again, he remarks: "The per-ceiving and knowing which arise from verbal contingencies are even more obviously products of the environment.... Abstract thinking is the product of a particular kind of environment, not of a cognitive faculty" (pp. 188-189). So why can't a psycholo-gist's parrot talk psychology?

There is simply no need to take sides between innate and outer factors in this way. We can study both. What behaviorism, it seems, still needs is to complete its metamorphosis from a dogmatic, fighting, metaphysical creed to an impartial method of study. The strength of behaviorism is that it is a form of empiricism, that is, an assertion of the primacy of experience over dogmatic theoretical principles in forming our knowledge. So, when it finds a dogmatic theoretical principle blocking our recognition of obvious and pervasive aspects of experience, its interests lie in ditching that principle, even when it happens to be a homegrown one. This has already been done in the matter of admitting data from private experience, something that Watson ruled out on metaphysical grounds as "the myth of consciousness." In *Beyond Freedom and Dignity* Skinner admits reality here admirably, speaking of "the indisputable fact of privacy; a small part of the universe is enclosed in a human skin. It would be foolish to deny the existence of that private world" (p. 191). The question is simply, as he goes on to say, how best to describe it, what conceptual scheme to fit it into. And the same thing is true of innate tendencies.

One thing that hampers a lot of other people besides Skinner here is the tantalizing notion of a single cause. Discussions on the cause of some phenomenon—say, Truancy, Wife-beating, or the Decline of the Modern Theater—often begin by listing a number of alternative possible causes, and go on to try to eliminate all of them but one. On this list there is often now something called "the genetic cause." But as it is not adequate alone to produce the effect, it gets eliminated in an early round of the competition and is heard of no more. But *everything* that people do has its internal as well as its environmental aspect, and therefore its causes in the nature of man as well as outside him. Picking out "*the* cause" often does mean, as Skinner suggests, looking for something that we can change. But in order to see what change is going to be any use to us, the internal factor ought *always* to be investigated, because it is not isolated, but connected with a complex system that will respond in one way or another to anything that we may do. Ignoring it because we cannot alter it really would be rather like ignoring the weather, or the shape of the earth.

I am suggesting, tentatively, that there has been a quiet, but on the whole benign, change in the meaning of the word *behaviorism*. People who call themselves behaviorists now often seem to mean simply that they study behavior. The *ism*—the defense of a creed—seems to have matured into a more modest *ology*—a name for the topic studied. Such gradual changes are benign because they allow crude positions to be made more subtle without a public outcry. But they are more benign still when they can become explicit. If one drops the general dogma that the only causal factor which can affect behavior is more behavior, there is really no reason why what affects it should not be inherited, why there should *not* be innate tendencies. Whether there *are* is an empirical question, not a matter of party loyalty.[23]

Behaviorists could afford to be less defensive. Their becoming so would be a great help in the joint exploring expeditions by various disciplines which are now needed to map the disputed area. At present, social scientists tend to appear on these occasions loaded with weapons and protective clothing—technical language, unnecessary assumptions, and control experiments of doubtful relevance—while Lorenz usually turns up speaking ordinary language and using a very wide frame of reference—wearing, as it were, only binoculars, jeans and a pair of old tennis shoes, but with an excellent homemade map.[24] I try not to let my delight at this spectacle bias me. I know he is in some ways oversimple, and has made mistakes. But I still think he has a far better idea of the *kind* of problem he is up against than most of those present. He has understood that it is no use, at present, trying to make anything look final. And the view he takes of professional rigor is the right one. Rigor is *not* just a matter of ducking down inside the presuppositions of one's own subject and defending them against all comers, but of understanding them so fully that one can relate them to those needed for other inquiries. We do not just have to verify our hypotheses carefully, but also to form them intelligently. As they are bound to tie up with matters that we do not know yet, and indeed with the general structure of human thought, this requires collaboration. It cannot be properly carried out in private, between consenting colleagues who stay within the confines of a single subject.

Lorenz and his party have, however, a difficulty about method

23. I shall say some more about behaviorism, and particularly about the question what behavior is, in Chap. 5.

24. This applies particularly to *King Solomon's Ring* (New York, 1952), which some people fail to recognize as a serious and seminal book, simply because it is nontechnical and delightful to read. In his technical papers Lorenz can be as hard to understand as any other scientist.

which also dogs me constantly in this book. The point of my discussion is to show how and in what cases comparison between man and other species makes sense, but I must sometimes use such comparisons in the process. I think the circle will prove virtuous, however, if it abides by the following rule: comparisons make sense only when they are put in the context of the entire character of the species concerned and of the known principles governing resemblances between species. Thus, it is invalid to compare suicide in lemmings or infanticide in hamsters *on their own* with human suicide or infanticide. But when you have looked at the relation of the act to other relevant habits and needs, when you have considered the whole nature of the species, comparison may be possible and helpful.[25]

This would not be true if the Blank Paper view that "man has no instincts," that there simply was no innate determining element in human behavior, were right. But it cannot be right. It is not even clear that it can be meaningful.[26]

25. The thorough, painstaking background surveys with which the field observers I quote support and explain their conclusions are a necessary supplement to what I say. I refer to only a few, for the sake of simplicity, but there are now a great many good ones. About the lemmings, see p. 58, below. About the principles for comparing species, I say a little more in Chap. 13, in the section on intelligence and instinct. For good and full discussions, see Eibl-Eibesfeldt, *Love and Hate*, chap. 3, also Lorenz, *On Aggression* (New York, 1963), chaps. 4–6, and many astute observations in Tinbergen's *Study of Instinct* (Oxford, 1961).

26. For an admirable and moderate discussion of the matter, see *Love and Hate*, chap. 2.

CHAPTER 2

Animals and the
Problem of Evil

Tradition and Reality

What then is the main point that emerges from the detailed, systematic, grueling studies of animal behavior that have been made by trained zoologists in this century, and have been given the name of ethology?

The general point is that other animals clearly lead a much more structured, less chaotic life than people have been accustomed to think, and are therefore, in certain definite ways, much less different from men than we have supposed. (There is still plenty of difference, but it is a different difference.) Traditionally, people have congratulated themselves on being an island of order in a sea of chaos. Lorenz and company have shown that this is all eyewash. There follow various changes in our view of man, because that view has been built up on a supposed contrast between man and animals which was formed by seeing animals not as they were, but as projections of our own fears and desires. We have thought of the wolf always as he appears to the shepherd at the moment of seizing a lamb from the fold. But this is like judging the shepherd by the impression he makes on the lamb at the moment when he finally decides to turn it into lamb chops. Recently, ethologists have taken the trouble to watch wolves systematically, between mealtimes, and have found them to be, by human standards, paragons of steadiness and good conduct. They pair for life, they are faithful and affectionate spouses and parents, they show great loyalty to their pack and great courage and persistence in the face of difficulties, they carefully respect one another's territories, keep their dens clean, and extremely seldom kill anything that they do not need for dinner. If they fight with another wolf, the encounter normally ends with a submission.[1] They have an inhibition about killing the suppliant and about attacking females and cubs. They have also, like all social animals, a fairly elaborate etiquette, including subtly varied ceremonies of greeting and reassurance, by which friendship is strengthened, cooperation achieved, and the wheels of social life generally oiled. Our knowledge of this behavior is not based upon the romantic impressions of casual travelers; it rests on long and careful investigations by trained zoologists, backed up by miles of film, graphs, maps, population surveys, droppings analysis, and all the rest of the contemporary toolbag. Moreover, these surveys have often been undertaken by authorities who were initially rather hostile to the wolf and inclinced to hope that it could be blamed for various troubles. Farley Mowat, doing this work in the Canadian Arctic, had his results rejected time and again because they showed that the sudden drop in the numbers of deer was *not* due to wolves, which had not changed their technique in a number of centuries, but to hunters, who had.[2]

1. Notice the word *normally* here. It has to be used or understood in describing the life of any plant or animal; there are always exceptions. Because putting it in every line is tedious, one sometimes omits it, and this must, it seems, be the reason why many people firmly believe that Lorenz said that animals never murder others of their species, or at least that wolves never do so. This belief is a complete mistake. Lorenz describes such inhibitions as needing to be *adequate* (that is, to the purpose of preventing extinction) and says that *the most reliable* ones are found among "the most bloodthirsty predators." But "the most reliable" examples of anything do not have to be infallible. And in fact he explicitly emphasizes that "there is no absolute reliance on these inhibitions, which may occasionally fail" (*On Aggression*, p. 129) and gives examples, including infanticide in foxes (p. 119). Similarly in *King Solomon's Ring* he writes of "the innate, instinctive, fixed inhibitions that prevent an animal from using his weapons *indiscriminately* against his own kind" (p. 196, my italics). Roe deer and solitary carnivores do use them indiscriminately; wolves and even hyenas do not.

2. *Never Cry Wolf* (Boston, 1963). See also Richard Fiennes, *The Order of Wolves* (London, 1976) and Lois E. Bueler's *Wild Dogs of the World* (London, 1974).

Actual wolves, then, are not much like the folk-figure of the wolf, and the same is true for apes and other creatures. But *it is the folk-figure that has been popular with philosophers*. They have usually taken over the popular notion of lawless cruelty which underlies such terms as "brutal," "bestial," "beastly," "animal desires," and so on, and have used it, uncriticized, as a contrast to illuminate the nature of man. Man has been mapped by reference to a landmark that is largely mythical. Because this habit is so ancient and so deep-rooted, we had better look a little more closely at its oddity before turning to the philosophic arguments in question.

I once read a chatty journalistic book on wolves, which described in detail how wolves trapped in medieval France used to be flayed alive, with various appalling refinements. "Perhaps this was rather cruel," the author remarked, "but then the wolf is itself a cruel beast." The words sound so natural; it is quite difficult to ask oneself: do wolves in fact flay people alive? Or to take in the fact that the only animal that does this sort of thing is *Homo sapiens*. Another complaint that the author made against wolves was their treachery. They would creep up on people secretly, he said, and then attack so suddenly that their victims did not have time to defend themselves. The idea that wolves would starve if they always gave fair warning never struck him. Wolves in fact, have traditionally been *blamed* for being carnivores, which is doubly surprising since the people who blamed them normally ate meat themselves, and were not, as the wolf is, compelled by their stomachs to do so.

The restraint apparent in wolves seems to be found in most other social carnivores, and well-armed vegetarian creatures too. Where murder is so easy, a species must have an adequate inhibition against it or perish.[3] (*Of course* this inhibition is not a morality, but it works in many ways like one.) Solitary animals

---

3. Again, *adequate* does not mean *total*. Since Lorenz wrote, much observation has been made of lions, a species whose inhibition is much less strong—but then, so is their sociality. For other carnivores and their customs, see *Sociobiology*, pp. 246–247. Wolves and wild dogs clearly are somewhat special. But the point here is not how widely the inhibition works in any given carnivorous species. It is that it does *not* work adequately in man. If it did, we should not need law or morality to restrain violence.

and those less strongly armed do not need this defense. Lorenz gives chilling examples from roe deer and doves, in both of which species stronger members will slowly murder weaker ones if kept in captivity with them, because in a free state these creatures save themselves by running away, not by relying on the victor's inhibition. And it is clear that man is in some ways nearer to this group than to the wolf.

Man, before his tool-using days, was poorly armed. Without claws, beak, or horns, he must have found murder a tedious and exhausting business, and built-in inhibitions against it were therefore not necessary for survival. By the time he invented weapons, it was too late to alter his nature. He became a dangerous beast. War and vengeance are primitive human institutions, not late perversions; most cosmogonies postulate strife in Heaven, and bloodshed is taken for granted as much in the Book of Judges as in the *Iliad* or the Sagas. There may be nonaggressive societies, as anthropologists assure us, but they are white blackbirds and perhaps not so white as they are painted. It seems possible that man shows *more* savagery to his own kind than most other mammal species.[4] Rats (which Lorenz mentions) are certainly competitors. They, it seems, will normally try to kill any rat they meet of another tribe, but in com-

---

4. See p. 49 for the nonaggressive societies. Wilson flatly denies that man shows *more* savagery, saying "murder is far more common and hence normal in many vertebrate species than in man ... even when our episodic wars are averaged in" (*Sociobiology*, p. 247). How does one check such things? Certainly, since Lorenz wrote, evidence has come in that some animals are bloodier than had been supposed. No doubt this should be cheering to the human race. Beyond this, Wilson suggests that a Martian zoologist, visiting "a randomly picked human population" would probably see little violence. But he probably would not see much theft or sexual activity either, yet both go on. Those of us who lead protected lives do not find it easy to believe in serious wife- and child-beating, but they are evidently quite common. And how would one compute the chances of his running into a riot, a raid, or a massacre, let alone a war? These cannot just be averaged in; they are qualitatively special. The main point however, is not to set up a contest of merit, but to make it plain that man resembles other species in having a serious problem to solve here. It is rather common now to resist this suggestion by claiming that the frequency of aggression is just an invention of the poets and historians. Were this true, it would be absolutely extraordinary: what motive, other than aggression itself, could account for such monstrous misrepresentation?

pensation they never kill or seriously fight rats of their own tribe. Rats cannot therefore compete with Cain or Romulus, still less with Abimelech, the son of Gideon, who murdered, on one stone, *all* his brothers, to the number of three score and ten (Judges 11:5). An animal that did anything remotely similar would (surely rightly) be labeled "dangerous."

Current fashion brushes off the suggestion of so labeling man by ruling that such conduct is not due to nature, but to society. This misses the point. We are not now asking the small question whether a particular man, or even a particular group, picked up a practice from others or invented it. We are asking a much larger one; how did these proceedings originate for the human race as a whole? How are they psychologically possible, and indeed hard to eradicate, when many culturally induced things come and go lightly, and many others cannot be culturally induced even with the utmost effort and good will? For this inquiry, nature and culture are not opposites at all. We are naturally culture-building animals. But what we build into our cultures has to satisfy our natural pattern of motives.

It is also suggested that any excess of savagery in us over other species is merely due to our general power of carrying everything we do further, through culture and technology, than they. We build more thoroughly and better than the bee and the beaver; thus, too, we kill more thoroughly. There is certainly much in this. But the question still remains: *which* things do we choose to develop in this manner? Not every activity receives this sort of attention; for instance, only lately has the physical science necessary for medicine been developed. But the glorification of fighting is extremely widespread and ancient. Now if we compare the value of these two things for human life, this glorification needs explaining. What culture has an epic poem celebrating the achievements of its great healer—or even of its engineer, architect, or inventor? Is not a creature with this bias rightly labeled "dangerous"?

Yet he has always believed otherwise. Man, civilized Western man, has always maintained that in a bloodthirsty world he alone was comparatively harmless. Consider the view of the African jungle given by Victorian hunters. The hunter assumed that every creature he met would attack him and accordingly shot it on sight. Of course he didn't want to eat it, but he could always stuff it (in order to triumph over his human enemies), and anyway he assumed it was noxious; it would be described in his memoirs as "the great brute." Drawings even exist of giant pandas cast in this totally unconvincing role—and shot accordingly.[5] Yet in these days game wardens and photographers habitually treat lions as familiarly as big dogs. It is understood that so long as they are well fed and not provoked they are no more likely to attack you than the average German shepherd. Much the same seems to hold of elephants and other big game. These creatures have their own occupations, and, unless seriously disturbed, are not anxious for a fight. Gorillas in particular are peace-loving beasts; George Schaller visited a tribe of them for six months without receiving so much as a cross word or seeing any quarreling worth naming.[6] In this case, and no doubt in others, Victorian man was deceived by confusing threatening behavior with attack. Gorillas do threaten, but the point is precisely to avoid combat. By looking sufficiently dreadful, a gorilla patriarch can drive off intruders and defend his family without the trouble and danger of actually fighting. The same thing seems to hold of the other simians, and particularly of howler monkeys, whose dreadful wailing used to freeze the white hunter's blood. Howlers have reduced combat to its lowest and most satisfactory terms. When two groups of them compete for a territory, they both sit down and howl their loudest, and the side that makes the most noise wins. That nervous white man, with his heart in his mouth and his finger on his trigger, was among the most dangerous things in the jungle. His weapon was at least as powerful as those of the biggest animals, and while they attacked only what they could eat or what was really annoying them, he would shoot at anything big enough to aim at. Why did he think they were more savage than he? Why has civilized Western man always thought so?

5. See *Men and Pandas* by Ramona and Desmond Morris (London, 1966). Giant pandas are of course wholly vegetarian, and defend themselves only if cornered.

6. See his book *The Year of the Gorilla* (Chicago, 1964).

I am not surprised that early man *disliked* wolves. When an animal tries to eat you, or even to eat your dinner, you cannot be expected to like it, and only a very occasional Buddhist will cooperate. But why did man feel so morally superior? Could he not see that the wolf's hunting him was exactly the same as his hunting the deer? (There are tribes that do think in this way, but it is Western thought that I am exploring.) And the superior feeling persists. As Lorenz remarks, people are inclined to disapprove of carnivores even when they eat other animals and not people, as though other animals all formed one species, and the carnivores were cannibals. "The average man," he says, "does not judge the fox that kills a hare by the same standard as the hunter who shoots one for exactly the same reason, but with the severe censure that he would apply to a game-keeper who made a practice of shooting farmers and frying them for supper."[7] This disapproval is very marked on the occasions when foxes do kill for sport or practice, destroying more hens than they can eat. You would not guess, to hear people talk at such times, that humans ever hunted foxes. In the same way, it makes a very disreputable impression when Jane Goodall reports that the chimpanzees she watched would occasionally catch and eat a baby baboon or colobus monkey, though they all lived amicably together most of the time and the children even played together.[8] But what else goes on on the traditional farm?

> Sing, Dilly dilly duckling, come and be killed
> For you must be stuffed, and my customers filled.

The reason such parallels are hard to see is, I suggest, that *man has always been unwilling to admit his own ferocity*, and has tried to deflect attention from it by making animals out to be more ferocious than they are. Sometimes the animals themselves have been blamed and punished. Such customs as the flaying of wolves were probably intended as punishments, though it is hard to separate this intention from magic. And certainly the wickedness of animals has often been used to justify our killing or otherwise

---

7. *King Solomon's Ring*, p. 183.
8. *In the Shadow of Man* (Boston, 1971). See her index, under *Predatory Behavior*.

interfering with them. It is a cockeyed sort of justification unless beasts are supposed capable of deliberation. We would probably do better to invoke our natural loyalty to our own species than to rely on our abstract superiority to others. Still, people do manage to think in this way. Their reasoning is certainly not always easy to follow. Ramona and Desmond Morris show, in a most interesting survey of medieval attitudes, how apes were regarded, not just as hideous, but as "evil and ridiculous"—as failed and degraded human beings. Moreover, "the ape's capacity for imitation gave rise to the odd notion that he deliberately copied human actions in order to convince people that he was really one of them. . . . He became the prototype of the impostor, the fraud, the hypocrite and the flatterer."[9] Once something is taken as the *prototype* of a particular quality, it is not easy to be convinced that it is not an *instance* of it. Nor do people seem to have tried hard to be clear on such points. The Morrises give interesting examples of the ritual execution of animals along with certain types of criminal, such as the medieval practice of hanging an ape and a dog on the gallows when a Jew was executed.[10] No doubt the animals executed were not exactly supposed guilty of a particular crime. But they were prominently pushed into the category of those for whom punishment was fitting; wickedness was deemed their climate. And there are not, I think, compensating instances of animals that symbolized virtue being *rewarded*. Nor do people seem to have hesitated to eat doves, lambs, nightingales, or any other creatures on account of their symbolic value.

Various philosophers have protested that I cannot be right in supposing that animals were thought of as evil. It would, they quite properly point out, be a gross confusion to mix up using something as the *symbol* of a vice with actually attributing a vice to it, and everybody knows that animals are as incapable of vice as they are of virtue. Why should I suppose that people were really as silly as this? Now because the evidence for a confusion tends to be confused, it is not always easy to clear up this kind of doubt. I

9. Ramona and Desmond Morris, *Men and Apes* (London, 1966), pp. 28, 35.
10. Ibid., p. 31.

was reflecting whether I was indeed wrong when a couple of things made me suspect that I was not. The first was a television documentary on sharks, which, though perfectly sensible on the whole, began, emphatically, with the words, "These are the world's most vicious killers." *Vicious?* (No evidence appeared in the film, incidentally, to suggest that sharks ever kill except in hunger or self-defense. The number of people they kill in the world yearly came out at twenty-six; the number of sharks people kill was not given, but was clearly vastly higher.) The second, nastier and more detailed, was a journalist's account of an expedition with a crocodile-hunter:

"Got him now," he cried. He shook water from his hair and beard. "We've got two wops [darts] in him; we can play him like a fish. Tire him out." Finally we made the crocodile drag the skiff with him. He had no respite.
   "That hook's caught right down in his gut. We'll have to be careful, or we'll kill him!"
   With the dawn the crocodile sought refuge in deep water. "He's trying to stay down, now," said Craig. "He doesn't like this daylight business. . . . Harass him like this, and he'll have to come up every half hour or so."
   "*He's got the morality of a laser beam,*" said Craig as we sat there. . . . "*The croc emerging from the egg will snap at anything that moves, no matter if it's a leech or a human leg.*" As he spoke he was tugging on a harpoon line, trying to *coax* the beast below to move. "He's a *dedicated* killing machine, the killer of any fish or animal or bird."[11]

This is ordinary, typical, present-day, vernacular speech and thinking; a great deal more like it has appeared in the public excitement over the film *Jaws*. If anyone can find a convincing meaning for it which does not involve dramatizing simple and primitive carnivores into conscious criminals just to boost human vanity, I shall be relieved and delighted. Terms like *machine* and *laser beam* ought to rule out such an idea. That they do not is an indication of the very confusion I complain of. Crocodiles, and particularly baby crocodiles, are indeed not highly advanced creatures; nor are sharks. For them, as for all carnivores, prey is

11. *Observer* color supplement, 15 February 1976, my italics.

simply food, not an enemy or a victim,[12] and to speak of their snapping reflex as *mechanical* would not be too misleading. But the words I have italicized leave no doubt that the hunter still manages to think of it as their conscious deliberate choice to outrage the known rights of others. And the only possible reason for mentioning *a human leg* is a persuasion that this is something at which even a newly hatched crocodile could, if not very depraved, be expected to draw the line. Of course this is silly. My point is that such silliness is neither rare nor unimportant. Consider again a very ordinary item from the *Guardian*, October 4, 1976. Under the headline "'ANIMAL' MOTHER GAOLED," the account began: "An unmarried mother who brutally beat up her three young children was told by a judge when he sent her to prison for two years on assault and wounding charges, 'You behaved like a wild animal.'" The judge could not, it should be noticed, have meant "wild animals too occasionally do the sort of thing you have done." He had to mean "usually." If wild animals usually did that, their evolution would have petered out long ago.

In case anyone feels that only the ignorant populace think like this, we might note too a passage in Wittgenstein's "Lecture on Ethics."[13] Wittgenstein is contrasting trivial accusations that can be laughed off with utterly serious ones where no such avoidance is possible. The serious case goes like this: "Suppose I had told one of you a preposterious lie and he came up to me and said, 'You're behaving like a beast. . . .'"

There is nothing unusual about confusing a symbol with the thing symbolized, about projecting a fantasy. It is so common and yet so deadly a fault that we need constantly to scan our thought for it, and can probably never do so enough.[14] We are always seeing people who are unlike ourselves as threats or monsters. Our children are to us symbols of hope—so we tend to expect them to be hopeful, and to be upset if they fail to do so. At other times we may see them as threats, symbols of a world

12. For the radical distinction between predation and aggression, see Lorenz, *On Aggression*, p. 24.

13. *Philosophical Review* 74 (1965), 3–12.

14. Iris Murdoch discusses this fault well in the second and third essays in *The Sovereignty of Good* (London, 1970).

that does not need us—and then we are inclined to attribute to them hostile motives. Parents too get treated as animated symbols, whether of repression or security, rather than as individuals. And the literature of misogyny, from the Christian Fathers onward, is a prize museum of this sort of muddle. Mixing up a symbol with an attribution is, in fact, normal, in the sense in which failing to think hard is always normal. Among human beings, it is often best checked by the victim, the walking symbol himself, who can say, "Hey, look—I am not that, but me." But though animals can demonstrate the same point clearly to those who will take the trouble to visit them at home, we urban people do not very often do so.

There is, moreover, a special reason for maneuvering animals into the position of instances and not only symbols of evil. We rightly connect the thought of virtue with that of our own species, because the virtues of that species are the ones that concern us. *Human* and *humane* are words of praise. Being *inhuman* is something terrible. It is easy from here to connect the notion of vice with other species. The use of words like *brutal*, *bestial, beastly* shows how readily we do this. And the temptation to treat the symbol as an attribution is the greater because distancing the quality protects our own self-esteem.

This way of thinking might, of course, have been balanced by *favorable* symbolizing, by occasions when we saw crocodiles, or still more, other animals such as lions, as embodiments of courage, patience, and other virtues. But favorable symbols too are read as attributions, and they tend to lead to venerating the beast, something that Jewish and Christian monotheism has always fiercely resisted. Monotheism does have a relatively hospitable side, a tradition in which animals can be seen as fellow-servants of God, or as aspects of his glory. But it has also a sharply exclusive and destructive side, in which the Lord tolerates no rival for our regard. In this mood, the church often and explicitly insisted that all plants and animals must be viewed merely as objects given to man as his instruments, that to have any sort of regard for them in themselves was sinful and superstitious folly. What is interesting is that many of those scientific humanists who most sternly rejected Christianity have continued this second tradition—but with man himself taking the place of the jealous God. Thus Marx in the *Grundrisse*, said that "the great civilizing influence of capitalism" lay in its rejection of the "deification of nature." Thus it was that "nature becomes for the first time simply an object for mankind, purely a matter of utility."[15]

The effect is an asymmetry about animal symbols. Favorable symbols are carefully demythologized, so that beasts shall not compete, first with God, then with man. It is not officially supposed that we ought to respect or be nice to actual lions or lambs on account of the Lamb of God or the Lion of Judah. But no similar trouble is taken in this tradition about unfavorable symbols. I do not mean that many learned persons would now say with the seventeenth-century writer Edward Topsell that "serpents are the most ungentle and barbarous of creatures."[16] But at the vernacular level the kind of remark I have just mentioned about sharks and crocodiles is very common, and very similar. Moreover the crack or fault in thought which it expresses runs through a great deal of much more ambitious thinking. The problem of how to relate man to other species remains unconsidered in a shadowy area where it naturally neighbors the problem of evil. Vapors from it float, uncriticized and hardly noticed, into arguments where they have no business. A common example is the way in which writers who want for some reason to praise or emphasize a particular quality in human life frequently say that it is "what distinguishes us from the animals" without trying even casually to get the facts of the comparison right. I shall have more to say about this habit in Chapter 10. But for the moment I am more interested in the philosophic use of the Beast Within than in our attitude to Beasts Without.

Beasts Within

The philosopher's Beast Within is a lawless monster to whom nothing is forbidden. It is so described both by moralists like

15. Quoted by Passmore, *Man's Responsibility for Nature*, p. 24, in a fascinating, if depressing, account of the process.
16. Quoted in Ramona and Desmond Morris, *Men and Snakes* (London, 1965), p. 41.

Plato, who are against it, and by moralists like Nietzsche, who are for it. Here is a typical passage from Book 9 of the *Republic*, where Plato is talking about our more unpleasant desires. These

bestir themselves in dreams, when the gentler part of the soul slumbers, and the control of Reason is withdrawn. Then the Wild Beast in us, full-fed with meat and drink, becomes rampant and shakes off sleep to go in quest of what will gratify its own instincts. As you know, it will cast off all shame and prudence at such moments and stick at nothing. In phantasy it will not shrink from intercourse with a mother or anyone else, man, god or brute, or from forbidden food or any deed of blood. It will go to any lengths of shamelessness and folly.[17]

Consider how odd the image is, in spite of its familiarity. Why not say, "*I* have these thoughts in my off moments"? Why not at least the Other Man within? What is gained by talking about the Beast?

Here is Nietzsche, speaking of the Lion he invokes to break the chain of convention:

To create for himself freedom for new creation—for this the Lion's
   strength is sufficient,
To create for himself freedom, and an holy Nay even to duty; therefore, my brethren, is there need of the Lion.
Once it loved as holiest Thou Shalt—Now it must see illusion and
   tyranny even in its holiest, that it may snatch freedom even from its
   love—
For this there is need of the Lion.[18]

But in the world there is no such Beast. To talk of a beast is to talk of a thing with its own laws. If lions really did not draw the line at anything—if they went around mating with crocodiles, ignoring territory, eating poisonous snakes, and killing their own cubs—they would not *be* lions, nor, as a species, would they last long. This abstract Beast is a fancy on the level of the eighteenth century's idea of a Savage, noble or otherwise.

Sensible eighteenth-century people reacted to Rousseau's suggestion of taking "savages" seriously very much in the same way that many sensible people today react to the idea of taking

17. *Republic* 9. 571c, tr. Francis Cornford.
18. *Thus Spake Zarathustra*, Pt. 1, "Discourse of the Three Metamorphoses," tr. Tille and Bozman.

animals seriously. They thought it obviously outrageous, because their notion of a "savage" was a totally unreal and standardized abstraction. They could not believe in any continuity between such mythical beings and real people—because, of course, a mythical being *is* something discontinuous with a real person. He differs in logical type.

Here are some of Dr. Johnson's comments:

A savage would as willingly have his meat sent to him in the kitchen, as eat it at the table here; as men become civilized various modes of denoting honourable preference are invented.

Pity is not natural to man. Children are always cruel. Savages are always cruel. Pity is acquired and improved by the cultivation of reason.

[On the question whether marriage was natural] Sir, a savage man and a savage woman meet by chance, and when the man sees another woman that pleases him better, he will leave the first.

And, in a rather fuller discussion:

A gentleman expressed a wish to go and live three years at Otaheite, or New Zealand, in order to obtain a full acquaintance with people so totally different from all we have ever known, and be satisfied what pure nature can do for man. JOHNSON. "What can you learn, Sir? What can savages tell, but what they have themselves seen? . . . The inhabitants of Otaheite and New Zealand are not in a state of pure nature, for it is plain they broke off from some other people. Had they grown out of the ground, you might have judged of a state of pure nature. Fanciful people talk of a mythology being amongst them, but it must be invention. They have once had religion, which has been gradually debased. And what account of their religion can you suppose to be learnt from savages?"[19]

By "savage" Johnson simply meant someone unfitted for society, without manners, virtues, friendly ties, skills, or sympathetic feelings, a negation of all that was admirable or interesting in people as he knew them. That this description actually applied to all primitive peoples seemed to him obvious. Yet in fact it applied to none. The last quotation shows the heart of the confusion—the idea that what is natural is to be discovered from isolation experiments, from observing creatures "grown out of the ground" instead of by using one's intelligence to sort out the

19. Boswell, *Life of Johnson* (Everyman ed.), 2, 253; 1, 271; 1, 241; and 2, 34.

innate from the acquired elements in existing social behavior. Comparison with other cultures is a help because, as Eibl-Eibesfeldt puts it in *Love and Hate*:

One may take as a starting-point that man's tendency is to vary culturally whatever can be modified. In New Guinea alone several hundred dialects are spoken. This is bound up with the tendency of human beings to isolate themselves into small groups.... But if one finds in spite of this, in certain situations, such as in greeting, or in the behaviour of the mother towards her child, the same behaviour patterns recur repeatedly and among the most different peoples, then it is highly probable that these are innate behaviour patterns. [p. 13]

This is quite different from expecting to find a mythical Raw or Unconditioned Man.

What anthropology did for this myth, ethology now does for the Beast myth. Kipling's Law of the Jungle is much nearer to reality than this fancy of the moralists. Beasts are neither incarnations of wickedness, nor sets of basic needs, nor crude mechanical toys, nor idiot children. They are beasts, each with its own very complex nature. Most of them fail in most respects to conform to their mythical stereotype. This is very marked in the matter of sexual indulgence, something to which the mythical Beast is supposed to be addicted. Desmond Morris really should not have needed to point out that, among animal species, it is *Homo sapiens* that gives an exceptional amount of time and attention to his sexual life. For most species, a brief mating season and a simple instinctive pattern make of it a seasonal disturbance with a definite routine, comparable to Christmas shopping. It is in human life that sex plays, for good or ill, a much more serious and central part. With no other species could a Freudian theory ever have got off the ground. Gorillas, in particular, take so little interest in sex that they shock Robert Ardrey: he concludes that they are in their decadence.[20] Yet Tolstoy, speaking of the life of systematic sexual indulgence, called it "the ideal of monkeys or Parisians."[21]

20. *African Genesis* (London, 1967), pp. 126–127. See also Schaller, *Year of the Gorilla*, p. 122.
21. In *The Kreutzer Sonata*. For further comparison of human sexuality with that of other primate species, see Wolfgang Wickler's book, *The Sexual Code* (London, 1969), and his article, "Socio-Sexual Signals" in *Primate Ethology*, ed. Desmond Morris (London, 1967).

If then there is no lawless beast outside man, it seems very strange to conclude that there is one inside him. It would be more natural to say that the beast within us gives us partial order; the task of conceptual thought will only be to complete it. But the opposite, *a priori,* reasoning has prevailed. If the Beast Within was capable of every iniquity, people reasoned, then beasts without probably were too. This notion made man anxious to exaggerate his difference from all other species and to ground all activities he valued in capacities unshared by the animals, whether the evidence warranted it or no. In a way this evasion does the species credit, because it reflects our horror at the things we do. Man fears his own guilt and insists on fixing it on something evidently alien and external. Beasts Within solve the problem of evil. This false solution does man credit because it shows the power of his conscience, but all the same it is a dangerous fib. The use of the Beast Within as a scapegoat for human wickedness has led to some bad confusion, not only about beasts (which might not matter) but about Man. I suspect that Man began to muddle himself at the point where he said "The Woman beguiled me, and I did eat," and the woman said the same about the Serpent.

Let us consider the predicament of primitive man. He is not without natural inhibitions, but his inhibitions are weak. He cannot, like the dove or the roe deer, cheerfully mince up his family in cold blood and without provocation. (If he could, he would certainly not have survived long after the invention of weapons, nor could the prolonged demanding helplessness of human infants ever have been tolerated.) He has a certain natural dislike for such activities, but it is weak and often overborne. He does horrible things and is filled with remorse afterwards. These conflicts are prerational; they do not fall between his reason and his primitive motives, but between two groups of those primitive motives themselves. They are not the result of thinking; more likely they are among the things that first made him think. They are not the result of social conditioning; they are part of its cause. Intelligence is evolved as a way of dealing with puzzles, an alternative to the strength that can kick its way past them or the inertness that can hide from them. And anger presents as tough a puzzle as any. The preoccupation of our early literature with bloodshed, guilt, and vengeance suggests to me that these problems occupied man from a very early time. I would add that only a creature of this intermediate kind, with inhibitions that are weak *but genuine* would ever have been likely to develop a morality. Conceptual thought formalizes and extends what instinct started.

To show that these suggestions about early man are not entirely off the mark, let us look at Bronze Age behavior as seen in the *Iliad*. I choose the *Iliad* because historically it lies behind Plato and Plato lies behind the modern tradition I complain of. I do not make the mistake of supposing it a genuinely primitive document, applicable to Early Man As Such—but what can we do? It is one of the earliest available in a shape we can come to grips with, and the tradition is our own.

I want to go back to the question of rituals of submission—to the wolf that cannot bite its conquered enemy. Lorenz remarks, "Homer's heroes were certainly not as soft-hearted as the wolves at Whipsnade. The poet cites numerous incidents where the suppliant is slaughtered, with or without compunction." This is true, but the interesting thing is that the appeals were made. Counting carefully, one finds that the score is indeed gloomy; in the *Iliad* there are six appeals and six failures. Moreover, all the suppliants are Trojans, that is, "the other side," and part of the point of the incidents clearly is to show Greeks in a position of power, exulting over an abject enemy. So far, so bad. But there is more to say. Achilles, refusing mercy, explains that before his friend Patroclus was killed, he used to *prefer* taking prisoners alive and selling them; it is grief and the desire for vengeance that stops him from doing so any more. In fact, most of these incidents take place just as the war reaches its climax; plainly it has had more desultory stages that Homer did not find worth singing about. There are two suppliants who offer large ransoms, and one of them nearly has his offer accepted, but his captor's brother intervenes and prevents the bargain. The *Iliad* is of course an aristocratic document, which is why little is said of the commercial spirit behind these transactions, but it is clear that that was working vigorously here in the cause of civilization.

Greed and laziness were, as often, good counterpoises to violence. Should we assume that they were the only counterpoises, that there was no direct objection to killing the helpless? I don't think we can, for this reason. The Homeric atmosphere is extremely honest and unhypocritical; nobody professes high sentiments just for looks, and nobody would believe him if he did. Yet throughout the *Iliad* runs a most ambivalent attitude to war and violence; although they are man's noblest occupation they are terrible, piteous, lamentable, miserable, a curse and a disaster to mortals. And this too has the ring of a perfectly sincere sentiment. The God of War is constantly abused as a plague and a mischief-maker, without whom everything would go well. And in spite of the failure of supplication on the battlefield, much is said of the rights of suppliants, much of the anger of the gods against those who trample on such rights. And later Greek writings show that these suggestions were not intended or received as humbug; the rights of suppliants are an extremely serious matter with the tragedians. Nor are they enforced by social contract arguments or by prudence, but simply by insisting on the horror of the act. Even the ineffective pleas in Homer are often extremely moving; in fact, it is this very ambivalence that makes the *Iliad* a great poem, instead of a butcher's catalogue. In short, the poem speaks with two voices; it deplores what it glories in, and so somebody must take the blame.

In the *Iliad*, beasts are not needed for this role; the answer to the problem of evil is always simple; if you cannot blame the enemy, blame the gods. I think this function of gods as scapegoats has been somewhat overlooked in the history of religion; it seems very important. Where a man feels guilty and is genuinely anxious to apologize to those whom he has injured, there is much to be said for having been misled by an irresistible outside force. This preserves his self-respect and also his friendship for the victim. We say today, "I just don't know what came over me," but the Homeric Greeks did know; they could specify Zeus or Ares. All the vilest and stupidest acts in the *Iliad* result from suggestions from the gods, and anybody who really wants to apologize simply states as much. The crudest case is that of Agamemnon who, when he finally wants to withdraw from his idiotic quarrel with Achilles, apologizes by explaining that Zeus drove him mad. At this the attentive reader will open his eyes, since the poem describes all about the beginning of that quarrel and it was one of the few occasions when no god *did* intervene. But Agamemnon's reasoning is simple: If I did it, I must have been mad, and only Zeus could madden a king. *Quem deus vult perdere, prius dementat.*[22] No thunderbolts strike him, for the explanation is universally accepted.

It almost seems a pity that the development of religion and morality should have put an end to this convenient way of thinking. They did, however, and as the Greek notion of the gods grew steadily more dignified and noble, the problem, 'Whom can I blame for my faults?' again became pressing. I do not think it is any accident that Plato, the first Greek who consistently wrote of the gods as good, was also the first active exponent of the Beast Within. Black horses, wolves, lions, hawks, asses, and pigs recur every time he mentions the subject of evil; they provide the only terms in which he can talk about it. This is not an idle stylistic device: there is no such thing in Plato. His serious view is that evil is something alien to the soul; something Other, the debasing effect of matter seeping in through the instinctive nature. This treacherous element clearly cannot be anything properly human; it must be described in animal terms—and those of no particular animal at that, since all particular animals have their redeeming features, but a dreadful composite monster combining all the vices: in short, the Beast Within, whose only opponent is the Rational Soul. Certainly good feeling is sometimes invoked too, and given body as a Good Beast, but its goodness is supposed to consist in its obedience to Reason, not in its contributing anything itself. The white horse willingly obeys the charioteer and helps him to restrain the black;[23] it is no Balaam's Ass that hazards its own suggestions. Accordingly the feelings named in this connection are shame, ambition, the sense of honor, *never, for instance, pity or affection, where the body might be held to make good suggestions to the soul*. Plato's map excludes such a

22. Whom God wishes to ruin, he first drives mad.
23. Plato, *Phaedrus* 254–257.

possibility. This exclusion has been both morally and psychologically disastrous. Fear of and contempt for feeling make up an
irrational prejudice built into the structure of European
rationalism.[24]

Aristotelian and Kantian Beasts

Aristotle, though in general he was much more convinced of
man's continuity with the physical world than Plato, makes some
equally odd uses of the contrast between man and beast. In the
Nicomachean Ethics (1.7) he asks what the true function of man is,
in order to see what his happiness consists in, and concludes that
that function is the life of reason *because that life only is peculiar to
man*. I do not quarrel for the moment with the conclusion but
with the argument. If peculiarity to man is the point, why should
one not say that the function of man is technology, or the sexual
goings-on noted by Desmond Morris, or even exceptional
ruthlessness to one's own species? In all these respects man
seems to be unique. It must be shown *separately* that this differentia is itself the best human quality, that it is the point where
humanity is excellent as well as exceptional. And it is surely
possible *a priori* that the point on which humanity is excellent is
one in which it is *not* wholly unique—that at least some aspect of
it might be shared with other beings. Animals are, I think, used
in this argument to point up by contrast the value of reason, to
give examples of irrational conduct whose badness will seem
obvious to us. But unless we start with a particular view about the
importance of reason in conduct, we shall not necessarily agree.
If we prefer, among humans, an impulsively generous act to a
cold-blooded piece of calculation, we shall not be moved from
our preference by the thought that the generous act is more like
an animal's. Nor ought we to be. The claims of reason must be
made good, if at all, within the boundaries of human life itself.
They could be strengthened by contrasts with other species only
if it were true, as sometimes seems to be suggested, that animals
were, in fact, invariably wicked.

24. I shall develop this point further in Chap. 11.

Arguments of this form have, however, flowed on unchecked. One of them is used by Kant in his early *Lectures on Ethics*, where, in the course of some rather sharp remarks about sex, he says, "Sexuality exposes man to the danger of equality with the beasts." [25] But how can there be such a danger? The logic of this complaint deserves attention. To be *like* the beasts is not always considered bad, since we share with them many habits, such as washing and nest-building, and the care of the young, which everybody approves of. The point might be that beasts give more time and attention to sex than people, or are more promiscuous. But even if this were true, it would not *alone* show that they were wrong to do so, or that people would be wrong to imitate them—not unless one had shown separately that animals always *were* wrong, or that people should never imitate them. This would be hard in face of such advice as "Go to the Ant, thou sluggard," or "Be ye wise as serpents and harmless as doves." There are many activities, such as eating bananas, where the accusation "You are behaving like an animal" could properly be met with the answer, "But I *am* an animal." We need to be shown—again, separately, and within the context of human life—*why* a particular activity is unsuitable to people. Otherwise the reference to animals here follows a form often used in popular morality when mention is made of any group considered inferior—we will call them Gonks. The argument runs:

Some Gonkish practices are abominable

This is a Gonkish practice

Therefore this practice is abominable.

The only thing that could make an honest argument of this would be a real universal major premise, and in the case of animals such a premise has often been half-consciously accepted. If one assumes that *everything* animals do is evil or inferior, then the argument takes on some force. The vices of the monstrous Beast Within are being projected on to actual animals.

Kant does not really need this argument at all. The dangers that he sees in sexuality can be, and are, much better expressed in terms more central to his ethics. They are dangers of treating

25. "Duties towards the Body in Respect of Sexual Impulse," *Lectures on Ethics*, tr. Louis Infield (London, 1930), p. 164.

people as things, treating them without respect, using them as means and not as ends in themselves. These are intelligible concepts. But the notion of humanity Kant uses in developing them is an odd one, and its oddity is again brought out by his attitude to animals. He wants us to respect humanity because it is rational, not because it is conscious. We wonder about lunatics, about the old, about babies. Kant is adamant that everything in human form must be respected, but has he any business to be so? Animals give an interesting test; can we treat them as things? Or are they too ends in themselves? Kant says they are not ends in themselves because they are not rational, so we cannot have any duties to them and we may treat them simply as means to our own ends. This does not mean that we may be cruel to them. But the reason for not being cruel is that cruelty would debase our own nature. It is therefore our duty to ourselves to avoid this defilement. But *why* it should be a defilement we don't know. There seems no official reason why Kant should not say, with Spinoza, that animals, though conscious, are entirely at the disposal of man, and can be used as suits his purposes. If these purposes are otherwise important, even if they involve giving great pain to the animal, no objection could arise on Spinoza's principles, nor as far as I can see on Kant's either.[26] There would therefore seem to be no objection to enjoying giving pain either. I do not just mean that the objections would be weak: I think they would be meaningless. This view seems very forced, almost as forced as Descartes' contention that animals are actually unconscious.[27] If you think cruelty wrong in general—which Kant certainly did—it seems devious to say that cruelty to animals is wrong for entirely different reasons from cruelty to people.

What I have said about Plato, Aristotle, and Kant has, I hope, shown that the use of animals as symbols of wickedness has done ethics no good, and that arguments based on it are irrelevant. But are they positively misleading? I think they are. In the first place, irrelevance itself misleads, because it distracts. Insofar as

26. Kant, "Duties towards Animals and Spirits," *Lectures on Ethics.* For Spinoza, see below, Chap. 13, pp. 351ff. I shall be pursuing the very important point raised by Kant both there and in Chap. 10, pp. 218ff.

27. For Descartes, see the second section of Chap. 10.

people looked for the source of evil in their animal nature, which was something they could not possibly alter, they were kept occupied by a contest they could not win. They either gave their energies to trying to jump off their shadows, or grew depressed at the difficulty of their position and gave up altogether. This defect is obvious in Platonism, in Stoicism, and in their influence on Christianity. The trouble is that animal nature is regarded, not just as containing specific dangers, but either as evil all through or at least as totally chaotic and without any helpful principle of order. It follows that there can be no sense in trying to organize it on its own principles and no sense in studying it to see what those principles might be. Order must be imposed from outside by Reason or Grace—again a hopeless task, for why should a chaotic animal take any notice of Grace or Reason? But of course such animal nature is an unreal abstraction. Every existing animal species has its *own* nature, its own hierarchy of instincts—in a sense, its own virtues. In social animals, such as ourselves and the wolves, there must be natural affection and communicativeness, and, in spite of our evolutionary gaffe in inventing weapons, it is plain that we are much better fitted to live socially than to live alone or in anarchy. Nearly all our most interesting occupations are social ones. Rousseau's or Hobbes's state of nature would be fine for intelligent crocodiles, if there were any. For people it is a baseless fantasy.

Nor does our richness in aggression disprove this.[28] It is one of Lorenz's most interesting suggestions that only creatures ca-

28. Recent discussions of this topic have been sidetracked by the suggestion that the word *aggression* properly has only a political sense, that it means only official, formalized warfare. This seems quite out of accord with usage. It has been in common use throughout this century as the name of a motive, that is, of the wish or tendency to *attack*—privately or publicly, physically or emotionally, literally or metaphorically. ("He is chock-full of aggression.") That is how I use it. Wilson (pp. 22, 242, 578) suggests reserving the name *aggression* for the act ("an abridgment of the rights of another"), while calling the motive aggressiveness. This will not work because (a) without the motive, an injurious act is not a piece of aggression at all (it might be, for instance, an accident or a piece of self-defense), and (b) if the motive is there, we can still show aggression by gestures and so on, even if we do no damage. Moreover, the notion of "rights" is quite obscure.

pable of aggression toward their own kind are capable of affection. In order to distinguish some of one's species as friends, it may be necessary at the same time to distinguish others as enemies. At the simplest level, in order to express one's love for A, it may be necessary sometimes to attack B, or at least to threaten him. Ambivalence may be ancient indeed. However that may be, he is clearly right in saying that aggression is directly bound up in most of the activities we value, and cannot simply be dropped like an old sock. It is part of our nature. But he does *not* mean that we cannot get along without bloodshed. For our nature is not Plato's and Nietzsche's Beast Without the Law. It is a complex, balanced affair, a structure like the Beasts Within other beasts, subject to a lot of laws, and rather more, not less, adaptable than others, because where they grew horns and prickles, we grew an intelligence, which is quite an effective adaptive mechanism. Where fighting is inconvenient, we can play chess or sue each other. Even the Beasts Within other beasts are much more adaptable here than has been believed. In particular, if they do not get what they want, they will accept something else instead. When they thirst for blood and cannot catch their enemy, they work it off by mock attacks on empty air or pieces of wood or the surrounding scenery, or by making noises, or by driving off neighbors or casual passers-by whom they do not usually hurt. This is called *redirection*.[29] Alternatively they turn vigorously to some apparently irrelevant activity; this is called *displacement*.[30] It is very clear that without these devices

29. See Lorenz, *On Aggression*, index under *Redirected Activity*. Of all the ethological concepts I have come across, this seems to me the most significant politically, for it is something we usually manage not to recognize in ourselves, telling ourselves that the people on whom we work off our anger actually *are* abominable. Yet bystanders can see our self-deception plainly. Victims often cannot escape, as passing animals usually can, because human society roots them in their place. Thus, dozens of human iniquities from wife-beating to racism are caused by the passing on of offense.

30. See Tinbergen, *The Herring Gull's World* (London, 1953), chap. 7. Displacement is also of great general interest in that, in a clear sense, it *explains* embarrassment—an essential job which I don't think has been properly done before. I suspect also that many of our activities are unsatisfying because they are really displacement activities. Overeating and much sexual activity may be examples.

most living creatures would long ago have pined away or burst from disappointment, since actually getting what one wants must be one of the world's rarest experiences. Of course these things are possible for people, and we all practice them constantly. (The behavior of anybody waiting impatiently for something will supply excellent examples.) But it is part of the mythical natural history of the Beast Within that it must have blood—that it will not be content to swear, break dishes, play squash, or write to the newspapers instead. The limits of displacement and redirection for the human species are not clear; we have all seen that they can stretch quite wide. The "nonaggressive" cultures cited by anthropologists provide some pretty examples. Margaret Mead's Arapesh, for instance, devote much of their lives to precautions against hostile sorcery,[31] and Ruth Benedict's Zuni Indians, while given to an apparently less sinister form of magic, openly use it as a means and a pretext for the control of aggression, which seems a rather different thing from not being aggressive in the first place.[32] ("The fundamental tabu upon their holy men during their periods of office is against any suspicion of anger.") Such ways of conducting the lightning are just the kind of thing that Lorenz wants us to study; he merely suggests that seeing them *as* displacement activities may enable us to understand them better, that ethological studies might well be useful here along with the obvious psychological and anthropological ones. But for this purpose we must honestly recognize our own pugnacity, and modify the notion of the characteristically human that has been accepted both by common opinion and by philosophers. Neither Beasts Without nor Beasts Within are as beastly as they have been painted.

31. Mead, *Sex and Temperament in Three Primitive Societies* (New York, 1935).
32. Benedict, *Patterns of Culture* (Boston, 1934), chap. 4.

CHAPTER 3

Instinct, Nature, and Purpose

Instincts, Closed and Open

I have been suggesting that animal life is much more orderly, and ordered in a way much closer to human patterns, than tradition suggests. People may grant this, and still ask what it means to attribute the order to Instinct. This question must be gone into before the word can sensibly be applied to people. It is a large topic, but I may at least be able to remove a few obvious confusions.

To begin with, people who dislike the *word* "instinct" can if they prefer often read *drive* or *program* for it, both of which are now in quite popular use. The substitution may help to make it clearer that what we are talking about is not a voice within, nor any supernatural being or entity, but a disposition, a set of causal properties. People tend to wave Occam's Razor around somewhat wildly here, because they think they smell entities lurking under all the abstract terms.[1] Considering some past uses of "instinct,"

---

1. Occam's Razor is the (medieval) empiricist principle that we must not invoke more kinds of entity than we need for an explanation. But just what counts as an entity is none too clear. There has been lasting doubt about whether the term applies to such things as gravitational attraction and the unseen particles of physics. (See for example, Berkeley, *Principles of Human Knowledge*, 102–117.) Are economic forces "entities"? We all need to use abstract nouns, and must be careful how we do so. But not all of them are vacuous. See note on p. 99.

For the quite clear and necessary use of *instinct* in modern zoology, see Tinbergen's admirable book *The Study of Instinct*. For a thoroughly antimetaphysical this is not surprising. But care is no more necessary here than it is with abstract terms like *society* or even *behavior*. Skinner sometimes writes of organisms "emitting behavior" as if it were some kind of gas.[2] No doubt he doesn't want to be taken literally.

Another source of trouble is, I think, the notion that a creature that is going to act on instinct must begin to do so as soon as it is born. Some instinctive behavior, such as human crying and sucking, and the baby kangaroo's extraordinary journey to the pouch, does work like this. Most does not; it happens when the occasion arises and the creature is mature enough. Sexual behavior, honey dances, birdsong, and all reactions to extreme and unusual threats appear later. There is nothing mysterious about this delayed action of inherent dispositions, any more than there is about a tree that, after continuing apparently inactive for many years, suddenly produces chestnuts, or indeed a human body that, at a certain point, stops growing. In the medical sector, nobody is surprised at this long-term innate programming. And since glands, brains, secretions, and so on are on anyone's view physical objects, it seems odd to be surprised at the same programming in the behavioral context.

Some people might, I think, accept this account for instinctive actions that are perfectly specific, such as nest-building or fairly standardized sexual conduct. What worries them is the notion that a more general pattern, such as aggression or sex generally, should be called instinctive. But the two things go together. Specific actions make sense only within a certain context, a particular way of life.

A useful piece of terminology here is that of closed and open instincts or programs. Closed instincts are behavior patterns fixed genetically in every detail, like the bees' honey dance, some birdsong, and the nest-building pattern of weaver birds. Here

---

discussion of its philosophical problems, see Lorenz's chapter, "The Great Parliament of Instincts," in *On Aggression*. See also Hinde, "Ethological Models and the Concept of Drive."

2. He introduces the phrase as an important technical term in *The Behavior of Organisms*, p. 20. Talk of "reinforcing behavior" also seems to imply that behavior exists, as a permanent stuff like concrete, between performances. But all there really is then is an organism, with certain dispositions or causal properties.

the same complicated pattern, correct in every detail, will be produced by creatures that have been carefully reared in isolation from any member of their own species and from any helpful conditioning. Such genetic programming takes the place of intelligence; learning is just maturation. Open instincts on the other hand are programs with a gap. Parts of the behavior pattern are innately determined, but others are left to be filled in by experience. Thus young birds are so constructed (or "programmed") as to follow, seek after, and obey whatever comes before them as their mother—but the mother's actual appearance cannot be in the program. Experience must "imprint" it. This is the simplest kind of "open" instinct, and it is very common. Even quite simple animals, however, perform activities where the gap left for experience has to be much larger, yet the general aim is still innately determined. For instance, in such general locomotive tendencies as the one to *come home*—which is common to many animals, including some very simple ones—an indefinite and unpredictable variety of ways of traveling, routes to be followed, and kinds of possible obstacle has to be provided for. Yet the creature must still have a general ruling motive. It cannot just wander at random till something "reinforces" a movement, since this is the surest way to an early death. For each kind of animal, a quite limited way of life is suitable, a range that it must quickly find and keep to. So "programming" includes a number of strong *general* tendencies, for example, to get home, to seek water, to hide by day, and to avoid open spaces. And the more complex, the more intelligent creatures become, the more they are programmed in this general way, rather than in full detail. Specific actions that are part of the species repertory occur, but they work only in the context of these general directives. These open instincts are general tendencies to certain *kinds* of behavior, such as hunting, tree-climbing, washing, singing, or caring for the young. Cats, for example, tend naturally to hunt; they will do so even if deprived of all example. They do it as kittens when they do not need food, and they will go on doing it even if they are kept fully fed; it is not just a means to an end. But their hunting is not a single stereotyped pattern, it covers a wide repertory of movements. A cat will improve greatly in its choice of these during its life; it can invent new ones and pick up tips from other cats. In this sense hunting is learned. The antithesis between nature and nurture is quite false and unhelpful here; hunting, like most activities of higher animals, is both innate *and* learned. The creature is born with certain powers and a strong wish to use them, but it will need time, practice, and (often) some example before it can develop them properly. Other powers and wishes it does *not* have and will find hard to acquire. For instance, swimming is outside the usual range of both cats and apes; in spite of their great agility it does not suit them, as it suits men and hippopotami; example will not usually bring them into the water, and they may starve if their food lies beyond it. And Cape Hunting Dogs, unlike most of the dog tribe, do not display dominance behavior nor exclusive selection of a mate. They are altogether less individualistic, more thoroughly welded into a society, than are most dogs. That is the character of their species. And every species has such a character.[3]

Now in this context, the notion of aggression as a general open instinct or tendency is perfectly sensible. Whether or not any particular species is aggressive is as clear a question as whether it burrows or builds nests. The range of behavior covered is wider, but still quite distinct. Aggression is a general tendency to attack members of one's species. It is not that much more particular thing, a tendency to kill. It is satisfied with driving away, though if it meets resistance there may be a fight involving injury or death. In any species that is aggressive at all, there are of course specific patterns of behavior used in attack and threat; dogs do not attack in the same way as terns or porcupines. So attack itself is not something generalized and standard. But there is still a unifying factor; threats are (necessarily) understandable across species barriers. In highly social species, the interpretation of threats is so far developed and refined that actual physical attack is very seldom needed, though it is always a possibility. What unifies cases of attack then is *not* (as people sometimes think)

3. See Schaller, *Year of the Gorilla*, pp. 58 and 103, and Bueler, *Wild Dogs of the World*, pp. 231–234. More on this general point in Chap. 11, pp. 273ff.

their all tending toward a specific act, namely killing. It is their relation to other motives connected with space and dominance. Aggressive creatures are commonly ones that want space around them, and once they have got somebody else out of it they are usually content to forget about him. Certainly killing him is one way of doing this, but in natural conditions it is a comparatively rare one. Much commoner is requiring his submission. An animal that gives way to a mild attack often does not need actually to vanish, provided that it *makes itself small*. It marks its submission by bowing down in some way, so that it does not intrude on the space surrounding the victor. If the submission is accepted, it does not have to go away; the winner often signifies this with a friendly gesture, and the quarrel is "made up." This whole range of behavior is extremely complex. But the capacity for it is still innate in a species, and forms a part of the species character.

Open instincts of this kind are the main equipment of the higher animals. It is to them that we must attribute all the complex behavior that makes the wolf's social life so successful; monogamy, cleanliness, cub care, and inability to attack the helpless are loose patterns, but they are built in. Open and closed instincts, however, are clearly not distinct kinds of things; they are extremes of a scale with many grades between. For instance, besides the birds with a fixed song pattern, there are others with various powers of imitation. Mockingbirds imitate other birds' song and also nonbird noises; their programming is obviously a more complicated matter than a cuckoo's, and must include some power of selection. But imitating itself *is* an instinct with them; they will do it untrained and you cannot teach them to compose instead. Nest-building with the higher animals is similar; unlike the weaver birds, they have no fixed stereotype, but a nest they will have, and if there is nothing to build it of they will do the best they can without. Rats will carry their own tails repeatedly into a corner, still showing the same peculiar movements they would use if they had proper materials.[4] In this way, every gradation is found from the stereotype to the quite

4. W. H. Thorpe (who gives other examples of this sort of thing) in the Introduction to *King Solomon's Ring*.

general tendency.[5] At the narrow end, perhaps we can say that no instinct can ever be completely closed. Even the weaver bird must vary things a little according to the branch and his materials; even the dancing bee adapts to the state of the hive and of her digestion. At the wide end, what shall we say? Will the notion of open instincts make sense when applied to people? Or does it then become so wide as to be vacuous?

When people such as Watson say that man has no instincts, they always mean closed instincts. They point to his failure to make standard webs or do standard honey dances, and ignore his persistent patterns of motivation. Why do people form families? Why do they take care of their homes and quarrel over boundaries? Why do they own property? Why do they talk so much, and dance, and sing? Why do children play, and for that matter adults too? Why is nobody living in the Republic of Plato?

According to Blank Paper theory, because of cultural conditioning. But this is like explaining gravitation by saying that whenever something falls, something else pushed it; even if it were true, it wouldn't help. Who started it? Nor does it tell us why people ever *resist* their families, why they do what everybody is culturally conditioning them *not* to do. I have never seen a proper answer to that on the Blank Paper assumption, but I gather it would be expressed in terms of subcultures and cultural ambivalences, of society's need for a scapegoat, and the like. It is a pleasing picture; how do all the children of eighteen months pass the news along the grapevine that now is the time to join the subculture, to start climbing furniture, toddling out of the house, playing with fire, breaking windows, taking things to pieces, messing with mud, and chasing the ducks? For these are perfectly specific things which *all* healthy children can be depended on to do, not only unconditioned but in the face of all deterrents. Just so, Chomsky asks Skinner how it comes about that small children introduce their

5. For the principles determining whether open or closed programming will occur in a given context, see Ernst Mayr, "Behavior Programs and Evolutionary Strategies," *American Scientist*, 62 (1974).

own grammatical mistakes into speech, talking in a way that they have never heard and that will be noticed only to be corrected. In dealing with such questions, the Blank Paper theorist's hands are tied by his *a priori* assumption.

The ethologist, on the other hand, proceeds empirically. When he finds some activity going on among the species he studies, he simply starts watching, photographing, and taking notes. From detailed observation of the context and comparison with other activities he gradually moves toward explaining its relation with other things that are done. (Thus, when herring gulls meet at the borders of their territories they constantly turn aside and pull grass. This is like nest-building behavior, but the birds do not use the grass. Instead they follow other patterns that commonly issue in fighting, and at times do fight. Having thoroughly studied all the things they do, and compared them with their conduct on other occasions, the ethologist tries the hypothesis that this is a displacement activity, undertaken to relieve a conflict between the motives of fear and aggression. But he does not accept this without careful comparison with other displacement activities and a full analysis of the term and its physiological implications.[6])

What Is the Nature of a Species?

Because of his methods of observation and his refusal to posit single explanations, the ethologist is better off than many previous people who have made use of the term "human nature." The term is suspect because it does suggest cure-all explanations, sweeping theories that man is basically sexual, basically selfish or acquisitive, basically evil, or basically good. These theories try to account for human conduct much as a simpleminded person might attempt to deal with rising damp, looking for a single place where water is coming in, a single

6. See Tinbergen's extremely careful and well-defended explanation, *The Herring Gull's World*, chap. 7.

source of motivation. This hydraulic approach always leads to incredible distortions once the theorist is off his home ground, as can be seen from Marxist theories of art or Freudian explanations of politics. The ethologist, on the other hand, does not want to say that human nature is basically anything; he wants to see what it consists of. (Even Robert Ardrey does not claim that man is *basically* territorial.) He proceeds more like a surveyor mapping a valley: he notes a spring here, a spring there; he finds that some of them do tend to run together (as, for instance, a cat uses tree-climbing for hunting and caterwauling in courtship.) If he finds an apparently isolated activity, with no connection with the creature's other habits, he simply accumulates information until a connection appears. Thus the "suicide" of lemmings turns out to be not an isolated monstrous drive, but part of a complicated migration pattern that results from their reaction to overcrowding.[7] Again, the grass-pulling gulls are moved not by a drive for destruction, but by the interworking of two patterns of motivation, fear and aggression, which are connected in certain definite ways in their lives in the context of nesting, and can be roughly mapped to show the general character of the species. *Understanding a habit is seeing what company it keeps.* The meaning is the use. The only assumption made here is the general biologist's one that there is *some* system in an organism, some point in any widespread plant or animal habit. This premise is justified by its success.[8]

The nature of a species, then, consists in a certain range of powers and tendencies, a repertoire, inherited and forming a fairly firm characteristic pattern, though conditions after birth may vary the details quite a lot. In this way, baboons are "naturally hierarchical animals," since they travel in bands with a leader and what is pleasingly called a senate of elders, and show carefully graded dominance behavior down to the meanest juvenile. This is not "disproved" by showing that a group does not have a

---

7. See W. Marsden, *The Lemming Year* (London, 1964); W. Elton, *Voles, Mice and Lemmings* (Oxford, 1942).

8. I shall discuss this assumption further in the last section of this chapter. See also pp. 153–154.

brutal "pecking order," nor that the details of the hierarchy vary a great deal with different species and conditions.[9] Investigating these subtleties merely strengthens and elucidates the idea of a natural hierarchical tendency. Nor is it disproved by finding an occasional baboon who is disrespectful or lax about his dignity; baboons "naturally" have fur, and finding a few going bald does not disprove it.

With this analogy in mind, let us face the fashionable question, is man naturally aggressive? First, what does it mean to say he is naturally aggressive? To the ethologist it certainly does *not* mean that he is basically aggressive, that that is his sole or overwhelming motive. It means that he is aggressive among other things, that in his repertory of natural tendencies there is one to attack other members of his species sometimes, without being taught to, without needing to as a means to another end, and without always having what seems to be adequate provocation. This has been hotly denied. Now the ethologist must try to proceed with man as he would with any other species, to look at its behavior impartially first and then search for causes and connections. He will find this easiest if he is not human himself, but is a member of another species coming here as an observer. So we will take him to come from Alpha Centauri, and call him for short the Centaur. This Centaur has at his command hundreds of years of observations on *Homo sapiens*. One of the things that strikes him is that the creature often deliberately kills or injures members of his own species—not, of course, all the time, but still much more often than other creatures on the planet. He has authentic records of the Hundred Years War, the Seven Years War, the Thirty Years War and all the rest, along with Armenian Massacres, ritual murder, cannibalism, capital punishment, tortures, pogroms, and holocausts, and he has no such records for other species. All this strikes him as quite as remarkable as the other distinguishing marks of the species, and he asks the human sociologist (whom we will call Jones to avoid scandal) for an explanation. Things proceed as follows:

9. For the variations, see T. E. Rowell, "Variations in the Social Order of Primates," in *Primate Ethology*, ed. Morris.

Jones. All aggression is due to cultural conditioning.[10]

Centaur. I beg your pardon?

Jones. They do it because their parents tell them to.

Centaur. Do they always do what their parents tell them?

Jones. They do so when their parents are powerfully convinced.

Centaur. Why then are the *parents* so powerfully convinced of the need for violence?

Jones. The parents are misled by wicked rulers, who find war in their interest. Modern techniques of brain-washing render this sort of deception very easy.

Centaur. I suppose then that this slaughter bears all the marks of a culturally imposed activity? It will be desultory, etiquette-ridden, reluctant, like church-going among people who are not religious? It will, in view of what you say about modern techniques, be a much more recent invention than these documents suggest? It will be undertaken with obvious boredom, simply to gain a living and satisfy the authorities? It will need to be disguised by association with something more attractive to render it palatable? It will be readily abandoned in any disturbance, and will be more popular with the old than with the young? *Now please show me films and records of various sorts of slaughter, in which these points are clearly brought out.*

Jones. Your approach is crude and you have not understood the subtlety with which society conducts its conditioning campaign. Most of it is unconscious. People think they are acting spontaneously.

Centaur. But I thought I had heard you complain, in discussing other schools of Earthling psychology, that they relied on hypotheses about unconscious proceedings? Did you not dismiss such hypotheses as unverifiable, and therefore meaningless, and their use as unscientific?

Jones. Certainly I did. But then, you see, their hypotheses, unlike mine, happen to be *wrong*. Mine are scientific because they are not just hypotheses. They are the principles of my science. . . .

10. Jones's arguments may be found well stated by, for example, the distinguished team of anti-ethologists collected for the symposium called *Man and Aggression*, edited by Ashley Montagu (Oxford, 1968), and throughout Montagu's own works.

That is one way the conversation may go. Another is this: instead of cultural conditioning, Jones says that violence results from *frustration*.[11] That is to say, men never engage in aggression if they are not frustrated:

Centaur. But do men ever live a life that does not frustrate them?
FIRST ALTERNATIVE:
Jones (emphatically). Never. Such a life is impossible.
Centaur. Then how do you know what they would do if they did?
Jones. Because what is natural is good, and aggression is bad.
Centaur. Species, however, are sometimes naturally prone to habits which for them are bad, as appears from your own records of the Irish deer, the argus pheasant,[12] and possibly the dinosaurs. Circumstances change, selection mechanisms are fallible, traits hypertrophy or stop being adaptive when the climate alters or the species invents weapons.
Jones. You do not appreciate the dignity of man. He is above such lapses.
Centaur. I apologize. Perhaps we had better leave aside the question of what would happen if he were *not* frustrated. *Are his reactions when he is frustrated not also a part of his nature?* Other species make full use of displacement activities; gulls pull grass, wolves growl, gorillas roar, sticklebacks stand on their heads and dig gravel. In this way actual slaughter is most often avoided. Man has displacement activities too (which seems in itself evidence of aggressive wishes), but they are not enough to keep him from slaughter. *Why not?*
Jones. It might possibly be allowable to describe this state of affairs in terms of an "aggressive instinct"—but only if we make clear that it is a *conditional* instinct, one that will come into play only if there is frustration and provocation first.
Centaur. *All* instincts are in some sense conditional. They all need

11. This side of the case is stated, much more systematically, in *Frustration and Aggression* by John Dollard et al. (New Haven, 1939).
12. See Wilson, *Sociobiology*, pp. 132, 262, 315, 548, and Lorenz, *On Aggression*, p. 40. The whole discussion there of how nonadaptive traits can be evolved and tolerated is relevant to my argument in the next section; see p. 74. For more about it, and particularly about the Irish deer, see pp. 133 (note) and 149.

proper occasions. Even to get hungry and thirsty, animals have to be in normal health and not preoccupied by some other, stronger motive such as fear. If the condition you have in mind is just the usual, inevitable measure of frustration and annoyance, this hardly means much. But you seem to be saying more. Do you seriously mean that *provocation* is always necessary? That aggression can only be reactive? That the occasions when men, like other creatures, appear to go out to seek a quarrel are always illusory? *If people attack only when they are provoked, who provokes them?*

SECOND ALTERNATIVE:

Jones. They hardly ever escape frustration, but that is because of a fault committed by nearly all parents and teachers, which deforms most human beings in early life.

Centaur. Then is not liability to commit that fault, and to be so easily deformed by it, part of the nature of the species rather than an outside accident? And please tell me more about the exceptional nonaggressive cases. Do they *never* want what they cannot get? And if they do, does their frustration never result in aggressive behavior?

Jones. Maybe, but then the educational fault in question, though unnatural, is always committed to some degree.

Centaur. What is the difference between saying this and saying that the fault in question *is* natural? You would then be recommending keeping it in check by certain educational methods, and of course you need not mean that those methods themselves are unnatural either. You would be using one part of the creature's nature to control another, just as you do when you cultivate a child's natural prudence to counter his natural tendency to take risks. That is how education works. All educable species are complex. If I may digress to the problems of centaurs. . . .

The Meaning of "Biological Determinism"

A third, rather more metaphysical variation of this argument has been added lately:

Jones. The notion that aggression is innate is biological determinism. This poses an intolerable threat to human freedom.

Centaur. Are you objecting to determinism generally, or just to the biological kind?

FIRST ALTERNATIVE:

Jones. To the biological kind. Physical determinism I can stand; economic and social determinism I positively welcome.[13]

Centaur. Please go on. If the behavior of living cells is not determinate, how will economic or social prediction be possible? At present we take such things as the pattern of crop growth or of the human metabolism, including people's digestive capacities, for granted. But these are surely the concern of biology? Or again, if the behavior of physical particles is determined, at what stage does indeterminacy creep in? Is the behavior of amoebae undetermined?

Jones. No, no. My objection is, of course, confined to the human scene. It might be better to describe it as aimed against *genetic* determinism. What I resist is the suggestion that a human life is completely predictable from genes, before the individual ever meets his society.

Centaur. Is there such a suggestion?

Jones. Your talk of innate aggression implies it.

Centaur. No, indeed—no more than talking of us as innately social implies that we must spend our lives going to parties, or saying that we are innately suggestible means that we must believe everything we are told—or, indeed, that calling us capable of sleep means that we have to sleep all the time. These are *general* dispositions. The room for particular developments within them and bargains between them is enormous.

Jones. Then you do not take your genetic factors seriously as causes.

Centaur. They are perfectly serious, but they are wide, and they are only one set of causes among others. No set of causes alone can be "fully determining." That, surely, is the weakness of all

13. This seems the minimum position for Marxists. It is usually extended into an enthusiasm for determinism generally. See for instance Engels, *Anti-Dühring*, Pt. 1, sec. on Morality and Law, Freedom and Necessity: "Freedom is the recognition of necessity.... Freedom does not consist in the dream of independence of natural laws, but in the knowledge of these laws, and in the possibility that it gives of systematically directing the work towards definite ends." He specifies that this applies as much to human minds as to lifeless matter.

forms of *hyphenated* determinism—economic, social, physical, or, indeed, genetic.

This point brings us to the SECOND ALTERNATIVE, to the possibility of dismissing determinism altogether. What would this mean?

Centaur. What actually *is* determinism? Your idea seems to be that there are two sorts of causes—hard and soft, determining and disposing, complete and incomplete. You want genetic causes classed as the incomplete, soft sort. But determinism is surely a view about *all* causes. And *all* causes are incomplete. If we pick out one set of them—economic, environmental, psychological, or whatnot—we are just making a selection, one that we hope will be helpful, from a vast set, all of which must be present. We are not claiming to unveil the secret spring of the whole.

So far as it goes, however, we must take each set seriously, or it is no use to us. Causes do not *force* effects to happen—that is a superstitious view—but they do help us to understand and predict them. Perhaps then, if we are to understand it, we must *for theoretical purposes* think of human behavior as predictable. Still, as that interesting humanoid philosopher Bertrand Russell makes clear, nobody could conceivably have the information that would make it predictable in practice. As he says, defining determinism, "Given *the state of the whole universe throughout any finite time*, however short, every previous and subsequent event can theoretically be determined as a function of the given events during that time."[14] Unless you think it conceivable that anybody should be given that, determinism remains something highly theoretical and remote. Like the assumption that questions have answers, it is a piece of apparatus for investigation, not the statement of a fact. But the contrary assumption, that our actions are not predetermined, is much less remote; it is one that we have to make every time that we wonder what to do. It is

14. "On the Notion of Cause," in *Our Knowledge of the External World* (London, 1914), p. 221, Centaur's italics.

another necessary piece of apparatus, used for a different purpose. This is the one that you need for human freedom. And you will find that it lands you in the same sort of difficulty about every other sort of cause as about genetic ones.[15]

Jones. I doubt that. Genetic causes are the only ones which are supposed to *constitute* me. I have to hold myself free, as something unconditioned, to deal autonomously with the conditions that my society thrusts upon me.

Centaur. How (if you will excuse the question) could nothing oppose anything? If you wish to be immune from genetic causes, do you not condemn yourself to be simply and solely a product of your society?

What you have here seems to be a quite general metaphysical problem, not something local about genetics. To solve it will call for careful work on such notions as cause, necessity, action, and the status of general principles. Centaurian metaphysicians have made some suggestions which you might possibly find helpful. . . .

Jones. I am not interested in metaphysics.

Centaur. Then may I ask you instead about some practical difficulties that you seem likely to raise for yourself in medical contexts? I notice that, when you are speaking medically, you seem fairly satisfied with determinism even on biological questions. You willingly excuse bad conduct where it seems that the offender has something wrong with his glands or his brain. Here you assume what seems necessary for all understanding of conduct: a continuity between the physical and mental aspects of people. And you accept the physical processes as determined.

But glands and brain are inherited. Must not their causal story be the same for the healthy and the sick? The difference seems to be that in the case of the healthy the range of possible action is a different one, and we can pay much more attention to the

---

15. The somewhat Kantian position I have sketched here, with brutal shortness, however popular on Alpha Centauri, will not suit everybody. (Determinism is, in fact, a much more obscure view, much harder to state, than people often suppose.) But this does not affect the central point that *whatever* view one takes about causes generally, there can be no possible reason for exempting genetic causes from it.

quite distinct questions that arise about their reasons. Reasons and causes are parallel ways of explaining conduct. They do not compete. That point, however, is certainly metaphysical.

To be practical, then: I have heard, somewhere on Earth, the suggestion that the best *practical* solution to the problem of free will is to treat oneself as free and other people as determined. This may well be the principle you are acting on in medical cases. And it may well be a good policy. But it does seem to raise some theoretical questions.

Anyone who thinks that the Centaur and I are contending against men of straw should look at an article by Stephen Jay Gould attacking *Sociobiology*. Gould, who is himself a geneticist, allows in principle that genetic factors might affect our social life, but is willing to suggest only extraordinarily general ways in which they might do so:

We would lead very different social lives if we photosynthesized (no agriculture, gathering, or hunting—the major determinants of our social evolution) or had life cycles like those of certain gall midges.... Unless the "interesting" properties of human behavior are under specific genetic control, sociology need fear no invasion of its turf. By interesting, I refer to the subjects sociologists and anthropologists fight about most often—aggression, social stratification, and differences between men and women. If genes only specify that we are large enough to live in a world of gravitational forces, need to rest our bodies by sleeping, and do not photosynthesize, then the realm of genetic determinism will be relatively uninspiring.[16]

And if they only specified that, newborn babies would be what bear cubs were once supposed to be—indeterminate lumps of animal protoplasm, needing to be licked into shape by their elders. As things are, babies start life with a species-specific nervous system, hitched to a determinate brain and at the other end to specific organs, muscles and expressive devices. This system is linked to glands producing secretions well known to have a great deal of influence over conduct. It is not clear how this could fail to be "specific control"—though obviously it is not the *only* kind of control that affects social behavior.

16. "Biological Potential vs. Biological Determinism," *Natural History*, May 1976, pp. 16, 18.

There are two reasons why Gould is unwilling to consider this range of causes. One is that he supposes the admission of innate tendencies to be inextricably linked with fascism. Unlike some people who believe this, however, Gould is not happy about making it his cornerstone. He sees that suppositions about facts ought not to be dismissed *merely* on the ground that accepting them might lead people to behave badly. He knows that evidence is relevant. Thus he says, "Scientific truth, as we understand it, must be our primary criterion.... If genetic determinism is true, we will learn to live with it." This is very proper. *But*, he goes on, "I reiterate my statement that no evidence exists to support it."[17]

Now if he means evidence for the view that genetic causes *alone* determine behavior, he will naturally find none, since that view is incoherent and no one holds it. If he means evidence for the view that they have *some* effect on behavior, that can be found in a vast range of activities which cannot sensibly and economically be explained on any other assumption. As random samples, we might name, on the negative side, all behavior in small children which displeases and startles their parents—since this, by definition, is *not* the outcome of conditioning. On the positive one, we could point to all aspects of sexual behavior which people are able to discover for themselves without instruction and sometimes in the teeth of general discouragement, and the specific talents (notably, but not only, mathematical) sometimes found in children who spontaneously take to, and excel in, an activity frowned on by or entirely unknown to those around them.

Is this *"evidence* for genetic determinism"? Is it *proof*? Gould is clearly worried by the question of what would count as evidence. Sometimes he seems inclined to say that there is no evidence either way. The first point to grasp here is that very general principles are *not* going to be proved by control experiments, which is what many people now seem somehow to expect. Experiments can only settle relatively small points, filling in the gaps in a general system of thought already devised because it is helpful in explaining a wide range of experience. The Blank Paper

17. Ibid., p. 22.

theory itself, as much as those that oppose it, stands or falls by this test.

This problem about the possibility of genetic explanation is not a detailed, factual question, of the sort that can be settled by experiment. It concerns our *ways* of thinking—the principles on which we interpret experimental results, and, what is even more important, the assumptions on which we select our questions. Patterns like these can never be shot down or set up at a blow. They are tested gradually, on complex principles, by their fit to the general shape of the facts available and to the other patterns of thought in use.

Though it hovers in the background, I am inclined to think that the metaphysical point raised by the question of "genetic determinism" is something of a red herring. When people object particularly to *aggression* as innate, they are commonly doing so on the assumption that human nature is good, and therefore that if slaughter is bad, it must be brought about by something other than human nature. But this is quite a different position from the official line that there is no such thing as human nature at all. Thus Ashley Montagu, one of Lorenz's most excited opponents, holds *both* that man has no instincts, and that he has a complex system of things called basic needs, the most important of which is love. Man naturally needs only what is good, says Montagu; everything evil, which includes all forms of physical combat, is alien to him and introduced from outside. He does however have a basic need to swear—swearing is a wholesome and proper activity, of which physical violence is possibly a perversion under the corrupt conditions of civilization.[18]

That such arguments conflict with any attack on instinct as such is obvious. On top of this (though they have often been useful in providing an excuse for treating delinquents decently) they are, when you think about them, vacuous. Where is evil coming from? Saying that society is to blame, not the delinquent, only shifts the blame from one set of human beings to another. If one goes on to say that *no* human being desires evil, who

18. Ashley Montagu, *Man in Process* (New York, 1961), esp. p. 161, and *The Anatomy of Swearing* (London, 1968).

started it? Rousseau, in his crude early work, gave the only possible answer. He said that evil results from bringing people together. (Hell is other people. . . .) While they were solitary, all was well and that was their natural state. Men in a state of nature had "no fixed home, no need of one another; they met perhaps twice in their lives, without knowing each other and without speaking."[19] It was when they left that stage and invented speech that society came into being and evil with it. Now Rousseau's description of these Pure Individuals is in fact almost the complete opposite of the behavior typical of primates. *They* spend almost all their lives in a group, leaving it perhaps twice in a lifetime; they need each other constantly, they know each other intimately, they communicate all the time ("one chimpanzee is no chimpanzee," as Robert Yerkes remarked). Even the fixed home is there in a sense; they wander, but over a definite range; they return seasonally to well-known places. That is the sort of context in which human speech and intelligence evolved; a solitary species could never have produced them. (Rousseau did see a difficulty about that; his suggestion was that in some uncommon natural emergency people turned to one another for help. Then, no doubt, the chairman convoked the congress of hitherto speechless elders, and raised the motion that the time had come to invent language. . . . Since Darwin, people ought not to talk like this.) Because society is the condition of man's living at all, let alone living naturally, and because there is some evil (namely, at least friction) in any society, evil too is in some sense natural to him; he has, like any other species, his own natural evils. This idea is difficult only if you insist on the black-and-white approach by which, if he is not naturally good all through, he must be (all through) naturally evil. These extremes have always been popular with the moralists. As Fielding described them in *Tom Jones*, "Square held human nature to be the perfection of all virtue, and that vice was a deviation from our nature, in the same way as deformity of body is. Thwackum, on the contrary, maintained that the human mind, since the Fall, was nothing but a sink of iniquity, till purified and redeemed by

19. *Discourse on Inequality*, Pt. 1 (Everyman ed., tr. G. D. H. Cole, p. 188).

Grace." But why take either option? It seems more reasonable to treat man's nature, his original constitution, as neither good nor evil, but simply the raw material for choice. A man is good or evil according to what he chooses.[20]

At any rate, this is the ethologist's position. Confronted with man's habit of slaughter, he does not throw up his hands in condemnation. He does what he did about the lemmings. He studies all the related patterns of conduct in order to understand the context. Lorenz, for instance, notes, first, that slaughter is often linked with some of the most precious elements in human nature, namely, loyalty and friendship. People often kill in defense of their friends and family; their pugnacity is often an aspect of their affection, and when they can be brought to see someone as a friend, it melts away. Also there are, in man's nature and not only in society, various trends contrary to slaughter. The wish for order is also natural; so is the horror of bloodshed. We are in conflict on that matter within ourselves, not waiting for the bidding of society. Were that not so, no society could exist.

Then we have to look at milder forms of attack, at aggression within a civilized society. Here Lorenz is very much interested in the *value* of aggression, in the relation of pugnacity to vigorous effort, in people who "fight unremittingly" on behalf of the truth, or to defend the helpless, in the struggle for reform and the battle against evil generally. Saying this is only suggesting a field for study. But it ought to make us wary of people such as Arthur Koestler who say that aggression is a disease and ought to be chemically treated by pills or the like. Nobody knows how much of human life might go with it if that were tried.[21]

I have suggested that it does, after all, make sense to say that

20. This remark states only one side of the truth; because of the ambiguity of "nature" it must not be taken as final. In a weak sense, "our nature" means, as here, our whole range of possibilities. In a stronger one, it stands for the pattern among those possibilities that guides us in choosing. See pp. 274, 299, 328.

21. For a fuller and more balanced view of the position about ambivalence, see Eibl-Eibesfeldt, *Love and Hate,* and also Anthony Storr's book, *Human Aggression.* Storr is admirably free from the unrealistic tendency many humane writers show to be shocked at the idea that anybody ever wants to be nasty to anybody.

man has a nature, and even that man has instincts. Why does this matter to philosophers? I shall return in a moment to the consequences for ethics, but first let us look briefly at a range of questions in the philosophy of mind which seem to be affected.

Traditionally, the distinguishing mark of man, and also his peculiar merit, is rationality. This is not an easy concept. It is not the same thing as intelligence, since you could show great intelligence in the pursuit of something quite irrational. "Rational" includes reference to aims as well as means; it is not far from "sane." Even "intelligent" is sometimes used to suggest something about aims, something beyond mere consistency of thought. If someone consistently aims at the destruction of everything or the greatest possible degree of confusion, people will tend to call him insane, irrational, and perhaps even stupid. (Yet you could presumably program a computer to aim at these things.) Why? Because rationality, like all our practical concepts, belongs to the vocabulary of a particular species with particular needs. The Existentialist, in talking about *total* freedom, is exaggerating quite as wildly as someone who might tell us to transcend the limitations of space and be omnipresent. We are not disembodied intelligences, tentatively considering possible incarnations. We have highly particular, sharply limited needs and possibilities already—in return for which restriction, of course, we have the advantage that our satisfactions, such as they are, are actual. There are quite narrow restrictions on what can possibly be rational for such a being—not necessarily limits to the possible particular desires, but to the policies, the schemes of life into which these can be built. Bobby Fischer, for instance, seems to have attempted a policy impossible to a human being in choosing Chess and Absolutely Nothing Else—impossible if only because chess, like nearly all our activities, needs cooperation *within* it and not only from outside. Certain extreme ascetics in attempting Religion Quite Alone have done likewise; so does the washing compulsive. Not every form of life can make sense for a given species. Our liberty is negative; we can reject the virtues and interests natural to us, but not acquire a new set. And even if, like Kant, you treat man's particular constitution as a contingent matter, you must still suppose (as Kant well knew) *some* system of needs, some particular constitution to give matter to the form.[22] There has to be something that counts as help, harm, interference, oppression, deceit and so forth. (The position of God and other spiritual beings has always been a problem here, since the idea of their having needs is felt to be peculiar, but it seems much odder to say that their preferences are arbitrary. I shall leave this headache to the theologians.)

Reasoning from Purpose

The notion of rationality I shall discuss in Part Four, along with some of man's other traditional distinguishing marks. But I must deal here with some questions concerning ethics, and practical thinking generally.

If we use evidence about our nature as a guide to action, are we arguing illicitly from purpose? Is this superstitious and unscientific? Does it commit us to believing in a creating God?

We had better notice first that we look to this guide all the time. Socrates, for instance, was reasoning in a completely ordinary way when he defended his decision to go on asking awkward questions on the ground that *an unquestioned life is no life for man*.[23] He meant not just that we are in fact creatures who spontaneously ask questions, but that it follows from this that inquiry is a good thing for us and therefore that we should pursue it. Is this wrong? Or can we indeed say that man should ask questions because he is made that way?

The words used here make a great difference to people's attitude. To take a fairly simple case of this kind: somebody who sees a seal out of water might be puzzled by its shape, and ask *why* seals are shaped like that. We answer that it is because they are *designed*, *adapted*, or *programmed* to move fast through water. And because of this, water is the right place for them. Water is

22. For example, in distinguishing the human from the holy will, he explains that the terms of morality apply only to the former, and therefore make sense only under some set of subjective limitations. God's position differs *formally* from ours (*Grundlegung zur Metaphysik der Sitten*, tr. by H. J. Paton as *The Moral Law* [London, 1948], chap. 2, secs. 75 and 85, pp. 95–96 and 100–101).

23. Plato, *Apology* 38a.

good, and a dry life would be bad. Now the word *design* may alarm people, because it is traditionally associated with God.[24] *Adapt* probably will not, because it is Darwin's word, given a clear meaning in nineteenth-century discussions of evolution. It stands for changes that are not supposed to have a designer, but are still to the species's advantage, since they take place through natural selection. *Programmed* has swum into popularity of late, and strikes many people as a still more scientific term. This is no doubt because genetics has advanced dramatically lately, at a time when computers have become both useful scientific tools and popular cult objects, and genetics often uses the language of programming. All the same, this term is actually less clear than *adapt* on the point that now concerns us—namely, not implying a designer. (If we believe in God, of course we shall want to raise all sorts of interesting questions about his part in the matter. But it will not do to bring them into the present argument. God cannot be used as a hypothesis within science.)

Suppose we agree, however, to use all these words as we use *adapt*, on the understanding that there is no designer. The interesting thing is that we must still argue very much as if there were one. What we want to say of the seals is that they are *well fitted* to cut through water, and that this fact is no accident, but is really what determines their shape. To make this clear, we simply have to use the analogy of a designing craftsman. (*Fit* is a craftsman's word as much as the others I have mentioned.) These creatures "are made" exactly *as if* they had been designed for the job of water-cutting. This is the only way to explain their shape, and therefore to express some essential facts about them. The sense of *why* used when we ask why they have this shape is enormously common in biology and completely legitimate.[25] It

24. The zoologist George C. Williams, however, chooses it firmly as the *mot juste* for adaptation conceived in the absence of a designer, in a most interesting and shrewd discussion of evolutionary concepts. See his book *Adaptation and Natural Selection* (Princeton, 1966), chaps. 1 and 9.

25. Explanations of this sort were what Aristotle was talking about when he spoke of what translators misleadingly call "Final Causes." "Explanations by function" would be much closer to his meaning. (See Max Hocutt, "Aristotle's Four Becauses," *Philosophy*, 49 [1974].) The term *teleology* has been so much knocked around that I avoid it entirely.

means "what good is it?" (Sometimes of course we cannot find the answer; sometimes, as in the case of the human appendix, the first answer may be "none now." But the question always arises, and "none now" is never a final answer.[26]) We can say that we are asking about *function*, which means *use*. But this is still a metaphor. Plants have functional shapes as well as animals, but noting this does not commit us to saying that there is somebody using them. The notion of function is a clear and useful one. But it too contains the slightly complicated notion that if someone *were* making or using a plant or animal, this is the shape he would have reason to make or use. Without being deceived, we need to think of organisms to some extent as if they were artifacts.

This requirement worries people. They have made various efforts to get rid of the schema. What cannot be got rid of, however, is the value judgment—"this is the good which *x* does." Saying that seals are well adapted to cut through water commits us, not just to a view about what is good and bad water-cutting, but also to saying that cutting through water is an advantage, something that can be worthwhile for creatures to do. We do not speak of animals as being well adapted to fall over cliffs, or get stuck in holes, or even neglect their young. If you try to replace talk of adaptation with neutral-looking formulas like "does *x* frequently" or "finds no difficulty in doing it," you lose the explanatory point. Domestic sheep, unlike their wild ancestors, may often fall over cliffs and find no difficulty in doing so. That does not make the habit an adaptation. To understand why they are as they are, we do have to look to the designer involved, the human breeder, and understand his purposes. Wild sheep have no designer. But we still have to speak as if they had—to the extent of forming a clear idea of what can be an advantage for each species—if we are to use functional arguments. This means that, most of all in the case of our own species, we have to have some idea what to count as plus or minus.

26. Cases like the Irish deer's antlers involve *conflicts* of good—something that genuinely serves one interest in the creature's life is damaging to another. Circumstances can also change so that one interest ceases to matter—apparently what happened with the appendix. I shall examine such conflicts further in Chaps. 9 and 11. For the deer, see note on p. 133.

If we had no such idea, we should be utterly stuck—not just, in particular, about how to study biology, but in general about how to act at all. Alien species, if we ever encountered them, might actually present us with this problem. Solving it would be a great deal harder than most science fiction so far has suggested. But for species on this planet we do have the idea. *Advantage* is not a mysterious alien notion, the name of a hitherto unidentified quality. It is a general name for thriving and prospering, for all the things that we and other species really want and value. Where we cannot identify these things, we cannot talk of function or adaptation. Different species, different cultures, and even different individuals make their own selections from the planetary menu, and drive their varying bargains. But our natural, instinctive tastes ensure that no moderately normal individual is helplessly ignorant about how to start doing this.

The odd suggestion that we are totally and incurably ignorant here (put forward in some twentieth-century moral philosophy) I shall discuss in Chapter 9. Here my point is the common-sense notion that our structure of instincts, as a whole, indicates the good and bad for us. I am saying that, if Socrates is right in his facts, he is right in his argument. That is, if it is *true* that people are naturally inquiring animals, and if that inquiring tendency has a fairly central place in their natural structure of preference, then it follows that inquiry is an important good for them, that they ought not to stop each other from doing it (unless they have to), and should do it themselves, to an extent in proportion to the other things they also need to do. And so on for our other tendencies. Of course there are conflicts between such tendencies. I shall discuss them shortly. But in settling them we do not decide things just by abstract reasoning or an arbitrary act of the will. We look at the facts, trying to size up the strength and importance of the natural tastes involved. This is how, for instance, we see the weakness of the family arrangements proposed in Plato's *Republic*. Plato hoped to get rid of the evils of competition by doing away with private property, most of all in what he rightly saw as its central case, attachment to one's own family. But though man is indeed a political animal, he cannot possibly become merely that. There is a natural balance of private and public, a relation of the two aspects of life, which simply defies distortions of this sort when they become extreme. Of course sacrifices of the private can be made, for instance in the religious life or on a kibbutz.[27] What I am pointing out is that they *are* sacrifices, that we cannot just decide to step up one element indefinitely and expect no trouble from the other. The price can be paid, provided that the goods secured really seem worth it to all concerned. But it will be paid with effort—the bargain will need constant attention—and there will be special dangers of emotional stunting and self-deception. This is because natural feelings like our strong and special affection for our children are not just loose facts about us; they are the sort of thing that constitutes our central good. Moral surgeons who want to cut them out because of their dangers misconceive their function. We are simply not in a position to replace them with something else which will not be worse. The choice we have is a choice between better and worse ways of expressing them. There is no such choice as dropping them altogether.

To consider an important example of such a feeling—important both because this feeling is so powerful and because its existence has lately been hotly disputed—let us look again at the case of Paul, who buys land because in general he wants privacy, and in particular he dislikes being overlooked. He might put the point more generally still, and say that he likes some space around him. Now this is a very common human demand. It operates (among other considerations) almost every time that people in our own or any other urban culture choose a house, apartment, vacation place, office, picnic site, or seat in a bus or library. If it is less influential among villagers isolated in the Amazon rain forest, that is largely because they already have

27. No one has tried at all consistently to put all Plato's suggestions into practice. Among points at which even the most drastic reformers quail are (1) the proposal at *Republic* 5. 460d that parents should never know which are their own children, mothers being expected to suckle, indiscriminately and without continuity, any baby that on any given occasion is handed to them, and (2) the one just before it (460a) that requires citizens to be ready to leap into sexual activity each time that the state confronts them with a breeding partner, but to be abstinent all the rest of their lives. The especially *unnatural* feature about both these demands is that they involve not just suppression, but an insolent and contemptuous *distortion* of a powerful emotional tendency. It is expected to work and make itself useful for the public good, while being denied its proper and natural place in the individual's life. More about this in Chap. 13.

space. People object to being overcrowded. It might seem to follow that overcrowding is bad for them. But this idea has met with strong resistance.

That overcrowding *is* bad for other social species has been shown experimentally many times. And people do not seem to find this statement doubtful. Overcrowding results in the breakdown of normal social patterns and makes for such things as constant aggression, cannibalism, and infanticide. It would be possible, of course, at this stage to take a starkly "objective" line, abstain from value judgments, and deny that these things are bad. But this pose is unconvincing, and adopting it would make biology impossible, which may be why people avoid it. Instead they reject any parallel between what happens to animals and what look like quite similar ill effects on people, on the ground that people are capable of culture and therefore not subject to natural evils of this sort, where the damage is not physical. It is supposed that they can accept without harm anything that their culture shows them to be worthwhile.

The general issue of people's incomparability I shall be dealing with throughout this book. But we must look at a particular point about this case right away. It concerns the relation of desire to excess. I do not think that, either for people or for any other species, there is a good thing that one could not have too much of. It would be extraordinary if the company of others were an exception. It is true that people can accept a good deal of crowding, that they often deliberately seek a crowd (company is, I am anxious to point out, a *natural* good), and that cultural conditioning telling us that it is all perfectly normal makes it more tolerable. But then that is true also of other excesses that harm people. Culture may help us to accept excess of work, of smell and other stimuli, of change or tranquillity, but it does not make them in themselves good or even indifferent. To speak of something as excessive is to use the concept (which we all in effect take for granted) of a level naturally acceptable to us. There is such a natural level for stimulation, and other people's company is inevitably stimulating to us. We react to it. Our power to react becomes exhausted, and after that no force of culture will stop us from either withdrawing or snapping. Wickler reports a relevant experiment.

Hutt and Vaizey have made careful studies of the effects of over-crowding in playrooms on children between three and eight. Each child was observed in three playgroups of different sizes. . . . The playroom was always the same size. . . . The tests showed that the number of social contacts between the children decreased the more densely the room was 'populated', although this was in fact when there were the most opportunities for social contacts. So the children avoided one another. When there were more than eleven children quarreling increased noticeably, as, incidentally, did the abuse and destruction of toys, which is interpreted as an open expression of aggressive tendencies worked off on the toy instead of the neighbour.[28]

The pattern is completely familiar in common life, and its effect can be seen in the design of towns everywhere, with their closed-in, defensive buildings. What is gained by saying that something so widespread is merely a matter of culture? In thinking about an individual it may make good sense to ask what came from his own nature and what from his culture. But the question makes no sense applied to the group. What its members have built up has to come from their own nature; there is nowhere else for it to come from. That is why we do not get rid of the notion of natural goods and evils by talking about culture, however important its particular forms may be.

Another useful point emerges from seeing that you can have too much of any good thing and that our natural demands are not, as people often think, insatiable and unlimited. If they were, it would be impossible to strike a bargain by weighing them against each other, and in that case there might be something to be said for the traditional picture of Reason or the Will as an arbitrary ringmaster or alien colonial governor, striding in to cow them all into submission. In fact, however, it is highly characteristic of natural tastes that they each have, as Bishop Butler put it, their "natural stint and bound."[29] There is a rough

28. *The Sexual Code*, p. 60, citing C. Hutt and M. J. Vaizey "Group Density and Social Behavior," in *Neue Ergebnisse der Primatologie* ed. D. Starck, R. Scneider, and H. J. Kühn (Stuttgart, 1967). Lorenz has an interesting discussion of the topic in his *Civilized Man's Eight Deadly Sins* (New York, 1974), esp. chap. 2.

29. Sermon 11, sec. 9. The fit between them is of course very rough; that is why we need morality. More on this topic in the first three sections of Chap. 9 and the last two of Chap. 11. For reason in the role of colonial governor, see Chap. 11, p. 260.

balance, naturally given, which Reason or the Will can come in to complete. They do not have to invent it from scratch. Natural tastes evolve as part of a whole. They do not, unless something has gone wrong, compete to take over entirely; each of them has some limits. What is *natural*, in fact, is never just a condition or activity—inquiry, say, or space around one, or sexual activity, or playing with children—but a certain *level* of that condition or activity, proportionate to the rest of one's life. This idea is important in resisting simple moralists. And it might well be necessary to say at some time to Socrates, or at least to Plato, that a life without the ordinary affections is no life for man either.[30]

Grasping this point makes it possible to cure a difficulty about concepts such as *natural* which has made many people think them unusable. Besides their strong sense, which recommends something, they have a weak sense, which does not. In the weak sense, sadism is natural. This just means that it occurs; we should recognize it. (We often express this idea by saying that something is *only* natural: it was to be expected; perhaps no blame is called for.) But in a strong and perfectly good sense, we may call sadistic behavior *unnatural*—meaning that a policy based on this natural impulse, and extended through somebody's life into organized activity, is, as Butler said, "contrary to the whole constitution of that nature."[31] Before sadists indignantly claim that this view is intolerant, let us get it clear. That consenting adults should bite each other in bed is in all senses natural; that schoolteachers should bully children for their sexual gratification is not. There is something wrong with this activity beyond the actual injury that it inflicts, something which would not be wrong with, for instance, negligence from which children accidentally suffered. Examples of this wrong thing—of unnaturalness—can be found which do not involve other people as victims; for instance, extreme narcissism, suicide, obsessive-

30. It is essential to notice that the existence of exceptions does not disprove this. People who want to do without a norm are usually saying that the *wrong* norm has been selected. They may also be making the point I make here—that what is normal is a *range*, not a point, and an oscillation within that range, rather than a single fixed position. Monotony is itself an abnormal extreme.

31. Preface to the Sermons, sec. 15.

ness, incest, and exclusive mutual admiration societies. "It is an unnatural life," we say, meaning that its center has been misplaced. Further examples, which do involve victimizing others, are redirected aggression, the shunning of cripples, ingratitude, vindictiveness, parricide.[32] All these things are *natural* in that there are well-known impulses toward them which are parts of human nature. When we withhold blame on these grounds, we may be contrasting them with iniquities at which it took some ingenuity to arrive, with vice so deliberate and carefully thought out as to be more or less artificial. Or again with *abnormal* impulses, wishes so appalling that anyone to whom they occur should, if sane, have written them off at once as having no place in life. But redirected aggression and so on can properly be called *unnatural* when we think of nature in the fuller sense, not just as an assembly of parts, but as an organized whole. They are parts which will ruin the shape of that whole if they are allowed in any sense to take over.[33]

Thus the notion of every passion having its stint and bound, which is well borne out by the behavior of other species, makes sense of the paradox of nature and allows us a clearer understanding of evil. What is evil must in a way be part of our nature, since what stands right outside it could be no temptation to us, would even be beyond our power. It has to be something possible for us, something for which we are equipped and to which we are drawn—but outrageous, damaging to the proper arrangement of the whole. If it prevails, it does so at a monstrous price, destroying what is more central. And perhaps the deliberate policy that it should prevail is what we mean by evil itself.

The point of Lorenz's book, *Das Sogenannte Böse*[34] (literally "*so-called evil*," translated with the rather misleading English title *On*

32. I use traditional examples. People who object to the *examples*—who want to defend the things named from the charge of unnaturalness—should separate this defense from the notion that no such charge can arise. Incest is interesting because it was an example given by Hume, along with parricide, of an artificial offense invented by man. But chimpanzees seem to avoid it (see Goodall, *In the Shadow of Man*, p. 182).

33. Aristotle's discussion of Bad Pleasures is throughout helpful in considering these conflicts (*Nicomachean Ethics*, hereafter called *Ethics*, 10.3 and 7.14).

34. Subtitled *Zur Naturgeschichte der Aggression* (Vienna, 1963).

Aggression) is to deny that aggression holds this position. Aggression, the general tendency to attack, is, he suggests, by no means a tendency to destroy—which in fact in normal conditions it seldom does. It is primarily a *driving away*, a demand for space, commonly on behalf of those belonging to one as well as of oneself. And this is something essential for most advanced creatures and deeply connected with the higher development of feelings—with social responsiveness and also with affection, loyalty, persistence, and enthusiasm. It is those who have become conscious of their fellows, and begun to make discriminations among them, who care who is near them. They cease to be able to ignore, and must respond, either with hostility or with friendship, often with a mixture or alternation of the two. This ambivalence, Lorenz says, lies deep in our nature. Attempts to root it out are misguided and wasteful. What we must do is to become conscious of our aggression, to study its various forms, and channel it where it does least harm and most good. He is showing aggression not just as an outlying part of our nature, like sadism, but as a central element, a structural factor that is involved in the development of many unquestionably valuable parts. Trying to get rid of it is something like sawing off a hand because it has held a sword.

Central factors in us *must* be accepted, and the right line of human conduct must lie somewhere within the range they allow.[35] Beings who would love everybody equally and unfailingly, having no preference among them and never wanting to drive anyone away, may be in a sense conceivable to us, but they are certainly not imaginable. Trying to behave thus would land us in the mess we always reach if we ignore the central structure of our feelings. We might get rid of the vigor that goes with aggression, but not of the ill feeling. Accepting aggression in this way does not, of course, commit us to approving all aggressive acts, any more than our general acceptance of sex or of the demand for power or pleasure commits us to endorsing everything

---

35. Jung's remarks about the need to acknowledge our Shadow, the futility of trying to reject those aspects of our nature which frighten and sometimes shame us, seem relevant.

in those provinces. These general motives are innate, but they are wide. Guidance within their limits comes from balancing their various possible expressions with one's other motives, in the light of a proper system of priorities.

As a crucial stage in my attempt to clean up concepts necessary for grasping our nature, I have been looking at the use of purpose arguments in biology, and suggesting that the notion of purpose is not itself a fishy one. It can be misused, but properly handled it is a valuable and necessary tool. In the next step of my argument, I shall discuss certain difficulties about using it properly, difficulties that particularly afflict those physical scientists who are most anxious to get rid of it altogether.

Part Two

ART AND SCIENCE
IN PSYCHOLOGY

Had I the time to write a book, I would make the human mind
as plain as the road from Charing Cross to St. Paul's.
—James Mill

CHAPTER 4

Directions without a Director

On Being Scientific

We do need some sort of notion of human nature. So far I have been meeting general objections to this idea and trying to clear up some difficulties about how we should shape it. I shall return to these problems in Part Three, and discuss more fully how the idea of our nature can guide us practically, how we must inevitably invoke it when we decide how we ought to live.

First, however, I must deal with a rather different set of difficulties. Granted that we have a nature, how should we study it? Is there a science available? There are those who would regard everything said so far as unscientific.

It all depends on what one means by a science.

I have suggested using comparisons with animals drawn from ethology—that is, from observations of individual animals, made by people skilled in such observing and in explaining the results. Suggesting that their findings are relevant to human life implies that that is a proper way to study us as well. And it is. We need to study people qualitatively as well as quantitatively, individually as well as statistically, in natural conditions as well as experimentally. For these purposes we need to use ordinary observation of the kind we can all make—but, of course, sharpened, refined, deepened, and organized into a proper psychology of motive. The field of this sort of psychology is, as I have implied, roughly that occupied by such people as Freud, Jung, Erich Fromm, Melanie Klein, and Eric Berne. It also properly uses contributions from the many novelists and dramatists, historians, poets, prophets, and sages who have struggled to understand man's nature since the dawn of human history, as well as facts from the physical sciences. Questions may be drawn from anywhere, though they will have to be related to those already on the table. And adopting somebody's question never commits us to accepting his answer.

Now, is such a study a science?

Unquestionably, it is an *art*. Some people think that what is an art cannot be any part of science, so that point must be considered first. By an art I mean a set of skills, which can to some extent be handed down, but which depend much on individual power, insight, practice, and personality. They do not reduce to any set of basic laws, (though of course they include skill in understanding relevant scientific laws) or to any single basic method. Law and medicine, linguistics, history, and geography are arts in this sense. So is philosophy. That does not stop them from being *scientific* in the sense of being systematic, effective, and well related to the findings of other disciplines. They certainly are not "scientific" in the sense of looking like physics. But that is a trivial sense. Each study has its own methods, and becomes deformed if it imitates another. *Science cannot be defined by contrasting it with art.* Practicing any science properly is an art.[1] When we use the word *scientific* as an important compliment, we mean "what increases our understanding of the world." The arts as well as the social sciences do this, and this is the proper sense in which the social sciences are called sciences. They are certainly arts as well. (We would probably be better off if, like the Germans, we had a neutral word to cover all serious studies; *Wissenschaft* takes no sides.) All "arts disciplines" have now to resist being seduced from their own peculiar ways of thinking, which they evolved to suit their own subject matter, to more fashion-

---

1. We can, if we like, distinguish science from art as Knowing That from Knowing How. But knowing how is the more fundamental notion, since simply parroting propositions is not valuable. See Gilbert Ryle, *The Concept of Mind* (London, 1949), chap. 2.

able "scientific" models. What is scientific is not what *looks* like physical science, but what *is* like it—in the sense of using the right methods for what it is trying to do. For large-scale investigations of whole populations, quantification is suitable, and insects, which hardly function as individuals, can be studied by that method most of the time. But for plenty of purposes it is quite unhelpful.

Edward Wilson, though he wants the study of people to be linked with that of other species quite as much as I do, wishes to turn the resulting subject into a "science" in the exclusive sense.[2] In *Sociobiology* he makes little of the need for art, for organizing one's concepts to suit a subject matter. Human psychology he hardly mentions. But he does speak repeatedly of ethology as something whose importance has been overrated; along with the comparative psychology of different species it is, he says, "destined to be cannibalized by neurophysiology and sensory physiology from one end and sociobiology and behavioral zoology from the other. . . . The future, it seems clear, cannot be with the ad hoc terminology, crude models and curve fitting that characterize most of the contemporary ethology and comparative psychology" (p. 6). Why not? The future will not "be with" anybody in the sense of falling to them as a conquest.[3] The need for many different methods is not going to go away, dissolved in a quasi-physical heaven where all serious work is quantitative.

Wilson makes clear what he thinks should replace these crude models: "When the same parameters and quantitative theory are

2. In his approach he represents a great number of distinguished people, many of whom he quotes and summarizes. But for simplicity I must treat him as their spokesman. I realize that this offends against the practice of certain disciplines where great importance is attached to attributing every opinion exactly to its originator. The trouble with this procedure is that a forest of names darkens counsel and promotes evasion.

3. This possessive attitude to the future is interesting. Wilson is confident enough to prophesy as follows: "*When* mankind has achieved an ecological steady state, *probably by the end of the twenty-first century*, the internalization of social evolution *will* be nearly complete. *About this time* biology should be at its peak. . . . Skinner's dream of a culture predesigned for happiness will surely have to *wait* for the new neurobiology. A genetically accurate and hence *completely* fair code of ethics must also *wait*" (pp. 574–575, my italics). If Wilson really knows all this, he should share his evidence with us, more particularly as he has himself shown that "Skinner's dream" and similar notions are in any case vacuous.

used to analyze both termite colonies and troops of rhesus monkeys, we will have a unified science of sociobiology" (p. 4). Now the aspiration to unity is fine, but the emphasis on quantification is ruinous. Quantification, like surgery, is an excellent thing in the right place, but a very bad topic for obsession. Unless you know just *what* you are counting, and have really grasped the principles governing how to decide whether it is what needs counting—unless you are sure that the things counted are standard units—and unless you understand what is proved by the results of your counting, quantifying provides you only with the outward show of a science, a mirage, never the oasis. The social sciences are littered with the debris of such projects. And Wilson goes on to add one to the number by naming as one of his parameters the division of labor. This is supposed to be something termites and monkeys have in common. Monkeys, however, do not labor. They toil not, neither do they spin. When we consider Wilson's discussion (p. 300), what is divided among them turns out to be *roles*, the headings under which percentages fall being: territorial display; vigilance and look-out behavior[4]; receiving friendly approaches; friendly approach to others; punishing intragroup aggression; and leading in group movement. Now it would be possible to say something general about the distribution of roles, but not by starting with this kind of distortion. Moreover, descriptions like "division of labor" cannot be applied even to termites without explaining the radical differences between laboring termites and laboring people.

The trouble is not—as people often think—that human concepts cannot be extended to other species. It is that such extension must be done sensitively. Apparently similar patterns can play very different parts in the lives of different species. But someone who is bent on quantifying across the species barrier cannot possibly do justice to these differences. Wilson in fact

4. Monkey sentinels, it should be noted, are not primarily there to give warning against predators and do not always do so. They are mainly interested in picking quarrels with members of other monkey bands. No doubt this habit has a *function* in distributing population. But it is not *work* any more than similar behavior on the part of small boys is work.

very often does note them, but fails to see how strongly they demand a nonquantitative approach. Ethologists and comparative psychologists specialize in understanding these differences. Grasping them is not an obstacle in the way of a unified study, but a condition of it.

All this trouble arises in relation to the "new synthesis" that Wilson hopes to organize among the studies concerned with the evolution of man as a social animal. To synthesize studies in the sense of relating them is excellent. As I remarked in my Introduction, the frontiers between them are often misplaced and sometimes just accidental. But anyone who hopes to tidy up such a confusion needs to find out what is actually going on. He had better not set out with the fixed intention of civilizing the natives, still less, perhaps, of cannibalizing them.[5] He has to have his own general concepts in excellent order. But certain chronic confusions prevent anybody hell-bent on imitating the physical sciences from talking sense about social evolution. These confusions I must discuss in the next five chapters. At their core is something that is not supposed to be on Wilson's agenda at all, namely, the notion of purpose. As I have already remarked, this idea, when officially outlawed, proves remarkably resistant and inclined to come back through the window. The damage this does to the scheme of sociobiology is my next topic.

The Exaltation of the Gene

The as-ifness of purpose language causes constant trouble. Taking it literally is strangely hard to avoid. New entities therefore are invented to be cast as designer. Schopenhauer's Will to Live and Bergson's *Elan vital*, popularized by Bernard Shaw as the Life Force, have been favored candidates. But they are currently being replaced by something much odder, namely, genes

---

5. An offer repeated on p. 575 of *Sociobiology*. A diagram of this distressing process appears on p. 5. It shows that by the year 2000 the python is to have digested comparative psychology without trace, and reduced ethology to a wisp; all remaining psychology is to be physiological. Cells and neurones will be fully studied; so will societies—but hardly anything in between. See the second section of Chap. 8, below.

and DNA. Thus Wilson begins *Sociobiology* with a chapter called "The Morality of the Gene." He there says of genes that "the individual organism is only their vehicle, part of an elaborate device to preserve and spread them with the least possible biochemical perturbation. Samuel Butler's famous aphorism, that the chicken is only the egg's way of making another egg, has been modernized; the organism is only DNA's way of making more DNA. More to the point, the hypothalamus and limbic system are engineered to perpetuate DNA" (p. 3). Now I am sure Wilson himself does not want to be interpreted as saying that the DNA is doing the engineering. But that is the impression readers get, and the quotation from Samuel Butler, which is being constantly repeated at present in this sort of context, can in fact bear no other meaning. It comes from his book, *Life and Habit*, and is part of a full-scale, uninhibited defense of Lamarck's view that evolution is brought about by effort—a view that Butler[6] was prepared to support by conceiving conscious thought, effort, and memory as present in even the very simplest organisms, and passed on, through a continuity of consciousness, from one generation to another. Even in this context, it is a paradox to talk of the genes as being *more* in charge of the operation than the individuals that embody them. Wilson and other population biologists do have a reason for talking of genes and DNA as being more influential causally than those individuals (I shall discuss it shortly). But constantly, as here, their language goes beyond this. It will bear no other meaning than that the genes or eggs are themselves the engineers. As a natural consequence—since engineers are usually viewed as being more important and valuable than the things they engineer, as containing the qualities that make those things valuable—these scientists slide on to treating the genes as containing the point of the whole operation.

Such language is much odder, much less defensible even than Life-Force talk. The Life Force was a name for something mys-

6. N. B., *not* Bishop Butler, nor the Samuel Butler who wrote the satire *Hudibras* in the seventeenth century, but his namesake, the nineteenth-century essayist who wrote *Erewhon*.

terious, vast, and structural; remarks about it were clearly remarks about how the universe in general works. Genes and
DNA, by contrast, are precise names given by scientists to specific little bits of complex goo. And little bits of goo, however
complex, cannot design or engineer anything. Of course it is
quite true that this particular consignment of goo is by ordinary
standards very special and important—but only because it is liable to turn into organisms, and organisms are, by ordinary
standards, important; indeed, they are the condition of anything's being important. If we contrast a world on which life is
still going on, though it will soon cease, with one on which actual
life is permanently extinguished, but the seed stores and the
sperm banks remain untouched forever, we cannot intelligibly
say that the real value lies in the second. Potentiality only matters
because of what will happen when it is actualized. Could we
think of the blueprints as more important than the building, the
mix than the pudding, the match than the fire?

Other entities too become involved. Wilson says (p. 4): "The
hypothalamic-limbic complex of a social species, such as man,
'knows,' or more precisely it has been programmed to behave as
if it knows, that its underlying genes will be proliferated maxi-
mally only if it orchestrates behavioral responses [properly]."
Rather more precisely still, it has not been programmed, it cannot behave (except in the boring sense in which gases do so), and
it is not the sort of thing that could conceivably know
anything—so it cannot behave as if it knew anything either. Like
our liver, it *works*. The language of purpose and agency cannot
possibly be the right one for describing the movement of working parts within a whole. Whether or not that language is in
order in its own proper place—for describing the behavior of
active, conscious beings—it is in order nowhere else.

Wilson and Samuel Butler are, however, saying certain admirable things here, which need to be pointed out.

First, they are *attacking* something really wrong and
dangerous—our grossly inflated idea of our own individual importance to the universe. We certainly are each inclined to think
that the whole concern was made for us, and to complain in
consequence that it has been made badly. We are also inclined to

take personal credit for our own character and talents, as if we ourselves had created them. This attitude of "infantile omnipotence" is indeed silly. It is quite reasonable to point out its silliness by the paradox of saying that to view everything else as made to perpetuate genes would be *as sensible* as to view it as made to gratify our individual sensibilities. Beyond that, Wilson has an extremely sound, more specific point to make about our emotional constitution. We cannot, he says, expect as a matter of right to be set up with a perfectly harmonious set of tastes and desires, all of which can be gratified. We could expect that only if that constitution had been evolved for, and adapted to, nothing but individual happiness. (Even then we would have no right to expect perfection.) But in fact selection has operated in many other directions at least as much. Species survive not merely by having happy members, but by having ones who do something about the next generation.

Continuing his account of the orchestrating that the brain-areas governing emotion have to do, he says that they must "bring into play an efficient mixture of personal survival, reproduction, and altruism. Consequently, [they] . . . tax the conscious mind with ambivalences whenever the organisms encounter stressful situations. Love joins hate; aggression, fear; expansiveness, withdrawal; and so on, in blends designed not to promote the happiness and survival of the individual, but to favor the maximum transmission of the controlling genes" (p. 4). Emotional conflict, in fact, is endemic and can never have a fully satisfactory solution.[7] The position our common moral tradition takes about this—that we must choose between different aspects of life, and that neither psychological nor social engineering will lead us to a conflict-free, simple path—makes evolutionary sense. Utilitarians and others who simply advise us to be happy are unhelpful, because we almost always have to make a choice

7. This emphasis on the inevitability of conflict is one of Wilson's most valuable points in relation to morality. He is especially interesting in discussing conflicts between individuals, notably between generations, and in showing that there is no reason to expect that evolution will iron these out (pp. 311, 341–344); it will only keep them below the level where they would do serious practical damage.

either between different kinds of happiness—different things to be happy *about*—or between these and other things we want, which have nothing to do with happiness.

The inevitability of conflict is a good reason for making the negative point: the purpose of evolution is not—or not just—to secure our individual happiness. *But need evolution have any such exclusive purpose?* Why is it better to say that the purpose *is* the proliferation of the genes? It seems equally irrational to pick on any stage of the species's continuation as containing the point of the whole thing. The genes are not little men. We are describing a very complex process, all stages of which equally (and not only reproduction) have been refined by evolution to contribute to the whole. The contentment of the individual is a necessary element in the whole cycle. Deeply discontented animals cannot reproduce—as is often found of those in captivity. And it is not only reproduction that depends on contentment, but also all the other activities necessary for species survival: eating, washing, nest-building, and the rest. In fact if somebody were called upon to advise an audience of conceited genes, as Wilson is advising an audience of conceited individuals, on how to survive, he would have to speak on very much the same lines, telling them not to behave as if they were the only element in the evolutionary cycle. "Remember," he would have to say, "that your welfare depends on that of the individuals which embody you. You must make it worth their while to keep going. If you depress them too much, or set them impossible problems, they will die out, taking you with them. And serve you right." It seems a pity that no gene is in a position to listen to such sound advice. Genes do not make decisions, so they cannot take advice. For the same reason, they can no more have a morality than they can play the trombone or write books on sociobiology.

The Need for the Long Perspective

Wilson's point is that the genetic perspective is more *important* than the individual one—that, as he puts it, "in evolutionary time the individual counts for almost nothing." Now importance is relative to purpose, and this vast and remote perspective cannot be primary for all purposes. There are, however, certain purposes for which it is indeed very important, and there Wilson is right to emphasize it. For instance:

1) The scientific need to extend our knowledge about the human race in general, and therefore to understand how it has developed. When the social sciences have abstracted their problems from genetic considerations, have assumed that they had all the facts they needed under their hands in the current scene, they have stultified themselves. They need evolutionary thought if they are to understand *what sort of beings these are* that confront current dilemmas.

2) The moral and psychological need to avoid creeping solipsism—"the speculative absurdity of considering ourselves single and independent beings."[8] This disease, though it is not as prevalent among philosophers as Wilson supposes, has indeed caused a lot of trouble. Hobbes, Descartes, and Freud, as well as Camus, have been centers of infection. (Kant had the cure, but not everyone has taken it.) It has commonly involved the belief that men are naturally unqualified egoists. Against this, Wilson convincingly shows that total egoism "pays" very badly genetically. If you richly fulfill yourself at the cost of destroying all your siblings and offspring, your genes will perish and your magnificent qualities will be lost to posterity. A consistently egoistic species would be either solitary or extinct. Since, therefore, we are social and not extinct, we cannot sensibly view ourselves as natural egoists. Still less could it make sense to say that we ought to be so.

3) The mystical angle. Wilson seems to view genes as in some sense immortal beings, the point of the whole cosmic concern, to which other beings are rightly sacrificed. There is something here that I greatly respect, and the long perspective is certainly in place in such thinking. But its value seems to collapse in absurdity when particular entities like genes stand in for the whole universe.

First, let us consider the scientific point, the need for the long evolutionary perspective. This is perhaps the central message of

8. Butler, Sermon 1, sec. 10.

Sociobiology to non-zoologists; it is argued in most careful detail. Man is a social species. Can he be understood in isolation from all other social species? Are his apparent likenesses to them really external and misleading, comparable to those between (say) birds and airplanes, tractors and elephants, or stars and diamonds? Or does he fall into place as one remarkable variation among many others on a vast but coherent evolutionary range?

Once you really begin to grasp the vastness and coherence of that range, it is scarcely possible to hesitate about these questions. People's difficulty about seeing themselves as members of the one creation has come from a crude, narrow, highly abstract notion of what the other members were like. Wilson does convey that vastness and coherence. He shows how the tendencies that make social behavior possible have evolved separately in many very different kinds of animals, how they vary greatly in different groups, yet how their variations converge to certain patterns which, for intelligible reasons, must tend to favor species survival—patterns such as altruism and the care of the young.

Against this enormous background, what does it mean to say that human behavior has no genetic cause *because it depends on society?* In the first place, society is not peculiar to humans. In all these species, an individual is "shaped by his society," in the sense that he needs it, he cannot grow up without it, and all the particular details of his life are filled in by it; they follow the path that particular society makes possible. Second, society is not an *alternative* to genetic programming. It requires it. To become a member of any kind of society, an infant must be programmed to respond to it. Others give him his cues. But he has to be able to pick them up and complete the dialogue.

This interaction has been shown experimentally again and again in the case of many animal species by bringing up young in a strange environment. Everywhere we find innate tendencies that make sense in one kind of society and not in another: not only closed instincts—detailed patterns—but also open ones, the kind of pattern found in the imprinted duckling. Ducklings take in, at first sight, the image of their mother from outside—"from society." But they must themselves contribute the power to select that image from their visual field and the very complex motor tendencies involved in following it, nestling, and so on. It is no use trying to imprint in this way a frog, or indeed a puppy, or a human baby. The last two have their own, much slower and more subtle, ways of forming social bonds. But these too involve *responding* actively to their elders. Babies do not only need to suck and cry to survive. A baby that fails, as time goes on, to smile and talk, laugh and weep, to meet the eyes of those around it, to seek and follow its parent, to treat those around it with affection, to want their company and approval, to play and to explore the world, cannot join its society. But these proceedings are thoroughly typical of those by which helpless young in other species secure the care and attention of their elders and are integrated into their society. They are normal patterns in social animals. In the evolutionary perspective, then, society and genetic programming imply each other. And the more complex the society, the richer the genetic programming has to be.

When we try to study human society without reference to that programming, we are abstracting from a species repertoire that we take for granted. Because it is so familiar, we can often quite well ignore it, as long as the views which we are taking for granted about it happen to be reasonably sensible, and in particular so long as no drastic change is looming. Change, however, can always bring out unsuspected tendencies latent in our nature, but played down by our culture. (Not, of course, only bad ones.) Nonhistorical, nongenetic psychology and sociology might be tolerably successful in stagnant times. But the more things change, the more we need to use the evolutionary perspective.

Against that perspective's enormous range of variation, the human species comes (as Wilson shows) as no surprise. Why should there not be, among all the other specialities, one social species that has specialized in developing docility and intelligence, one that has used open instincts to make its societies more versatile than the rest? Social species range already over a vast gamut of complexity, from the very simple, closely joined coral polyps through the much more complex and independent ants and bees, and so on through the most various birds and mammals to our own area. *Each* species has its own peculiarities, its own special kind of structure, and each has to have its own special set of inherited tendencies to maintain them.

Wilson's contribution here is concerned with correcting our perspective. He points out how we limit our insight if we do not think about genetic causes, how refusal to consider them commits us to standing far too close to the social pattern, taking as absolute what are really passing features of our own society, and as relative the underlying structures that cannot easily be fitted into them. We cannot know ourselves in this way. And if we insist on making this mistake, evolution will indeed make a monkey of us.

The Absurdity of Forgetting the Individual

These considerations bring us naturally enough to the next point, the effect of the genetic perspective on our conception of an individual. Can he possibly be thought of as naturally separate from his society? Could he so separate himself? Is "society," in forming him, working across the grain of a nature originally entirely self-regarding?

This question of Egoism is one many people have found difficult. Wilson does not make it easier by mixing it up with the quite different and more general problem of conflicts between feeling and thought. He begins:

Camus said that the only serious philosophical question is suicide. That is wrong even in the strict sense intended.... Self-existence, or the suicide that terminates it, is not the central question of philosophy. The hypothalamic-limbic complex automatically denies such logical reduction by countering it with feelings of guilt and altruism. In this one way the philosopher's own emotional control centers are wiser than his solipsist consciousness, "knowing" that in evolutionary time the individual counts for almost nothing. [p. 3]

I suppose he is speaking *ad hominem* to admirers of Camus. But even they would do well to separate the issues. He is in fact saying two perfectly sensible things:

1) In general, we often find that the intellectual schemes we have invented for understanding ourselves do not work, because they fail to take account of our complex emotional needs; and

2) In particular, if our scheme is a solipsistic or egoistic one, we shall be in trouble because it will not fit our social nature.

But by mixing them he makes it sound as though *all* intellectual schemes were necessarily as silly and faulty as solipsism, and correction of them could only come from an outside source, the personified HLC. Thus he presents the individual himself, "the philosopher," as something separate from, and at odds with, his own emotional centers. But we—individual people—*include* our emotions as part of us. Insofar as we do not grasp or allow for them, we are confused individuals and bad philosophers. The "individual" that Wilson is setting over against the genes, the emotional centers, and other heroes of the piece is a vicious abstraction, "the intellect." This should be plain from the fact that the parts allotted to thought and emotion here can easily be reversed. It is *possible* to represent selfishness as rational and altruism as emotional—but it is also possible to invert the script and say, with common morality, that to treat oneself as the only thing that matters is irrational or crazy, though our feelings may lead us to try it. Thought and feeling, in fact, are both involved on both sides. It is evident that what Camus says is an expression of feeling as much as thought. (One can say, as Wordsworth did, that "our thoughts are the representatives of our past feelings."[9])

Insofar as we can make the distinction, however, we do, no doubt, often need to say that our feelings are sounder or more important than our thoughts. *But to say this we need not leave the regions of ordinary consciousness and start talking neurology.* Representing the dispute as carried on between the HLC and the cerebral cortex will not help us (even if we could be sure that neurologists were not about to discover that some quite different organs were involved instead). If evolution has left us disposed to have certain feelings, then we have those feelings. All we need is to be freed from cockeyed intellectual systems that prevented us from acknowledging them. Egoism is certainly one of these. Our consciousness is not solipsistic. Why should it be? Solipsism is a philosophical muddle, the fruit of confused thinking. We have lived all our lives in a public world; we are adapted to it and used to it; we could not live elsewhere. But that world is not a world of genes and HLC. It is a world of other people. And it is *we*, not our HLC, that live in it.

9. Preface to the *Lyrical Ballads*, first section.

The point I am making is not ontological.[10] It has nothing to do with wanting to add the soul as a detachable spare part. It concerns category logic and the proper use of concepts. Anyone who speaks of a small part as doing something that can only intelligibly be done by the whole grinds his logical gears, producing a frightful noise that obscures all the implications of what he is trying to say. (Very few scientists treat their cars as badly as they treat their conceptual schemes.) If I claim that this car-buretor won the Monte Carlo Rally, or that Eclipse's left hock won the Derby; if I say that my small intestine has digested my lunch; if the boy soprano's family remark that he has just sung the *Messiah*—we speak confusedly. Verbs must have their proper subjects. It was Caesar, not just Caesar's brain, that crossed the Rubicon. And what took the decision to do it was again Caesar, not his HLC or his cerebral cortex.

People find it hard to grasp this point because they see it as antiscientific. Must not the *real* account of what is happening, they say, be the physical one? Are we not speaking only indi-rectly or superficially, if not superstitiously, whenever we de-scribe an event in any other terms than as the movement of electrons? Is not everything else in some way *unreal*?

Asking different kinds of questions produces quite different *kinds* of answers; they are usually not reducible to one another, though they must be compatible.[11] Slicing the world in different directions reveals different patterns. Jelly rolls, sliced down-ward, have a spiral structure. Sliced across, they have stripes. Stripes are not reducible to spirals, nor vice versa, and will not become so by further analysis. Both are real, and the two pat-terns can be related if we understand the relation between the two slicing angles. In just the same way, other things are real as

10. An obsession with ontology, with cataloging the items in the universe, is not actually very useful. Philosophers rightly make less of it than they used to do. Occam's Razor, the principle used for slicing off such items when too many accumulate, is accordingly rather a crude instrument. Before we can ask *whether* the world contains (say) minds, dreams, purposes, thoughts, and so on, we need to ask what we mean by saying that people mind, dream, intend, think. See p. 51.

11. A common situation, well discussed by Ryle in *Dilemmas* (Cambridge, 1964), esp. chaps. V, VI, and VIII.

well as electrons. Brains are also real—but so are the colors we see and the pains we feel, though they could never figure in books on physics or neurology. And someone with a moral conflict has a *real conflict*—granted that it is not unreal in the way that conflicts can be so (that is, fictitious, imaginary, or self-induced). All real features of the world can be studied directly, on their own terms. They do not have to be approached indirectly, by finding their mirror images in a pattern studied by physicists.

I shall return later to this question, to the absolute necessity of taking seriously the perspective of ordinary life, as well as the echoing vistas of evolution and the microscopic view of the neurologist. I must first, however, examine something else, which works to push aside that ordinary perspective. This is the third point I mentioned, the suggestion that genes or DNA should in some sense displace ordinary individuals as furnishing *the point* of the evolutionary process—further, that they can be seen as immortal beings, entitled to reverence.

What, then, about the gene as immortal being?

One highly honorable thing Wilson is expressing here is simple awe and wonder. The sense that the complexity of what he studies, its incredibly intricate adaptation, makes it something stunning and miraculous in its own right is an entirely proper reaction. Such wonder is a motive with every good scientist; those incapable of it are mean and limited.[12] DNA undoubtedly calls for this response. Here is a string of molecules, varying down its length the arrangement of a few common elements. Yet it contains the entire blueprint for every detail of an elephant, and also the power (given suitable nutrients and so forth) to produce an elephant. Moreover the parts of this blueprint will be dispersed and reassembled again to serve for the offspring of this elephant; they will survive it and pass on indefinitely (if all goes well) to generate a further series of elephants till the end of the story. Words fail us. And so they ought to.

But saying that is quite another thing from saying that we are

12. For the value of wonder as a motive, see the Introduction to Aristotle's *Metaphysics*, Bk. 1, chap. 2, 982b11.

dealing with a *being* here which we should respect more than the particular individuals that will spring from it. (If we follow the lead of our initial wonder into an explicitly religious context, we shall see God as that being—but if we have no such context ready, the thought that the gene itself is that being can follow. It is that thought which I am discussing.)

In the first place, as I have suggested, our wonder at the gene *depends* on our wonder at its descendants. In the second, we need not respect it for being immortal. Genes are immortal only in the boring sense in which amoebae are; they reproduce by dividing, so they do not actually die. But then neither do they live, not in the full sense in which more complex organisms do. One crowded hour of glorious life as an individual is worth an age as a gene. Can genes be seen as Souls? Wilson prefaces his book with a quotation from the Bhagavad Gita: "He who thinks this Self to be a slayer, and he who thinks this Self to be slain, are both without discernment; the Soul slays not, neither is it slain." I do not want to keep on about what may seem a harmless religious idea, especially in view of the admirable motive that is linked with it. But unluckily this issue brings up the whole question of our relation to others, and of how to approach psychology. *We need a psychology for individuals, not for genes.*

There *are* angles from which all the details of everyday life and the entire fates of individuals shrink into negligible importance. They include the speculative one I have mentioned, where we study, theoretically, social movements and developments on a large historical scale. They include too the position people reach in certain contemplative human states, such as those Spinoza meant when he spoke of seeing things under the aspect of eternity, and those discussed in the Bhagavad Gita. A Creator, should there be one, might well occupy both these positions. But they do *not* include the position in which we find ourselves in everyday life. We are members of the species we study, and we live here and now, not in evolutionary time, where "the individual counts for almost nothing." If we start identifying ourselves with the Eternal Designer and regarding the other human beings around us as dust on the lens, we shall qualify not for the throne of the universe, but for the asylum.

It is clear that those who invented and favored the idea of the Life Force did put it to illicit emotional use, as a device to justify contempt for the unappreciative crowd around them. Bernard Shaw, a fastidious man with a numbing fear of human contact, used the remote perspective to rationalize that fear. He liked, more and more as time went on, to view people as puppets, and the notion that they were really only passing manifestations of the Life Force made this easy for him. He used his position as dramatist to distance the whole human race, and he saw the Life Force as a fellow dramatist, a collaborator. (This is especially plain in *Back to Methuselah* and *Man and Superman*.) Both Samuel Butler and Schopenhauer too were lonely and timid people, tempted to identify with the universal life of the species by the quasi-divine status their perspective allowed them, the excuse it gave for regarding the people around them as beneath their notice. I was sharply reminded of this habit recently by hearing a well-known writer on evolution speak on a television program, bizarrely entitled *The Selfish Gene*, during which he repeated with relish Samuel Butler's remark about the egg and assured his audience gleefully that they were *really* only their genes' way of producing more genes. His tone was not (as Wilson's is) one of awe at the glory that outlives us. Instead it expressed only the simple glee of the intellectual who has found a way to put down his public. This kind of motive is, unfortunately, stronger than people realize. It can lead, with startling ease, to a confident belief that all the concerns of daily life are somehow "unscientific," that the scientific thing to do is always to find some extremely remote standpoint and insist that only what is seen from it shall count as reality. Middle-sized phenomena, such as we must always deal with in our lives, are dismissed as beneath explanation, while the scientist makes off with the speed of light, either to use his electron microscope on ultimate particles, or to gaze through his telescope at remote perspectives, in terms of which indeed the individual counts for almost nothing. Now both these things must be done, but they are no *more* scientific than working on patterns seen in the phenomena immediately before us. The scientific temper is one that looks for the appropriate method in each field, that carefully distinguishes different sorts of questions for differing treatment. To become obsessed with a method for its own sake and try to use it where it is unsuitable is thoroughly unscientific.[13] And the purpose of all *explanation* must be, ultimately, to illuminate the chaotic world with which we are actually surrounded. That is what we have to explain.

13. "It is the mark of an educated man to look for just as much precision in each enquiry as the nature of the subject allows" (Aristotle, *Ethics* 1.3).

CHAPTER 5

On Taking Motives Seriously

Behavior Includes Motive

I am attacking here a very general notion which is by now deep-rooted among people who want their psychology to be scientific. It is the notion that motives must not be examined and explained *as motives,* but always reduced to something else. Those who choose, as their explanatory something else, movements in the brain and nerves are physicalists. Those who choose outward body-movements are behaviorists. The two fail for the same reason. They distort what they are supposed to be explaining. Their analyses can seem plausible only where they rely covertly on concepts that they officially claim to explode. I have said a little about the way this happens with Wilson's physicalist suggestions. I must now expose the similar worm in the behaviorist bud, and show how alike is the fate of the two doctrines. What I say here about behaviorism is intended to supplement my earlier criticisms. Like them, it is aimed at the more extreme and dogmatic forms of the view; subtler versions designed to meet such arguments may escape it. But Wilson, like many other people devoted to the idea of science, drifts into behaviorism quite as often as physicalism, and when he does so, he uses it in a crude and unregenerate form, as I shall show.

In discussing the central importance of motives, I shall make no special distinction between man and other species, because I think the problem is the same for both. There is nothing anthropomorphic in speaking of the motivation of animals. It is anthropomorphic to call the lion the King of Beasts, but not to talk of him as moved, now by fear, now by curiosity, now by territorial anger. These are not the names of hypothetical inner states, but of major patterns in anyone's life, the signs of which are regular and visible. Anyone who has to deal with lions learns to read such signs, and survives by doing so. Both with animals and with men, we respond to the feelings and intentions we read in an action, not only to the action itself.[1]

It is, however, rather widely supposed that psychology must not use these methods because they are in some sense unscientific. This is a confusion. It is not unscientific to talk *about* feelings. What is unscientific is being unduly influenced by them. Scientists certainly ought not to become too emotional over their work or too emotive in discussing it. This is true whatever the topic. But it is no reason for tabuing investigation *of* the emotions. Again, to talk about the experiences of a thinking subject, as well as his outer behavior, is quite a distinct thing from *becoming subjective*. We can study the experiences of thinking subjects as objectively as we study anything else, and can, on the other hand, become extremely biased, subjective, and emotional about the state of the oil trade.

Because they deem inner experience indescribable, behaviorists have tried to describe the outer manifestations of behavior alone, abstracting them from any experiences of the behaving agents. This experiment has been interesting, and well worth making. Yet it fails. It fails inevitably, because most of the terms in which we can describe behavior effectively do refer to the experiences of the agents as well. Reference to a conscious subject always slips in, whatever the disinfecting precautions, simply because language has been so framed as to carry it. If all such references were really strained out, most descriptions of behavior would become either misleading or unintelligible. When we speak of either a human being or an animal searching or finding, attacking or defending, eating or drinking, laughing

---

1. For anthropomorphism, see Chap. 13.

or crying, we are not just describing standard, outward movements—any more than we are *just* describing states of mind—but such movements made with certain sorts of feeling or intention. Often the movements are not standard at all, but a mixed set, united only by the fact that they are all movements that someone in a particular state of mind would naturally make.

Take laughter. What do we mean if we say that Smith laughed at somebody? From an outer, disinfected point of view, laughing is just making a peculiar, convulsive noise. Very similar noise can be made by physical objects, such as a saw, and by animals such as hyenas and kookaburra birds. But someone who makes this noise while sawing is not laughing at anyone, nor are hyenas and kookaburras. And, on the contrary, someone who has not had this noise made at him at all, but has been treated with complete outward courtesy and perfectly suppressed smiles, can still have every justification for saying "they were all laughing at me," and can be right. It is also quite possible, if somebody thinks he has been laughed at, to say to him, "Yes, I laughed, but not at you," and this can be true or false.

If we want to understand such notions, there is no substitute for grasping the kind of subjective, conscious state in which such noises are typically made, and for this you need to be capable of something like it yourself. Someone who does not grasp that state at all will be simply unable to recognize a laugh—to distinguish it reliably from coughs, sobs, snorts, and other noises—let alone to interpret its point and meaning. Someone who grasps it only in a rudimentary way will make constant mistakes about just what *kind* of laugh it is. And we do find this occurring with people who have a peculiar or defective sense of humor.

What happens with laughter is typical of the very wide range of terms that describe what can be called expressive behavior. Frowning, weeping, smiling, waving, pouting, bowing, nodding, stamping, slouching, grunting, and so forth are *not* just names for bodily movements, but for those movements carried out with certain general kinds of feeling or intention. Often they are stylized by convention to become recognized signs, and then we must interpret them as messages from another conscious being, just as we do language. Often they are involuntary; a person then *betrays* his state of mind rather than deliberately conveying it. But if they turn out to be quite out of his control—if, for instance they are due to muscular spasm—their meaning is sharply altered. That is the only situation where it ceases to matter that they are made by a conscious being. And in that case, we may very well say that the movement, though it looks the same, is not a real smile, laugh, or whatever, at all. (Technical terms like *rictus* are invented especially to make this important distinction clear.)

The child accused of laughing at his grandfather can quite properly reply "I didn't," whatever the appearances. In some cases it may be unlikely that he is telling the truth. But there is still an aspect of the truth that he is in a better position to tell than the bystanders, namely, what it felt like at the time.[2] The reason this does not isolate us altogether from one another's understanding is that we are sufficiently alike by nature for similar outward signs to indicate similar inner states in everybody much of the time, and that we can watch a good deal of our own outward behavior as well as have inner experience. Bystanders watching a hysterical child can, if they happen to have experience of hysteria, know a good deal about him that he does not know about himself. And every normal person shares to some degree in a common pool of experience that enables him to judge, at least roughly, and often with surprising subtlety, what sort of inner state a particular piece of outward behavior signifies. When the correlation gets out of gear—when what should be expressive behavior ceases to give us the slightest guide to a particular person's state of mind—then, even if there are outer regularities, we say that we can no longer understand him, and we look around for some sort of help.

Not all behavior is expressive. But a great deal of what is not is purposive. This means that it can be understood only if we suppose the agent to have some sort of purpose or intention. Thus

2. As Skinner says (*Beyond Freedom and Dignity*, p. 191), "a small part of the universe is enclosed in a human skin." But the human skin is remarkably pervious to language. Even novels like Virginia Woolf's, which emphasize the privacy of experience and the difference between people, work only because language is public and we *do* understand each other. See also p. 346, below.

countless ordinary verbs that describe actions—hurry, fetch, seek, find, place, offer, call—are most naturally used to describe conscious deliberate activity carried out for some end. To say that a physical object (say, a hurricane or a tree) did any of these things sounds odd; it is either arch and affected, metaphorical, or symbolic. And depriving these words of their purposive implication is really hard. This becomes clear if we think (for instance) of someone accused of an illegal action who wants to excuse himself by showing that he did not know what he was doing. Granted (say) that he can be shown to have *sought out* the documents, to have *found* them, *carried* them to the apartment of the person to be framed, *looked up* the combination of the safe, *opened* it, and *hidden* them under other papers inside, it is not very intelligible for him to plead that he did not know what he was doing. Such words as these make sense only if they are used of conscious agents. And very many others—such as approach, catch, collect—though they can be used of material objects like avalanches or falling trees, have as a primary sense that in which they apply to people, and in that sense do carry the notion of intention.

That language works in this way has long been a subject of grievance to behaviorists. Thus, Skinner complains that "the vernacular is clumsy and obese" because it does more than record what is actually before us. "Many of its terms," as he says in *The Behavior of Organisms,* "imply conceptual schemes. . . . The term 'try' must be rejected because it implies the relation of a given sample of behavior to past and future events; but the term "walk" may be retained because it does not. The term 'see' must be rejected, but 'look toward' may be retained, because 'see' implies more than turning the eyes toward a source of stimulation, or more than the simple reception of stimuli" (pp. 7–8). But this is sweeping back the sea with a feather duster. "Walk" is no better for this purpose than "try": how could one be said to walk without any implication of earlier and later walking? We see a figure in a certain posture and say "he is walking." This is to class him as someone who *can* walk (so that, for instance, if he later excuses himself from other walking on grounds of incapacity, he is lying), and it is to place him as going from A to B. (If we later find that in fact he was simply posing for a statue called "Walker," we shall say we made a mistake.) Thus we are relating his behavior to past and future events. More than that, however, we are also relating it to his intentions. You can scarcely walk inadvertently. If his movements are important—if, for instance, he is going across the road to inform on his friends—it will not be easy for him to claim that he did it under compulsion if we saw him *walk* across alone rather than being pushed, carried, or threatened. If he wants to plead sleepwalking or blackmail, he must complete that story, referring again to the past and future, to answer implications about them which "walking" normally holds. In just the same way, "look toward" is no better than "see." It has implications about the past and future in that you cannot *look* anywhere if you have not for some time had eyes, and it is not very intelligible to say you do so if you do not want to see something. This again involves your intentions. And in fact only conscious creatures, capable of intentions, can be said to *look toward* anything in a literal sense. The commonest figurative sense for the term is that used in connection with windows and telescopes, which enable people to look in a particular direction.

Far more drastic efforts would be needed to avoid these implications. One would have to proceed by using, as far as possible, words that apply naturally to physical objects rather than people. Thus, instead of "he walked across the road," one would have to say something like "section of protoplasm," measuring 1.76 meters vertically, emerged at 2:06 P.M. from hole in building at point *x* on plan and moved northward, its extremities landing alternately on concrete substratum, finally entering hole in further building, at point *y* on plan, at 2:09 P.M." The effect of this kind of thing is disappointing, since the listener's only chance of making any sense of it is to grope around for a usable conceptual scheme, which will make it possible finally for him to shout, "Oh I *see*—you mean that a man walked across the road."

What Describing Is

It is not the vernacular that is clumsy. It is Skinner's notion of *description* that is misguided. Describing involves selecting what matters, and what matters always tells us more than we now see. Description is not meant to record all that is before us. In fact it records very little of it—just enough to bring into use a conceptual scheme that tells us enormously more. This is its purpose. We describe what we see as a Cow or a Table. Because we know what these things are, this credits them, at a stroke, with a whole complex history of the kind suitable for cows or tables and also a whole set of capacities for the future. This bonus is not contraband. It is the legitimate fruit of our previous experience and our powers of reasoning.

Certainly we can, if we like, pick out, among the possible descriptions, one that says less about the past and future of an object—one, say, in terms of colored patches. But doing this is not being disinterested. It is showing a different interest, namely, one centered on the passing experience itself rather than on the cow. Talking that way substitutes for implications about the cow's past and future others about the visual field, the relations of shapes and colors, sight, our eyes and our power of perception. These things can be very interesting, for specific reasons, to a painter, a psychologist of perception, or a student of optics. But this is true because they each have a conceptual scheme into which the detail will fit. Within that scheme, what seems like an isolated report about colored patches will tell them, too, a great deal more than explicitly appears in it. Because of the need to select, there cannot be a totally disinterested description, answering no particular question and arising from no special angle. The question for a describer is always: which conceptual scheme do we need?

Now in dealing with human behavior, we find intentions, motives, and feelings enormously important. It usually concerns us very little to know the exact details of a man's outward actions. But it can concern us vitally to know his intentions. We see his action; he has left the house. But is he angry? Is he considering leaving for good? Did he misunderstand what we said? Would he inform on us? Or has he just gone shopping? These are the kinds of questions which have shaped our language. *All* the terms in which we speak of human behavior have this bias, including, indeed, *behavior* itself. If someone asks, "How did she behave at the meeting?" he cannot be properly answered by a neutral screed, however complete, beginning "First she entered at the door on the left, then she sat down in the large chair," and so on to the end. The kind of answer called for will be: well or badly, arrogantly, diplomatically, savagely, feebly, confusedly. Nor is such language in the least *imprecise,* as Skinner seems to think. "The privacy which seems to confer intimacy upon self-knowledge," he writes in *Beyond Freedom and Dignity,* "makes it impossible for the verbal community to maintain precise contingencies. Introspective vocabularies are by nature inaccurate" (p. 192). But saying that somebody behaved savagely, or that I myself feel savage, is no more *imprecise* than saying that an apple is green. There are many shades, both of green and savagery. There are also borderline areas: green shades into yellow, savagery into peevishness. The terms are general. If we want to be more specific, we say more. Calling such terms *inaccurate* is still odder; how could you be inaccurate if accuracy were not possible? Someone who has been through a particular nasty experience can perfectly well say that a certain novelist describes accurately what it felt like to undergo it. (The silly word "introspection" is certainly no help. It seems meant to describe seeing one's feelings rather than feeling them—but then we don't need it.) As I have said, there would certainly be trouble if we were forced to *choose between* describing outer actions and inner experience—if we could not have both. But we do have both. People have insides as well as outsides; they are subjects as well as objects. And the two aspects operate together. We need views on both to make sense of either. And, normally, both are included in all descriptions of behavior. This means that we can constantly use what look like bare descriptions of outward acts to tell us important and interesting things, as well as the boring and pointless ones they overtly contain. If we answer the question about behavior at the meeting by saying, "She raised objections to every motion," or "She sat throughout with her head on the table," or, "She threw her shoes at the chairman," we convey quite clear and reliable information about motives, intentions, and states of mind. It is not so far at all detailed, but then nor is the information about the outer performance. And more detail can always be provided.

There is nothing fishy about trying to study motives, and a great deal that is fishy about trying to avoid doing so. Motivation is a central human concern, a thing that gives constant trouble when it is not understood. And the "scientific" way to understand it is, as with everything else, to take it on its own terms and find concepts suitable for bringing out its typical patterns. We all need and use terms like fear and anger, interest and desire, hope and repression; we all look for motives that are not apparent and for ruling patterns of motivation. What we need, therefore, is to do these things in a clearer, more organized way, not to outlaw them, or try to reduce them to reports of outer action, since they exist to explain these, not to summarize them. Nor is it the slightest use trying to substitute for them neurological reports of what goes on in the nerves and brain. These (again) describe something different, however interesting and helpful. There is, in fact, no need for these rather desperate measures of flight from the obvious subject matter of psychology. All they have done is to castrate that subject. It has been reduced, for fifty years or so, to the state in which the study of teapots would be if one half of the people engaged in it were sworn as a matter of professional pride never to mention the inside of a teapot, while the other half were just as unwilling ever to mention the outside.

Communication and Consciousness

Choosing the first of these options, Wilson in *Sociobiology* scrupulously avoids any discussion of purpose, motive, mind, consciousness, feeling, intention, or any related notion, and omits them from his index. Not mentioning things, however, does not necessarily make them go away. The method has its usual effect; sometimes strange gaps appear in the argument, at other times the banned concepts appear anyhow in a ghostly and uncriticized form. The trouble is worst over the problem of altruism, one that he regards as central. But it crops up all the time. One notable example is his discussion of communication. He defines this as "action on the part of one organism (or cell) that alters the probability pattern of behavior in another organism (or cell) in a fashion adaptive to either one or both of the participants" (p. 10), and later remarks contentedly that "this definition conforms well both to our intuitive understanding of communication and to the procedure by which the process is mathematically analyzed" (p. 176). Now this definition is actually so wide as to include almost any kind of interaction between cells or organisms. It seems to be satisfied when a donkey crops a thistle, when the thistle pricks the donkey, or when any one part of the donkey's digestion acts upon another. Yet, as Wilson worriedly notes, it is *not* necessarily satisfied by human communication: "In human beings communication can occur without an outward change of behavior on the part of the recipient. Trivial or otherwise useless information can be received, mentally noted, and never used. But in the study of animal behavior no operational criterion has yet been developed other than the change of patterns in overt behavior, *and it would be a retreat into mysticism to try and add mental criteria*" (p. 176, my italics). Trivial or useless information, however, is only the fringe of the problem. This way of treating human communication is altogether a dead end, an imposing signpost leading to a blank wall. Speech only "alters the probability pattern" of people's behavior if it is *understood*. That is what distinguishes it from infections, blows, flea bites and most of the other ways in which organisms interact.[3] That is what terms like *communication* are needed to mark. And the reason we pick out some interactions between animals as being communications is because that is true of them too. Threats, greetings, infantile appeals, submissive gestures have to be *understood* as such if they are to work. They are sometimes misinterpreted. And to explain the response to them one must always know what they are being understood *as*—what impression the receiver has formed of the signaler's motives and intentions. This is not true of infections, flea bites, or any sort of interaction between cells. And it is true of blows only insofar as blows are, among other things, a form of communication—they signal the striker's social attitude. Understanding communica-

---

3. "The experimental animal which *eats* the dinner-bell has misinterpreted the sign."—Max Black. See pp. 234–239.

tion therefore *is* interpreting it—whereas understanding causal interaction is no such thing. Communicating *is* conveying information and social attitudes. And this is something that it makes sense to talk only of conscious beings as doing.

Wilson's eccentric definition does not do him much harm, because he very sensibly ignores it, and goes on to decide what is and is not communication by common sense. But he can do this only by following, without acknowledgment, the everyday principle of confining it to beings which can reasonably be treated as conscious, and as *noticing* each other's signals. Far from being a retreat into mysticism, this provides the only context within which words like *communication* can have any kind of sense. Someone who genuinely thought of animals as unconscious automata would have to stop speaking of what they do as communicating. As that would lose us a most valuable distinction, nobody seems likely to try it.

CHAPTER 6

Altruism and Egoism

Different Notions of Selfishness

I have been suggesting generally that if we are to understand the behavior of conscious beings, we must take their motives seriously and not try to reduce them to something else. I must now illustrate this in an important case: that of altruism and selfishness.

Many people have found altruism a problem, and Wilson is among them. In fact he speaks of it as "the central theoretical problem of sociobiology; how can altruism, which by definition reduces personal fitness, possibly evolve by natural selection?" (p. 3). But two totally distinct problems are combined here. There is, first, the traditional problem of selfishness in human life, which is a problem about motive. It runs "Can a conscious agent deliberately choose to do things that *he thinks* will not pay him?" This problem can be considered only by people willing to take motives seriously. Second, there is a problem about evolution, which runs "Can a species survive if each member of it sometimes does things which do not (*in fact*) pay him?"

Both problems arise from the obvious point that people, and animals too, often do seem to do nonpaying things. The first inquirer is asking, can they know what they are doing? Do they perhaps understand their interest differently from the observer? He wants to make their acts *intelligible* in the sense of imaginable from the inside, from the angle of another possible agent—to grasp their reasons, to see what makes them tick. The second, by contrast, is viewing action from outside, from a very remote standpoint indeed. The sense in which he wants to understand it is that of fitting it into the theoretical scheme of evolution, which means reconciling it with natural selection.

Taken separately, neither of these problems is too hard. Taken as a tangle, however, they become almost impenetrable.

They differ not only because they arise from different inquiries and use their terms in distinct senses, but because they point to quite distinct ranges of example. No doubt the acts that a conscious agent believes will pay him often actually do so. All the hard work of prudence is devoted to making this happen. But it is always an uncertain business. Gamblers may win fortunes while the most careful accountants overwork and die of thrombosis. And even if outer events turn out as expected, feelings may not. Both the successful (surviving) accountant and the successful gambler may find that they do not know what to do with their success. Things are liable to turn to ashes in people's mouths. There are therefore constant difficulties in deciding what "really pays." And what pays at one time of life or in one situation may be disastrous at another. When should the payoff be declared? People fall into Solon's paradox; they find themselves saying "call no man happy till he is dead," and then reflecting that that hardly seems the time to do it either.[1]

Let us now consider the two questions separately. First, can a conscious agent deliberately choose to do things that he thinks will not pay him?

The answer to this simply depends on what we mean by "pay" (or by advantage, benefit, or whatever similar word we fancy). If we use such words in a very wide sense, the answer must be no, but the point becomes rather trivial. What we deliberately choose must certainly in *some* sense please and satisfy us. But this is as true of suicide, martyrdom, alcoholism, and unprofitable vengeance as it is of eating and drinking. What we choose must somehow attract us. But it need not in any normal sense pay us. Saying that it does is trivial because it stretches such words as *pay* beyond their normal use for the sake of paradox.

1. Aristotle, *Ethics* 1.10

The question has a much more ambitious and interesting point if we use words like *pay* in their direct and obvious sense, meaning "deliver a competitive, outward advantage." This is the way in which people making cost-benefit analyses use them. We now ask: can people deliberately do things that they believe will shorten their lives, lessen their income, damage their health, or diminish their power? Can they, that is, deliberately do such things for the sake of doing them, not trading off one advantage against another—say, losing income in order to increase health—but genuinely ignoring all such advantages? To keep this question clear of the earlier trivial one, we ought to have a list of publicly recognized advantages. It would probably be drawn from the list of our basic needs.

What we have now is a question of fact. And a brief glance around shows the answer to be yes. People do, sometimes, knowingly commit suicide. They do sometimes pursue vengeance, inquiry, or amusement that is sure to injure them. They smoke. They gamble, even against what they well know to be hopeless odds. (Think of Dostoevsky). They indulge in futile competition. In fact, we all do some of these things sometimes. Prudence is not universal. Certainly no one is imprudent all the time. But even if imprudence were quite rare, its existence would still destroy the position of philosophic Egoism, for that position is that "expecting payment" in the full outward sense is essential to the notion of wanting or choosing, that to want something necessarily *means* "to believe that you personally will profit from it," means making a favorable cost-benefit analysis.

Now our selfishness does not work like this. We are far too lazy-minded to do so much calculation. Mostly we do either what we have to or what we feel like doing. And quite often what we feel like doing is helping or pleasing other people—though of course not so often as they, or bystanders, might hope. If we never felt like doing this, the word *selfish* could never have arisen, since it describes a person who does not have these feelings or is not moved by them to action, and distinguishes him from other people who do and are. But the first point to insist on is how little we actually calculate.

Even in cases that do lead to solid, visible benefits, such as eating, what moves us is not usually the calculation of the benefit, but direct desire. This becomes obvious when illness or distraction destroys the appetite; we then find it really hard to eat. And people put on a diet for their health can have great difficulty in keeping to it. But the same holds for more complex desires, such as sociability, friendliness, curiosity, the taste for music, vengeance, or crime. Someone who tries to pursue these things without a genuine, spontaneous taste for them, merely for social advantage or because his doctor has told him to, will fail. His only hope of succeeding comes if he manages to *wake* a genuine taste.

It is true that many of the things we and other species like doing do eventually pay, and this fact is of great interest to the evolutionist. And it is true that we try to calculate our own interests. Calculation of this kind is even one of the things we have a taste for, as can be seen from the impractical lengths to which some people carry it. We are creatures naturally interested in the future, and it is a part of our rationality to be so. But neither our rationality nor our motivation can be limited to this tendency. The taste for future security is one taste among others, a taste that is often overborne.

The same thing is clear when we think how people choose their way of life. This choice is real—even in the most restricted life there is something worse that we try to avoid—but it is never undertaken by making a list of all conceivable modes of living and then doing an impartial cost-benefit analysis of their likely effects. Innumerable ways of life do not occur to us, and of those that do, many are marked "not for me." We use calculation of consequences only to choose among those that may seem initially possible and equal.[2] There is nothing irrational about this. We have to live in the present, not the future. The payoff pattern, the relation of means to end, is much less important in motivation than people suppose. What matters is the relation of part to whole. To give meaning to life, we want to see what we do as an element in something that, as a whole, satisfies us.

Naturally, this something does not have to be edifying. It may

2. See a very interesting discussion by Bernard Williams in J. J. C. Smart and Williams, *Utilitarianism: For and Against* (Cambridge, 1973), pp. 82–92.

be vengeance or destruction quite as easily as friendship or discovery. But—and this is the point for my discussion of Egoism—because it needs to be something larger than our own life, something worth participating in, almost necessarily it involves other people. Even the most hell-bent financier usually needs somebody to share his wealth with. Failing to find someone, or finding only the wrong kind of people, he is frustrated. Even the most solitary artist or thinker hopes to find, eventually, a public that will understand him. Certainly some people are natural recluses, but—leaving aside the difficulty of finding out whether they are actually pleased with their lives—they do seem somewhat abnormal.[3] I am not criticizing them, but pointing out that they can hardly provide an escape for the rest of us from the dilemma endemic to a social species; awful though other people may be, most of the activities that we really care about must involve them. Solitude is necessary for many parts of our life, but it cannot be the climate of the whole. Nor do we need other people merely as scratching-posts, *means* to the adjusting of our own states of consciousness. Our nature demands for its fulfillment ends to aim at which lie outside ourselves.

The Use and Misuse of Egoism

At this point champions of philosophic Egoism tend to cry "humbug!" and stop listening. This is not very bright of them, since the point that I have made holds just as strongly for sinister motives such as revenge as for decent or heroic ones. (In fact the demand for real outward action is just what makes revenge such a dangerous motive; you cannot get people bent on it to accept psychotherapy or enlightened self-interest instead.) But the

3. Proust, himself a thorough recluse, remarks, "In the case of the solitary, his seclusion, even where it is absolute and ends only with life itself, has often as its primary cause a disordered love of the crowd, which so far overrules every other feeling that, not being able to win, when he goes out, the admiration of the hall-porter, of the passers-by, of the cabman whom he hails, he prefers not to be seen by them at all, and with that object abandons every activity which would force him to go out of doors" *(Within a Budding Grove,* tr. C. Scott Moncrieff, Pt. 2 [London, 1924], p. 123).

humbug difficulty must be met, because the whole trouble about evaluating Egoism is that people see the problem not as a real problem at all, but as a mere clash of styles and attitudes. William James pointed out how we often dramatize an argument as a clash between tough-minded and tender-minded attitudes, between partisans, as it were, of science and sympathy. This habit chronically infests and distorts certain philosophical controversies, particularly about such tough-seeming but confused positions as determinism, hedonism, egoism and behaviorism. Role-playing of this kind paralyzes our thinking because it makes thought seem unnecessary; the positions are ready-made for us. Once they have imagined themselves to be tough-minded, people are quite liable to accept the loosest and most vacuous ideas uncritically, provided they are put forward in the right contemptuous tone of voice, while those who have cast themselves as tender-minded sometimes accept very brutal suggestions, provided that they sound familiar and traditional. But, as a minute's thought will show, science and sympathy cannot be alternatives, much less opponents. Anyone who treats them as such has forgotten the point of both. They are distinct aspects of life, and we all need both of them.

Looked at without this bias, Egoism is not a plausible account of motivation. And if we refuse to accept Egoism, the traditional problem about selfishness is not particularly difficult. We ask: can anyone deliberately act just for someone else's interest? This seems strange if we have already decided that the only reason he can act for is his own interest. But, as we have seen, people can and do constantly act for other reasons; they even act directly contrary to their own interests.

The point about hypocrisy, however, is important. For hypocritical distortion does *exaggerate* the claims others have on us, and play down the claims of self-fulfillment. That distortion is what philosophic Egoists—notably Hobbes, but also Aristotle, Spinoza, and Nietzsche—protest against.[4] They want to redress

4. Aristotle has an extremely interesting attempt to derive the love we feel for others from our love of ourselves (*Ethics* 9.4,8). This has been a very popular line with philosophers, but I think it is ultimately perverse. See the last two sections of Chap. 13.

the balance. Hobbes put the position particularly strongly because he had a crucial political point to make. As he saw it, if people attended better to their own interests instead of showing off, they would avoid doing many of the terrible things they do; in particular, they would altogether give up waging wars of religion. The humbug of chivalry was therefore Hobbes's prime target, and the *Leviathan* is, among other things, the *Catch 22* of its day. Look, he says, at the realities. Death is not a joke. It is the end of you. Does not all other value, therefore, depend on, and perhaps reduce to, your power to avoid dying?

Now it is perfectly true that enlightened self-interest is often a far better guide in politics than posturing and *machismo,* both for our own interest and for other people's. Self-preservation is not only a strong general motive with us, but also a positive duty. What it cannot be is our only duty or our only motive. While we survive, we must *do* something. And further, the point of all we do cannot be (as the subtler "tough-minded" theories suggest) to manipulate our own state of consciousness. Even in politics, there are other things that concern us besides finding the best means either to staying alive or to self-stimulation. And in private life, this is still plainer. People do an enormous range of things "as ends in themselves"—that is, not as a means to anything else, and certainly not to adjusting their own state of consciousness (which is a delicate job, and perhaps could only be efficiently performed by the pharmacist or the hypnotist). Football players want to win their games, and supporters want them to win them. Neither will accept, even from the most skilled pharmacist or hypnotist, the offer of *the sensation of a won game* instead. Avengers do not want the sensation of avenging; they want people's blood. And similarly, rescuers and benefactors do not (if they are real ones) just want the sensation of rescuing and benefacting. They want to help people. This involves wanting the people actually to be helped. If somebody else does so first, they will usually be quite satisfied.

The question of hypocrisy must be considered here, because we have a kind of suspicion that all these people are pretending. This, however, can hardly be right. You cannot have fake Vermeers unless there are some real Vermeers. This is not because it is *difficult* to copy without a model, but because nobody could want to. The existence of fake rescuers and benefactors, far from disproving the existence of the real thing, actually establishes it.

Again, consider the arts. A real actor or musician is not trying to tinker with his own subjective state. He is trying to practice his art properly. If he is interested in altering anyone's state of mind, it is that of his audience. Feedback will please him, but only insofar as it shows that he has got across what he was trying to do. (If what he wanted was simply the sensation of being applauded, the simplest thing would be to go through the motions of playing, while running a recording of an excellent performance by someone else. What's wrong with that?) The payoff pattern is quite unsuitable here. These actions point outward; they buy no round-trip ticket.

Art and sport are good areas, too, for showing how much shallower and less useful the payoff pattern of means and ends is than the pattern of part and whole in understanding human motivation. Is the play in the first half of the game just a means to that in the second? Or is all the play just a means to goals? Why not shoot them right away and save time? If the positions in the league table are the point, why not determine them by calculating the probabilities, or with a randomizer?[5] Are the first bars of the *Appassionata* just a means to the last cadence? Again, within the life of a player, actor, or musician, at what point is the payoff to be declared? If the actors who play the bit parts in the first scene of *Hamlet* are each doing so merely as a means to playing Hamlet some day themselves, they will play them very badly. The bit parts may *be* a means to that, just as they are certainly a means to a paycheck. They may also be a means to diffusing a weird atmosphere that will produce the right emotional effect later in the play. But had the director treated that problem as someone editing a horror film would have to treat it—as an isolated practical problem in emotional manipulation— he would go wrong in much the same way as a Martian might if asked to organize an ice hockey game. Understanding that

5. A possibility ingeniously exploited in Michael Frayn's novel, *The Tin Men* (London, 1972).

goals are the point, he takes twenty pucks down to one end of the ice and fires them into the cage from a cannon. It is not going to be easy to explain to him—or to ourselves—just what is wrong with this. But activity for its own sake is a pattern that pervades human life. Researchers like Masters and Johnson have documented the sad effects on people's sex lives of treating the whole business of sex merely as a means to a quick orgasm; it is well known that things do not go much better if you treat it as a means to quick production of an heir. Payoffs are a part of our lives, but not at all such an important one as may appear. The misleading point is, perhaps, that where the whole extends through time, we naturally have our eye on the part we can still influence, and this is the future. But there is no moment when the payoff can be declared, and the search for one leads to confusion and despair. John Stuart Mill's adolescent breakdown was, it seems, a result of his entrapment in this feature of Utilitarianism.[6] Attempts to use the pattern consistently and exclusively must, as far as I can see, lead to this sort of barren desolation. The attraction of Egoism, in fact, vanishes if you are consistent about it. It has only the momentary impact of suggestions that demolish isolated pieces of humbug. Its most heady pronouncements are often combined with others pointing a very different way—as when Nietzsche, so often eloquent for Egoism, remarks all the same, "Man should be trained for war, and woman for the recreation of the warrior; all else is folly."[7] What's she supposed to get out of that?

How to Misunderstand Altruism

For great areas of human motivation, then, Egoists are forced not just to distort their account, but to make it meaningless.

6. "It occurred to me to put the question directly to myself, 'Suppose that all your objects in life were realized, that all the changes in institutions and opinions which you are looking forward to could be completely effected at this instant, would this be a great joy and happiness to you?' And an irrepressible self-consciousness distinctly answered, 'No!'" (Autobiography, chap. 5).

7. *Thus Spake Zarathustra*, Pt. 1, "Of Womankind." He even adds "The man's happiness is, I will. The woman's happiness is, He will." Perhaps in fact egoism is always a sex-linked doctrine.

Hobbes and Aristotle do this repeatedly. Two examples are all I have room for. Aristotle, considering the case of somebody who dies to save a friend, asks whether this must count as acting for the friend's sake, and answers, no, the man has merely secured for himself a benefit greater than his friend's, namely, glory. He "prefers a short period of intense pleasure to a long one of mild enjoyment."[8] But if we believed this, we should not be especially impressed with him for doing what he did, and the glory he is after could never have attached to his act. (Even if the fellow fails to think this out, of course, his cost-benefit analysis is miserably shaky; how can he be sure of enjoying himself enough in the time available?)

Again—Hobbes defines pity as "Grief for the Calamity of another, arising from the imagination that the like calamity may befall himself" (that is, the person who feels it).[9] But if the only thing we ever felt on seeing the disaster of another was fear, our behavior would show only fear. There would then be no such word as pity, since there would be no such thing. And Hobbes could never have been called upon to define it.[10]

This is the traditional pattern of distortion. Anyone who doubts its power may be interested to watch Wilson falling into the very same hole. In *Sociobiology* he considers the case of someone who dives into water to save a drowning stranger, and remarks:

The reaction is typical of what human beings regard as "pure" altruism. However, upon reflection, we can see that the good Samaritan has much to gain by his act.... If such episodes are rare, the Darwinist calculus would predict little or no gain.... But if the drowning man reciprocates at a future time, and the risks of drowning stay the same, it will have benefited both individuals to have played the role of rescuer. Each man will have traded a one-half chance of dying for about a one-tenth chance. [p. 120]

Now this passage might merely be saying that *in fact* they will, on average, have benefited themselves, or at least done them-

8. *Ethics* 9.8.
9. *Leviathan*, Pt. 1, chap. 6.
10. See Butler, two long, very astute footnotes, on Sermon 1, sec. 6 and Sermon 5, sec. 1.

selves no harm. As we shall see, this is the most that the argument can possibly call for. But the language constantly implies more. It unmistakably refers to motivation, and analyzes it in the traditional distorting Egoistic style. The word that does so most plainly in the passage above is *traded*. *Trading* is a name for something that can only be done deliberately, and with appropriate motives. Traders must know what they are doing. To do something that merely turns out to benefit you is not trading, but if you make a deal, you have still traded if it turns out badly. Whatever the upshot, a rescuer was not "trading" unless his motive was a calculation of profit. Of course it could have been so. But people do in fact quite often rescue strangers *without* first checking that these strangers are husky, loyal, useful allies who will stay around until a counter-rescue becomes necessary. And a rescuer who finds that he has pulled out of the water a nonswimming old gentleman who lives at a distance does not necessarily react as he would if he had spent a lot of time salvaging a whiskey crate and then found it to be empty—that is, by throwing him back in again. He may still reckon that he has done what he set out to do.

The word "trade" does not stand alone. All Wilson's key terms are drawn from the language of conscious motivation. *Altruism, selfishness,* and *spite* are his names for activities that benefit (respectively) other people, the agent, and nobody. (It might have been better to talk of other-benefiting, self-benefiting, and purely injurious activities). The dictionary, however, defines altruism as "regard for others, as a principle of action," which is a motive. And this is certainly its normal use. Selfishness and spite, still more obviously, are never names for what actually happens, but for the agent's state or habit of mind. A spiteful action does not cease to be spiteful because it is frustrated, nor is accidentally injuring somebody a piece of spite. Similarly, in opening the section on what he calls "reciprocal altruism," Wilson remarks, more in sorrow than in anger: "The theory of group selection has taken most of the good will out of altruism. When altruism is conceived as the mechanism by which DNA multiplies itself through a network of relatives, spirituality becomes just one more Darwinian enabling device" (p. 120).

The stern tone, suitable for one revealing unsuspected nepotism in the charities of a presidential candidate, suggests that we have examined the motives of all rescuers and have found that they are not what they seem. But no attention has been paid to these motives. In what sense can the theory of group selection "take the good will out of altruism"? It is supposed to do it by showing that traits will survive only if they benefit the group. But one cannot "take the good will out" by showing how good will evolves. *Good will* is a term describing a kind of motivation whose occurrence is what we start from. People do sometimes rescue those who cannot benefit them. The theory of group selection is there to show that such motives could not have been passed on if they had undermined the survival of the group—perhaps that they must have promoted it. This is an entirely different thing from showing that they actually never evolved at all, that what looks like them is in fact only a cleverly disguised form of calculation. It seems important to notice that, if this were true, calculation of consequences would have to be immeasurably more strongly developed, commoner and more efficient than it actually is in man, let alone in other species. Hobbes's picture not only deprives us of our actual virtues; it credits us with others we do not have, at least in the necessary degree—a steady, unfailing prudence, a persistence in calculation, a stern intellectual honesty and consistency, a brisk readiness to act on extremely remote probabilities, such as we never actually see. (Since these really are important virtues, of which we are partly capable, the appeal of Egoism lies partly in celebrating them, as well as in attacking hypocrisy). If Hobbes's picture were accurate, the phenomena on the human scene would be totally different, and the "problem of altruism" in other less calculating species would remain quite insoluble.

This brings us back to the point with which I began this chapter—that we have two distinct problems before us. Wilson's kind of account—which is now extremely widespread—is weak in that it constantly carries into the evolutionary discussion an irrelevant and uncriticized Egoism. Officially it ignores motives, but in fact it makes constant reference to them, and because this reference is unacknowledged, its errors go uncorrected.

There is a real puzzle about the transmission of altruistic behavior. But that puzzle is solved by showing that it benefits one's kin and one's group. The further problem of inventing some way in which it can seem to benefit the agent himself arises only for Egoists, because only they have ruled that it has to do this to make him act. Wilson and his colleagues, however, take the Egoist stance, by pointing out that those benefited are often the agent's kin and suggesting that this makes it somehow possible for him to identify with them, since they will proliferate his genes for him if he does not live to do it himself.[11] Thus they give kin selection a much more prominent place in their argument than group selection. The general point about identifying with one's kin I shall be discussing shortly. But it is worth remarking here that altruistic behavior can extend far beyond kin. It is true that those surrounding an animal very often are its kin, and that this makes a great difference to the actual transmission of its genes. But its behavior does not systematically alter when the surrounding animals are not kin at all, as in the case where a creature leaves its home group and joins another before breeding. And even if it stays put, much of its behavior benefits, and some is meant to benefit, non-relatives. The social insects are indeed a special case. For them, group and kin are effectively the same. But this is just what makes them a misleading model for studying the overall relationship of the two concepts.

Beyond this, however, the whole notion of identification is uncalled for and useless. Only a very intelligent and well-informed agent could *plan* successfully to act so as best to proliferate his genes. But we are dealing, mostly, with agents who do not plan at all, including, usually, the human rescuer. It is important that we understand such actions for what they are, as done with the motives that they actually are done with, rather than distorting them to fit a tidy theory. The motive has to be one that can function independently of planning.

11. Notice how this at once takes us away from the normal notion of *selfishness*. If someone said, "He is utterly selfish, he thinks of nothing but the prosperity of his relations," or (as we must shortly substitute), "He thinks of nothing but how many descendants he will have in five centuries' time," we could hardly fail to reply, "But why do you call that *selfish*? You surely mean that he is either (1) clannish or (2) crazy."

There might, perhaps, have been an intelligent species somewhere which did not develop direct social impulses at all, but depended for all its social activity on calculation of consequences. We are not it. It would have done many of the things we do, but for quite different reasons. Others it not only would never have done, but could never have understood at all. But it is this alien species that is demanded by people who think of intelligence as the source of all social development. Thus Wilson writes: "a strong impelling force appears to generate social behavior in vertebrate evolution. . . . This force, I would like to suggest, is greater intelligence. The concomitants of intelligence are more complex and adaptable behavior and a refinement in social organization that are based on personalized individual relationships. Each member of the vertebrate society can *continue to behave selfishly* . . . but it can also *afford* to co-operate more" (p. 381, my italics). If intelligence had really been the only "impelling force," most of the concomitants would never have been found necessary. Why affection? Why time-consuming greeting procedures, mutual grooming, dominance and submission displays, territorial boasting, and ritual conflict? Why play? Why (on the human scene) so much time spent in nonproductive communication of every kind—idle chatter, lovemaking, sport, laughter, song, dance, and storytelling, quarrels, ceremonial, mourning and weeping? Intelligence alone would not generate these ends. It would just calculate means. But these things are done for their own sake; they are a part of the activity that goes to make up the life proper to each species. Insofar as there is one "impelling force," it is sociability. From that comes increasing power of communication, which provides the matrix for intelligence.

The Mystery of the Unconscious Altruist

Let us look now at our second question, the evolutionary one. Can a species survive if each member of it sometimes does things that do not *in fact* pay him?

Here, too, the word "pay" must be taken in its normal sense, as referring to outward, competitive advantage, not to subjective satisfaction. And again, we should start from the phenomena. But which phenomena? The notion of what does pay will not be easy to delimit.

Animals do quite a number of things that can be called *altruistic* in the full and natural sense, because they are actually *aimed* at serving others. Many creatures take great trouble over rearing their young, and also defend them vigorously, sometimes getting killed in the process. Many also defend and rescue young that are not their own; some will adopt orphans.[12] Some (for example, dolphins and elephants) also help and rescue adults of their species in difficulties, and some, such as wild dogs, will also feed sick and injured adults. Many babysit, and some (such as wild dogs) will bring food to the babysitter. Beyond these things, however, there is a very wide and heterogeneous set of further activities that appear to pay others and not the agent: for instance, mobbing predators, giving warning cries, taking risks in finding new homes or food sources, and even leaving the nest when you are injured, so that (or rather, with the result that) your fellow worker-ants are not inconvenienced by your dead body.[13] Many of these things clearly are *not* done with any view to helping others, though there are borderline cases. But Wilson's method lumps them all together as altruism.

Now it is quite true that creatures take risks in doing all these things. The puzzle from the evolutionary angle is that dangerous practices should tend to eliminate themselves by natural selection. Inquisitive rabbits that tend to investigate predators do not leave many descendants. Ought "altruistic" tendencies to have been eliminated in the same way? Are they unaccountable?

Two things can make them seem so. One is a devotion to the

---

12. The widespread tendency of social creatures to help, favor, and delight in young that are *not* their own fits most awkwardly with the notion of "the selfish gene." If we were really concerned only with the competitive success of our descendants, ought we not to get busy suppressing the other competitors? In fact this habit is rare enough always to call for explanation when it happens. See Tinbergen, *The Herring Gull's World*, p. 169.

13. *Sociobiology*, p. 121.

Egoistic model. If you are convinced from the start that all motivation can aim only at the agent's own advantage, you certainly cannot make sense of action aimed at someone else's. But I have suggested that this model is wrong.

The other is an atomizing approach to impulses. If you believe that the tendency to each specific sort of action is inherited separately, then all tendencies carrying personal danger are surprising, because it should have been possible to eliminate them while keeping all the rest. But in fact there seems no reason to suppose that these tendencies are inherited in such small units, however convenient that arrangement might be to games theorists.

As for Egoism, the notions of group and kin selection make it quite unnecessary, and it ought to be dropped from the argument. Selection does not work by cutthroat competition between individuals, but by favoring whatever behavior is useful to the group. People with crude notions of "Darwinism" make an intriguing blunder here. They confuse the mere *fact of competing*, that is, of needing to share out a resource, with the *motive of competitiveness* or readiness to quarrel. Where creatures are competing (as a fact), their success will be decided by whatever tendencies they have that best help their predicament. These need not be quarrelsome tendencies at all. A species may prevail because it is better at finding food or turns to a food that is more plentiful, or because it grows protective coloration, or indeed because it becomes *less* quarrelsome and more cooperative. Very often the best means (whether it counts as "prevailing" or not) is to move aside, finding a slightly different habitat, food, or mode of escape—inventing for oneself a new ecological niche. Now among the possible ways of prevailing, quarreling can certainly figure. But there are pretty sharp limits to its usefulness, and usually other methods are used. "Contests" between species are in general entirely figurative. Those involved need not even know what is going on. They come to the feeding place and find it bare; they find their eggs gone, or they unwittingly nurture a cuckoo. What they do is done for its own sake, not as part of a response to a challenge.

Competitiveness, as a motive, then, need not be involved at all in "competition" between species. And even where it is, it has to be limited sharply by prudence and common sense. Animals must avoid fighting that leads to serious injury; they have no doctor. Thus even a very hungry lion will abandon its kill to hyenas when the odds are against it, and vice versa. This is even more true of competitiveness within a species. While it has its uses, it can easily turn out very badly. The rival-fights of deer, for which they have evolved their antlers, are useful because they select powerful fathers for the young. But as the system develops, and the few strongest stags begin to monopolize the mating, things go less well. The gene pool is unnecessarily narrowed, and the job of protecting the young becomes harder. More serious, selection operates to produce good fighters rather than deer of good all-around capacity. This favors size, and particularly size of antlers. (Deer do not use their antlers against enemies outside their species; they drive them off with their forefeet). Unless predators or other modes of selection intervene, stags then head towards the fate that seems to have overtaken the enormous Irish deer—a seven-foot spread of antlers and extinction.[14] Where the motive of competitiveness is strong, it is hard for a species to get out of such a cul-de-sac. Strong fighting stags simply will not allow others to mate.

Thus the sort of "competition" involved in natural selection gives no support for an Egoist account of motives. All the same, some notion of possible motives is needed here. The question how a creature can come to rescue others of its species, or to give

14. For various views on this entrancing topic see Stephen Jay Gould's article, "The Origin and Function of 'Bizarre' Structures," *Evolution*, 28 (1974), 191–220. Gould quite rightly points out, (1) that the great creature prospered very well for a time—it was not some sort of Thurber animal which never made sense; (2) that the horns are not disproportionate to the body, but near the average proportion for deer. He adds the interesting fact that (3) they seem adapted for display rather than actual fighting. He concludes that they were not in fact impractical at all, but just an ordinary useful adaptation. Now he is clearly right to reject the view called *orthogenesis*, namely that such features develop in a straight line because of some mysterious force, regardless of value. Such forces are meaningless. But does it follow that sexual selection could not *continue* to favor large forms at the point where (whether for reasons of fodder shortage or of thicker forests) they were becoming impractical? This sort of thing does occur in birds (see Wilson, p. 132, on grackles, Lorenz *On Aggression*, p. 40, on argus pheasants). It seems plausible that it could prevent the changes needed to delay extinction.

warning cries, is a genuine one, calling for an answer that makes genetic sense. We cannot treat these acts just as cultural phenomena, induced by precept or example. Could they just be imitated? As far as warning cries go, this is partly an empirical question about a particular species's power of mimicry. Some have none. But it is also about their kind of awareness, the sort of things they attend to, and the sort of reaction they are capable of. About rescuing, the point seems still plainer. Many species could never consider it, whatever examples might be shown them. We are dealing here with a difference in emotional *range* among species, with a capacity, found only in the most social species, to be so deeply concerned for others as to take drastic action. (A familiar example of this difference in emotional range is that between dogs and cats, which does not yield to cultural interference.) Now this gap has in fact somehow been bridged in evolution; this kind of active concern for others has—in several groups, separately—somehow become possible. And, since most of this bridging has been done well before the human stage, or quite independently of it, it has *not* been done by conscious calculation of the human type, but by adaptation. So it does seem likely that it carried a selective advantage. Of course, among human beings, example and training can help the reaction and make it much commoner. But they could not do this if the capacity were not there in the first place, just as it is in dolphins and elephants, although not in polar bears or hamsters. No purely cultural development could have generated it.

How to Make the Whole Study of Motives Impossible

The necessary complexity of such capacities points up the wrongness of an atomizing approach to impulses. It seems unrealistic to talk as though the tendency to rescue people were something that could be carried by a single gene. Something like a tendency to give warning cries might conceivably be so. But rescuing is plainly far too complex a phenomenon to be governed in this way. This is true partly because the kinds of danger, and therefore the kinds of rescue possible, do not follow a single pattern—but also because, in any fairly complex creature, the undertaking of dangerous actions *must* involve other traits in the character besides the impulse in question; the whole character has to be such as to permit them. Such behavior cannot stand alone.

Wilson in fact knows this perfectly well and sometimes says it. But he still does not give it enough weight, because he pays too much attention to the mass of speculation on these subjects generated recently by games theorists. (I do not say that this is all useless, but it is only useful so far as we can apply a binary model of winning and losing, pinned to a single, separately heritable characteristic while everything else is held constant, and this does not seem to be very far, with anything more complex than fruit flies.[15]) Thus, though he may not actually make the blunder of which his critics complain, of positing separate, single genes for spite, altruism, and so on, he much too readily accepts the language of those who do treat behavior as a mere mass of discrete units inherited separately.[16] This raises quite unnecessary problems. "Granted a mechanism for sustaining reciprocal altruism," he writes, "we are still left with the problem of how the behavior gets started. Imagine a population in which a Good Samaritan appears for the first time as a rare mutant" (p. 120). The passage goes on to cite calculations of the "critical frequency of the altruist gene, above which the gene will spread explosively. . . . How critical frequencies are attained from scratch remains unknown. Co-operative individuals must play a version of the game of Prisoner's Dilemma."

15. E. B. Ford (*Ecological Genetics* [London, 1964], pp. 9–10) spells out clearly the hopeless weakness of *a priori* genetics, conducted by "mathematicians who sit at home and deduce how evolution ought to work." He points out too the sharp limitations imposed on the work even of laboratory experimenters by what he calls Drosophilosophy—obsession with a few standardized lines of investigation concerning the black-bellied fruit fly. This animal (long the rat of genetics) does have certain advantages from the experimental angle, but Ford is clearly right to stress that no single species should ever be deemed typical in this way and studied in isolation both from comparison and from its own ecology in the wild.

16. For the great complexity of this situation—the extent to which one gene can influence many characteristics and one characteristic depend on many genes—see, for example, Dobzhansky, *Mankind Evolving*, chap. 2. Failing to

What is the problem? All the creatures that it makes sense to suppose could develop positive altruism are already caring for their young. And the first element of parental care which develops is defense and rescue from danger. (Even some fish and reptiles do this, as well as the social insects.) All that is needed is to extend the pattern to adults. Now the development of sociability proceeds in any case largely by this extension to other adults of behavior first developed between parents and young— grooming, mouth contact, embracing, protective and submissive gestures, giving food.[17] In fact, wider sociality in its original essence simply *is* the power of adults to treat one another, mutually, as honorary parents and children. It is enriched later with other patterns largely drawn from the interactions *between* infants: hence the enormous importance of play as a source of social sophistication. But quasi-parental interactions come first. They work well because they are adapted to soothe, to conciliate, to forge a bond. Once forged, why should this bond not carry its usual consequence of protectiveness? Besides this, in a stable group, many adults present will actually *be* descendants of the others, and others will be those whom they have known as young, so that quasi-parental bonds are already formed. (Friendly behavior to young who are *not* one's own is very common.) Add, too, that those who, from whatever cause, are especially protective and good at rearing young, are likely to leave a disproportionate number of descendants in relation to those actually born. Again, the cry for help which a creature in danger

---

stress complexity invites incredulity about the central point, which must still remain valid—namely that natural selection does manage to take place in spite of it, and sometimes to produce what appears the most refined adaptation of means to ends.

For the problems concerning "supergenes" (blocks of genetic material locked together by a twist in the DNA) and "switch mechanisms" (genetic factors making possible a kind of jump in evolutionary direction), see Ford, *Ecological Genetics*. The effect of such things can, as he points out, sometimes speed up evolution remarkably. In any case, *a priori* estimates of pace are useless, since, as he says, "it is completely unrealistic to consider the behavior of a large interbreeding community under constant conditions, since that situation, far from being realised, is not even approached in nature!" (p. 33).

17. This is a dominant theme in both Eibl-Eibesfeldt's *Love and Hate,* and Wickler's *The Sexual Code.*

gives is likely to resemble that of a young animal. Even if there has been no selection for the similarity, he suddenly finds himself in a position of infantile helplessness. Why should it not release the same behavior? What need is there of a drastic mutation? What compulsion to play at Prisoner's Dilemma?

That game would, no doubt, well represent the situation of an "altruistic" mutant in a nonsocial species, say a codfish or even a hamster. The effect of his distinctive actions would depend entirely on luck; he could not (for this is the point of the game) count on any understanding cooperation from other players. As Wilson says, "he rescues but is not rescued," so he is not likely to leave very many descendants.

But could there be such a mutant?

If there was, it seems that much more than just a single gene must have mutated. It is not clear how, starting cold, with the emotional equipment of a nonsocial species, he could become endowed at one leap with all the capacities for so complex a performance as a rescue. What is needed for such a change seems to be an alteration in the general programming system, a metamutation that would produce, not just one new behavior pattern (such as cries of warning) but a whole set, adjusted to a new way of life. If such changes are possible (as some have suspected they must be), the fact is of great importance and needs discussion; in particular, it would totally alter the rules of the games-theory game in this area.

What this supposition brings out is the absolute necessity of treating altruism as an aspect of motivation, and therefore as something that makes sense only in the context of a given emotional constitution. It cannot be dealt with if it is defined merely by results. The higher animals—unlike, perhaps, the social insects—have characters, general forms of life typical of their species. Their particular behavior patterns have to fit into these. When a particular species puts something high on its priority system—for instance, dominance, territory, or the care of the young—then it will face danger for that. Many species have at least one such thing that they are willing to take risks for, though others specialize in running away and living to fight another day. Understanding a particular motive is seeing what set of motives it belongs to, and then what importance that set has in the life of the species. To see how each element can have developed, therefore, we need to think how the set as a whole developed. No doubt for a complex pattern like the care of mammalian young to be formed, many mutations have been necessary, but there are also other factors—for instance, the mere ordinary exchange of genes to form new combinations,[18] better feeding, or worse dangers, the stimulation of new environments, and the effect of other changes in the creature's life. And we have to ask about the effects on group and species survival of the whole set—not just of a particular action. It does not seem likely that the power to rescue others from severe danger makes much difference directly to a species's survival, though it can certainly do so to that of a small group. What does make an enormous difference, however, is the power to form the strong social bonds that make rescue possible. When we consider what is involved in the relation of parent and child in a slow-developing species, and remember that this bond shapes the early experience of every member of that species, further gradual progress to mutual help among adults does not seem too hard to imagine. And in that context, rescue is intelligible enough. It has to be explained not as an isolated gamble, but as part of a whole pattern of motives, which as a whole is advantageous. Explaining it is showing what company it keeps.

Wilson, however, would like to explain such habits in a much more simple and ambitious way—namely, by reconciling them somehow with the Egoist model, which he takes to be self-justifying. He feels it necessary to show altruistic behavior as somehow benefiting the individual who displays it. He goes about this by treating the behavior as contributing to that individual's *genetic fitness*—which means simply and solely his chance of leaving offspring.

18. "The very lowest estimate of the number of variable genes in human populations will still be in the hundreds, and this is amply sufficient to make the potentially possible gene combinations far more numerous than can ever be realized in people now living or those to be born in the future. The mechanism of the Mendelian recombination of genes thus confers on a living species a capacity to produce a prodigious abundance of ever-new genetic endowments" (Dobzhansky, *Mankind Evolving,* p. 31).

This must be noticed at once as a disastrous move. The notion of fitness has long been a loose cog in arguments about evolution. Wilson greatly increases the strain upon it, without giving it the kind of support that that strain calls for. As it is such a central and widely invoked concept, it seems necessary to make clear the dangers of his treatment.

The trouble with words like "fit" in these discussions is that, if taken in a wide sense they are liable to become vacuous and if taken more narrowly they easily become tendentious. Thus the phrase "survival of the fittest" does not mean much if it means only "survival of those most likely to survive." If on the other hand it means "survival of those whom we should admire most" or the like, it describes a different state of affairs; we shall need different arguments to persuade us that this is happening. In just the same way, Wilson equivocates with the notion that to be "fit" is an advantage to anybody. If it means "healthy" or "able to do what he wants to do" then it usually is so. But if it only means "likely to have many descendants," there is no reason for treating it as an advantage at all. Yet for Wilson the latter meaning quickly becomes, not just *an* advantage, but the only advantage that matters. Thus he defines selfishness as "raising one's own fitness by lowering that of others" (p. 117), this fitness being genetic fitness. Again, of insects that discourage predators by tasting nasty, but can hardly do so without dying in the process, he writes, "it pays to stay around as long as possible to teach predators not to eat one's offspring. In contrast, cryptic saturniids have a short postreproductive life; it does *not* pay to teach predators that one's relatives are good to eat" (p. 125). *Whom* does it pay or not pay? The creature in question is no longer there to be paid. It is wrong to put the perfectly sensible point about the conditions under which a trait can survive in this highly metaphorical way. As we have seen, it can lead to personifying the gene itself, or the DNA, in order to find a candidate for the vacant position of plotter and payee. Just as often, however, the individual itself is nominated for the job of plotting, and that in some fairly surprising species:

One of the most promising circumstances in which to search for *voluntary* population control is the evolutionary reduction of virulence in parasites. Virulence often (but not always) comes from the capacity to multiply rapidly. Thus the condition is likely to evolve by individual selection. But too high a level of virulence kills off the hosts, perhaps before infection of other hosts is achieved, so that virulence will be opposed by interdemic selection. *It may stretch credulity to think of an altruistic bacterium or self-sacrificing blood-fluke,* but in the sense that feeding ability or reproduction is curtailed in spite of competition from other genotypes, a parasite can be altruistic. [p. 116, my italics]

What is stretched is not credulity—the facts described are perfectly easy both to believe and to understand—but the use of words like "altruistic" and "voluntary."

Another awkward flaw in the scheme is that an individual shares genes with many others who are not his descendants. Since the proliferation of these genes too is supposed to benefit him, the notion of simple genetic fitness is expanded to that of *inclusive fitness*—"the sum of an individual's own fitness plus the sum of all the effects it causes to the related parts of the fitnesses of all its relatives" (p. 118). Thus, the care or rescue of any relative becomes compatible with egoism—provided that the arithmetic works out right: "If only first cousins were benefited $(r = \frac{1}{8})$ the altruist who leaves no offspring would have to multiply a cousin's fitness eightfold; an uncle $(r = \frac{1}{4})$ would have to be advanced fourfold, and so on" (p. 118). But if we are *really* to regard this "inclusive fitness" as representing our own interest, can these bargains be called altruistic at all? The answer seems to vary; thus, on the page before: "Self-sacrifice for the benefit of offspring is altruism in the conventional, but not in the strict genetic sense, because individual fitness is measured by the number of surviving offspring. But self-sacrifice on behalf of second cousins is true altruism at both levels." The mind reels. Genes identical to ours are scattered among all our relatives— indeed, if we move in a small stable group, over the whole population. What is special about the specimens passed through our own progeny? It is not as if we could keep them together in a *block* with which we can at all identify. Human inheritance systems obscure how fast these blocks break up. When that arch-dynast, Louis XIV, died and left the throne to his great-grandson, one-eighth of his genes remained to help rule his country. Seventy years later, Louis XVI carried about one-thirty-second of them to the guillotine.[19] Anyone who tries to separate out his own interest as something persisting through these changes has forgotten how utterly dependent his own genes must be, at every stage, on the others that are incorporated with them. Thus, when Wilson proceeds from mentioning the second cousins to say, "and when directed at total strangers such abnegating behavior is so surprising (that is, "noble") as to demand some kind of theoretical explanation" (p. 117), he seems to make a rather arbitrary point. No man is an island; we can never tell whose life has been, or will be, bound up with ours. But apart from local kinship systems, which depend on culture, how could there be different *kinds* of motivation for rescuing first cousins, second cousins, and strangers? Cousins, after all, can *be* strangers; so, indeed, can uncles and brothers. (Wilson touches on the problem of unrecognized relatives on p. 247 of *Sociobiology*, but he does not seem to recognize its explosiveness.[20]) The demand for "some kind of theoretical explanation" arises only from the Egoist position. And from that position, offers of an increase in "inclusive genetic fitness" will be received with proper contempt. The agent himself is getting no sort of advantage at all.

In the second part of this book I have been discussing how we can best set about understanding human nature, granted that (as I argued in Part One) there actually is such a thing. One chief reason why humanely minded people have been unwilling to admit that we do have a nature has been the fear of a crude and unperceptive psychology.

If we want our psychology to be "scientific" in any sense that matters, we must not aim at a superficial likeness to the physical sciences, but at an intelligent adaptation of our concepts to a

19. Or possibly much less, since the half of his genes which a parent passes on to any particular child does not necessarily include a fair quarter from each grandparent, but varies indefinitely.

20. It is worth noting, for instance, that in such species as the chimpanzee, multiple mating makes it impossible in principle for father and child *ever* to recognize each other as relatives. And in many species, an individual never knows as relatives anyone but his parents and the siblings of the same brood.

distinct subject matter. And we should not expect to build a single monolithic science, but to use a number of different approaches, intelligently related.

Any such psychology ought indeed, as Wilson suggests, to make full use of the evolutionary perspective as a background. But it is equally necessary that it should be capable of dealing with the foreground—of abandoning the long perspective and looking directly at the motives of individuals. We must therefore take these motives seriously in their own right and not try to reduce them either to neurological phenomena or to behavior patterns. All such reduction must fail because it distorts essential characteristics of its subject matter. It only looks persuasive when it surreptitiously uses ordinary motive-concepts to flesh out its artificial schemes.

Motives have their importance in evolution and their own evolutionary history—but they have also each their own internal point, and it is virtually never a wish to bring about some evolutionary event, such as the maximization of one's own progeny. Confusion between the aims of individuals and the "aims" of evolution—if there can be said to be such things—is ruinous.

I shall move on to the question of how far evolution itself can be said to have aims in the next chapter.

Part Three

SIGNPOSTS

The feather'd race with pinions skim the air—
Not so the mackerel, and still less the bear,
But each, contented with his humble sphere,
Moves unambitious through the circling year;
Nor e'er forgets the fortunes of his race,
Nor pines to quit, or strives to change, his place.
Ah! who has seen the mailéd lobster rise,
Clap his broad wings, and soaring claim the skies?

—George Canning, *The Progress of Man*

CHAPTER 7

Up and Down

Is There an Evolutionary Ladder?

In what sense, if any, can evolution be said to have a direction or a purpose? It is hard to see whom we could credit with such a purpose, unless we call upon the Lord. Yet the word "evolution" commits us in some sense to taking what happens, or at least much of it, as being *in order*. To evolve means to *unfold* or *unroll*. It suggests typically the opening of a scroll or a bud, bringing into action what was only potential within them. This means both that certain definite potentialities were present from the start, greatly limiting what could emerge, and that these, rather than many other changes that must have been possible, were in some sense the right or suitable candidates. A bud eaten by a caterpillar has fulfilled some of its potentialities, since it always was potential caterpillar food. But it has not fulfilled those proper and central to it. Ought we to say, similarly, that evolution would have failed, fallen short, or become deflected if it had followed a different path? Would there be something wrong if, for instance, birds or ants, snakes or people had never developed?[1]

---

1. There are obviously related problems about the word *develop* itself, and also about a whole range of concepts like *growth, progress, advance, modernity, primitive,* and *the avant-garde*; also *the Future* when that is used as a term of admiration (see p. 159).

This is an alarming question. But we commit ourselves to some kind of answer to it whenever we mention *higher* or *lower* life-forms. And the matter becomes far more pressing if we start, like Wilson in *Sociobiology*, to map the relative heights of different kinds of societies, and to say things like

Four groups occupy pinnacles high above the others, the colonial invertebrates, the social insects, the nonhuman mammals, and man. Each has basic qualities of social life unique to itself. Here, then, is the paradox. Although the sequence just given proceeds from unquestionably more primitive and older forms of life to more advanced and recent ones, the key properties of social existence, including cohesiveness, altruism and co-operativeness, decline. It seems as though social evolution has slowed as the body plan of the individual organism became more elaborate. [p. 379]

How do we decide which are *the key properties of social existence?* Apart from man and the mammals, none of these groups is descended from any of the others, so we are not following any actual development.[2] How can we evaluate and compare patterns that play totally different parts in their lives? It seems vacuous to grade different kinds of cohesiveness except in relation to the different kinds of creatures which have to cohere.

Bees, coral polyps, people, and other mammals do not provide alternative solutions to the problem of the clash of interests between individuals. People and other mammals share that problem. Bees and coral polyps have not reached the stage where it can arise. Bees do indeed readily run into danger, benefiting their community by doing so. The reason they do this is that they have never developed the power to know that they are doing it. A bee that labors ceaselessly for the larvae, or rushes out to sting an intruder though it cannot extract its sting, or serves its own egg to the queen as food, undergoes no conflict and exerts no virtue. It just reacts to the pheromones. (This is quite clear from

2. Wilson has a quite remarkable reason for omitting birds from his list of the highly developed. Birds, he says on p. 148, rank as social beings below the ants, because of their failure to form castes. As no other creature, and certainly not man, has castes in the insect sense, that seems to leave the insects a walkover. Anyone who doubts that birds have a rich and complex social life can read Lorenz's discussion of jackdaws in *King Solomon's Ring*, or of geese in chapter 11 of *On Aggression*. Or he can simply watch the maneuvers of a flock preparing for migration.

the ease with which such habits can be distorted to become use-less or detrimental—for instance, in ants, by nest-parasites which exploit the whole behavior, displacing and sometimes eating the larvae.[3])

If we ask how creatures that act so elaborately against their private advantage can have evolved, the answer lies in their mode of reproduction. Most workers are sterile. The unit of selection is normally the whole community. Its prosperity de-pends on the efficiency of the workers. An uncooperative strain would simply revert toward the solitary life these insects started from and in which many of them still remain. This would lose them enormous advantages in food storage, brood defence, and so forth. So it is natural to understand their evolution, as we would that of a plant, without reference to the plans or wishes of individual bees.

But a dedicated egoist can, if he chooses, look at it differently. The notion of genetic advantage supplies a goal which the crea-ture can actually be said to reach. If—just for the sake of argument—it *were* an intelligent creature, and its wish *were* sim-ply to proliferate its genes, it might (it seems) do just what it does at present. For, Wilson says, with the system of reproduction that bees use, "it is genetically more advantageous to join a sterile caste and to rear sisters than it is to function as an independent reproductive" (p. 381). This is because they share more genes with their sisters than with their offspring. (The ratio is about three-quarters to one-half, but see the very complex calculations on p. 416. It is evident that a bee which did plan like this would have to be a pretty good statistician.) Throughout this argument words like *trade, prefer, advantage,* and even *investment* constantly recur. What seems to happen in evolution can, it emerges, be represented dramatically as a possible outcome of quite dif-ferent causes—namely, the planning of a dedicated and monomaniac conscious agent, addicted to dynastic ambition.

Now this parallel fantasy may very well have its uses. But it cannot help the argument about selection, which has to stand on its own feet. And it is liable to mislead us badly as soon as we start to compare these societies with those of other creatures. For it

3. *Sociobiology,* pp. 375–376.

suggests, quite unrealistically, that the genetic standardization of the insects is some sort of solution to the problems of conflict: "Absolute genetic identity," Wilson says, "makes possible the evolution of unlimited altruism" (p. 380). But, as he sees elsewhere, it also makes it quite meaningless: "Altruism is easy for genetically identical individuals, in fact, in them such behavior is technically not even altruism" (p. 33). Genetically *identical* individuals are in fact only found at an even simpler level than the insects, in such things as coral colonies or composite jellyfish like the Portuguese Man of War. Wilson calls these "perfect societies" (p. 379). This is probably more like talking of a perfect circle than like making a moral judgment. Still, he goes on to say that human beings, since they "approach the insect societies in co-operativeness and far exceed them in communication," have "reversed the downward trend in social evolution that prevailed over one billion years of the previous history of life" and to ask "Why has the overall trend been downward?" (p. 380).

Rightly did Darwin pin up a paper warning himself to be careful about using such words as "higher" and "lower." What is *downward* about the trend that has produced elephants, chimpanzees, wolves, dolphins, and jackdaws, by comparison with ants and bees? Upward, in this graph, must represent only one value: harmony. The point cannot be just survival, nor even survival in numbers. Survival is just as well achieved by much less ambitious creatures which go in for sheer number. (In fact a cost-benefit-conscious gene that really understood its business would, no doubt, have remained on board something like the amoeba; it will probably be among the last to go.) Nor is it survival-as-a-society, since many animals achieve this in spite of a lot of bickering. It seems to be the elimination of friction. But the impressiveness of this achievement must depend on the complexity of the parts.

Is there any sense to questions like, what is it all for? which way are we going? what constitutes "upward"?[4] Scientists, on seeing

4. For confusions and obscurities in the notion of "orthogenesis"—steady one-way movement running through all evolution, or even through the history of a particular group like horses—see George G. Simpson, *The Major Features of Evolution* (New York, 1953), pp. 268–269.

these questions naked, will probably want to sweep them aside and claim that they are irrelevant; the whole inquiry must be value-free. But we cannot do this. The scheme of evolutionary thinking ceases to work at all if we insist on sitting on the fence about what we count as an advantage. Think of the state of affairs in the future when life is becoming impossible on the earth. If "evolution" simply means "whatever change takes place," the changes that occur in those days will have to count as evolution too. In this spirit, Schopenhauer suggested that the purpose of anything was what came at the end of it, and therefore that death was the purpose of life.[5] As I have already suggested, the point of evolutionary talk is to help us to distinguish between useful and damaging developments. We can make no such distinction without committing ourselves to some notion of what constitutes an advantage. The same necessity becomes plain in two much more familiar situations: one, where zoologists discuss developments that seem to them to be *maladaptive* (that is, disadvantageous to the species), and the more striking one where they commit themselves, as Wilson does here, to some sort of hierarchy of evolution, to the view that something is *higher* or *lower* than something else.

The first point can be pushed under the rug fairly easily by speaking of survival. What is maladaptive, we say, damages the species's chance of surviving. But at what level of survival are we aiming? Even here we do not find value-free, antiseptic, guaranteed neutral standards. A species that proliferates very widely is doing more surviving than one whose numbers remain relatively constant, but how long will it be able to continue? It is idle to talk here as if one could calculate the chances. Changes of circumstances outside the species itself may make "calculations" that would have looked perfectly safe at one stage turn out disastrously at another. It is now widely held that what went wrong with the dinosaurs was not any sort of nemesis called forth by their mistaken investment in size—that they were not, in fact, unwieldy and ill-designed at all, but were probably overtaken by

5. A thought quoted, and used to ruinous effect, by Freud in discussing the Death Wish (*Beyond the Pleasure Principle, Complete Psychological Works,* Vol. 18, p. 49).

some quite general and unforeseeable climatic change, such as was bound to spell the end of all but very small and unambitious animals.[6] And here we come back to my point about the amoeba. If the "aim," the steady, impartially determined advantage, were just surviving, amoebas would be the thing to be. But evolution cannot possibly be seen as a progress toward this, since it is largely a progress away from it.

I think it may be this difficulty of locating the advantage which pushes zoologists toward egoism—a pattern familiar in human life, and one which seems to let us shelve the attempt to "find a purpose" in evolution. We just accept each creature's tendency to work for itself, and take the sum of these as constituting the aim of the whole. But can they form a sum when they so often conflict? Besides, as we have seen, creatures do not have this simple and elegant tendency to work each for themselves. They do not "maximize" survival, nor in any clear sense aim to do so. They survive, or they don't. If that is all, perhaps we must renounce the habit of dealing in evolutionary hierarchies, must stop talking of "higher" and "lower" life-forms.

What do we mean when we speak (as Wilson does in his inquiries about "social evolution") of higher and lower animals, of upward and downward trends, of evolutionary regression, and of maladaptation? A ready answer is that the question is just one of *complexity,* that the higher is simply the more complex. This is part of the point, but it cannot be the whole; only some sorts of complexity are relevant. If any sort would do, some plants would qualify; indeed, the complexity of anything *can* be viewed as infinite. Among living things, termites rate high, and some of the colonial jellyfish, such as the Portuguese Man of War, seem unbeatable. But we need a kind of complexity typical of living things, and one in which the traditionally classed "lower" animals rank as simpler than the "higher" ones. Now the favored suggestion for this property is *intelligence,* and this is what makes Wilson's suggestion so interesting. He puts bees and ants higher than any other species but man, in spite of their lack of intelligence—in spite, indeed, of naming that lack as the factor

6. See Simpson, *Major Features of Evolution,* pp. 292 and 302.

that brought them to a dead halt in evolution "between 50 and 100 million years ago" (p. 434). It is quite true that he speaks only of *social* evolution. But how can one isolate that? To talk of the "evolution of societies," without any reference to changes in the kinds of individuals that compose them, is to abstract one set of patterns for attention and approval in a way that needs justifying. Different sorts of individuals would seem to call for different sorts of arrangements. What is so good about complete harmony and cooperativeness, as opposed, say, to a looser grouping of individuals who pursue their own ploys much of the time, but have arrangements to avoid serious friction? I am not saying that this question cannot be answered. I am pointing out that it arises; therefore, we are *not* dealing with a neutral, antiseptic, value-free problem here. What, too, about communication (a respect in which, Wilson says, we much exceed the insects)? What is so good about communicating? How are we sure that it constitutes an excellence? Is it even clear that in this respect we *do* exceed the corals and the colonial jellyfish? With them, there are no internal barriers; information flows freely from unit to unit wherever it is needed. The *unrestrictedness* of the communication much exceeds that among people. Why does this fail to impress us?

Sharply it emerges, when we face such questions, that the impressive element lies in *what* you communicate, not in the mere fact that you are communicating. Among people, we are not most impressed by the person who talks most, nor by him who can be shown to have passed on the greatest number of distinctly enumerable "bits" of information. Such people can be pests; they may merely represent a disastrous increase in confusion. What we value is not communication in itself, but certain human activities within which it is an essential element—love, friendship, inquiry, play, worship, exploration, laughter, mourning, facing danger, the arts and crafts. Because we need to do these things together, we need communication as we need light or sound. A human being who cannot communicate is as hampered as one deaf or blind in respect of his deepest emotional needs. What he suffers from is that *his faculties cannot be used;* they are *unawakened.* So he is either deprived altogether of the life proper to him, or, if his faculties work partially and are then frustrated, he is unhappy. But for a creature naturally solitary—a hamster, say, or a polar bear—this does not happen; solitude is his element. He has no unused faculties. The riches of his life lie elsewhere.

It is possible to construct a ladder on which polar bears rank lower than coral polyps, just as it is possible to construct the reverse one. We do not have here that simple pattern (so dear to academics) which we represent in the examination system, of a one-way one-dimensional grading, by a standard that has already been established. We appeal to a number of standards. They can diverge and sometimes conflict.

Survival Is Not Enough

We cannot reduce all these standards to the one basic one of efficiency in surviving. All existing species are surviving. What interests us when we draw distinctions among them is not this fact, but *what* their life is: what each of them *does* while it survives. This point has been obscured by a slick simplification, plausible for a time after Darwin, which suggested that the kinds of life we value most are also those most likely to secure survival. It showed man as the supreme survivor, and other species as mere precursors, amateurs at this important art. But this was never more than a self-deceiving fancy. The relations between survival and the qualities that we find admirable are far more complex than that. Three points will make this clear.

1) Man is not the supreme survivor. Rats and spiders, termites, ants, earthworms, slugs, and barnacles will almost certainly outlive him, however well or badly he may do, and amoebas will outlive them. Moreover, it is quite possible for man to shorten his own term of survival by exercising those very qualities he most admires. Those who rest all values on survival have to ask: If we go first, will it prove that rats and the rest were after all the higher species?[7] Rats are an interesting case, because

7. As G. E. Moore pointed out, using the American Indians as an example, being higher can hardly *mean* just that "we can kill them more easily than they can kill us" (*Principia Ethica* [Cambridge, 1948], p. 47).

they share a quality widely held to be the key to human success: they are extremely adaptable. We certainly cannot make about them the rather patronizing judgment we often make about creatures that become extinct, namely, that they are over-specialized. Extinction has overtaken mammoths and great auks; it looms before gorillas, giant pandas, and manatees; over-specialization has no doubt something to do with all these cases. Does it follow that rats are "higher" than these animals? Cannot an animal (say, the gorilla) be vulnerable because of a specialized habitat, and yet be highly developed?

2) This brings us to the fact that not all nonsurvivors have been evidently "low." For instance, it no longer makes sense to patronize the dinosaurs. The smaller ones, it now seems, may have been as spry and active as many mammals, and some of them at least were quite intelligent. How they lived we cannot now know in any detail. But it seems that many of them cannot possibly have led the monotonous, fixed, incurious, unenterprising life that we usually have in mind when we grade a creature low.

3) Finally, supreme survivors can be very "low" indeed. *Lingula,* a modest but contented brachiopod, has apparently remained virtually unchanged from the Cambrian age to the present. As for the amoeba, not only has it long been unchanged as a tribe, but since it reproduces by division, its first members are in a sense still here in person. There's survival for you. If that is what interests us, we need never climb that evolutionary ladder. The dramatic language used in much talk about evolution obscures this point. Ruthless marches, relentless pressure, brutal cutthroat competition and all the rest of it sound like a mode of ensuring that whatever does not climb that ladder is bound to perish. It isn't. It can just stay at the bottom. Nor, therefore, is there the kind of poetic justice that people often find in the evolutionary process, whereby inertia is punished by extinction. Certainly countless species have perished, and some of them were inert. But just as many have been those who *did* vigorously develop a way of life, and had it fold up on them.

There is a serious snag here, affecting the whole business of functional thinking in biology. *We have a right to look for the best, but we do not have a right to expect it.* The arrangements we find do *not* always seem the best possible. We must constantly proceed by asking "what is the good of *x*?", which means that we assume there will be an answer. This, however, does not amount to assuming, with Leibniz, that "everything is for the best in the best of all possible worlds."[8] Yet discussions of evolution often do seem to proceed on something like this extreme assumption. For it to work, we would have to have clear information about both what was possible and what was best. We have neither. To deal first with possibility, let us consider the question, how far does the actual fall short of it? What are the obstacles to evolution?

Very often we have not the slightest idea, and this means that evolutionary thinking ought often to be a lot more modest than it is. Superlatives like *optimize* and *maximize* only have a clear sense where the whole range of possibilities is known. What limits them? Wilson gives what seems like a non-answer. Failure to adapt, he says, is due to "phylogenetic inertia," which, "similar to inertia in physics . . . consists of the deeper properties of the population that determine the extent to which its evolution can be deflected in one direction or another, as well as the amount by which its evolution can be speeded or slowed" (p. 32). If there really were such a property, genuinely similar to those of physics, it ought to be directly testable and it would be of enormous interest. The examples Wilson quotes, however, suggest no such thing. What they amount to is: sometimes we can see how a creature's reproductive system makes it hard to develop the appropriate adaptation, but mostly it seems that the creature in question just doesn't happen to have the genes.[9] And any

---

8. This principle is not actually the fatuously cheerful falsehood it may appear; it only says that all other possible worlds would be worse. But it is still an obscure and exaggerated way of putting the quite genuine point that, when we are dealing with living things, we have a right to expect that existing arrangements will have *something* to recommend them over *some* alternative possible ones.

9. Simpson discusses various kinds of explanation which can be helpful here (*Major Features of Evolution,* p. 298). But they are so diverse that lumping them together under the head of "inertia" would obscure and not clarify them. He makes a particularly useful point in noting the ambiguity of "specialization" when that is conceived as an evolutionary trap.

attempt to explain *why* it doesn't may have to do what the analogy with physics suggests and examine detailed causes. But they will be different in each case. An explanation may have to show how, by bad luck, this animal simply is not capable of making the required adaptation, rather than how valuable not doing so is to it. Many species, after all, do become extinct. Everyone has to allow for failure. And this is the final, crucial objection to supposing that the highest qualities, those we ought to admire most, are always those that maximize survival. Believing this would require an enormous Leibnizian act of faith in the optimization system, combined with a most un-Leibnizian conviction that surviving was the only thing that mattered.[10] It is not clear what could bring anyone to such a position.

We cannot, then, see our way to giving any sort of clear answer to questions about what is evolutionarily possible. And the notion of a quasi-physical force working for evolution is somewhat vacuous. Much more so, then, is the notion of a quasi-physical inertia called in to stop it. Dormitive force is not much help in accounting for the effect of opium, nor is phylogenetic inertia here. Quasi-physics in fact seldom does help anyone. Turning from questions about possibility, then, to the other difficulty, can we say anything about what "best" would mean here?

The notion of evolution has always carried some sort of assumption about values. This was expressed crudely in various forms of "evolutionary ethics," most of which fully deserve the

10. This seems to be implied by Wilson's somewhat obscure remark about our emotional constitution: "According to genetic theory, desirability is measured in units of genetic fitness, and the emotional centers have been programmed accordingly" (p. 551). This must mean that we feel each desire in exact proportion to the use it has had in promoting survival. But, even if there were such units, no part of our constitution is tested *alone* in this way. Selection works on the creature as a whole, strength here compensating for weakness there. Giant pandas have many weaknesses, but have made up for them until now by having a remote habitat with few competitors. As Wilson elsewhere freely says, evolution is not infallible even in ensuring such general bargains, much less in every detail. Here he is greatly exaggerating a true and valuable point. Our emotional nature *has* been subjected to natural selection along with the the rest of our capacities, and we can use this fact to help us understand it—but only on condition that we do not overstate it.

blasting G. E. Moore gave them in *Principia Ethica*.[11] They proceed by picking out some one favored pattern from the thousands that could be traced in evolution and using it as a pointer for the future. They claim that, because events have moved in direction *x*, they ought to go on further in that direction, and that we must therefore take all possible steps to push them that way, lest they fail. The trouble with these theories is not so much that (as Moore said) they are using natural facts as a guide to values. It is that they have picked out quite unsuitable natural facts.[12] Not only do they confine themselves to facts about evolution, but among the vast range of evolutionary facts they select a single strand, arbitrarily, in response to standards they have already accepted for other reasons and do not criticize. If this were not so, no call to action could follow. A genuine, impartial diagnosis of an evolutionary trend could lead only to prediction. Such trends, if believed in at all, would have to be things that, like the weather, will take their course whatever we do. The frenzied anxiety about *promoting* what is supposed to be inevitable can spring only from an uneasy consciousness that we *are* taking sides—that the trend we have picked is only one contender among many, and by no means a sure winner. If we try to support it, we do so *not* because it is inevitable, but because we have found some reason to prefer it, and that reason cannot be a belief in evolution. Other grounds are needed. (Something of the same dilemma afflicts Marxism; the inevitability of the Revolution can hardly, of itself, be a reason why we should help it along.)

Thus, the unbridled nineteenth-century capitalist who thought of himself as the spearhead of evolution did so because he liked the sound of a few things he had heard about the place of competition in natural selection. Had anyone pointed out to

11. Pp. 46–58.
12. For the suitable ones, see Chap. 9. The intuitionists' idea that *no* facts are relevant, that there is always a "naturalistic fallacy" involved in reasoning from them, is quite incoherent. Many people have now made this plain, starting perhaps from A. N. Prior's admirable *Logic and the Basis of Ethics* (Oxford, 1949). My own contribution to this demolition job is a paper called "The Neutrality of the Moral Philosopher," *Proceedings of the Aristotelian Society,* 74 (1974).

him that he was not affecting the genetic situation, or that his
kind of competition could not be compared with that between
species, or that cooperation within the species was the characteristic strength of man, or that his nearest analogy in real evolution was probably the Irish deer, he would simply have stopped
listening. And other claimants to the position of spearhead,
though they differ from him in detail, fall just as surely into one
of two classes, the vacuous and the totally disreputable.

Must all talk of value in an evolutionary context be like this?
Can anything better be made of the evolutionary ladders?

One feature about them might rouse the interest of our Centaur. By a strange coincidence, they all end at man. Does this
have to be so? Could there be a species that did *not* put itself at
the top of its own evolutionary ladder? Perhaps, people may say,
the question hardly arises, since to be considering it at all, you
have to be intelligent. But might there not be two intelligent
species that knew of each other? In principle we could meet
intelligent alien life; should we know how to place it in relation
to ourselves? Moreover, are we sure that we would always recognize intelligence if it was of a different kind from our own? if it
were exhibited by creatures with different interests? Could we
ever really deal, for instance, with the question how whales rank
in intelligence? It is hard enough to compare different kinds of
intelligence sensibly even in human life. Intelligence tests are
desperately blunt instruments for doing so, answering only the
crudest purposes, because so many kinds of faculty and interest
go to make up human intelligence. Artists and scientists, farmers, grandmothers, children, engineers, civil servants, Eskimos,
and explorers constantly overlook the evidence of one another's
intelligence because they are looking for it in the wrong places.
And the sort of intelligence on which intelligence tests concentrate tends ineluctably toward that needed by the people who
devise them, namely, experimenters and statisticians. Does every
intelligent creature have to do things of which we can see the
point and show its intelligence in ways which we can recognize?

These difficulties about comparing different kinds of intelligence may not impress everybody. But even those unmoved by
them will probably feel uneasy about saying that "intelligence,"

whatever it may be, is the *only* kind of excellence required by evolutionary grading. This point comes out well in the many science fiction stories stemming from H. G. Wells's *War of the Worlds,* which confront the human race with aliens much more intelligent than itself, but inferior in "humanity," that is, roughly speaking, in the richness of their social, emotional, and imaginative life. But these qualities are much harder to measure even than intelligence, and much harder to penetrate in creatures very different from us. So the judgment that places us at the top becomes not only harder to make, but less and less meaningful, more obviously like the notoriously unsatisfactory sort of ranking that people sometimes try to make between different kinds of human beings—between musicians and engineers, active and contemplative natures, young and old, men and women.

Understanding the Metaphor of Height

The truth is, there can be no evolutionary ladder. Creatures diverge, each to its own way of life, each finding its own characteristic sort of fulfillment. Shall we then speak rather of a tree? People may be inclined to accept this, feeling that a tree has a clear vertical axis, and that we must still be placed at the top; who else would be there? But what I am asking about is the meaning of that same vertical axis. Suppose that we think rather of a bush, which does not have a main trunk, nor, therefore, a dominant direction of growth; is there any reason for treating the *top* of the bush as especially important?[13] Or we might take something whose growth is not vertical at all: a spreading strawberry plant. Or indeed the biosphere itself, producing life of many kinds in many directions. Is this a worse image for evolution?

We have to unpack the symbol of *height.* And to do this, we have to see how it has become entangled in the notion of evolution.

Height is a natural symbol for value. Before anybody thought of evolution, this was expressed in the idea of a Great Chain of

13. Acknowledgments to the palaeontologist A. L. Panchen for this bush, a most helpful and liberating piece of symbolic vegetation.

Being—a scale of creatures reaching from the least to the most important. From inanimate matter the chain led through the simpler living things to the more complex, then on through man and the Heavenly Beings to God. It was eternal and unchanging.

When, however, people began to think about evolution, they made (as commonly happens) no more changes in their ways of thinking than they were forced to. They did not scrap the Great Chain of Being. Instead, they simply unhooked the top end from Heaven and slung it ahead into the Future. Its axis now was time. But its associations with value did not vanish. For good reasons and also bad ones, they proved tenacious.

Among the good reasons was the desire to have values located somewhere. In an age of change it became increasingly difficult to locate them in the past; people could no longer confidently say "It is good because our fathers did it." So they began to say, "it is good because our descendants will do it." Hence the bizarre cult of the Future itself as a kind of mythical subsistent realm enshrining value—a cult invented by Nietzsche, filled out by Wells and the Futurists, and still very influential.[14]

Among the bad reasons were sheer human arrogance, ambition, and greed, a contempt for other life-forms (unluckily encouraged by some Christian thought) which aspired to the total "conquest" of nature, now that God, formerly controller of the whole Chain, had been deposed.[15] If the hierarchy of values could be seen as a linear progress away from other life-forms toward *exclusively* human values, respect for other living things was a waste of time. They "belonged to the past," and this was now an expression of disgrace.

This disastrous tangle between the ideas of time, height, and value had many important effects that I cannot touch on here. My topic now is, in what sense do we have to consider our own species as the paradigm of value? There is a sense in which we of

14. C. S. Lewis has some excellent remarks on the way people have used this idea to obscure to themselves their own responsibility for shaping events, and on the general oddity of treating the future as substantial, as "a promised land which favoured heroes attain—not as something which everyone reaches at the rate of 60 minutes an hour, whatever he does, whoever he is" (*Screwtape Letters*, XXV).

15. See pp. 254 and 358.

course must do so, namely, that we must live according to the values of our own species, not those of any other. No *other* candidate for the top of the tree can be set up for us to imitate. *Humanity* is for us a term that quite rightly sums up all that we have to value and aim at. It signals our own area of the bush. But this by no means implies that the things we value are not found elsewhere or that we have yet listed and understood everything that should be valued; we plainly have no monopoly on many valuable elements, such as kindness and affection. We did not, personally and unassisted, invent every aspect of humanity. Much of it is drawn from a common source, and overlaps with dolphinity, beaverishness, and wolfhood.[16]

It is quite possible that any creature capable of raising the question would find it necessary to place itself "at the top" in this sense and to this extent. Such a need is no coincidence, and also no scandal so long as we understand clearly what it means. It should not stop us from understanding the distinct natures of other species, if we are willing to make the effort. If the qualities that count as excellences in our life really had nothing to do with theirs, things would be different. This would be the case if, for instance, we were colonists on a totally alien planet, or if Descartes had been right in his speculations about the human soul, making it altogether an alien to the rest of the animal kingdom. But Descartes was wrong.

The figure of the bush, in fact, is useful in several ways. First, it allows for the branches' diverging. Second, since they all still grow on a common stock, it emphasizes their connection, their mutual dependence, their relevance to one another. Third, it shows up well the central fallacy of evolutionary ethics, which is to treat evolution as a straight progress in a single direction, and to imagine that, having quickly found the road, all we need do is to drive along it as fast as possible. Branches diverge and can curve to and fro quite sharply. And even the straightest branch must stop somewhere, or it will break.

16. For beavers, see Lars Wilsson, *My Beaver Colony* (New York, 1968), and entries under *Castor* in the index of *Sociobiology*. They are particularly interesting because, being rodents, they have less intelligence than most of the animals we commonly rate highly, but still possess many traits that we think central to humanity. For this general problem, see Chaps. 10 and 11, below.

This is a much better figure for what we find in evolution. Curves constantly appear; the "progress" or "advance" of any group can zigzag and double back repeatedly. Snakes, for instance, have gone "back" from their ancestral life as lizards. Abandoning their ears and even their legs, they have slid away into corners. Yet it would be hard to deny that they have made something of themselves; pythons and cobras are hardly creatures to be sneezed at. Are they higher or lower than the lizards? Another fascinating case concerns the eyes of mammals. The strong development of primate intelligence is probably a result of an upsurge of dependence on eyesight. You need good sight to survive if you move through treetops, and that calls for a large cortex. But, long before that development, the earliest mammals seem almost to have abandoned sight for smell. All mammalian eyes are degenerate in comparison with those of birds and reptiles; perfectly good mechanisms for accommodation have somehow been lost, and replaced later by much less adequate substitutes. Mammals have made most of their advances while relying on smell. Should we say, then, that improved sight constitutes an advance, or that it does not?

The sensible way to deal with such questions seems to involve treating all such things as responses to particular difficulties and opportunities. In the treetops, you need sight; in creeping around under thick cover at twilight, you need a nose. One such strong development tends to exclude another. And nobody needs every speciality:

> Why has not man a microscopic eye?
> For this plain reason; Man is not a Fly—[17]

There is, in fact, no such thing as fitness in the abstract, only fitness for certain conditions, and these may change.[18] Moreover, all such developments have their limit, and, for any species, there are limits to the specialities it can combine. There is not, and could

---

17. Pope, *Essay on Man*, Epistle 1, lines 193–194.
18. The notion of "inclusive genetic fitness," in fact, seems to have lost touch with that of *fitness* altogether, and to be merely a name for long-term fertility or the like. Thus the "survival of the fittest," in this context seems to mean just that those who have the most descendants will, as a matter of fact, have more descendants than the others. This is not a very inspiring proposition.

not be, an indefinite progress in any direction, much less in all directions. Size has many advantages, and species tend to advance in it, but it has its limits, particularly if (like the Irish Deer) you combine it with an impractical shape. The problem is evident even in the simplest cases of evolution, such as that where predator and prey perfect each other through competition in speed. Cheetahs, in their extraordinary brief sprint, can rise to 70 m.p.h. and still do not always catch their gazelles. It does not seem likely that flesh-and-blood creatures which have other aspects to their lives could become more specialized in this direction. (As it is, because cheetahs are solitary, pregnant females have serious problems, and the shape of that tiny, beautiful head could probably not be altered to add another trifle of brains without spoiling the sprinter's balance.) There are those who hold that the typical human hypertrophy of the cerebral cortex is not a specialization of this kind, does not take its toll of other faculties, and can therefore be increased without limit. I find this a startling act of faith.[19] But even if it should be true, it would not show that it is the *best* thing that could happen to the creature—the right way for it to go. At any point in evolution, a development that has so far been profitable may reach its limit, may need to be balanced by other developments that have been neglected, may begin to produce dangers of its own against which the species has no defense.

People hope, I think, that the brain will turn out to be an exception because it is an all-purpose development, one on a different level from all the others, which helps all our remaining powers impartially, and so does not destroy the balance. But we cannot rely on this, because intelligence genuinely *is* impartial. It magnifies dangerous tendencies as well as helpful ones; it makes it much easier for us to do lasting damage. As we know by now, very intelligent people can be very destructive. Brains alone will

19. I am cheered to find George C. Williams too asking, "Do we really understand the function of man's cerebral hypertrophy?" (*Adaptation and Natural Selection*, p. 14). It is too simple-minded to assume, on the tree pattern, that the production of just such a creature must have been the goal of evolution from the start, a result so obviously right that the mere natural upward movement was bound to reach it.

not produce harmony, and they make conflict much more dangerous.[20]

No doubt this is why Wilson represents social evolution as a march toward greater harmony. In wanting a corrective to an obsession with intelligence, he is certainly right. But *all* such obsessions have to be resisted. There can be no single direction for social evolution any more than for evolution generally. So we cannot sensibly name a single "impelling force." Nor, therefore, can we sensibly talk of "phylogenetic inertia," or any other quasi-physical force, as needed to account for its limited success. Some species become social, others do not. To some extent we can see why they were likely to do as they did and what sort of good it has done them. But this is a situation far too complex for the crude push-and-pull language of physics. Talk of general forces adds nothing to the more subtle terms of specific observation. Thus, Wilson's remark that "high inertia implies resistance to evolutionary change, and low inertia a relatively high degree of lability" (p. 32) is vacuous. They do not *imply* it, they are names for it. He goes on, "Sociobiologists have found examples of phylogenetic diversity that are the outcome of inertial differences between evolving lines. One of the most striking is the restricted appearance of higher social behavior among the insects." But this takes it for granted that the *proper* development, the one to be expected, is that toward more complex societies. And throughout this discussion, Wilson lumps together as examples of "inertia" cases where creatures have failed to make a change that would manifestly help their survival with cases where they have simply failed to form a society. But why? Again, I think the insect model is misleading. To a human eye, insect societies stand out strikingly; they "excel" solitary forms of insect life dramatically. What does this mean, apart from the fact that they are superficially more like our own? If we take examples nearer to ourselves, where imagination can get a better grip, can we put the point clearly? Is it *better* to be a wolf than a polar bear, a jackdaw than a wandering albatross, or a human being than

---

20. Nor can they prevent silliness, the sheer constant waste of time and power. Intelligence alone is not rationality. See Chap. 11.

any of them? Well, we are inclined to say, it is certainly more interesting. But for whom? There is surely only one answer: it depends on who you are in the first place. What test have the lives of these creatures failed? The answer, though embarrassing, seems simple—they have failed to become more like ours. If man wants to set up a contest in resembling himself and award himself the prize, no one will quarrel with him. But what does it mean? All he can do by these roundabout methods is perhaps to assert a value-judgment about what matters most in *human* life. But, now as always, the only proper way that such value-judgments can be arrived at is by considering carefully the very complex claims that arise within human life itself.

CHAPTER 8

Evolution and Practical Thinking

Where Evolution Is Relevant

Evolution cannot furnish a test to resolve our clashes of values. The reason for studying it is not to come up with a simple one-way pointer, but to fill in some of the background necessary for understanding our own nature. That is bound to make us see it as *more* complex than we thought at the start, since it is the business of any culture to simplify, to narrow down the options considered to those that the times most call for. This point has been obscured during the recent surge of interest in human evolution and animal studies, by the natural tendency of critics to concentrate on the controversial. If someone writes a book, primarily emphasizing the complexity of human nature, but saying that a certain impulse plays a certain rather unexpected part within that complexity, it is the second point that will hit the headlines and polarize the controversy that follows. But what needs attention is still the first. The issue is not between bad guys who use an "adversary" approach and good guys who are scientific and impartial (as Wilson suggests). Everybody, including himself, is partial in the sense of starting somewhere, of selecting something for emphasis. The fatal thing is not this. It is being confused about one's reasons for doing so. Particular insights and principles of inquiry must be set in the context of other possible alternatives. The reasons that might lead someone to start elsewhere, with different selections and emphases, must be understood and answered. Unfavorable evidence must be dealt with. These are very hard requirements. In this age of intense specialization, when scholars can easily avoid ever speaking to someone in a neighboring field, they seem to many people simply impossible. On balance, I do not think they are any better met by those who regard themselves chiefly as "scientific" than by popular writers. Simply not considering an alternative case is no better than inveighing unfairly against it. And the consequences are worse, since what is unfairly inveighed against does at least get heard of.

Sociobiology is certainly on the side of the angels here, since it makes an enormous effort to be comprehensive, and much of it is easily readable. It is aimed at a fairly general audience; it recognizes their right to a share in the insights of zoologists about animal nature and the way evolution works. Now what, beyond a simple signpost, does such knowledge contribute to our practical thinking?

The answer is, I think, plain. All moral doctrines, all practical suggestions about how we ought to live, depend on some belief about what human nature is like. (This includes doctrines that we "have no nature," since that means that we are—naturally—quite plastic.) Very often these beliefs are wrong. When they are so, they are often evolutionarily implausible. Some understanding of ourselves as an animal species can therefore help us to avoid subscribing to them. Human life is full of conflicts. In dealing with them, we are often advised by people of the sort I will call moral surgeons, to make a clean break and eliminate an aspect of life entirely. And they do not regard this—as physical surgeons generally do—as an unusual and somewhat deplorable measure, called for only in emergency. The more determined kind of moral surgeon remarks that he is *not* just prescribing for an emergency, but revealing our essential nature, telling us that what he disapproves of is actually an accretion, no true part of us, something alien. Thus, Tertullian observed that the world in general was a heap of filth containing a single pearl, the human soul, to be extracted from the polluting body and saved for Heaven. And thus today solicitous people want us to disown the aggressive and possessive impulses we feel within us, to treat them as alien accretions, rather than to acknowledge and understand them, recognizing, as Jung said, our own Shadow.

To resist such advice we do not need to invoke evolution. People could resist Tertullian at once. The sense of our own wholeness is both natural to us and expressed in our culture. Still, because conflict is painful, such people have a disproportionate influence. Besides, these doctrines need to be answered. *Why* should it be right to regard the world or ourselves in this way rather than some other? Here argument is called for, and here moral philosophy starts. It differs from straight moralizing in that it uses argument to deal with conflicts, and even where its conclusions are bad, this difference makes it much less dangerous and more helpful. Arguments can always be answered. Moral philosophy, unlike straight moralizing, arises from and thrives on plurality of values.[1] Yet perhaps even moral philosophy has been too ready to endorse moral surgery, too eager to simplify man. The crudeness of Egoism, which I have already discussed, is a fair example. There were good reasons for emphasizing the distinctness of human individuals; there were political purposes for which such emphasis was necessary. But that does not justify grossly generalizing partial observations and saying that man is altogether incapable of seeking anything but his own advantage. Now it so happens that evolutionary considerations strongly reinforce this point. It is not clear how a species could evolve which did what Hobbes supposed, and became calculating before becoming social. This I have said already. What I now want to emphasize is how necessary Hobbes found it to back his analysis of man's predicament by a story about his nature and his early history. The State of Nature and the Social Contract are not just literary devices, nor are they merely metaphors about people's present psychology. They imply something about human origins, namely that we *are as if* the Contract story had

---

1. That is why it arose in Greece at a time of great distress and political confusion, which had made all simple, one-sided moral attitudes untenable. Socrates did not invent the habit of questioning established values to reveal the contradictions beneath them. He just tried to work out better ways of doing it.

been true, and therefore cannot (for instance) have evolved from the reverse direction. To that extent they form an empirical hypothesis about the past, which has been falsified. Similarly Rousseau, when in the *Discourse on Inequality* he spoke of primitive man as solitary, as "meeting other men perhaps once or twice in a lifetime, without knowing each other and without speaking," was not just adding illustrative embroidery to his analysis of political obligation. Certainly what he says is primarily meant as a piece of timeless psychology, as a claim about what people are like now in their deepest motivation. But it does also have a literal, historical meaning, because such accounts of how people are now are not compatible with just any story about their past.

Further examples could be given, including, of course, the Christian story about God's Creation, which Hobbes and Rousseau were implicitly resisting. But the general point is perhaps clear. Major moral insights are not independent of psychology; they imply a view about how people essentially are. And these psychological views are not independent of history; they all imply some view, however general, about how we came to be that way. It is not, therefore, the student of evolution who brings this topic into the controversy. All he does is to suggest some better ways of handling it. And the point he must chiefly make today is that the reductive simplicity so dear to moral surgeons will not do. The motivation of living creatures does not boil down to any single basic force, not even an "instinct of self-preservation." It is a complex pattern of separate elements, balanced roughly in the constitution of the species, but always liable to need adjusting. Creatures really have divergent and conflicting desires. Their distinct motives are not (usually) wishes for survival or for means-to-survival, but for various particular things to be done and obtained while surviving. And these can always conflict. Motivation is fundamentally plural. It must be so because, in evolution, all sorts of contingencies and needs arise, calling for all sorts of different responses. An obsessive creature, constantly dominated by one kind of motive, would not survive. That, in fact, is one thing hopelessly wrong about the Freudian picture, and also about the Nietzschean one of a species totally bent on power. You have to have a wider emotional repertoire than that if you intend to keep going.

The next step, then, is to ask: is there any reason to think that this requirement had dropped away, had become unnecessary by the time the human race evolved? Now we do not know *a priori* the limits of what is possible for evolution. But we do know, on the one hand, that very deep, ancient, and general patterns like this plurality are the hardest to get rid of, and, on the other, what sort of impression our species makes now. To start with the latter point, we can ask: do we find ourselves a species naturally free from conflict? We do not. There has not, apparently, been in our evolution a kind of rationalization which might seem a possible solution to problems of conflict—namely, a takeover by some major motive, such as the desire for future pleasure, which would automatically rule out all competing desires. Instead, what has developed is our intelligence. And this in some ways makes matters worse, since it shows us many desirable things that we would not otherwise have thought of, as well as the quite sufficient number we knew about for a start. In compensation, however, it does help us to arbitrate. Rules and principles, standards and ideals emerge as part of a priority system by which we guide ourselves through the jungle. They never make the job easy—desires that we put low on our priority system do not thereby vanish—but they make it possible. And it is in our working out these concepts more fully, in trying to extend their usefulness, that moral philosophy begins. Were there no conflict, it could never have arisen.

Why Neurology Cannot Replace Moral Philosophy

The traditional business of moral philosophy is attempting to understand, clarify, relate, and harmonize so far as possible the claims arising from the different sides of our nature. Here I believe that we can be helped by the insights the evolutionary context provides, alongside many other sources of insight. Wilson, however, believes like many other scientists that this is a job for neurologists. He says, "Scientists and humanists should consider together the suggestion that the time has come for ethics to be removed temporarily from the hands of the philosophers and biologicized" (p. 562), and, more enthusiastically,

The transition from purely phenomenological to fundamental theory in sociobiology must await a full, neuronal explanation of the human brain. Only when the machinery can be torn down on paper at the level of the cell and put together again will the properties of emotion and ethical judgment come clear. Simulations can then be employed to estimate the full range of behavioral responses and the precision of their homoeostatic controls. Stress will be evaluated in terms of the neurophysiological perturbations and their relaxation times. Cognition will be translated into circuitry. Learning and creativeness will be defined as the alteration of specific portions of the cognitive machinery regulated by input from the emotive centers. Having cannibalized psychology, the new neurobiology will yield an enduring set of first principles for sociology. [p. 575]

And again, if with less brio, in his opening paragraph, "What . . . made the hypothalamus and limbic system? They evolved by natural selection. That simple biological statement must be pursued to explain ethics and ethical philosophers, if not epistemology and epistemologists, at all depths" (p. 3).

Now the reasons why these suggestions are romantic fantasy are rather simple, though not widely enough known. You cannot *explain* a piece of behavior by digging into the body of the behaving person, unless your attempts to explain it in more immediate ways have reached a point where that information is called for. As a first step in verifying this, it will be wise to read through these passages again, substituting each time the words *mathematics* and *mathematical* for *ethics* and *ethical*. Do they look as convincing? Mathematics, too, is a branch of human thought, affecting conduct, for which no doubt certain specific parts of the brain are needed. And the evidence for these parts being genetically determined is much plainer and more striking than it is in the case of ethics, since mathematics is a sphere particularly noted for infant prodigies, children capable of extraordinary feats in it, even when they come (as they often have done) from uneducated families. So these capacities have been subjected to natural selection. That much is true. But it cannot follow that *the* way to "explain" mathematics and mathematicians—the "fundamental" way—is to dissect the brain and watch the neurones.

Such a study could certainly be important for its own purposes. As a part of our understanding of the brain itself it could be most weighty. It might have an interesting bearing, too, on the psychology of mathematics—the causal relations of this faculty to others, the fact that it is sometimes found almost isolated from other forms of intelligence, its frequent failure in later life, and so on. But there is no way in which this can be made into an explanation of mathematics itself. Understanding mathematics involves, being able, first, to *do* mathematics—to perform this sort of reasoning; second, to grasp the standards that govern it (a stage sometimes beyond the power of the infant prodigies); and, third, to relate mathematical standards to other standards of thought, to work out the place of mathematics in life. It is a shocking, though common, abuse of words like *fundamental* to call this sort of explanation less fundamental than the examination of the brain. Each inquiry has its own purposes, which determine its questions. A "fundamental theory," for each, just *is* one that gives the kind of explanation which those questions call for.

At this point, if the example of mathematics is fairly clear, it would perhaps be useful if the reader would play the substitution game again, but would this time read, instead of *ethics,* the name of his own favored subject. *Ad hominem* to Wilson, this requires reading *neurology* or *sociobiology.* For, in the sense in which a neurologist "explains" anybody else's activity, he can also explain his own. Neurology too, like ethics, is a branch of thought which can affect conduct. And in the brain of the working neurologist, too, fascinating evolutions are going on. So, if what we want is an explanation of neurology, why not abandon our interest in what he thinks he is doing, and, by concentrating on the physiological story, "explain neurology and neurologists at all depths"? Only, since the bystanding and examining neurologist too must be treated in the same manner, what finally emerged might not be much of an explanation.

It ought to be plain that there is something wrong with the program. "Cognition" cannot be "translated into circuitry." Learning and creativeness cannot be "defined as specific portions of the cognitive machinery." They cannot be, because *trans-*

lating and *defining* are operations performed, not on the meat in any thinker's brain, but on language. Learning, knowing, and so forth are words that describe the relation of a thinking subject (as a whole) to the things he thinks and talks about. Defining these words is clarifying their proper use, so as to get rid of whatever ambiguities and confusions dog them. Since these words describe functions of the whole thinking subject, they cannot be used to describe changes in "portions of the cognitive machinery" he uses to perform them. This would again be like saying that the carburetor had won the race, instead of the car or the driver. Carburetors do not even know how to enter races, let alone win them. Winners need carburetors, and thinkers (including neurologists) need brain cells. But that is a different story.

We can turn now to the original suggestion about "explaining ethics and ethical philosophers." Suppose that somebody is worrying about a moral problem—say, how to help a resolutely self-destructive friend or relative, who has just told him to go away and mind his own business. He wonders, what more can he do? Has he, perhaps, really no right to interfere? And even if he has the right, is he actually wasting his efforts when there are other things he ought to attend to?

He thinks about this. And here, too, no doubt there will be activity in the neurones. Here, too, (as Wilson rightly says) that activity will need an inherited apparatus. Not every creature is capable of scrupulous attachment to a friend, and most of those that are cannot deliberately organize their plans for dealing with it. But even though that apparatus is there, here again, investigating it will not be the slightest help in understanding or solving the problem. What we need for that (apart from knowledge of the facts) is sympathy and a firm grasp of the principles, standards, and ideals involved. Everybody has some such principles, standards, and ideals, however confused or misguided. But when a hard, unusual case like this turns up, we have to work them out further, beyond the area where they are already clear. We must face unconsidered possibilities and ask ourselves alarming questions—for instance, must we perhaps let the self-destroyer go if he really wants to? Trying to answer this by collecting information about our own neurones would be no more use than doing it, like a Roman augur, by inspecting the entrails of a goat. What we are looking for is not any sort of fact about ourselves—or, indeed, about anybody else. It is the relation of proposed acts to certain standards, principles, and ideals that we accept as binding, *not* just on ourselves, but on anyone else who becomes involved with them.[2] That is why the moral problem is public—why someone else, a friend, or a moral philosopher, or the man himself on a later occasion, when he feels quite different, can think about it, as well as the person in the dilemma. (This is not true of, for instance, questions about the taste of food, or about noise tolerance.) "Explaining the ethical philosopher" might very well mean grasping this fact—seeing how general, public discussion of these intensely personal issues becomes possible. It *is* possible—and it is practiced everywhere, from bars to pulpits, because the standards and ideals are public property, and we all need to work them out together. Now there is another aspect to the publicness, which Wilson quite rightly emphasizes, in the likeness of our emotional constitutions, which makes us able to sympathize to some extent with one another's dilemmas. We can all feel respect, guilt, horror, admiration, regret, and the like. And though we do not feel them in unison, we are sufficiently within shouting distance in the matter to be able to understand one another's reactions if we try, and to exchange reasons for thinking one of these responses suitable. Here, too, I would agree with Wilson that the general willingness to think and talk in this way shows a jointly inherited physical basis. There are creatures quite incapable of these feelings. But here too it is the subject's experience, and not any examination of the organs involved, which we must rely on. If dissection showed identically shaped bodies where the conscience was supposed to be based, but social experience showed no agreement on who should ever be blamed and praised, morality would be impossible. If it showed differently shaped bodies, but agreement prevailed, morality could go forward. *Understanding ethics* means, in the first place, as with mathematics, being able to follow an ethi-

2. See Ryle, *Dilemmas*, chaps. V, VI and VIII for these problems.

cal argument. Next, as with mathematics, it means being able to state and generalize the standards involved. Third, it means being able to relate those standards to other forms of thought, to say something about the place of ethics in life. The second stage leads into ethical philosophy; the third completes that journey. So someone who wants to "explain ethics and ethical philosophers" in the most natural and useful sense needs to follow that program. Certainly there is another kind of explanation, the causal one which explains how this process is physically possible. But that is no use; if what you want is to *take over* a subject, grasping the causes of its occurrence will not make taking over possible. (Moreover, at that game, evolutionists have no monopoly. If they press their point, historians and physiologists between them can take over all of us. Cannibalism is a game that more than one can play at.)

Are we to say, then, that ethics belongs to philosophers or to biologists? The kind of territorial claim that Wilson makes in these passages is quite meaningless. Philosophy and biology are not in competition; they are different aspects of one inquiry. "Biologicizing ethics" does not involve "removing it from the hands of the philosophers"; it means philosophizing better. What we need is to attend more, in moral argument, to the biological facts. But this does not make philosophy unnecessary; it just makes it harder. Philosophy *is* the sorting out of very general concepts, the organizing of them into usable schemes. The relation between biological facts and questions about how to act is not simple. Concepts like nature, duty, freedom, motive, and creativity need analyzing and cleaning up. Doing this is plainly no part of neurology. This is not to say that neurologists cannot contribute to it. Clearly they can, if they are interested—as perhaps they should be—in the relation of their subject to other ways of thinking. But if they contribute, it is philosophy that they are doing. All important and original biological thinking involves some philosophy.

Philosophy is needed in these areas because the conceptual tangles are terrible, and "philosophy" is simply the name for the effective sorting of them, whoever does it. This said, I and many other professional philosophers willingly admit, or rather vigorously claim, that moral philosophy was in many ways done badly during the first half of this century. The moral problems arising from violent cultural change were very tough. In some areas philosophers made a reasonable stab at solving them, but in far too many they retreated into nitpicking and evasion. The trouble arose (so far as English-speaking countries are concerned) in the early years of the century, with a brief vogue for Intuitionism—the indefensible view that moral truths can be directly seen, so that any disagreement can only be due to dishonesty, laziness, or confused questioning. One thing that makes it hard to grapple with Wilson's arguments on the nature of ethics is his apparent conviction that moral philosophers always hold this belief. In fact it was an extraordinary aberration, intended (as the fighting language of its proponents makes clear) to be a completely new departure, altogether displacing moral philosophy as previously understood.[3] And its popularity did not last long. Intuitionism served for a time as a stick with which to beat more positive traditional forms of moral reasoning. But it was so obviously bankrupt of positive suggestions for replacing them that it soon gave way to its more vigorous successor, Emotivism. This view at least took the reality of disagreement seriously. But it too was committed to the futile and unhealthy attempt to isolate values from facts, in particular from the facts of our own nature. Why this is futile I must discuss in the next chapter.

3. G. E. Moore said this explicitly in *Principia Ethica* (see, for instance, p. ix of the Preface), and so did H. H. Prichard in the other manifesto of the movement, his paper "Does Moral Philosophy Rest on a Mistake?", *Mind,* 21 (1912). They thus produced a bliss-was-it-in-that-dawn-to-be-alive atmosphere which for a time distracted attention from their vacuousness.

A certain numbness strikes me when I find that Wilson seems to think *Kant* was an Intuitionist (which is roughly equivalent to calling Darwin a champion of the Genesis creation story) and also to equate Intuitionism with Social Contract ethics (*Sociobiology,* p. 562).

CHAPTER 9

Facts and Values

Goodness and Wants

How can our nature guide us?

Concepts such as *nature,* which seem to combine reports of fact with judgments of value, have worried moral philosophers. (There are plenty of other obvious examples, such as Importance, Dirt, Danger, Injury).[1] Calling something *natural* is sometimes just reporting that it happens; but usually it is also making a suggestion about how to treat it. Often it recommends some sort of acceptance, sometimes strong approval. Putting the point another way, we all believe that understanding what we are naturally fit for, capable of, and adapted to will help us to know what is good for us and, therefore, to know what to do. Common sense takes this view; so does Freudian psychology. So does traditional moral philosophy. Thus, Bishop Butler says that the Empiricist method in morals begins "from a matter of fact, namely, what the particular nature of man is, its several parts, their economy or constitution; from which it proceeds to determine what course of life it is, what is correspondent to this whole

---

1. For an excellent discussion of *injury* and *danger,* see Philippa Foot's article "Moral Beliefs" in *Theories of Ethics,* edited by her (Oxford, 1967), pp. 87–90. Julius Kovesi sorts out the logic of such terms in the opening chapters of *Moral Notions* (London, 1967) with a sharpness that ought to be an example to philosophers. (He deals with *dirt* on p. 38.) I discuss *importance* in the third section of this chapter.

nature."[2] And the reason this works is that we can indeed only understand our values if we first grasp the given facts about our wants.

Moral philosophers in the first half of this century, however, made great efforts to discredit all reasoning that assumed this connection. Half the trouble in this controversy resulted from a mistaken notion of *facts*—from assuming that they were simple neutral things, easily defined—matters seen and described infallibly, without reference to standards, which arose separately as a kind of practical convenience or even luxury. Actually, as I have already suggested in talking of *description*, we are never neutral even in what we "see"—we must always select, interpret, and classify. This is just as true of scientific observers as of ordinary ones. By *facts* we usually just mean "data," that is, everything we count not as part of the particular problem before us, but as what is safe enough to be taken for granted in solving it, and needed to do so. But *facts* are never confined to the raw data of sense, and seldom to "physical facts" (the kind that can be stated in terms of physics). It is a *fact* that this is food or poison, that it is dangerous, dirty, unique, or legal, that it is an ancient totem pole or the flag of my country. Yet standards quite alien to physics must be grasped before we can "see" these facts. They are thus never logically isolated from some kind of "evaluating."[3]

These philosophers nonetheless suggested instead that evaluating was always an independent process, isolated from all judgment of facts—that there was never a logical or conceptual link between them, only an external association. When we value anything, we are (they said) conferring on it an abstract approval that could just as intelligibly be conferred on anything else. Argument is irrelevant.[4]

The point of this move was essentially a negative one. The

2. Preface to the *Sermons*, sec. 12.
3. See G. E. M. Anscombe's article "Brute Facts," *Analysis,* 19 (1958), G. Warnock's admirable little book, *Contemporary Moral Philosophy* (London, 1967), and Kovesi's *Moral Notions;* also my own article, "The Neutrality of the Moral Philosopher," *Proceedings of the Aristotelian Society,* 74 (1974).
4. See Moore, *Principia Ethica,* and Prichard, "Does Moral Philosophy Rest on a Mistake?"

Intuitionists wanted to expose weaknesses in certain contemporary ways of reasoning from facts to values, notably utilitarian ones. But they extended their point, by the usual exaggeration, into a sweeping general ban on all moral reasoning. Thus, G. E. Moore proclaimed in *Principia Ethica* that the business of ethics must be confined to examining moral judgments of the form "this is good," and establishing that this "good" was indefinable. This meant that "no relevant evidence"[5] could ever be brought for such judgments. Attempts to introduce any were futile and misleading; he stigmatized them as "naturalistic." Once the surrounding rubble of mistaken argument was removed, we would, Moore said, be able to see directly what was good or bad, just as we see what is green or yellow.

His Emotivist successors disputed this confident conclusion. They demoted the bold "seeing" to a mere feeling or attitude. But they accepted, and insisted on, the isolation of moral judgments from every kind of evidence. The moral scene narrowed strangely. All the traditional interest in aims, motives, and desires, in good and bad reasons for action, in freedom and responsibility, in society and the nature of man, was dismissed as merely factual or metaphysical. Notions such as justice, happiness, and humanity were treated as just confused cases where the judgment of fact had not yet been disentangled from that of value.[6]

The original Intuitionists held that once questions about values were properly understood and squarely faced, disagreement would vanish. In taking this line, each of them in fact merely expressed his deep confidence in his own moral views. In Prichard's case the confidence was misplaced. He does not seem to have had any attitude to offer which could make his blank conventionality usable. Moore, however, did have an extremely interesting contemplative and aesthetic moral position of his own, one that gave a key importance to art. But its impressiveness cannot support his intuitionism. People who accept Moore's

5. *Principia Ethica,* Preface, p. viii.
6. See, for example, C. L. Stevenson, *Ethics and Language* (New Haven, 1945), chap. 1.

values are no better insured than anybody else against the constant disagreement which is a fact of life. They must dispute, both with those who share their general views and with those who do not.[7] And Moore's views themselves cannot be defended except by reference to psychological facts. *If* Moore was right about the supreme importance of contemplation, it can only be because man is essentially a contemplative animal. This position cannot win in a walkover. It has to be defended against such views as Kant's exaltation of the Good Will, and Aristotle's of activity, not to mention all manner of minor and more specific claims. Far from being "simple" and indefinable in the way that color-words are, goodness is simple only in the very different way in which the most completely general and abstract ideas are.[8] And this is not the kind of simplicity which eliminates dispute. People do disagree about what is good; it is, indeed, the kind of thing that makes them argue.

Intuitionism crumbled against the reality of disagreement. It was followed by Emotivism, the view that disagreement on values is real and important, but nonrational. It is merely a clash of feelings and attitudes. No standards of logic or relevance enter into the business of resolving it, which is essentially a matter of persuasion, that is, of emotional engineering. This position was worked out during the Thirties[9] and converged after the war with something apparently very different, Existentialism. The

7. Moore himself never did so. He just laid down his views with the massive, undoubting simplicity that always made him so influential. Many people swallowed the message whole, especially in the field of art criticism. (Clive Bell's *Art* is a sustained hymn of celebration on the themes proposed in chap. 6 of *Principia Ethica.*) Some disciples, however, did later realize how odd it all was. Maynard Keynes, one of the shrewdest and least complacent of them, discussed the matter most interestingly in response to criticisms by D. H. Lawrence (Keynes, *Two Memoirs* [London, 1949]). For a delightful description of the difficulties of arguing *within* the Intuitionist tradition, see his pp. 84–88.

8. It is worth noting that Moore also proposed to treat *reality* as a simple, indefinable notion like goodness. (See his paper, "Objects of Perception," in *Philosophical Studies* [London, 1948], pp. 72–78.) The roots of this confusion are probably present in Locke, who similarly piles together as "simple ideas" particular perceived qualities like the taste of a pineapple and the most abstract structural ones like Existence *(Essay Concerning Human Understanding,* Bk. 2, chaps. 1–8). Two totally different kinds of "simplicity" are involved.

9. Largely by C. L. Stevenson, using suggestions drawn from Wittgenstein,

common element is the rejection of argument. In meeting moral dilemmas, both Emotivist and Existentialist stress the gap between choices. Both concentrate on extreme binary decisions—approve or disapprove, join the Free French Army or save your mother[10]—instead of mentioning the more complex, less dramatic attempts to find a third course *by thinking* which occupy so much of common life. Both exclude solution by reasoning. The great difference between them is one of point of view. Existentialism speaks in the first person, for the participant: if reasoning will not help me, what am I to do? I jump in the dark. Emotivism is a second- or third-person solution adapted to rather less drastic cases. You persuade him or he persuades you; let them persuade each other. We disapprove of Hitler; do so also.[11] You do not persuade him, nor does he persuade you. The aim is unanimity; it can be called "understanding," but only on condition that we do not mean that it is cognitive. *Relevance* is just a name for persuasiveness.[12]

Both these positions, again, express moral views, convictions about the importance of independence or of a tolerant "understanding." And, again, a sympathy with these convictions may make people accept the analysis of "moral judgment" which goes with it. But it should not do so. Both positions are, unquestionably, a response to the increasing difficulty of reasoning morally in a changing world. Hard work is called for, and many useful traditional positions need revising. Instead, we are told to stop thinking altogether. This is vacuous. So is the suggestion that actually we never were thinking, though we thought we were. The proper response to the claim that we cannot reason effectively in moral matters is that of the passenger to the steward

particularly from the *Lecture on Ethics*. What was wrong with Intuitionism was, however, perhaps best exposed by P. H. Nowell-Smith in his *Ethics* (Penguin, 1954). A brasher, more dramatic form of Emotivism appeared in A. J. Ayer's *Language, Truth and Logic* (1935). Stevenson's key notion of "emotive meaning" was, I think, effectively exploded by Max Black in "Some Questions about Emotive Meaning," *Philosophical Review*, 57 (1948), reprinted in his *Language and Philosophy* (Ithaca, N.Y., 1949).

10. Sartre, *Existentialism and Humanism*, p. 35.

11. Translation into Stevensonian terms of "Hitler is evil."

12. A point explicitly and repeatedly made by Stevenson. See, for example, *Facts and Values* (New Haven, 1963), pp. 4 and 85.

who tells him, "You can't be sick here, sir."[13] And there is absolutely no reason why anybody should be impressed by the romantic aura that has been cast round Existentialism, with its singular position that there is something particularly virtuous about denying the possibility of virtue, or that the one secure moral judgment is that it is wrong to make moral judgments. Thought is not a luxury from which we must heroically refrain. It is an essential aspect of life.

I have suggested that, when we wonder whether something is good, common sense will naturally direct our attention to *wants*. And it is because our wants conflict that we have problems. We often need a priority system by which we can say, "both are good in different ways, but this good matters more than that one." So the full facts of conflict are essential to understanding the meaning of terms like *good*. Thus *these* facts are not irrelevant to values. If we say something is good or bad for human beings, we must take our species's actual needs and wants as facts, as something given. And the same would be true if we were speaking of any other species. It is hard to see what would be meant by calling good something that is not in any way wanted or needed by any living creature. Should we therefore say that everything we want is good? In a minimal sense this is right; everything we want has to have something good about it, otherwise we could not want it. But of course we cannot stop there, or *good* would simply mean *wanted*. We must go further because of conflict, because of the clash and competition among our various wants. What is good in a stronger, more considered sense must be wanted, not just by someone's casual impulse, but by *him as a whole* and on grounds conveyable to those around him.

Moreover, our basic repertoire of wants is given. We are not free to create or annihilate wants, either by private invention or by culture. Inventions and cultures group, reflect, guide, channel, and develop wants; they do not actually produce them. Thus, if twentieth-century people want supersonic planes, they do so because of wants that they have in common with Eskimos and Bushmen. They want to move fast, to do their business

13. Passenger: "Oh, can't I!" (He is.)

quickly, to be honored, feared, and admired, to solve puzzles, and to have something bright and shiny. We are innately "programmed" to want and like such things. And those wants are not scattered loose, but must be held together as expressions of one personality. This is why it is wrong to say that we just establish the facts, and then, quite separately, take up an attitude to them, view them as good or bad. Thought and feeling must go together throughout. We all have to have a conceptual frame within which wants are related. We cannot treat them as chance particulars, which might be assigned any value and which we might decide to invent or discard.

Since wants are bound to conflict, right from the start we need a system, a scheme of priorities to help us think about them. And we are born equipped to form one. Even the rudimentary personality of a small child already includes a policy for choice, for comparing wants. And a culture (something without which no child can develop) is a device for coordinating, fixing, and developing those systems. No human being therefore can possibly find himself going out to shop for values for the first time, without any idea what he is after. He cannot be a Creator who, before creating, would have to decide what wants to create in himself. (The notion of "creating values" is a piece of nonsense—all that anybody can do is to adjust, develop, and extend them.) The question is never which wants to have. It is always what to do about conflicts between existing ones. That question arises all the time, and it is the only context that can give meaning to discussions about *good* and *value*. But it can arise only for somebody who has already developed some sort of policy, who has started practical thinking.

Wants are not random impulses. They are articulated, recognizable aspects of life; they are the deepest structural constituents of our characters. Someone who has two random impulses—say, to finish a particular job and to run away—does not yet have a conflict. The conflict starts only when he tries to decide on one of them. Deciding involves thought, because it does not just mean jumping one way or the other. It means becoming clear about the meaning of the two acts, about what is involved in doing them, and finding in that meaning something continuous and coherent with one's previous policy. Unless the decider can see what he decides to do as *his* act—as the act of the person he is now, however much he may want to change himself—he has not *decided:* he is still drifting. If he moves at random, that is still a drift. The alternative to deciding is disintegration of the personality, a form of suicide with little to recommend it.

What goes on in choice is therefore not just any inexpressible brute clash of feelings. That may well happen for a start. But it is the problem, not the solution. The solution needs articulate thinking. What we have to try and do is, first, to discover the facts about our own wants and other people's, and understand them for what they are. We then have to set them in some order of priority which makes sense in the context of our whole lives. At this point we may be said to be valuing. We decide, for example, that affection matters more here than honor, or science than safety. And this is taking sides. But it is also forming a factual judgment about what are actually our deepest needs.

Because these conflicts are so complex, it is unrealistic to suggest that they are solved by the pulling and hauling of mere unordered feeling. (There is something comic in Hume's picture of Reason as the slave of *the Passions*—how is it supposed to know which of them to obey? Slaves have a bad time in such circumstances.) Still less can they be solved by "the Will," in the sense of blind push. In this sense you cannot will until you have decided what to will. Of course the use of our will in the sense of being resolute can help us, and so can experiment—a partial gamble, deliberately taken when thought can get us no further. But the initial work has to be done by thought—by painfully and methodically searching for an order that will make the scene more intelligible.[14]

On Using Our Knowledge

It is hard, in fact, to see how we could solve such conflicts except by studying the wants concerned in more detail. When we wonder whether, or why, or how far something is good, we are

14. On the unsuitability of the will for this job, see Iris Murdoch, *The Sovereignty of Good*, essay 1.

not connecting it externally with an abstract property called goodness. We are not asking for evidence of its goodness in the sense of an extra fact, as we might cite a man's being seen with a bloody knife as evidence for his having committed a murder. We are asking for *specification,* the point of which will be to connect it with a particular want. In what way is it good? What's good about it? What kind of goodness has it? Thus (dealing for the moment only with good actions) a suitable answer might be that it is, say, an act of friendship—not, that is, of justice, prudence, courage, or general charity. What sort of act of friendship? Sharing a friend's trouble. Details again? Well, Captain Benwick's sweetheart had died while he was at sea, just when at last they should have been able to get married:

"The news must follow him, but who was to tell it? not I. I would as soon have been run up to the yard-arm. Nobody could do it but that good fellow (pointing to Captain Wentworth). . . . He . . . wrote up for leave of absence, but, without waiting the return, travelled night and day till he got to Portsmouth, rowed off to the Grappler that instant, and never left the poor fellow for a week; that's what he did, and nobody else could have saved poor James." [*Persuasion,* chap. 12]

Here, it should be noted, we cite *facts.* But the facts are not logically loose from the description "sharing a friend's trouble," as they would be from the term *good,* nor is that description loose from the next above it, "act of friendship." They are of the sort that naturally fall under it. By contrast, it would be no use saying that the action was good because it was frequent, brisk, or noisy, or that it was an act of friendship because it involved surprising him, or that it constituted sharing his trouble because one repeatedly wrote his name. And so forth. These explanations are gibberish. But to call them gibberish is to recognize that there is here a clear standard of sense. It is, I think, important that this same standard would naturally come into play at the point in discussion when Hume and Bentham say we reach a terminus—namely where someone says "I do it because it gives me pleasure." [15] *"What sort of pleasure?"* we ask. And we really do

15. See, for example, Hume, *Enquiry Concerning the Principles of Morals,* Appendix 1, sec. 244; Bentham, *Principles of Morals and Legislation,* chap. 1, sec. 244, and chap. 4, sec. 8.

not understand him until we know the answer. Pleasure is not an abstract stuff.

If people did not (in fact) *want* their friends with them when they were in trouble, if they did not mind bereavement or were not liable to despair, or if that despair could not be helped by companionship, Captain Wentworth's act would not be an act of friendship. Nor would it be half so impressive a one if giving that companionship were always easy and pleasant, if we had no preference for emotional peace and comfort. ("I would as soon have been run up the yard-arm.") Again, if people did not, in general, want or need friends, the notion of an act of friendship itself would be vacuous. Computers, ignorant of human nature, could never arrive at it or specify a content for it. That is why understanding facts of this kind is absolutely necessary in building up the ideas of the various sorts of human goodness, and why the general term *good* remains totally vacuous till that has been done.

To return to problems about the double function of terms like nature: if I say for example, that noninformative conversation or playing with one's children is *natural,* I am not just describing an action and then adding, after a pause, "hurrah," or "and incidentally I approve, do so also." I am noting the *sorts* of advantage that it has, and also the *sorts* of dangers likely to attend forbidding or neglecting it. If it is natural, in the strong sense, it fills a need, and one that cannot easily be filled with a substitute. What we need is not necessarily something we die without, but it is something without which we shall be worse off. People who think they are too busy for play and conversation will find their affections atrophy, will lose that source of wisdom and vitality which consists in the free play of our social faculties, will become incapable of friendship. Does saying this amount to *general disapproval* of their policy? Hardly, because we have not asked what their alternatives are. We have named only one factor in the sum; there may be a multitude of others.

Disagreement, then, is not to be resolved by slinging general approval and disapproval to and fro. We cannot treat it as a mere blank clash of attitudes, to be resolved emotionally, whether by bullying or seduction. We want the *right* solution. To find it, we want relevant evidence, and we know that relevant does *not* just mean persuasive. We do not take the blank clash of attitudes as ultimate, except in the trivial, contingent sense that both sides may give up from sheer unwillingness to try. In this sense, of course, we certainly can say that we can get no further with a particular dispute, that the answer simply depends on where you start from. But this is obviously a fact about the disputants, not the dispute, and there is nothing in it peculiar to disputes about value. Exactly the same thing happens in "factual" disagreements—say, between two economists, psychologists, or historians of different schools, or between a Marxist and a Freudian account of motives. Nobody supposes that these failures are logically necessary, that the disputants are not really discussing the same world. They possess distinct conceptual schemes, which have not yet been properly related, but ought to be. Their position is somewhat like that of people who, seeing those diverse maps of the world that appear at the beginning of the atlas, might pick on one of them as right and dismiss all the others as wrong. They would then defend physiographical boundaries against political, isobars against isotherms, instead of trying to relate them.

The absolutely unanswerable objection to taking value conflicts as ultimate and immune to reason is that they do not just occur *between* people, but *within* them. Normally, Mr. Pro and Mr. Con[16] are actors on our inner stage. Each one of us has to fit together somehow for himself ideals that seem to conflict, and to find some sort of path between great and admitted evils. We are all, to some extent, in the predicament of Anthony Powell's character, X. Trapnel:

Trapnel wanted, among other things, to be a writer, a dandy, a lover, a comrade, an eccentric, a sage, a virtuoso, a good chap, a man of honour, a hard case, a spendthrift, an opportunist, a *raisonneur,* to be very rich, to be very poor, to possess a thousand mistresses, to win the heart of one love to whom he was ever faithful, to be on the best of terms with all men, to avenge savagely the lightest affront, to live to a hundred full years and honour, to die young and unknown but recognized the following day as the most neglected genius of the age. Each of these

16. Characters disputing in Stevenson's *Facts and Values,* p. 85.

ambitions had something to recommend it, from one angle or another.[17]

The only way in which Trapnel was exceptional was in being a shade or two less clear even than the rest of us about the impossibility of combining these things. Most of us do, at some level, more or less know that we must choose. But how? Considered as a decision-procedure for this problem, self-persuasion is absurd. We must decide before we can persuade anybody, even ourselves. Nor is it much help to tell us, as some Existentialists would, that we are simply faced with an inexpressible choice, which we must be brave enough to make without justification. This piece of advice too is suitable only for people who have already decided what to do or that it does not matter what they do, but are hampered by hesitation in actually doing it. To get that far, they have to have accepted some reasons as good ones. Typically, such people have two or more conceptual schemes that they have not meshed properly together—personal and political loyalties, work and family, love and self-respect. Meshing them is what they need to do next.

When we "want help" with decision, we are not illicitly asking for somebody to carry the can, or for a rule-book from which to read off the answer. What we want help with is building a wider conceptual scheme, within which the partial ones that distract us can be related. These wider schemes can be worked out, but not instantly. They need time, trouble, and a good deal of cooperation. They are not purely private enterprises, any more than a language is; they are meant to serve everybody. As we can see again and again when we look back into our history, in the end they can work. An obvious example is the dilemma basic to so many seventeenth-century tragedies, of Love versus Honor. Here was an agonizing clash of ideals, the strain of which eventually produced its own partial solution in a revision of both notions, a better understanding of both love and honor. Of course revision of this sort will not eliminate these conflicts. There really are divergent ideals. But what vigorous thinking does is to find better ways of stating the options, less misleading

17. *Books Do Furnish a Room* (Boston, 1971), pp. 144–145.

symbols for the values involved. This helps us also to alter institutions that make things gratuitously harder (such as dueling, arranged marriages, and a rigid vengeance code).

Our Nature Is a Whole

In dealing with such conflicts, we have, I repeat, no option but to reason from the facts about human wants and needs. When we ask, "how should this institution be altered?" we can approach an answer only by asking the further question, "what does human nature demand?" Both love and honor are essential elements in life everywhere. There is no society where it is not a clear explanation of someone's misery to say that he is universally despised, ignored, or hated. That this is so depends on our emotional constitution. We inevitably need and value love and honor in themselves, not just as means to any further and simpler good. Life has many elements just as irreducible and autonomous—speaking broadly still, laughter, knowledge, art, play, order, freedom and many more.[18] Their multiplicity has often bothered people who want rationality to consist in simplicity of aim. These people have in fact sometimes tried to eliminate either love or honor as distinct elements in life. Thus Hobbes wrote: "*Honourable* is whatever possession, action, or quality, is an argument and sign of Power . . . . Honour consisteth only in the opinion of Power," the importance of power being, as he explains, that it keeps us safe. So that here, as elsewhere, "the passion to be reckoned upon is Feare."[19] Just so Swift, (following the Stoics) showed his Purely Rational Horses as simply immune to all personal affection, dismissing it as a pointless weakness.[20]

But there is nothing rational about using simple premises for a complex subject matter. The claim to be especially rational or

18. I deliberately do not choose examples that are easily comparable, because I want to stress that the things we need are of varying logical types. In particular, we have *formal* as well as material needs. We can need life arranged in a certain way. This is why, as Aristotle remarked, good things can be found in all the Categories (*Ethics* 1.6) and why Moore was so wrong to treat goodness as a simple, ground-floor quality like yellow. Only visible surfaces can be yellow.

19. *Leviathan,* chap. 10.

20. *Gulliver's Travels,* Pt. 4 (the Houynhnhms), chap. 8.

logical because one is ignoring half the facts before one and basing a hasty argument on the rest is often met in common life; it should be resisted and particularly by Empiricists. Simple premises that distort our problems can only lead to irrationality and confusion.

Human needs are multiple. *Bonum est multiplex;*[21] we have many sorts of good because we have many wants. Yet we have to make sense of them all somehow by a scheme or priorities. We get nowhere by ignoring their complexity or by pretending to reduce them to one. Instead we have to follow the working of that deep need for unity which is luckily to be found at the center of them. People have a natural wish and capacity to integrate themselves, a natural horror of being totally fragmented, which makes possible a constant series of bargains and sacrifices to shape their lives. These bargains we need to understand as fully as possible. For instance: the man who really does have to choose between love and honor, art and prosperity, freedom and order—who cannot find a way to combine them by tearing down some piece of humbug or devising a new solution—can make a proper choice only if he realizes that on both sides are real goods. He actually will have to sacrifice one part of his life, and of other people's lives too, to another. And the only ground on which he can do it is that the one want is more fundamental, more central to him and to humanity, than the other. He has in effect to decide what sort of person he wants himself and other people to be, what his life and his society should be like. But he does not have to decide this alone. He can use the whole range of experience his society has stored for him, and the responses of those around him, to settle what is after all not just his private question, but one that concerns everyone—the scheme of priorities on which we shall relate these wants. And it is here that the more general, weighter senses of *good* and *bad* begin to come in.

21. See G. E. M. Anscombe, *Intention* (Ithaca, N.Y., 1957), sec. 39, a fascinating discussion of such phrases as "Evil be thou my good." That Saint Thomas should prove a better Empiricist than Moore may surprise some people, but that is the position. He paid more attention to the phenomena. Good is *not* simple. I shall say some more about its complexities in Chap. 11.

To ignore the multiplicity of wants, and therefore of goods, to talk as though value were a simple one-dimensional quantitative matter, has two bad consequences. First, discussion may become so unreal, so far from any use in understanding our practical problems, that it becomes merely a detached game; we may even pride ourselves on this detachment. Second, we may simply root for our own favored good, our chosen aspect of human life, under the flag of neutral analysis. Conflict of goods is the heart of our problems. Love clashes with honor, order with freedom, art with friendship, justice with prudence, kindness with honesty[22]—and not just in the rare, melodramatic cases of major decisions, but in the constant, quiet grind of everyday living. Somehow we manage to balance their claims, by bargain, compromise, sublimation, partial combination, and sacrifice. If you like a somewhat dramatic conclusion, these methods may sound less impressive than a final victory where one contestant is utterly routed. That kind of climax is often used in literature, but not in the best literature because it cannot be used in life. To write off entirely any of the contestants named, we should have to amputate a part of our nature. This is the simple ascetic solution, often tried but never successful. (It is interesting that, while few Western people now favor it if it is undertaken in the name of religion, many seem to be quite hopeful about it if it is undertaken in the name of art or freedom.) The trouble with asceticism notoriously is that what you sling out at the door comes in through the window, in a worse form. Thus, on Swift's issue of eliminating personal affection, Butler remarked:

Experience will show that, as want of natural appetite to food supposes and proceeds from some bodily disease, so the apathy the Stoics talk of as much supposes, or is accompanied with, somewhat amiss in the moral character, in that which is the health of the mind. Those who formerly aimed at this upon the foot of philosophy, appear to have had better success in eradicating the affections of tenderness and compassion, than

22. It is because we have some idea of the range such goods cover that we are not (as R. M. Hare suggested) helpless in arguing against narrow-minded fanatics like his Trumpeter and Nazi (*Freedom and Reason* [Oxford, 1963] p. 112). Fanatics have to give reasons why the (perfectly well known) goods they want to ignore shall cease to matter.

they had with the passions of pride and resentment; these latter at best were but concealed, and that imperfectly too.[23]

The best you can hope for by this method is a partial death. To avoid this, we try to do justice in some way to what we must renounce: to avoid complete specialization. In such attempts we always call on some notion of balance or proportion. In forming theories, however, people often brush this consideration aside as if it were something necessarily limited, bourgeois, and conventional. It is not. Being bourgeois (in the bad sense) means aiming at one particular sort of balance—namely, one not designed to do justice to the full capacities of either the individual or his society, but sacrificing everything to prudence. Notoriously, this can mean as drastic a cutback as any religious asceticism; its terminus is the miser. Being conventional (in the bad sense) means sticking to the notion of balance already prevailing, whatever it may be. This may have been badly designed in the first place, and become still worse with outside changes. Beech trees trimmed down to make a hedge are a fair model for either of these policies. They are probably less likely to be blown over in a gale than a natural beech tree; nevertheless, they are much less well balanced and proportioned. Balance, in fact, is not just a negative matter of not falling over; it is a positive one of attaining one's full growth. This same point is usually missed in discussions of Aristotle's doctrine of virtue as a mean. Aristotle certainly was not recommending a cautious or conventional policy; he never said that the mid-point was where it was safe to go or where everybody else was; he said explicitly that virtue might involve dying for one's friends.[24]

The notion of balance and proportion does not exclude, either, a life devoted to some overriding aim. In fact, it is especially relevant there. For even the most specialized person is still a person; he has the whole range of faculties to dispose of. Thus the monk does not totally reject love; he is not trying to become a Houyhnhnm. He concentrates with peculiar intensity on the love of God and the general love of mankind as his creatures. He

23. Sermon 5, sec. 11.   24. *Ethics* 3.9, 9.8.

does not reject freedom either; it is to avoid servitude to the World, the Flesh, and the Devil that he accepts the obedience of the cloister. How human nature will respond to such bargains is a factual problem; evidence about it is quite essential for choice.[25] And such factual questions have of course their philosophic angle: what conceptual scheme shall we use? How do notions like love and freedom work here? What way of describing things will make the problem most intelligible?

In struggling through these thickets, we are usually, as I have suggested, trying to decide either in what way something is good, or which of several (good or bad) things is the more *important.* And importance itself is, of course, not a blank abstract "simple" quality, but a relation to our lives. Calling something important means that it *concerns* us deeply, that it *means* or *imports* something essential to us, is linked with a central part of our nature. So to decide which thing is more important, we have to weigh the facts about that nature and look for its central needs.

Suppose (for comparison) that the question were a physical one: someone asks whether sleep or sunshine is more important to the human body. The answer will certainly be that they are so in different ways; there is no neutral stuff called importance which can be extracted and measured. But by considering the facts about how we get along without either, we can decide priorities for practical purposes if the two needs conflict. The same is true of love and honor, art and friendship, order and freedom. Different sides of our nature demand them; the disasters springing from their withdrawal are of different kinds. Where there is conflict, we have to resolve it by deciding which disaster strikes nearer the core of our being.

---

25. The price is not counted only in strain and effort. There is also the renouncing of alternative ways of life—of skills and qualities hard to combine with those on which we concentrate. And if enterprises turn out so hard as to be "unnatural," there is an inevitable reliance on some rather doubtful allies. Vanity, conceit, aggression, pigheadedness and sheer blind habit are probably necessary collaborators in carrying through any large enterprise; they may do little harm so long as we recognize them. But where things are very hard, they tend to take over. This is why there are limits to how far we can go from a "natural" balance.

This is how we work our way up from an understanding of particular goods and particular needs through the more general notions that we need for comparison, and so toward the most general notion of all, *good,* which completes and orients the formal framework. It is, as Plato rightly said, a central notion, because it expresses our belief that all the other things we call good do in some way at some remote point *converge*—that our nature, in spite of its conflicts, is not radically and hopelessly and finally plural, but essentially one.[26] The notion of good is central to us, because of its place in the structure.

But this reason for attending to it is about as different as can be from the one given by moral philosophers from Moore onward, which exalts it just on the grounds of its isolation. They represent it as floating free, a kind of mysterious exotic pink balloon, a detached predicate, high above all possible attempts to entrap it and connect it with life by any conceptual scheme whatever.

In this chapter, I have argued that there is not (as has been suggested) any special difficulty about "reasoning from facts to values." So we are not prevented from putting our understanding of human nature to practical use. At present, when we wonder what to do, we simply take for granted a wide range of facts about natural human wants and needs. We also take for granted that they give genuinely relevant and sometimes compelling logical grounds for our practical conclusions. We are right in this. But when different *kinds* of life, different balances of needs come into question, we have to become conscious of what we were formerly assuming.

We Are Not Tourists Here

To complete this brief outline of the ways in which we can and must reason from facts to values, we must consider one more serious current misconception. This concerns the sense in which we are, or are not, *at home* in this world or in the universe. It has been for some time a commonplace of Romantic thought that,

26. *Republic,* 6.501–end. See also Murdoch, *The Sovereignty of Good,* last essay.

since the Copernican Revolution, we are not at home in it, because we have lost the medieval world-picture that placed us at its center, and assured us that the whole thing was in some sense made for us.

Now in fact I doubt whether that world-picture ever had great influence outside intellectual circles; most people most of the time have enough to worry about with what is around them, without thinking of the stars. But my present point is a much wider one. What we need, in order to feel at home in the world, is certainly *not* a belief that it was made for us. We are at home in this world *because we were made for it.* We have developed here, on this planet, and are adapted to live here. Our emotional constitution is part of that adaptation. We are not fit to live anywhere else. (The possibility, such as it is, of surviving briefly, and at ruinous expense, in space-craft and the like is just parasitical; it depends on extending the conditions we are used to into a few bizarre corners, not on our being able to live in *other* conditions.)

To demand that this universe—all of it—should be made *for us* was at all times a childish and megalomaniac notion. Christian thought on the matter was not, of course, really megalomaniac, because it regarded man, as well as other creatures, as existing under God's direction and for his glory. Man thus ranked below the whole host of Heaven; moreover, the scheme in which he ruled on earth was God's, not his own. Sharp bounds were set to his conceit. But if we try to retain the pattern without God as its kingpin, we are attempting something crazy. It is not surprising that those who do this become confused and distracted. Anyone who expects a personalized, custom-built world is certainly likely to find the existing one absurd.

The notion of being *at home* is actually something much more modest. It does not mean having an environment that has been especially designed for you. It means having one where you belong. A strong element in Christian thought stresses that we do not belong on earth—"here is no continuing city." But it does so on the grounds that we belong somewhere else; we come from Heaven, can go back there, and are adapted for it. This way of thinking is not open to people who do not believe in Heaven. Where do they think we do come from?

I think this question points up a real difficulty about our complex nature. Certain developments of our faculties do set us terrible problems. In particular, we can notice and reflect on the incongruities of our situation in a way that gives us special trouble, even though those incongruities themselves are, I suspect, no worse than those that beset many other species. For example, the horror with which death afflicts creatures capable of lifelong affection is something we share with, among others, many birds which mate for life and many of the dog tribe. Mourning and desolation are not our inventions. But because we can anticipate them, can think about them and experience them widely in imagination, we have a graver problem—one, of course, which forms part of the price we pay for the joys and uses of imagination. But the way to face this problem cannot possibly be the dualist one—the way of identifying our real selves exclusively as soul or intellect, while drawing up the ladder that connects this aspect with the rest of our nature. We cannot dismiss our emotions and the rest of our nonintellectual nature, along with the body and the earth it is fitted for, as alien, contingent stuff. We have somehow to operate as a whole, to preserve the continuity of our being.

This means acknowledging our kinship with the rest of the biosphere. If we do not feel perfectly at home here, that may after all have something to do with the way in which we have treated the place. Any home can be made uninhabitable. Our culture has too often talked in terms of *conquering* nature. This is about as sensible as for a caddis worm to talk of conquering the pond that supports it, or a drunk to start fighting the bed he is lying on. Our dignity arises *within* nature, not against it.

I have suggested that we ought not to feel that dignity threatened by our continuity with the animal world. And I have compared the threat people feel here with the threat Christian thinking detected in the Copernican Revolution and in the theory of evolution. All three alarms indeed are connected; all depend on the confusion that results from taking symbols literally. One of the lasting nightmares caused by Copernicus was the fear that *up* and *down* could no longer function properly. From the notion that we are perhaps in free fall, sea-sickness follows.

But it ought not to. *Up* and *down* concern our relation to this planet, which is where we are. It is no threat to us that we might feel seasick in a space ship; we could also feel so if we went to sea, and no one attributes any cosmic significance to that. And life goes on tolerably in the Antipodes.

The notions of *up* and *down*, however, also function as symbols. To worship is to look up. And for God to be in the sky, looking down on a universe of which we occupied the center, was certainly a satisfying symbol. Before the Copernican Revolution, as afterward, it was not supposed to be relied on as literal truth, but seen, like all images of God that man could conceive, as provisional, as expressing men's ignorance as much as God's glory. So the Copernican Revolution ought not to have injured religion. Nonetheless it did, partly because the church chose to persecute Galileo, partly because people do easily become dependent on symbols. They need time, care, and help to disentangle themselves from them. The sense of God's providence as encompassing and explaining everything became, from these and other causes, greatly weakened.

But people by no means learned to dispense with it, to be contented, as the Enlightenment advised, with human life as explaining and justifying itself. Their lack of success in doing this is one reason the notion of evolution provoked such passion. On the one hand, it showed human beings as growing naturally out of creatures which they had despised, which they had regarded as symbols of wickedness, weakness, or at best of the Passions. It linked them more firmly to the earth, which was unquestionably Down. On the other, however, it offered them a new upward direction into the Future. And this provided a new and potent symbol.

People did not proceed—as the theory of evolution really requires—by demythologizing their symbolism about animals and the downward direction. Instead they either resisted evolution at all costs, or accepted it with the proviso that the Future was to lift them out of the degrading company that admittedly contaminated their past. The Future was seen as leading man away from the rest of nature as fast as possible, as giving him the hope of escaping continuity with it after all. Those who felt a sense of pollution at the thought of kinship with other animals could dwell on the hope of becoming less like them. Since both animals and the earth were still used, quite uncritically, as symbols for evil, weakness, *and* emotion, this distancing usually meant becoming less emotional, more intellectual and technological. In Nietzsche, with his violent poetic imagination, this arid intellectual *machismo* is balanced by some emphasis on feeling as well. But in the future fantasies of Shaw and Wells, and in the mass of science fiction that has followed them, it cavorts instructively. Robot worlds, purged of natural emotions, replace flesh and blood. And the idea of space travel itself acts as a symbol for the storming of Heaven. Man, having "conquered" his own world, is supposed to rise up and conquer the sky as well, thus putting down all his rivals, divine as well as terrestrial. But if God is alive, will ray guns bother him? And if he is dead, why dress up in his clothes?

The temptation to play at being God, which seems sometimes to afflict atheists, is something I must discuss later.[27] My present concern is the strong symbolic barrier that still makes it hard for many people who officially believe in evolution to accept its consequences, to see the kinship between man and other species that becomes so obvious once we start to observe both dispassionately. Kinship is not identity. But even kinship may be hard to admit if you are convinced that the other party is essentially evil, or if you think of your only path to salvation as leading away from him as fast as possible. Does our salvation really lie that way? Is the extinction of the normal human affections really an essential part of the better Future to which we are hurrying? (Shaw, Wells, and sometimes Nietzsche made it so.) Those affections link us with the animals. And animals are constantly, perhaps inevitably, used as symbols for them.

Camus remarks, "In a universe divested of illusions and lights, man feels an alien, a stranger. His exile is without remedy, since he is deprived of the memory of a lost home or the hope of a promised land." This is nothing but the fantasy of a child who, because he is disappointed in his actual parents, decides to view

27. Chap. 11, p. 254.

himself as a kidnapped and disinherited prince. We have either to accept the idea of God or not. If we do not, the lights of the world are no illusion. They are the earthly realities which we mistakenly projected onto Heaven. To dramatize our own position, as Camus does, by picking self-flattering aspects from both alternatives is bad faith. The "stranger" or "outsider" of Camus's novel is indeed a kind of alien. But he is so because he is an emotional cripple, someone apparently incapable of sharing human feelings—though it struck me even when I first read the book that he didn't seem to try very hard.[28] He can be no sort of an ideal for others. If people without his handicap imitate him, they lose the really excellent and central point of Existentialism: the acceptance of responsibility for being as we have made ourselves, the refusal to make bogus excuses.

Has the universe gone dark and silent on us? Pascal had that idea. He said, "The eternal silence of these infinite spaces terrifies me."[29] Why should it? Silence is frightening if it comes where there ought to be noise—silence in the nursery, in the dining hall, in the woods when the birds ought to be singing. But we do not live in the sky. If we had to, that would be very frightening indeed, for it would kill us. Much science fiction consists in scaring oneself into fits with this nightmare. But nothing need take us up there—unless we have the idea that we are called upon to take over from God, and that up there is where he used to live.

We have lost the music of the spheres, and that was certainly a very gracious symbol. But if there is a God, that symbol is quite

---

28. The Stranger's impressiveness springs from the courage and honesty with which he accepts an incurable handicap. But from those of us who have no such handicap, honesty demands an equally hard but quite different thing—the admission that we have normal powers and feelings. There is nothing stoical about *acting* lame. The pretence of being (spiritually) lamer than one is is Byronism. It is not necessarily Byronic to *write* stories like *The Stranger/The Outsider*—or indeed like Herman Hesse's *Steppenwolf;* such stories demand to be told. But for uncrippled people to make a cult of, and identify with, these figures *is* Byronic, that is, bogusly romantic. When we are so lynx-eyed for the bad motives that can underlie ordinary morality and religion, we had better watch these less advertised forms of hypocrisy as well.

29. *Pensées,* sec. ii, 162.

unnecessary for him, and if there is not, the music of real life, which that outer music reflected, is still here for us on earth.

There is no reason why we should be frightened of the heavens. If we think of them, not as a haunted church, nor as the home of alien demons, nor as a terrifying and impossible home for ourselves, but simply as they are—as the spacious and splendid setting in which our world properly belongs—what threat do they pose? They do not concern us, except that they are glorious.

Part Four

THE MARKS OF MAN

He fell in love with himself at first sight, and it is a passion to which he has always remained faithful.

—Anthony Powell, *The Acceptance World*

CHAPTER 10

Speech and Other Excellences

The Lure of the Simple Distinction

Man has always had a good opinion of himself, and with reason. What, however, is essentially the ground of it? What finally (you may ask) does distinguish man from the animals?

Nearly everything is wrong with this question.

First—as I have been saying—unless we take man to be a machine or an angel, it should read "distinguish man *among* the animals," and animals of this planet at that, with no extraterrestrial nonsense to give us all the drawbacks of religion and none of its benefits.

Second, as the question is usually put, it asks for a single, simple, final distinction, and for one that confers praise. This results, I suppose, from the old tradition of defining things by genus and differentia; that is, by naming first the class to which each thing belongs, and then the characteristic which marks it out from other members of that class. This rather hopeful scheme is supposed to enable us to find a formula stating the essence of each thing (or rather of each natural kind). And the differentia ought indeed to be in some way the thing's characteristic excellence, its central function—since that, and not just some chance quality (as in "featherless biped"), is useful in helping us to place it sensibly, in telling us, therefore, what it is really like. The old, more or less Aristotelian, definition of man as a rational animal follows this pattern and is its best-known example.[1]

Now most people today would with good reason reject this scheme as too ambitious to use outside the human scene. We cannot expect (they would agree) that things not made by man will necessarily have an essence we can grasp and a simple characteristic excellence we can see the point of. Evaluating snails from the human point of view is a fallible process and should be taken as such. We can certainly find marks that will help us to classify and understand them. But we had better not claim that by doing so we have finally expressed their true nature in a simple formula.

People are slower, however, to see that the same obstacle blocks us when we ask *What is the characteristic excellence of Man?* If we mean "what would seem distinctive about him to a nonhuman observer?" we would need first to know that observer's frame of reference, and what contrasts would strike him. If we mean "what is the best and most important thing within human life?" the question is a real one, and we can try to answer it. But it is not about biological classification. It is a question in moral philosophy. And we do not help ourselves at all in answering it if we decide in advance that the answer ought to be a single, simple characteristic, unshared by other species, such as the differentia is meant to be. Why should a narrow morality necessarily be the right one? Why should not our excellence involve our whole nature? The Platonic exaltation of the intellect above all our other faculties is a particular moral position and must be defended as such against others; it cannot ride into acceptance on the back of a crude method of taxonomy.

Oversimplicity, in fact, is what wrecks the notion of essence. Grading qualities as *more* and *less essential*—that is, more and less important to the species concerned—is not silly at all. Aristotle

---

1. Aristotle himself did not give this definition, though his argument at *Ethics* 1.7 and elsewhere does suggest it. Nor (certainly) did he ever proclaim that everything should be defined in the way described. He disliked such sweeping schemes and, if asked how things should be defined, would probably have answered that "it is the mark of an educated man to expect in each subject the sort of precision of which it is capable" (*Ethics* 1.3).

was doing this when he rejected two-footedness as a proper genus for man. It simply was not central enough in the life of the species; "Bird and Man for instance are two-footed, but their two-footedness is diverse and differentiated."[2] Birds and men, in fact, have dispensed with the support of forefeet for distinct though parallel reasons; if one mentioned those reasons, calling birds winged or flying animals and men handed or manipulative ones, one would be saying things of much greater interest. Flying and having hands are fairly essential properties, in that they make a great difference in the characteristic life of the creature. They are helpful in explaining it, where the negative "two-footed" is not. Similarly, Lorenz criticizes Desmond Morris for "over-emphasizing, in his book *The Naked Ape,* the beastliness of man.... He minimizes the unique properties and faculties of man in an effectively misleading manner. The outstanding and biologically relevant property of the human species is neither its partial hairlessness nor its 'sexiness', but its capacity for conceptual thought."[3]

Lorenz's point is that conceptual thought is a *structural* property, one affecting the whole organization of the life of the species, while hairlessness and "sexiness" in his view are minor, more local properties that affect it much less pervasively. And because each species does have its own way of life, structural properties can indeed be unique to a species. But not all of them are, and even where they are unique, that does not prove them excellent, even from the species's own point of view. Any species can have pervasive and characteristic bad habits. Conversely, what is good does not have to be unique to a species. For instance, in describing beavers, we should certainly say that their engineering capacity was one of their most outstanding features. But this does not isolate them. The elements of this capacity are present in their heritage: beavers are rodents, and gnawing, burrowing, and building industriously are a part of rodent life. And termites build, moles burrow, bees are industrious. What

2. *De Partibus Animalium* 1.3.
3. *Studies in Animal and Human Behaviour,* tr. R. D. Martin (London, 1970), vol. 1, p. 14.

makes beavers special is a particular *combination and further development* of these basic faculties. Again, if we consider the extraordinarily keen and effective eyes of birds of prey, we are not forced to isolate them. We need to know that all birds have pretty good sight, which is necessary to flying, and that predators in general have to be sharper and better equipped than their prey. Or again, if the talk is of elephants, we can do justice to the miracle of the trunk without pretending that nobody else has a nose.

Structural properties, then, do not have to be exclusive or necessarily excellent. Nor do they have to be black-or-white, yes-or-no matters. And certainly no one of them is enough alone to define or explain a species. We commonly employ a cluster of them, whose arrangement as *more* or *less essential* can be altered from time to time for many reasons. And what is really characteristic is the shape of the whole cluster.

The various things that have been proposed as differentia for man—conceptual thought or reason, language, culture, self-consciousness, tool-using, productivity, laughter, a sense of the future, and all the rest—form part of such a cluster, but none of them can monopolize it or freeze it into finality. There are always more that we have not thought of mentioning yet, and among them the most obvious. What would we say about someone who had all the characteristics just mentioned, but none of the normal human affections? These, of course, are plainly very like those of many other species, so they do not get named as the differentia. But shortage of them is the commonest reason for calling people inhuman. Because of this sort of thing, it is really not possible to find a mark that distinguishes man from "the animals" without saying *which* animals. We resemble different ones in different ways. It is also essential to remember how immensely they differ from one another. In certain central respects, all social mammals, including us, are far more like one another than any is like a snake or a codfish, or even a bee.

The logical point is simply that, in general, living creatures are quite unlike mathematical terms, whose essence really can be expressed in a simple definition. A triangle without three sides ceases to be a triangle. But a flightless bird does not cease to be a bird, nor a flying fish a fish. What is special about each creature is not a single, unique quality but a rich and complex arrangement of powers and qualities, some of which it will certainly share with its neighbors. And the more complex the species, the more true this is. To expect a single differentia is absurd. And it is not even effectively flattering to the species, since it obscures our truly characteristic richness and versatility.

People therefore need not act as if they were threatened every time something that has been supposed an exclusively human attribute is detected in other creatures. Considering the carelessness, and the real ignorance about other animals, which reigned when these criteria were set up, and also the still persisting reluctance to look at them dispassionately, we are bound to keep finding such attributes. The effect of dodging the situation by resetting the criteria each time in a way that it is hoped animals will be unable to penetrate is to separate the human differentia further and further from our central faculties. Nobody doubts that plenty of tests can be invented for aspects of language, tool use, foresight, and so on, which only man will be able to pass—though, as has already become clear, we cannot know in advance which they will be. But what reason could there possibly be for supposing that the faculties for passing those tests would be man's central and most important faculties? Is man perhaps centrally a test-passing animal? To read some of the literature, you might think so.

This notion of the human differentia has been misused in various ways. For instance, early in *The German Ideology,* Marx said: "Men can be distinguished from animals by consciousness, by religion or anything else you like. They themselves begin to distinguish themselves from animals as soon as they begin to *produce* their means of subsistence. . . . By producing their means of subsistence, men are indirectly producing their actual material life. . . . As individuals express their life, so they are. What they are, therefore, coincides with their production." In what sense do other animals *not* produce their means of subsistence? Two interpretations of *producing* suggest themselves: one, the processing of materials rather than simply gathering them; two, the free and deliberate planning of what one does, whether it be gathering, processing, or anything else. On the first criterion, bees, beavers, and termites do at least as well as the simpler hunting-and-gathering human tribes, which shows, again, that you have to consider *which* animals you are distinguishing yourself from. On the second, man is indeed in a special position, but then he is so for everything he does, not just for production. Which did Marx mean? A passage from the *Paris MS* is just as ambivalent: "Productive life is species-life. . . . The whole character of a species, its generic character, is contained in its manner of vital activity, and free conscious activity is the species-characteristic of man." This, however, gives the main emphasis not to production, but to free conscious choice. That is something found over a much wider range of activity than mere production, and certainly is a human structural characteristic, though by no means our only one. Conscious choice seems to be what Marx meant by contrasting men's "beginning to distinguish themselves from animals" with their merely being distinguished from without to suit the special interest of some classifier. Marx, however, wanted to combine this general Kantian point with something much more specific, a concentration on man as Maker. Anthony Quinton, to whom I owe these quotations, remarks: "This conception of human essence is Marx's materialist correction of Hegel's idealist and more or less Aristotelian notion of man as an essentially rational being. Man is, indeed, essentially rational for Marx but his reason is actualized in productive activity."[4] This is certainly right, but I think the point must be put more widely. *Everybody* after Aristotle who proposed this sort of definition of man was arguing with Aristotle, was commenting in one way or another on the definition of man as a rational animal, and was taking previous contributions for granted. Marx did not want to deny the rationality; he wanted to give it a different twist. But to do this effectively we need a quite different frame of argument, one where a number of different elements, all recognized as essential parts of human life, are explicitly considered together and set out in an intelligible order

4. *"Has Man an Essence?"* in *Nature and Conduct*, ed. R. S. Peters (London, 1975).

of priority. To do this, we have to drop the simple differentia scheme and leave any question of distinctness from other species right out of the argument. If another species were, in fact, found which did just what Marx meant by producing, it would not damage his argument about the structure of human life at all. The insistence on exclusiveness, in which so much intellectual capital has been invested, does no work whatever in the argument.[5]

Descartes: Reason and Language

The very great influence of one metaphysical scheme has, however, long made dropping the idea of the differentia impossible. This is Descartes' view of mind and body as radically divided in such a way that animals other than men cannot possibly have minds. Since this scheme places everything of value in the mind, it makes the human differentia a necessary piece of apparatus. And it has widely survived his view of the mind or soul as immortal, because it has a great appeal for mechanists.

Descartes, arriving in the course of his systematic doubt at the conclusion that he himself (since he could think) existed, asked next *what* he was. He at once rejected the suggestion, "a rational animal"—"What then did I formerly think I was? A man. But what is a man? Shall I say 'a rational animal'? No, in that case I should have to go on to ask what an animal is and what 'rational' is and so from a single question I should fall into several of greater difficulty."[6] He concluded that he *himself* was simply a thinking thing, not an animal at all. His body, though attached in some way to this soul or self, was no part of it, but a distinct physical mechanism. But all the physical processes occurring in an animal belonged to the body. Animals, then, since they did not properly speaking *think,* had no souls.

5. Sartre seems to be making just another move in the same game when he says that "man as the Existentialist sees him is not definable" till he "defines himself" (*Existentialism and Humanism,* p. 28). The notion of *defining* here seems very cloudy.

6. *Meditation 2,* in *Philosophical Writings,* tr. P. T. Geach and G. E. M. Anscombe (London, 1954), p. 67.

Descartes therefore regarded animals as automata, operating without consciousness. They did not, he said, really *act* themselves at all; they were acted upon: "it is nature that acts in them according to the arrangement of their organs, just as we see how a clock, composed merely of wheels and springs, can reckon the hours."[7] For this view he gave two reasons: their failure to talk, and the unevenness of their apparently intelligent performance. Let us take the second first.

Apparently intelligent performances by animals, said Descartes, could be shown not to proceed from real intelligence, because the same animals could at other times act stupidly. But of course the same unevenness is found in people. A horse,[8] which finds its way home cleverly, may be foolishly frightened of something that is not dangerous. A man, who sees through the false danger cleverly enough, may foolishly lose his way home. (Descartes, like others who use his model, never seems to consider what sort of a showing a human being would make if tested by members of a *more* intelligent species. Human beings are judged by their ideal performance, animals by their actual one.[9]) Relatively stupid conduct by a fairly intelligent being on an off-day is not in the least like the "stupidity" of a machine. A car cannot even try to find its way home; a clock will not make even a bad shot at identifying danger. Stupid solutions show a consciousness of the problem.

For this and related reasons, most people today would probably not follow Descartes in thinking animals unconscious. (If they are the kind of behaviorists who think consciousness itself an obscure notion, they will do so for people as well.) Nevertheless, many still regard animals as automatic in a way in which

---

7. *Discourse on Method,* Pt. 5, in ibid., p. 43.
8. For horses, see Bernard Grzimek's essay, "On the Psychology of the Horse," in *Man and Animal,* ed. Heinz Friedrich (London, 1972). People concerned with trying to compare the intelligence of various species commonly agree that it differs so much in kind that it is misleading to conceive it as the same stuff, varying only in quantity.
9. The Hippo's feeble steps may err
    In compassing material ends,
    While the True Church need never stir
    To gather in its dividends.   [T. S. Eliot, *The Hippopotamus*]

people are not; "they act not from knowledge but from the disposition of their organs," as Descartes says.[10]

What does this mean?

It is not just that a causal explanation "from the disposition of their organs" can in principle be given. This, many of us might agree, is true of people too. Where people are concerned, however, even the most rigid determinist must use other sorts of explanation as well. If we ask why a woman has suddenly rushed out of the house, the explanation may be, "to catch her little boy; she just saw him on the ice." This gives her *reason;* she acted "from knowledge." It does not compete with or deny causal explanations from her history,[11] but it must precede them; they are explanations *of* her rushing to save him from the ice. But now what about the action of a mother elephant who, caught with her baby in a flooded river, repeatedly saves the baby from being washed away and eventually manages to lift it with her trunk onto a ledge out of the water?[12] Again, the first explanation must be one of what she is trying to do, namely, to save it from drowning. And in doing that, how could she too not be "acting from knowledge"—knowledge that it is in danger and would be safer on the ledge? In both cases alike, motives and in some sense reasons must be mentioned before we can talk of cause.

To some people this seems obvious sense; others feel that some deep principle is being betrayed. The trouble, I am sure, is in Descartes' notion of reason as a single, indivisible, yes-or-no thing without degrees; his insistense that "brutes not only have a smaller degree of reason than men, but are wholly lacking in it," because, as he says, "reason is a universal tool that may serve in all kinds of circumstances"[13]—so that failing to use it shows one does not have it. But to have a universal tool is, of course, not the same thing as using it universally. And though reason can indeed in principle be used anywhere and on anything, it unluckily does not follow that everybody can in fact so use it. Someone

10. *Discourse on Method*, p. 42.
11. Including "the disposition of her organs"—hormones and so on.
12. Richard Carrington, *Elephants* (London, 1958), p. 60.
13. *Discourse on Method*, p. 42.

ignorant of, or stupid at, mathematics or Russian, cannot do a particular advanced problem or piece of translation. A prejudiced or infuriated man cannot criticize his aims. A quite impractical person cannot deal intelligently with a burst pipe, nor can a fanatical flat-earther understand eclipses. And at any given time there are problems that no human being can solve. Reason, in the sense of logic, certainly can be called a universal tool. But considered as a *faculty*—as something we are gifted with—it is not so at all. It is a set of highly varied mental capacities, practical and theoretical, which are separable and unevenly distributed among human beings, and are shaped in specific ways by their lives. This set cannot be reduced to, or derived from, the full, conscious, critical understanding of logic. That is not the differentia of men, but of logicians, and even they do not have it completely. Part of the trouble certainly is that Descartes, like Plato, saw pure, speculative reason of the logician's or mathematician's kind as lying at the core of human life—so that he was really defining man not so much by his consciousness or general intelligence as by his capacity for mathematics. But this again is a special view of what *matters* in life, of what our ambitions should be. It is not the normal meaning of reason.

In normal contexts, in fact, these speculative powers are not at all central to the notion. Someone who is plainly producing correct and even original mathematical work can still give us good grounds to wonder whether he is rational or reasonable. As I suggested earlier, these words mean much more than "consistent." A man who reasons consistently, but from the premise that he alone matters, is the type of unreasonableness. "Irrational" is a rather wider term, whose main use, I think, is to say that something has gone wrong with a person's system of priorities, with his sense of what is important. It can certainly be used to refer to a mere failure in speculative reasoning—say, the groundless expectation that things will still come out right whatever we do to our environment. But I do not think we use it to classify such an erroneous attitude as a *mere* failure to get the facts right. We do this by calling it stupid. "Irrational" makes a more general criticism, connecting that local failure with some general confusion about what is important. It suggests something wrong in the valuing system, as well as in the mere calculating power.

That suggestion I shall pursue in Chapter 11. The point here is that this sort of criticism can be made of animals as well as people. Rationality involves sanity. And a mad dog differs from a normal dog in just the same way as a mad man from a sane man. On the matter of knowing one's onions, understanding what one is about, there is not (as you might think from Descartes' remarks) a single scale reaching down from the most intelligent man to the stupidest and stopping short there, leaving all beasts equally nowhere. There are a number of scales on which both people and animals can be found variously arranged, as well as some others that are exclusive to people, and undoubtedly others peculiar to different types of animals. Of many elephants and gorillas, as well as of many unintellectual humans, we can very well say that

> He knows what's what, and that's as high
> As metaphysic wit can fly—[14]

a compliment that cannot be paid to every scholar. As for the use of the *word* reason, there is certainly a case for confining it to man, if we want to emphasize the importance of conscious, deliberate choice, just as there is a good case for confining the word "language" to sets of conventional signs and not extending it, except metaphorically, to "the language of the eyes" and other natural ways of communicating. Still, reason and sanity are often nearly synonymous. Jane Goodall, describing a chimpanzee under stress, says, "there was a time, toward the start of this battle for dominance, when Hugo and I feared for Goliath's sanity."[15] I think that we would probably not use the phrase "feared for his reason" here. But the gap between the two notions in such phrases is not very large.

Altogether, in ordinary speech, "having reason" or "being rational" is not a yes-or-no business like having a hammer. It is much more like having insight or energy or initiative or

14. Samuel Butler, *Hudibras,* 1.1.149.
15. *In the Shadow of Man,* p. 115.

imagination—things that can be possessed in varying degrees and also in very different forms. So we are not saying, if we concede some sort of knowledge, reason, intelligence, or purpose to the elephant, that we expect to find the next minute that it has written a Beethoven sonata or taken over the government. Nor, indeed, that it is taking legal action against the ivory trade.

People do feel a threat here: what is it? Human achievements are secure; they are unparalleled, they are all around us; there is no doubt about them. They cannot be shaken by an inquiry into their roots, elements, and origins. Yet there undoubtedly is a sense of outrage, varying from the disgust of one who finds a caterpillar in his salad to the terror of one who finds King Kong in his back yard, in people's insistence on a firm, simple differentia—a sense that is often felt to make all argument unnecessary. Might it perhaps be relevant to ask here, who is really threatening whom? On quite sober and conservative estimates, we are now moving steadily toward exterminating *all* the other most intelligent species on the planet, except possibly the dolphins—great whales, great apes, elephants, all the large predators. They meanwhile can do nothing to us except (it seems) what the Yahoos did to Gulliver—show us a mirror for what we do not much want to see. (Gulliver's horror when his clothes began to wear out and deprive him of his differentia sums up the situation.) But, in expecting this exposure, our guilt distorts the matter. No animal is what the Yahoos were, a mere projection of human vileness. Their species have each their own nature, each different from and mirroring ours in a different way. Elements of what we value will be found in all of them.

I return now to language. Descartes seems to have thought of it as a separate capacity, parallel to that for general intelligent performance. But perhaps it is only one area among many where intelligence can be shown.

Language is possibly our favorite human distinguishing mark. On the one hand, it seems an unmistakable, unsplittable single thing. Like the clothes that mattered so much to Gulliver, you cannot miss it. On the other hand, unlike the clothes, it is both really valuable and intrinsic to us. It plainly calls for innate powers, which are linked to the main structural properties of our life. Human talk involves thinking conceptually, having a sense of things absent, being capable of abstract calculation, conscious of self, and all the rest of it. So we naturally see it as the key to our castle.

This, of course, is why the recent experiments in which chimps have undoubtedly in some sense been taught a language have upset people so much. The facts are briefly these.[16] Between 1966, when she was a year old, and 1971, a chimp called Washoe was taught a sign language called Ameslan, commonly used by the deaf-and-dumb and consisting of hand gestures, roughly speaking one to a word. She took to it like a duck to water. She acquired in five years a vocabulary of about 150 Ameslan words which she could use, and another 200 which she could understand. Moreover, she uses it constantly, freely and spontaneously in casual conversation, not just for tests or when rewarded. Since then other chimps have also been taught the language, with much the same degree of success. Four of them have now been placed with Washoe in a community on an island, watched but not interfered with. They use Ameslan constantly and spontaneously to talk to one another. And their use of it is increasing. Moreover, they talk to themselves, and, without having been taught to, they swear. (The favored swearword is the Ameslan sign for "dirty.") One chimp, Ally, has been deliberately exposed to both Ameslan and spoken English, and can give the Ameslan sign for an absent object when its name is spoken. This involves something linguists have called "cross-modal transfer," which has been supposed impossible for animals.

Earlier attempts to teach apes to talk had failed, resulting in their knowing only a few words after many years' work. This was put down to the general weakness of their intellects. But the remarkable difference between these results and the Ameslan ones suggests, offhand, that the trouble lay not so much in the intellect as in their lacking the innervations from the brain to the larynx which are necessary for speech.

16. Events will certainly have overtaken me before this book comes out. I can only use the information I have, which is drawn largely from Eugene Linden's sensible and perceptive little book, *Apes, Men, and Language* (New York, 1974).

This would mean that language, or the power to speak it, is actually not the unsplittable, single, unmistakable thing people had supposed. A lot of intellectual capital, however, has been invested in the idea that it is so. Defenders of the castle therefore reply that Ameslan, at least as spoken by chimps, is not really a language at all. It does not, they say, have the right structural properties, so its use does not require the rational faculties that language is normally thought to imply. Chimps may have been handed the key, but they cannot turn it. The argument here has been largely concerned with word order, and is heavily dependent on the definition of abstract terms like "syntactical," which were devised by linguists in the first place entirely for use in a human context and are not easy to apply in this new area. (If pressed, this kind of argument is liable to prove that a lot of human beings do not talk either.) A number of objections of this nature made in response to Washoe's early efforts have already been withdrawn by their proposers, after further study both of her performance and that of human children.[17] The inquiry goes on, and rightly; new and more detailed standards are set up for the chimps to spar with.

But we need to ask some quite different questions as well.

First, *what follows if the chimps can, in some sense, talk?* Why does it matter so much? There is something most fishy about the idea that big questions could hang on the result of these experiments *alone.* The experiments matter only if they bring to our notice an important and pervasive fact about the world. If they do so, there must be other evidence for it. The sense that these educated chimps somehow threaten the whole fabric of human superiority must mean that the notion of human superiority itself is badly confused. Neither linguistics nor human dignity can certify *a priori* that language is confined to humans. Whether it is clearly an empirical question.

After discussing this question, I shall move on to one that supplements it and is equally necessary whatever comes of the experiments, namely, *if they are not talking, what are they doing?* Or, more generally, if the seemingly intelligent actions of the higher

17. See Linden, pp. 54 and 74.

animals are never really intelligent, what are they? Notions of mechanical, imitative, or reactive explanations are usually held in the background of such discussions as if they were the obvious and simple ones. I believe they are, on the contrary, incoherent and obscure as explanations of what actually happens. They would never have been put forward except to save a received theory from disaster.

First, then, what requires *a priori* that only humans should talk? The answer is not linguistics or human dignity, but simply a piece of bad metaphysics, namely, Descartes' dualistic view that the world is divided sharply, without remainder, into lifeless objects on the one hand and human, fully rational, subjects on the other. This position cannot in any case be reconciled with evolution. For if it were true, there would have to have been a quite advanced point in animal evolution when parents who were merely unconscious objects suddenly had a child which was a fully conscious subject. And that situation makes no sense.

Language and Morality

What makes the bad metaphysics much harder to unravel is, however, the traditional entanglement of this view with morality. I must therefore discuss this confusion now although, as I shall try to suggest, it need not really concern language at all.

We can have duties to people, but not to things. So if animals are things, it does not matter how we treat them. This crude and simple reasoning ought of itself to be enough to show what is wrong with metaphysical dualism. The argument simply reverses itself. Since it *does* matter how we treat animals—since cruelty is vicious in its own right, and not just because it might lead to ill-treating people—the sharp division into object and fully rational subject cannot be right. And as we have plenty of duties to people which do not depend on their being rational either, this consideration does not stand alone.

The tradition, however, took the other path. In Kant's moral philosophy, the distinction between *people* and *things* is central, and is admirably used. His main moral point is that we must distinguish between them. We must not treat people as mere things to be manipulated, but with respect, as free beings, as ends in themselves. This respect is the central dynamic of his system. But he considered it to be simply a tribute to their rational status. Although he defined it rather generally as "the consciousness of a worth which thwarts my self-love"[18]—the mere sense of something of value independent of ourselves—he thought that only rational beings could possibly have that sort of unconditional value. So it could not be extended to animals. Their position between the two opposing forces had been overlooked, and they were simply pushed into the class of Things to avoid complicating the system.

Kant's discussion of the matter is interesting because he is so clearly sensitive to aspects that go far beyond his official view. He says, for instance, "The more we come in contact with animals and observe their behaviour, the more we love them, for we see how great is their care for their young. It is then difficult for us to be cruel in thought even to a wolf."[19] This points toward something which I shall discuss in Chapter 11—the importance of mere steady, constant, structured, good feeling in our ordinary notion of what commands respect, and indeed of rationality. Another example goes further. "Leibniz," says Kant, "used a tiny worm for purposes of observation, and then carefully replaced it with its leaf on the tree, so that it should not come to harm through any act of his. He would have been sorry—a natural feeling for a humane man—to destroy such a creature for no reason."[20] This cannot in Kant's terms count as *respect*, but it would be natural to describe it in terms like Albert Schweitzer's, of "respect for life."

It is certainly a "natural feeling," and one that passes Kant's test for a serious, rational motive. It is not a mere inclination, it is a feeling *that we must not* destroy certain things—and one that is not isolated, but forms part of our central system of standards.

---

18. *Grundlegung*, chap. 1, sec. 16, note (Paton tr., pp. 66–67). See also p. 354 below. For admirable recent discussions of this issue, see Peter Singer, *Animal Liberation* (London, 1976), and Stephen Clark, *The Moral Status of Animals* (Oxford, 1977).
19. "Duties towards Animals and Spirits," *Lectures on Ethics*, p. 241.
20. Ibid.

Kant, I think, was simply mistaken in supposing that we could have this sort of feeling only toward creatures that were themselves rational. Christianity, anxious to destroy primitive paganism, had made great efforts to exclude plants and animals from the area proper to such feeling by positive propaganda. Thus Saint Augustine wrote, "Christ himself shows that to refrain from the killing of animals and the destroying of plants is the height of superstition, for, judging that there are no common rights between us and the beasts and trees, he sent the devils into a herd of swine and with a curse withered the tree on which he found no fruit." Jesus, Augustine goes on, was deliberately trying to show us that "we need not govern our behaviour towards animals by the moral rules which govern our behaviour towards men. That is why he deliberately transferred the devils to swine instead of destroying them, as he could easily have done."[21] Kant himself was thinking within this Stoic and Christian tradition, which makes it a positive duty for man to recognize his superiority over, and lack of indebtedness to, nature: "As the single being on earth that possesses understanding, he is certainly titular lord of nature, and, supposing that we regard nature as a teleological system, he is born to be its ultimate end."[22] But the sense that indiscriminate destructiveness of living things is really evil cannot be dismissed like this. It crops up constantly, both in our own culture and in others, notably in Buddhism, as a necessary corollary of "humanity to man." Even the bloodiest societies draw the line somewhere. There is nearly everywhere a horror of killing *certain* creatures, or too many creatures, or creatures in certain circumstances. Totem animals are a good example, but they do not stand alone. Even Western culture is full of examples like Saint Francis and Saint Hubert. Remarkably, in view of the public involved, "it is recorded that at the [Roman] Games put on by Pompey in 55 B.C., in which a

---

21. *The Catholic and Manichean Ways of Life,* chap. 17, quoted with comment by John Passmore, *Man's Responsibility for Nature,* p. 111. Clearly Christians today seldom think like this, but the tradition was in its time most influential, and its effects are still with us in secularized form.

22. Kant, *Critique of Judgement,* Pt. 2, sec. 431. See the last two sections of Chap. 13, below.

number of elephants and hundreds of lions and leopards were entered, the crowd booed and cursed Pompey for having the elephants attacked. . . . Cicero wrote to a friend about the incident and stated that the crowd was aroused by pity and 'somehow felt that the elephant was allied with man'.[23] Again, Antony Alpers quotes from Oppian's *Halieutica*, "The hunting of dolphins is immoral, and that man can no more draw nigh to the gods as a welcome sacrificer nor touch their altars with clean hands, but pollutes those who share the same roof with him, who willingly devises destruction for the dolphins." Alpers remarks, from a quite wide survey of the sources, "Looking over all the known facts, I rather think that Oppian's view of cruelty to dolphins, even though he is alone among Greek writers in expressing it so fervently, may have been fairly widely held."[24] Again, "In his *Apology for Raimond Sebond,* Montaigne argued that it was absurdly presumptuous for men to set themselves up above the animals. In his *Essay on Cruelty* he drew the conclusion that 'we have a general duty to be humane, not only to such animals as possess life, but even to trees and plant'."[25] And there is Blake—

> A robin redbreast in a cage
> Puts all Heaven in a rage—

and many similar remarks in *Auguries of Innocence* and elsewhere. In saying that even Western culture is full of such thoughts, I mean, of course, that there are many and that you may find them anywhere. I do not mean that they were systematically assembled into a doctrine. They were not, because there was a powerful and positive resistance to their being so treated on the part both of the church and the central rationalist tradition. They remained as isolated notions, scruples felt and communicated, but not supported by any official framework. *But it is out of such scruples that our whole morality is built.* They are its raw material. It is quite wrong to dismiss as "sentimental" those for which

23. Ivan Sanderson, *The Dynasty of Abu* (London, 1960), p. 272. For further details see Cicero, *Ad Fam.* 7.1, and Pliny, *Natural History* 8.21.
24. *Dolphins* (London, 1965), pp. 43 and 158–159. See also p. 158 for the Australian aborigines' prohibition on dolphin-slaughter.
25. Passmore, *Man's Responsibilty for Nature,* p. 114.

no framework has yet been provided. They are indeed *sentiments* or feelings as well as thoughts, and until the concepts involved in them are developed into a proper framework, their status as thoughts remains slightly shaky—we have still to relate them to the rest of our morality. This sort of relation was made by Bentham, and it is noteworthy that he did it in the context of insisting that our duties extended to a number of perhaps imperfectly rational *people,* people whom it had previously seemed sentimental to have any scruples about—primitives, slaves, women: "The French have already discovered that the blackness of the skin is no reason why a human being should be abandoned without redress to the caprice of a tormentor. It may come one day to be recognized, that the number of legs . . . or the termination of the *os sacrum* are reasons equally insufficient for abandoning a sensitive being to the same fate."[26]

In the main tradition, however, what prevailed was Kant's official view, the more or less contractual one, that rights and duties have meaning only where there is a social convention expressible in language. Thus in Kant's central example:

If a dog has served his master long and faithfully, his service, *on the analogy of human service,* deserves reward, and when the dog has grown too old to serve, his master ought to keep him until he dies. Such actions *help to support us in our duties towards human beings, where they are bounden duties.* . . . If a man shoots his dog because the animal is no longer capable of service, he does not fail in his duty to the dog, *for the dog cannot judge,* but his act is inhuman and damages in himself that humanity which it is his duty to show towards mankind.[27]

But there are many human beings who for this or that reason cannot judge either, for instance, babies. And where they do judge, their judgment is not sufficient to determine whether we actually have a duty toward them, nor can it be the ground of that duty. This contractual or legalistic attitude is the weakest side of Kant; all his best moral philosophy proceeds without it and is often directly contrary to it; true autonomy demands that we judge without any reference to the other's attitude. But his

26. Introduction to *Principles of Morals and Legislation.* Chap. 17, sec. 4, note *b.*
27. "Duties towards Animals and Spirits," *Lectures on Ethics,* p. 241, my italics.

contractual approach has been widely imitated. People find it neat and simple to reduce the basis of obligation to its institutional form. And no doubt within a given civilization many duties (though never all) do acquire institutional forms. Natural trust is strengthened by contract, and the duty a parent owes to a child can be represented crudely as flowing from the social contract, because that contract shores it up. For political purposes there is often a point in looking at things this way: politics must stick to the enforceable. But if we consider this as a *comprehensive* account, it is crass and futile. We have plenty of duties to our children which do not concern society, or which conflict with its rulings. And someone who has a child outside a society does not cease to have a duty to it. Similarly, the whole point of the story of the Good Samaritan is to get rid of the contract notion when discussing our duty to our neighbor. Kant shows his limitations by suggesting that the whole obligation to the dog is contractual, and also by suggesting, unintelligibly, that decent behavior to the dog is not real decent behavior, just practice for real decent behavior to people; that we cannot have a duty to the dog itself.[28] But at least he does not add the more sinister error of supposing that language has to be present for the matter to concern us at all, that there are really no other considerations to restrain us from gratuitous cruelty and destructiveness toward any nonhuman creature, nor from exterminating species. This position seems to me, again, so obviously and crudely immoral that it simply discredits the moral theories that are intended to defend it. As Bentham rightly remarked, when you are wondering whether it is all right to hurt somebody, the question you have to ask is not whether they can talk, but whether they can suffer.

People readily become suspicious of suggestions that they could have any duty to animals, because they see this as likely to lay on them an infinite load of obligation, and they rightly think

---

28. It is interesting that he gives just this same merely preparatory status to our "duty" toward works of art. Following him, some people now say that our regard for animals must be an "aesthetic" one, since it cannot be moral. This won't wash. See the concluding sections of this book.

an infinite obligation would be meaningless.[29] *Ought* implies *can*. Indefinite guilt is paralyzing. The position, however, is actually no worse than the one we are already in with regard to people. We already have the idea that we owe some sort of obligation to any human being. But it is not infinite, because what each of us ought to do is limited by the alternatives he can reach. We have to consider priorities. Conflicts of interest must be recognized both within the human species and outside it. We have to take sides, and are entitled to put our own species first. All species do this. No creature can in fact subsist without killing some others, if only by competing with them for food. The point is not that we can hope to avoid injuring either animals or people. It is that we ought to recognize that such an injury matters, and to try to avoid it where no adequate reason justifies it. Suffering inflicted on experimental animals, for instance, is not just a null term that can be dropped right out of the moral equation. It has a weight, and that weight ought to be proportioned to the demonstrable value of the research. Not just anything justifies absolutely everything. Some scientists may be brutal, but that does not make brutality scientific.

The entanglement of this moral difficulty with language, however, is one thing which I think makes people uneasy about the chimpanzee experiments, so uneasy that they feel that the results will simply have to be negative.[30] This special anxiety, I suggest, is out of place. We already have, and have long had, evidence that the great apes are complex and sensitive creatures, with a full social life and close personal ties, therefore capable of great suffering. If they turn out able to pass tests in language use which are of special interest to linguists, it will make no dif-

29. Albert Schweitzer did say that we have a "responsibility without limit to all that lives" (*Civilization and Ethics,* tr. C. T. Campion [London, 1946], p. 244). There is a real difficulty about words like *responsibility, right,* and *duty* since they are used sometimes in a minimum sense ("he did no more than his duty") and sometimes, as here, in a looser and wider one, for the whole range of claims that may come upon us—"the whole duty of man," or "I am responsible for him." Any useful discussion must distinguish these senses.

30. As Linden puts it, "If she is not a dumb beast, what right have we to treat her like this?"

ference to this conclusion. Their complexity emerges plainly from the carefully recorded accounts of the people—by now quite numerous—who have spent long times with them in the wild, observing their lives in natural conditions. It emerged, before that, from the accounts of those who, like Köhler and Yerkes, kept them in cages for research, but who were sufficiently interested in them to *look* for it, rather than simply viewing them as raw material for establishing something. It will not emerge simply from isolated experiments, because it is a structural characteristic. People determined to "explain animal behavior" on some simple scheme will always be able to find their own way of accounting for any isolated performance, however impressive, as mechanical, imitative, coincidental, or whatever. But this is vacuous, since "explaining behavior" *must* refer to structural principles, therefore to long stretches of it and many partial parallels. It *is* relating it to a context.

Many people fail to grasp this point, apparently because they think of "scientific" evidence as only that produced in laboratories by control experiments. This leads them to treat field studies, however careful, thorough and well-documented, as "anecdotal"—mere preparation for the real thing, therefore properly ignored till it bears fruit entitled to be considered by learned persons. This attitude is much like that of cavalry generals in the First World War, waiting impatiently for the infantry to clear the ground so that they could make the dashing charges that alone they thought properly entitled to the name warfare. Because these creatures *are* complex, only a tiny fraction of the important truths about them can ever be seen in laboratories or expressed in control experiments. The same, of course, is true of the human race.

On the special issue of proving experimentally that one is an intelligent being, it is interesting to think, again, how human beings would make out. I once read a pleasing science fiction story about some people who were captured by aliens much more intelligent than themselves, and caged in a sort of galactic zoo, along with other inferior creatures. They made desperate efforts to demonstrate their rationality by various activities which seemed impressive to them, but which were dismissed by their keepers as quaint forms of dominance or courtship displays. At last they despaired, and decided to occupy themselves, since they could not get out, by trapping and keeping some insects they found in their quarters. They were promptly released with apologies, since it was recognized at once that the trapping and caging of other creatures was a sign of rationality.

What then is the actual importance of language?

It is not just the fact that a human being talks which gives him a claim to be treated with respect. It is what his talk shows—and he shows the same things in other ways as well, through his actions. If the chimps turn out able to talk well, this can be of enormous interest and tell us much about both their nature and ours. But whatever is true of their moral status is true also, and will continue to be true, of many other fairly advanced creatures. Educated chimps would not form, along with man, an exploitative elite, exalted above all other life-forms as subject above object. The only intelligible arrangement is to regard *all* animals as subjects of some kind, though with a life that varies greatly in its kind and degree of complexity.

What Goes with Language? Other Structural Properties

People oppose this very natural way of thinking not only, of course, because of the moral difficulties I have been mentioning. They do so because of a peculiar current view of the relation of subject to object, which affects the whole idea of science. This is the view that to consider everything equally as object is the only proper and scientific way of proceeding. But the term "object" is ambiguous.

Being "objective" in our thinking is indeed an intellectual virtue. It means that we overcome our private prejudices, see ourselves and our concerns as others see them. What this involves is interchanging (grammatical) subject and object *within the human scene.* The terms are used here as they are when Booth (subject) kills Lincoln (object). Both are people, and the transaction would be of the same kind if it were reversed. But the distinction of *people versus things* is of a quite different kind. The word "objective" is not rightly applied to someone who treats live human beings as if they were *lifeless* objects. Lack of discrimination of this kind has no sort of practical merit and is not "scientific" either, since the difference between living and lifeless things can have great theoretical as well as practical importance.[31] Nor is there anything clever about failing to recognize that living things range along a great scale of complexity from the simplest to richly social beings, who share with us many of the needs and capacities on which speech rests.

Language, then, is perhaps not, any more than reason, a yes-or-no business, a hammer that you are holding or not holding, a single, indivisible, sacred heirloom guaranteeing supremacy. It, too, is a rich and complex range of skills. (Compare the question: Has man, yes or no, a sense of smell? Or a sense of direction? Would charitable dolphins consider that he could swim, or not?) "Having language" in the sense in which human beings have it is having a large and versatile tool kit. But kits containing some of the same tools are found in much less ambitious quarters. Or, to return to the image of the key—there is no question of keeping the chimps out of the castle. They and many other animals have always been inside, and only our conceit and prejudice have stopped us from seeing them. They are all over the ground floor, which is still a central area of our life as well as theirs. But there are many other floors to which they do not go and cannot, because they have never wanted to enough, and so have never developed their powers beyond a certain rudimentary point. They have, undoubtedly, other powers and other interests of their own, but we are not at the moment considering those.

Apes and other creatures can count a little, but they do not much care to do so.[32] They are not going to arrive at the differential calculus. It is much the same with tool use. Chimps are

31. This confusion seems to bedevil discussions about treating people "as sex objects." There is nothing at all wrong with being the object of a normal human feeling—being at the receiving end of it—but a great deal wrong with being treated as a piece of equipment, a thing.

32. Throughout I am emphasizing interest rather than capacity because that side has been neglected. Clearly there must be a chicken-and-egg relation between the two. But I find it interesting that chimps apparently have more capac-

not greatly interested in it; they will never make power tools. But they do use stalks to fish termites out of their nests, and they prepare those stalks in advance.[33] They also use crushed leaf bunches as sponges to soak up water and egg. And sea otters use stones to break open shellfish. Elephants do various things with branches. Outward skills of this kind are fairly easily observed, and the rudiments of them are certainly found outside man.

When we turn to more abstract, structural properties like "self-consciousness," it is much harder to know what counts as proof. Jane Goodall is, rightly I think, impressed with a response of Washoe's which seems relevant here: "For the first time, Washoe was asked (in sign language) 'Who is that?' as she was looking into a mirror. Washoe, who was very familiar with mirrors by that time, signaled back, 'Me, Washoe.'" Jane Goodall comments: "This should not be disturbing. . . . It is only through real understanding of the ways in which chimpanzees and men show similarities of behavior that we can reflect, with meaning, on the ways in which men and chimpanzees *differ*. And only then can we really begin to appreciate, in a biological and spiritual manner, the full extent of man's uniqueness."[34] Equally significant is the response of Lucy, another Ameslan chimp, to the "swallow game":

Roger will take a pair of sunglasses and pretend to swallow them by turning his head in profile to Lucy and sliding the glasses past his open mouth on the side of his face that Lucy cannot see. Lucy thinks this hysterically funny. . . . Promptly after Roger finished to-day's performance, Lucy grabbed the glasses, and taking her indestructible mirror hopped across the living room to another couch. Holding the mirror with her feet, Lucy, to her own vast amusement, performed the swallow trick, passing the glasses along the obscured side of her face exactly as Roger had done. Then she signed, "look, swallow."[35]

---

ity than they now use, so that merely coming to possess more of it (by mutation?) would not necessarily produce increased use of it. If it is not used, there can hardly be selection for it. See later, p. 249, and for the facts, the chapter on intelligence in Morris and Morris, *Men and Apes* (London, 1965).

33. See Goodall, *In The Shadow of Man*, index entries under *Tool-using*. Wolfgang Köhler reported this sort of thing in 1925, but no one seems to have paid any attention. See *The Mentality of Apes* (Pelican ed., 1957), pp. 72 and 78.

34. Goodall, *In the Shadow of Man*, pp. 250–251.

35. Linden, *Apes, Men and Language*, p. 97.

This connects, of course, with the old and quite sensible suggestion that *laughter* is a sign of intelligence. A certain detachment, a power of looking *at* a thing and sizing up its incongruity, is needed to see even the simplest joke. And Lucy has the rudiments of this. As Linden's drawing shows, she was watching herself in the mirror. Again, Vicki (one of the earlier chimps who failed to learn human speech) when given photos and told to sort them into human and animal, did so successfully, but placed her own picture in the human file, while leaving her father's in the animal one. She, like other apes brought up by people, regards herself as a person. But to "regard oneself as" something seems to be a mark of self-consciousness. It might be right to connect with this one of Lucy's most interesting reported remarks, a comment on her own emotion. When her human foster-mother drove away during a training session, Lucy ran over to the side window to watch her drive off, and as she did so, signed to herself, "cry me, me cry."[36] Natural expressive movements were no longer enough for her.

But consciousness of self as an object that other people can look at has long been evident in apes who drape trails of greenery and other things over themselves. Köhler remarks:

The meaning of these things can be clearly seen in the circumstances and behaviour of the animals. They play, not only with the things they have hanging round themselves, but with other animals' also, and their pleasure then is visibly increased by draping things round themselves. It is true that one often sees an ape walking about alone and yet draped, but, even under these circumstances he is most impishly self-important or audacious, as on the occasions when a decorated chimpanzee, with all signs of being in the best of tempers, will strut about among his companions or advance upon them menacingly.[37]

There is the same sort of difficulty over what we mean by "conceptual thought." Of course its higher reaches are exclusive to man; no other animal thinks about relativity theory or even social history. (But nor do a lot of people.) What are conceptual thought's lower limits? Passing information about things absent

36. Ibid., p. 111.
37. *The Mentality of Apes*, p. 85. See also p. 268 on mirrors, and Schaller, *Year of the Gorilla*, p. 186, for gorillas adorning themselves.

is certainly one part of it, but not the whole. Bees do that in their honey dances, which do not show thought. We demand perhaps that a new and unfamiliar example should be brought under a general heading. So what about the dolphins whose trainers ask them simply to "invent a new trick," and who promptly do so?[38] ("There's certainly somebody in there," as one trainer observed, peering anxiously at his dolphin.) Or what about Mike, the thrusting chimp who rose from low status to dominate his group by learning (quite spontaneously) to bang kerosene cans together to enhance his displays, eventually managing to keep three four-gallon cans going ahead of him for a sixty-yard run, and sometimes hurling them forward?[39] Again, the language experiments have shown many cases where an ape makes up a suitable name for something whose proper name it does not know. Thus Lucy, who hates radishes, calls them "cry hurt food," and calls a watermelon "candy drink" and all citrus fruits "smell fruits." And Washoe, who also regards herself as an honorary person, when first introduced to other chimps, called them "black bugs."[40] Another aspect of conceptual thought is being able to think of something not present when you need it for some new purpose, following out clues of true relevance instead of merely associating or following present stimuli. In tool-using, Wolfgang Köhler showed that chimps could do this. But he also showed that their ability for it was very limited. Only the brightest of his chimps, and they only sometimes, could remember to think of and fetch a stick or box that was not actually in their view. It is right to notice here, however, that tool use, like counting, is rather alien to a chimp's natural *interests*. His problems are not usually physical, but social, and his attention in a difficulty goes at once to a social solution. Thus, Köhler re-

---

38. I saw this happen on a TV documentary and can unfortunately give no references. It seemed, however, a perfectly sensible documentary, made by Dutch scientists, and the fact seems to fit well enough with other information about dolphins. Compare too this from Ivan Sanderson; "Elephants are very amenable to learning tricks, *and in fact they often seem to think them up themselves*" (*The Dynasty of Abu*, p. 266). Grasping what is involved in "a trick" seems fairly "conceptual."

39. Goodall, *In The Shadow of Man*, p. 114.

40. Linden, *Apes, Men and Language*, pp. 106, 10.

marked that he had trouble in keeping his apes to the task of getting the suspended bananas themselves, since their first idea in this predicament was to lead him to them and ask him to lift them down. Other experimenters sometimes report the same sort of thing as a nuisance and embarrassment to their work. But as "experimenting" is a notion nobody has explained to the chimps, what they do here is by no means stupid, and they might well think of the unresponsive humans as stupid or mulish. (This is one of many ways in which the artificial experimental situation interferes with the subject matter. When everything is geared to experimental purity, what is going on is bound to become unintelligible to the animal, which is expecting a normal personal approach, and has grounds for doing so, since it is in general treated with friendship. The fact that it is puzzled and flounders when this friendship suddenly gives way to something mysterious does not show stupidity—rather the opposite. A child would do the same.[41]) Jane Goodall describes a number of successes in solving problems by "social engineering," often scored by Figan, an enterprising youngster who found that, being small and weak, he did not get the bananas that the humans were putting out while the larger apes were around.

Figan suddenly spotted a banana that had been overlooked—but Goliath was resting directly underneath it. After no more than a quick glance from the fruit to Goliath, Figan moved away and sat on the other side of the tent so that he could no longer see the fruit. Fifteen minutes later, when Goliath got up and left, Figan without a moment's hesitation went over and collected the banana. Quite obviously he had sized up the whole situation; if he had climbed for the fruit earlier, Goliath almost certainly would have snatched it away. If he had remained close to the banana he would probably have looked at it from time to time. Chimps are very quick to notice and interpret the eye movements of their fel-

41. To discover that someone whom one had taken for a friend is in fact using one as an experimental subject is a very bad experience. Stories in which people do so use their nearest and dearest (such as that of Patient Griselda, and *Cymbeline*) have an extremely unpleasant flavor; it comes from *using people as objects* in a strong sense. I cannot help feeling that this fact brings an element of falsity into the chimp experiments. We are waiting to see how far they can respond like people, while treating them in a way in which people could not possibly be treated. I do not mean that there is any unkindness—quite the reverse; but the situation is very artificial.

lows, and Goliath would possibly, therefore, have seen the fruit for himself. And so Figan had not only refrained from instantly gratifying his desire, but had also gone away so that he could not "give the game away" by looking at the banana. . . . But there was more to come.

Commonly when a chimpanzee gets up from a resting group and walks away without hesitation, the others will get up and follow. It does not need to be a high-ranking individual—often a female or a youngster may start such a move. One day when Figan was part of a large group and, in consequence, had not managed to get more than a couple of bananas for himself, he suddenly got up and walked away. The others trailed after him. Ten minutes later he returned, quite by himself—and naturally got his share of bananas.[42]

It is probably worth remarking that in Descartes' day, not only was evolution unthought of, but examples like these were totally unknown. The great apes had not even been discovered, let alone studied, nor did anyone but hunters watch any animal in its natural habitat, which is how we watch people. "Animals" were primarily farm beasts, vermin, dangerous predators, game for hunting, and the dogs, horses, and others that served man. The last, of course, were much the most familiar. But domestic creatures are always kept in situations that cramp initiative and are systematically bred to be as unassertive as possible. (For instance, their natural patterns of courtship and mate selection are bred out of them for human convenience. The effect of this is that people get the idea that brutal, hasty, and unselective mating is typical of "the animals" as opposed to human beings— whereas actually it represents as great a distortion as the bulldog's nose and the dachshund's back.) In general, any spontaneous, enterprising behavior on the part of an ox, dog, or horse tends to strike its owner as wasteful, stupid, or obstreperous, not as evidence that it has a mind of its own. He views the animal mainly in its functional light simply as a thing, an implement, and partly (sometimes) in its light as a member of the human hierarchy, where it occupies a very low place, the servant of servants. The deeply hierarchical nature of dogs makes this easier, and other domestic creatures simply fall into place below dogs. It is worth noticing that when Mill, for instance, said that it

42. *In the Shadow of Man,* pp. 96–97.

was "better to be a man dissatisfied than a pig satisfied,"[43] he clearly had in mind the farm pig, carefully bred for maximum inertia and imprisoned in a sty. His whole point was the acceptance of inactivity. Yet this sort of pig is almost as much a human artifact as the farmer's tractor. Wild boars are quite another matter. The contrast he was pointing to was really one between *free and imprisoned.* Yet it passes for a standard case of the contrast between man and beast.

The only primates known in Descartes' day were the little North African macaques, "Barbary apes," which were sometimes kept as pets. As Ramona and Desmond Morris most interestingly show, these creatures were seen in a light that could only reinforce man's self-esteem, as inferior *imitators,* making themselves ridiculous by their vain efforts to share the grandeur of human status.[44] In a human household, they were naturally somewhat destructive and "mischievous"; their behavior did much to strengthen the notion of animals as derisory failed human beings. Other, more exotic animals would occasionally be seen, bored and inactive, in menageries, prisoners to enhance the glory of a monarch or amaze the populace—showing about as much of their own nature as a human being might be expected to do if kept in solitary confinement for years by an alien species with no understanding of its needs. Added to this, learning was essentially an *urban* matter—serious thinkers, up almost to the time of Darwin, tended to take Socrates's view that "it is not fields and trees which will teach me anything, it is men in the city."[45] Finally, the Christian church, following its early tradition of attacking nature-worship, positively opposed any attention to the claims of animals.[46] Altogether it is not surprising that a perfunctory attitude to the question of animal intelligence became commonly accepted. That this attitude has lingered so long is also understandable, since a tradition *that a certain topic does not matter* is one of the hardest things to get rid of—discussion of it tends to be tabooed before it starts.

43. *Utilitarianism,* chap. 2.
44. *Men and Apes,* pp. 28–35.
45. Plato, *Phaedrus* 230.
46. See p. 219, and for further examples and a fuller history, Passmore's book.

Why the Machine Model Cannot Work

If, however, we do consider seriously the sorts of examples I have just been mentioning, and the mass of others from which I have picked them, what shall we say about Descartes' suggestion that animals were indistinguishable from robots?

If there were machines with the organs and appearance of a monkey, or some other irrational animal, we should have no means of telling that they were not altogether of the same nature as those animals; whereas, if there were machines resembling our bodies, and imitating our actions as far as is morally possible, we should still have two means of telling that, all the same, they were not real men. First, they could never use words or other constructed signs. [Second, their performance would be unreliable.][47]

If this were right, we ought to wonder how we ever got the idea that animals were *not* machines, but something conscious. Could it perhaps be something to do with their movements and gestures? Descartes answers, "We must not confuse words with natural movements, the expressions of emotion, which can be imitated by machines as well as [manifested] by animals."[48] But here we begin to see the syndrome that has continued to distort all understanding of this subject. Descartes is simply not concentrating on the animal side of his comparison; he has thrown it off hastily as a contrast to the human side without working it out. Certainly expressive movements can be imitated by machines; but then so (as he points out) can words. So the mark of the conscious, intelligent speaker is not that he answers, but that, by contrast to the machine, he answers *appropriately*—"arranges words variously in response to the meaning of what is said in his presence," as Descartes says. *But this is also true of both animal and human gestures.* We would in fact quickly catch out any gesturing robot for this reason. Whether it was animal or human, speaking or silent, would make very little difference. The sense of appropriateness is prelinguistic. It is also prehuman; dogs would not be taken in. Descartes, worried about the frontier status of the deaf, says, "Men born deaf-mutes . . . usually invent for themselves signs by which they make themselves understood to those

47. *Discourse on Method,* p. 41.
48. Ibid., p. 43.

who are normally with them."[49] They can thus count as rational.
(It seems therefore that Descartes ought to be interested in
Ameslan.) But such pre-set signs are, of course, only a part of
the communicative equipment of the dumb. Harpo Marx does
not need them. And dogs and horses, hawks and elephants, also
"*make themselves understood* to those who are normally with them,"
whether members of their own species or human beings. And
the human beings return the favor. "Making oneself understood" is an immensely wider field than "talking." It supplies the
context, and the only possible context, within which human talking makes sense.

   This brings me to my second question. If animal behavior
(including "speaking" Ameslan) which looks intelligent is not
really intelligent, what is it? In what way are we being had? What
is the alternative, and sounder, way of understanding it?

   It should be made clear at once that *imitation* cannot be the
answer. Imitation is not a substitute for intelligence; it is one way
of applying it. Unintelligent imitation does not work. Intelligent
imitation, the sort that partly grasps the principle of what it is
doing, is one thing among others which intelligent beings can
do. It is obviously an essential element in human learning. In
Apes, Men and Language Linden makes some good remarks about
this, commenting on an occasion when Lucy, having seen him
taking notes, later grabbed his pad and scribbled on it:

> Critics have suggested that any preferences for word order shown by
> the chimpanzee result from imitation of human models without any
> understanding of the significance of word order. Many people are
> tempted to write off any evidence of simian cognitive ability as dumb
> mimicry; however, the job Lucy did in transcribing my notes . . . would
> not have caused me to hire her either as mimic or stenographer, and
> would leave me to doubt that Lucy could precisely imitate behavior if
> she did not know what she was doing. Moreover, Fouts has demon-
> strated that imitation is the least effective method of instruction. [pp.
> 96–97]

Köhler makes the same point that successful imitation involves
insight,[50] and I shall say more about it myself later. Imitation, in

---

49. Ibid., p. 42.
   50. *The Mentality of Apes*, pp. 189–193. This chapter gives a most shrewd and
lucid view of the whole issue. Köhler did what so few experimenters manage to

fact, is only a halfway house, an implausible form of the more general hypothesis that really does appeal to people as simpler and more economical, namely, *mechanism*.[51] Like Descartes, they want to treat the behavior as a stock reaction to a stock stimulus. There are obvious difficulties about using this sort of pattern for spontaneous behavior like that of Mike and Figan. I shall return to them shortly. But the problems are just as grave for nearly all forms of communication, because *interpretation* is needed to produce an appropriate response. Linden quotes from the anthropologist Gordon Hewes, a witness quite sympathetic to the apes, who, however, makes the remark, typical of the common view, that their audio-vocal system is basically an "alarm-system," and adds, "Sound systems only seem to trigger various holistic 'emotional' responses, such as alarm, attention, fear . . . followed by more or less stereotyped behaviour patterns such as flight, attack, protective mothering, submission, and the like."[52] What does it mean to call submission or protective mothering a *stereotyped behavior pattern?* These are immensely wide ranges of behavior. There is no stock item instantly produced, as there should be if "triggering" was an appropriate word. All the details vary according to how the individual sizes up the situation. Certainly there are some sorts of gestures typical of the response, and likely to occur in some form sooner or later. But then that is true for people also. What probably does happen instantly is indeed *attention*. The creature looks up. But this is not a "holistic emotional response," if that is a phrase suitable for alarm and fear. It is a preliminary to taking in the message, not an actual response to it. The response itself takes time, because the message has to be understood before it can be acted on.

The word *response* has, I think, given a quite misleading look

---

do, he really grasped and mapped the range of alternatives he had to deal with. Every word he wrote seems to me still relevant.

51. By *mechanism* I do not mean any metaphysical view on how the world is, but simply the methodical principle of interpreting things by regarding them as if they were machines. This goes far beyond the "reasoning from purpose" I mentioned in Chap. 3, because it assumes that we grasp *completely* the aims for which the thing was designed, and have a right to expect that *nothing will be present except* the minimum means to those ends. This is true of machines, not of organisms.

52. *Apes, Men and Language*, p. 160.

of plausibility to this sort of view, because it has naturally such a wide range of meaning. It can quite rightly be used for the highly sensitive *answering* of a conscious being, but also for entirely mechanical movements:

> The boat responded
> Gaily, to the hand expert with sail and oar.
> The sea was calm, your heart would have responded
> Gaily when invited, beating obedient
> To controlling hands.[53]

The flexibility in the word *respond* is, I think, what makes it possible for people to accept what is in effect a mechanical account of behavior in a being that they do not officially regard as unconscious, without seeing how atrociously this works. The most plausible place for that account certainly is in Hewes's example of *alarm* succeeded by *flight*. But even here two quite different things are possible. If a conscious being always hides himself on hearing a certain alarm cry, it does not follow that this is a "holistic emotional response," that the cry simply and automatically terrifies him into hiding, without reflection. It is also possible that he *interprets the sign,* that he understands the cry as an utterance—whether as a cry of pain or as a warning. The first pattern, the automatic unthinking act of self-protection, obviously is the proper one for some cases. It fits, for instance, the innate hiding response that many young birds show to dangers they have never met before.[54] It also fits the quick response of perfectly sensible adults in intelligent species (including man) to very sudden and violent stimuli, like loud noises. But these are exceptional cases. It is not clear whether they are even rightly called cases of *communication* at all, even if the loud noise does happen to be a cry of alarm. In communication, it should not be the sign itself that directly produces the response, but the reading of the sign. This is clear from the evident possibility of various readings, and particularly of mistakes. George Schaller records: "One female [gorilla] had the tendency to scream loudly every time I arrived near the group. The others ignored her

---

53. T. S. Eliot, *The Waste Land,* 418–422.
54. Described by Tinbergen in *The Herring Gull's World,* p. 215, and also in *The Study of Instinct.*

warning, even when she was out of sight, indicating that they recognized her voice. Apparently she cried 'Wolf!' too often."[55] He remarks that in general "their reaction depends not only on the sound but also on the condition under which it is given and the member of the group who gives it." There is *not*, in fact, a standard "holistic emotional response." Just so, Jane Goodall describes a nervous old female chimp who often misinterprets the expressive movements of those around her, reacting as if to a threat when no threat is present. In the same way, an inexperienced mother will not let other chimps look at her baby, interpreting as threat what is really curiosity. Conversely, chimps may get into trouble by failing to take threats seriously enough. Learning to size them up is an important part of their education and occupies a lot of their attention.[56]

One point that Hewes properly makes is that for apes vocal communication is much *nearer* to mere automatic prodding, because much simpler, than gesturing is. This is evidently true, particularly for gorillas. Schaller, after explaining that the rather small repertory of gorilla noises *are* used and understood as signs, remarks that all the same they do not say much: "In general, vocalizations draw attention to the performer so that he can then impart further news through postures and gestures."[57] They can be viewed, in fact, as rather like human interjections. But even the simplest interjections are not just mechanical stimuli. They are still words, signs addressed to conscious subjects, meant to be understood.

Nor can communications that are answers to others be treated just as mechanical reactions to stimuli. They pose exactly the same problem as the spontaneous activities I have already mentioned; they can be explained only by reference to the views and feelings of the individual concerned. This is every bit as true of animals as it is of people, and everyone who actually has to deal with an animal, however briefly, must unthinkingly assume it. It is not that either animals or people are necessarily always less predictable in their general behavior than physical objects. Some

55. *Year of the Gorilla*, p. 230.
56. *In the Shadow of Man*, pp. 81–82, 146–147, 175.
57. *Year of the Gorilla*, p. 229.

physical objects (such as old machines and thunderstorms) are quite hard to make predictions about; some living beings quite easy. It is that, to make the predictions, we have to, and do, take into account the individual's state of mind, which it makes no sense to do for an alarm clock or a thunderstorm. It is quite true that—as Chomsky points out—people's words are unpredictable, because there is not a finite set of possible remarks, nor a system for calculating them. People's sequences of gestures, however, are unpredictable for exactly the same reason. It would obviously not make much sense to list possible gestures and predict one's friend's performance from the list. This is true not only for exceptional people, but for everybody, including babies. And it is true for animals as well.

Anyone who doubts this should attend to the phenomenon of play. Neither human nor animal babies begin their lives at all as the mechanistic reactive theories would wish, by waiting passively to be acted on, and then imitating mechanically what is done around them. Instead both equally take the initiative. And among all the more intelligent species, they play—that is, they act, quite spontaneously and entirely for fun, in ways *not* current among the adults around them. As machines do not do this, they are little use as models for explaining it. The machine model may well fit what is happening inside the nerves and brain. But this is little help to us at the stage where we ask, for instance, "What on earth is that child doing?" The answer may be, "He is play-growling and trying to pull the rug away to tease the dog." But exactly the same answer is possible for the dog's play-growling and pulling the rug away to tease the boy. Both, equally, let you know what they are doing by their gestures. For both species equally, every individual performs differently, and differently each time. For both equally, a true stereotype, an unchanging response, is *alarming*, is a symptom of something wrong. For both, failure to be appropriate, to respond sensitively to variations in social behavior around them, is also alarming, and so is apathy—simply sitting around and waiting for a stimulus to respond to. Equally from children and young animals, we expect a steady fountain of fairly unpredictable behavior, which will have to be interpreted in the light of their characters and feelings, not just attributed to causes. And we are seldom disappointed. Young creatures of all intelligent species are essentially creative and innovative.[58] This spontaneity is not what is peculiar to man. People who want to assert the uniqueness of language will do better to look, first, to the conventional nature of its signs, second, to the extraordinary thoroughness with which their possibilities have been exploited.

Understanding What Language Does

People concerned with the specialness of language may, however, answer that it is nothing to do with all I have been describing, but something quite different again. Thus Chomsky says that studies of animal communication only "bring out more clearly the extent to which human language appears to be a unique phenomenon, without significant analogue in the animal world."[59] In some ways, of course, it *is* unique, but why must it be "without significant analogue"? He goes on that "assuming an evolutionary development of language from simpler systems of the sort that one discovers in other organisms" has no more basis than "assuming an evolutionary development from breathing to walking" (p. 60); they are simply not stages of the same process. He concludes that it must be "an example of true emergence— the appearance of a qualitatively different phenomenon at a specific stage of complexity of organization" (p. 62). He observes therefore that "it seems rather pointless, for these reasons, to speculate about the evolution of human language from simpler systems—perhaps as absurd as it would be to speculate about the evolution of atoms from clouds of elementary particles."

Now incomprehension is not an advantage. We should put up with it only when it is really necessary. And this particular piece

58. I use these words in the wide and quite proper sense in which Chomsky constantly uses them, applying them to speech generally—not in the narrower and stronger one in which they would only apply to geniuses. Chomsky quotes von Humboldt's splendid remark that "the speaker makes infinite use of finite means" (*Language and Mind* [New York, 1968], p. 15). All I am pointing out here is that the player does the same.

59. *Language and Mind*, p. 59. All Chomsky quotations in this chapter come from this book.

of incomprehension seems to me simply the nemesis of treating language with peculiar narrowness, as though nothing mattered about it except certain abstract patterns. If the evolution of speech were really incomprehensible—if nothing in human life provided a particularly suitable setting for it—it ought to be just as conceivable that it should arise in any other species, say, crocodiles. The question of *understanding* it is not one of tracing the mechanics of evolution, of saying just what mutations or selections were necessary to bring about the change. ("Emergent evolution" describes a sudden large change whose mechanics are uncertain—for example, beginning to fly). But understanding a habit is, I have suggested, seeing what company it keeps, what it does for us, what part it plays in our lives.

Chomsky concedes that "the examples of animal communication that have been examined to date do share many of the properties of human gestural systems, and it might be reasonable to explore the possibility of direct connection in this case" (p. 62). But this seems to leave gestures totally divided from language—insulated from it by an immense evolutionary gap like that between atoms and clouds of elementary particles. Descartes' wedge, here as so often, tries to split the unsplittable. You can only accept this idea, I think, if you have your mind entirely on *printed* language. It is a splendid and remarkable feature of human language that it *can* be printed—its fruits are not only larger than those on other communication trees, they also keep. They can be picked and transported and used a couple of thousand years later, and this is indeed glorious. But it does not make irrelevant the tree on which they grew in the first place, and on which each new example must still grow. Most human language, even for the most literate of us, is spoken, not written. And when it is spoken, the words themselves are only the peak of a pyramid, of which tone of voice, gestures, facial and bodily expression, pace, timing, silences, and the relation of the whole to what is going on at the time form the major part. To see what I mean by *major*, anyone can try the experiment of saying his words in a tone and with gestures which do not suit them. This is not easy to do. It is difficult in just the same way as making two consecutive remarks that do not make sense together, or saying the words in the wrong order. Our habitual sense of order and meaning protests against it. But if it is done, one thing is certain—the hearer can not just accept the words at their face value. A conflict is set up, and the words are not going to win it. The tone, gesture, and so on will be taken as probably *more* informative than the words. And in a natural example, this will nearly always be right. (One such example is the familiar case of the person being asked for help, who speaks at great length and apparently helpfully—but whose manner conveys instantly to the practiced observer the real message, "I cannot do anything for you and am not even going to try.") The relation between the words and the way they are spoken is *not,* I am suggesting, just that between any two chance aspects of an organism, like "breathing and walking." It is conceptual; they are parts of the same meaning-system. We use them as complementary tools for the same job. Is that meaning-system then impoverished when the speaker is not present? It would be, if our imagination were not so prompt and active in reproducing him. This is plain when people reading letters from someone they have been missing are delighted to "hear his voice" in the written words, or pained when they fail to do so, and also in the difficulties of telephone communication. Again, in reading good novels or plays, we may not attend much to the inner dramatization by which we bring the ink marks to life—but that it has been going on becomes suddenly and painfully manifest when we see bad stage or television performances of them. "Darcy was never like that," we howl, and rightly. It is worth remarking too that until this century novels were always meant to be read aloud.[60]

With nondramatic prose—straight description or argument— things are a little less simple, but I think essentially the same. We feel the difference between a mincing, artificial style and a direct, straightforward one as a difference in tone. We do "hear the writer's voice," and it affects us *not* just with an irrelevant liking or disliking for him, but with a sense of his

---

60. These aspects of speech have surfaced into the interests of linguists in the last decade and are now receiving a good deal of attention. See David Crystal, *The English Tone of Voice* (London, 1975) and the index to Linden's book, under *Paralanguage.*

whole personality which modifies the meaning of what he says. Hume's or Plato's tone of voice comes through the centuries, sharp and unmistakable, filling in for the imagination a whole immense background of personal reaction that completes the sense of what they are literally saying, making all the differences between an isolated argument and a comprehensive view of life, between, in fact, a little philosopher and a great one.

Even quite simple informative prose is never wholly detached from its writer. We always need to know enough about him to grasp how reliable he is and what he can be relied on *for*. Style helps to sort out the honest but unimaginative informant from the smart aleck, the dispassionate from the prejudiced witness, the original investigator from the zombie. The great flexibility of language allows everybody to leave his private mark. But the more we need to check on his reliability, the more anxious we are not to stop at mere words, but if possible to meet the writer face to face.

I am making the fairly obvious point that speech is only part of the way in which a person communicates. The creative and innovative recombining of signs, which Chomsky so rightly emphasizes in our use of words, appears also in our joining of them to particular gestures, facial expressions, looks, silences, whistles and nonverbal activities of every kind. "Human gestural systems" are not separate, self-contained entities. They are aspects abstracted from the one great communication system. The relation of gestures anywhere to the local language is organic. A foreigner must grasp them, as much as the tense structure and the polite forms of address, if he does not want to misunderstand and be misunderstood. What makes the grasping easier, and often stops us from noticing that it is taking place is that, though there is a conventional element, the basis of gesture is innate and universal. Local variation is not very great. But while our general basic equipment of expressive movements is innate,[61] we are also innately equipped to vary the details in any context indefinitely, for both cultural and private reasons. That

---

61. See Eibl-Eibesfeldt, *Love and Hate,* for a careful and convincing analysis of the range.

is how we are able constantly to signify our changing attitudes to one another. Now it seems reasonable to say that our power of varying our words and their order is a further special development of this basic communicative power. Speech makes sense only for a species that is already constantly communicating by expressive movements.

Understanding What Expressive Movements Do

I have suggested that one thing that obscures the continuity of language with other ways of communicating is a too abstract notion of language. But a too abstract notion of what animals are up to is also disastrous. Chomsky says that all animal communication either "consists of a fixed, finite number of signals, each associated with a specific range of behavior or emotional state, as is illustrated by the extensive primate studies that have been carried out by Japanese scientists for the past several years; or it makes use of a fixed, finite number of linguistic dimensions" (p. 61). Now the "fixed, finite number of signals" is obviously a contribution of the classifying observer. If he is piling up statistics, he must count such things as bows, retreats, and charging displays as standard units. His account will thus mislead casual readers in the same way as the townsman's observation that all sheep are exactly alike, or the Westerner's similar observation about Chinamen. To see this, we need only set up our observer from Alpha Centauri with his notebook to watch the guests arriving at a scholarly conference. Those who meet, he records, may ignore or avoid each other, or they may nod, bow, smile, wave in passing, or sometimes stop, shake hands, pat each others arms, or even embrace. (He is not concerned with talk, and neither need we be.) It is a fixed, finite number of signals. He cannot distinguish their qualities, and can take little account even of intensity. Where he does note it, he is in no position to deal with the real nerve of a communication system, the relation of each act to expectations in its background and context. He observes two smiles and waves that seem perfectly standard. But one was actually the first stumbling and painful move toward reconciliation of two people who have been quarreling bitterly for years; the other was a carefully formal greeting between colleagues who are beginning to hate each other to the point of open violence. Nor does he know anything about Jones, who typically just gives us that distant wave though he has known us for twenty years and is really fond of us. A novelist would get the point quickly enough, because he is interested in his characters' fate and behavior in depth and through time. So will an ethologist, when he is concerned not with the initial process of classification but with the subtler discrimination that must follow it, and eventually with the histories of individuals. He is not *merely* a classifier. But of course his business, like that of a sociologist or anthropologist, does call on him sometimes to classify. And like them, when doing so he can give a very crude impression.

Chomsky's point about "linguistic dimensions" is similar. This means ranges of signal corresponding merely to ranges of intensity in single dispositions of the sender. So, for instance, in the robin, "rate of alternation of high and low pitch is a linguistic dimension correlated with the non-linguistic dimension of intention to defend a territory" (p. 61). The robin, that is, can give you *more* or *less* of a keep-out-or-else signal, but nothing more. What there shall be more or less of he cannot vary.

This account is misleading even for birds. Directly signaling a *hypothetical intention* of the form, "if x, then I shall do y to extent z" would actually be a quite sophisticated performance. (Plenty of people, after all, deny that animals can have intentions at all.) And territorial birdsong goes on whether anyone approaches or not, very much as a baby's crying does. There are people who interpret the baby's crying too as an expression of intention ("He's just letting you know who's master") or a device for dominance ("He's just trying it on"). But crying can be put to these secondary uses only if it succeeds in its original and deeper function, which is expressing discomfort. Any baby must begin by crying for that reason alone. Just so, the bird's song is not just a mechanical advance indicator of the violence with which intruders will actually be repelled. The bird has to have a feeling to express *before* intruders appear, and he keeps it up even when they are clearly not going to. The song must be primarily expressive. What it says is, "Hurrah, hurrah, it's me, it's mine, I've got it, I am the greatest," with marked variations according to personality and mood in every case, so that, as the ethologist Bäumer put it, the message is not just "here is a cock," but "here is the cock Balthazar." [62] The song *does* warn off possible trespassers, and this can rightly be said to be its function *from the point of view of the species*. But the bird does not stand at that point of view. He has a different sort of reason for singing.

When we come to the more advanced mammals, moreover, the simple functional notion is no more true than it is for human beings. (The idea of "animal communication" in the abstract, as something standard, found equally in bees, birds, apes, and dolphins, is terribly misleading). Human smiling certainly can be treated as having a "linguistic dimension," since, by and large, it signals a degree of friendliness. But there are so many kinds of friendliness, and the smile can be combined in so many ways with other expressive elements, that the linear pattern of degrees only is quite misleading. Exactly the same is true of friendly gestures in dog or ape. No doubt there is a linear dimension of intensity, but there is so much lateral variation, there are so many other aspects of life involved, that it is never a standard unit.

There is something odd, too, in the move Chomsky makes to get this linear dimension right out of human speech: "When I make some arbitrary statement in a human language, say, that 'the rise of multi-national corporations poses new dangers for human freedom,' I am not selecting a point along some linguistic dimension that signals a corresponding point along an associated non-linguistic dimension" (p. 61). But this statement, if seriously meant, is a *warning*. Someone who makes it, if he is not just talking for the sake of talking, ought certainly to have, and to mean to communicate, an idea of how grave a warning he means it to be. He takes his stand somewhere on that dimension. Serious remarks, even in print, are intended to commit the writer to a certain position. And, of course, they often plainly signal, among other things, the intention to attack or defend a

---

62. Lorenz, *On Aggression*, p. 34.

territory with a certain degree of intensity. (An excellent example is the opening sentence of *Language, Truth and Logic*—"The traditional disputes of philosophers are for the most part as unwarranted as they are unfruitful. . . .")

In denying this, Chomsky is rightly resisting the idea that language is simply a manipulative device: "If I speak with no concern for modifying your behavior and thought, I am not using language any less than if I say exactly the same things *with* intention. If we hope to understand human language and the psychological capacities on which it rests, we must first ask *what* it is, not how and for what purposes it is used. When we ask what human language is, we find no striking similarity to animal communication systems" (p. 62). *What* it is however must include its own essential function; it just excludes alien functions. And even speech that has no concern for modifying other people's behavior and thoughts still has to have a meaning. In talking to himself, or talking just to relieve his feelings, a speaker still tries to make sense. He is his own listener. And this is quite as true of expressive speech as it is of other kinds. As R. G. Collingwood pointed out, *expressing emotion* is not just a mechanical operation like pouring milk.[63] It is a crystallizing, a defining of the indefinite; it makes clearer and firmer what was chaotic and only half-recognizable. We can "find out what we mean when we see what we say," that is, at the same time as other people, if any are present. This is one of the essential jobs of speech, not just a secondary exploitation of it. *But the same is true of human gestures.* Throwing something down on hearing a piece of news does the same clarifying job, both for the thrower and for others, as swearing. It manifests his feeling, not just as an undifferentiated flood, but as a certain kind and degree of annoyance, indignation, despair, or whatever. In such ways do we "make ourselves understood," both to ourselves and each other. Now human gestures are, both in their general arrangement and in many details, far too close to primate gestures[64] for it to make any sense to deny that this is true of apes as well. I think the wish to

---

63. See his discussion of expression in *The Principles of Art* (Oxford, 1938).
64. As Eibl-Eibesfeldt and many others have shown in careful detail.

deny it comes from the traditional notion that apes are essentially mechanical, which is not dispelled by essentially classifying accounts. We need to look instead at some of the detailed descriptions of behavior, particularly behavior that is mainly expressive—for instance at accounts of those remarkable activities that throw a sharp and sudden light on the origins of human sport and dancing:

At about noon the first heavy drops of rain began to fall. The chimpanzees climbed out of the tree and, one after the other, plodded up the steep grassy slope toward the open ridge at the top. . . . At that moment the storm broke. The rain was torrential and the sudden clap of thunder, right overhead, made me jump. As if this were a signal, one of the big males stood upright and as he swayed and swaggered rhythmically from foot to foot I could just hear the rising crescendo of his pant-hoots above the beating of the rain. Then he charged off, flat-out down the slope toward the trees he had just left. He ran some thirty yards, and then, swinging round the trunk of a small tree to break his headlong rush, leaped into the low branches and sat motionless.

Almost at once two other males charged after him. One broke off a low branch from a tree as he ran and brandished it in the air before hurling it ahead of him. The other, as he reached the end of his run, stood upright and rhythmically swayed the branches of a tree back and forth, before seizing a huge branch and dragging it farther down the slope. A fourth male, as he too charged, leaped into a tree and, almost without breaking his speed, tore off a large branch, leaped with it to the ground, and continued down the slope. As the last two males called and charged down, so the one who had started the whole performance climbed from his tree and began plodding up the slope again. The others, who had also climbed into trees near the bottom of the slope, followed suit. When they reached the ridge, they started charging down all over again, one after the other, with equal vigor.[65]

This went on for twenty minutes. Jane Goodall remarks that only twice more, in the course of ten years, did she see such a performance; "often, it is true, male chimpanzees react to the start of heavy rain by performing a rain dance, but this is usually an individual affair." Wolfgang Köhler recorded many equally striking goings-on; this passage is typical:

Tshego and Grande were playing together on a box. Presently Grande rose upright, and . . . began to stamp first one foot and then the other,

65. *In the Shadow of Man*, pp. 52–53.

till the box shook. Meanwhile, Tschego slipped from the box, rose upright, and slowly revolved round her own axis in front of Grande, springing clumsily and heavily—but springing—from one foot to the other. They appeared to incite each other to these antics and to be in the best of tempers.... I have frequent notes of such behaviour.... The whole group of chimpanzees sometimes combined in more elaborate *motion-patterns*. For instance, two would wrestle and tumble about playing near some post; soon their movements would become more regular and tend to describe a circle around the post as centre. One after another, the rest of the group approach, join the two, and finally they march in an orderly fashion and in single file round the post. The character of their movements changes; they no longer walk, they trot, and as a rule with special emphasis on one foot, while the other steps lightly; thus a rough approximate rhythm develops, and they tend to 'keep time' with one another. They wag their heads to the steps of their 'dance' and appear full of eager enjoyment of their primitive game. Variations are invented time and time again; now and then an ape went backwards, snapping drolly at the one behind him.[66]

If one described children doing these things, no one would find it in the least surprising, and the connections with the development of social communication on the one hand and of art on the other would pass as obvious (though I do not know that they would be well understood).[67] How could a totally different kind of explanation be called for in the case of apes?

Naturally, this sort of thing is not just what goes on at the Bolshoi Ballet. But it does something to indicate on what bush, growing out of what soil, ballet is a flower. Again, the ape paintings collected and discussed by Desmond Morris in *The Biology of Art* are not being set up to compete with human paintings—though it is a matter of some interest that both Picasso and Herbert Read admired and bought Congo's pictures. Since they were done without reward, they do show two things, however: first, how deep-rooted in our ancestry is the spontaneous interest in certain sorts of arrangements of form and color, and the delight in producing them, and second, how the ape's natural

---

66. *The Mentality of Apes*, p. 266.

67. See for instance Huizinga's suggestions in *Homo Ludens* about the seminal place of play in human activities. Caroline Loizos has a most thoughtful paper on primate play in *Primate Ethology*, ed. Morris, in which she raises central questions about the function and meaning of play. See also my article "The Game Game," *Philosophy*, 49 (1974).

emotional and expressive tendencies readily flow through devices of human invention to expand their range. The chimps' eager acceptance of Ameslan is only another example of this. And I am myself much more impressed with how eagerly they do accept it, how much they want it, than concerned about whether their use of it corresponds exactly with human use. The *wish* to communicate more freely is the interesting factor. But this wish, though interesting, should be no sort of surprise to anyone who has read or heard about the highly sociable life that apes already lead. The surprising thing is how successfully theorists seem to have managed to resist this information, which has long been freely available. Linden cites the view of linguist Charles Hockett that only after man invented language did communication acquire "a life of its own, . . . [it] left man with an additional consuming drive beyond *the drives of hunger and sex*—a need to communicate. . . . Lack of communication, says Hockett, will blight the human spirit, and, he claims, this is not true of any other animal."[68] The total falsity of this last remark is obvious to anyone who ever comes back to a dog that has been left alone for an afternoon, let alone anyone who reads about the problems of keeping solitary monkeys. The suggestion seems to be that man invented loneliness. For this, he would have had to have invented love. A quite unjustified ambition to be credited with that invention may have something to do with these claims.

Chimps pose a special problem. They have, and often reveal in experiments, a good deal more intelligence than they normally use in the wild. How did they develop it? Some zoologists suspect that they are degenerate, that increasingly easy conditions have led them to slip some way back on the evolutionary path they once traveled. The Ameslan experiments, if they go on without serious setback, seem to suggest that, if they did backslide, they did so just about the point when our own ancestors somehow made, instead, their great leap forward. If one supposes chimplike creatures among whom there occurs a mutation, providing all at once much better control of the larynx, does that give us speech? I am inclined to think that it might, granted two other things which both seem possible. One is that

68. *Apes, Men and Language,* p. 147, my italics,

there must already be a clear advantage in communicating orally rather than by gestures. A number of things could bring this about, such as the need to be heard at a distance, or having one's hands otherwise occupied. Any slightly ambitious cooperative scheme, tool use and manual dexterity generally, or indeed swimming,[69] could make the use of speech rather than gestures pay instant dividends. The other requirement, and it is the one central thing that people forget, is intensity of motivation. To compel a general change as strenuous as learning to use conventional instead of natural signs, it is not enough for an exceptional individual or two to be born capable of starting the game. All must take the trouble to join in it. Here I am impressed by a detail in the history of an Ameslan-using chimp called Bruno: "At first, he had little interest in mimicking these strange movements he was asked to perform. Fouts says that when he first started to teach him 'hat' . . . Bruno would look at him with mild curiosity as if to say, 'I'd really like to help you, but I can't for the life of me understand what it is you want me to do.' After a while Fouts got exasperated and threatened Bruno. Bruno immediately started signing, 'hat, hat, hat.'"[70] The pressure here was quite slight and artificial, but it worked. It seems plausible that some genuine emergency must have performed the same trick, have made the use of conventional signs fearfully pressing, whether before or after the human larynx became usable. But it could only have done so in a species uncommonly determined to solve its difficulties socially. What we need to make the origin of speech intelligible, in fact, is a line of hominids which does not just have a lucky mutation, but has in general the right temperament—is exceptionally cooperative, persistent, and thorough in using what it gets. They must not just be lucky opportunists; they must be stayers. As Desmond Morris has pointed out, this kind of disposition is less common in

69. The suggestion that man may for a time have been aquatic is attractive in a number of ways, though it does not yet have (as far as I know) the archaeological evidence it needs for acceptance. See Elaine Morgan, *The Descent of Woman* (New York, 1972: a useful book in any case to counterpoise the *machismo* of Ardrey and Desmond Morris), and also Morris himself, *The Naked Ape* (London, 1967), pp. 43–45.

70. Linden, *Apes, Men and Language*, p. 126.

primates, who do not usually work hard for their living, than it is in carnivores. The special development of people has led human life to converge in many structural properties with those of the big dogs and cats. They have become (everywhere, not just in certain cultures) much more persistent, cooperative, strenuous, territorial, pugnacious, constant, acquisitive, and given to pair-bonding than most other primates—not just more intelligent. And that same tendency to persist in and thoroughly *use* every faculty, instead of pottering around contentedly at the rudimentary stage, would be needed also for their success in language. One way and another, in fact, sheer stout-hearted persistance could be the crucial distinctive factor that led the species to out-distance and eventually put out of business all its near relatives and competitors, thereby leaving itself in that strange isolation which has made it so deeply confused about its status.

This kind of explanation seems to me not only to leave quite undamaged the serious points that matter to linguists like Chomsky, but actually to suit them much better than Descartes' dualistic account. Chomsky, quite rightly, insists that our linguistic faculties are *innate*. But if they are, they need an inherited physical basis. It would be very strange for them to occur in isolation, in the absence of other complex innate faculties. Had we been otherwise blank paper at birth, it is hard to see how language could have come out of us. Blotting paper does not talk. But if we are beings with a rich and complex nature, containing many innate needs and capacities—if our whole emotional and imaginative constitution unfolds according to certain general patterns that shape our social life and make communication possible—then language ceases to be a kind of unaccountable miracle. Along with tool use, mathematics, and the arts, it is just one case, though an impressive one, of a skill natural to us, and essential for the structure of human life.

CHAPTER 11

On Being Animal as well as Rational

The Unity of Our Nature

I have suggested that, instead of a single distinguishing mark for man, we look rather for a knot of general structural properties, and have considered how language might form part of such a knot, instead of being an isolated miracle. This chapter will do the same for that other most venerable and impressive candidate for the position of distinguishing mark, rationality.

This discussion of rationality may strike hasty readers as perverse, because its purpose is so different from that of most treatments of the subject. They are usually concerned essentially to *celebrate* reason, and to stress what is unique about it. This celebration I wholeheartedly accept and take for granted. (It ought, I think, to be obvious by now that I am not short of respect either for reason itself or for the great Western tradition of using it.) My present purpose, however, is the distinct and supplementary one of asking how this unique thing, rationality, is possible in a being that is not just a disembodied intellect, but also and among other things some kind of animal, how it fits into such a life. Thus it will constantly be my business to look at the pattern on the other side of the carpet, at the continuity. I am asking about reason what I have been asking about language, namely, what links it to the rest of nature? what part does it play in our life? To understand this, I shall examine, through animal parallels, what conditions must have been necessary in a prerational creature if reasoning was to develop and what, therefore, must be retained as a setting for reason? I do this, not in the belief that reason can be "reduced" to nonrational elements, but from the desire to make sense of our nature as a whole—to find how each of us can regard himself as one thing, not two, when part of our nature is prerational. I have said that it is not clear how a creature such as Plato and Descartes described could ever have evolved without celestial interference. Amputating the Cartesian Immortal Soul and leaving the rest of the compound untouched does not, as some people think, help us. The intellect is still left as an alien intruder in the world.

As for celestial interference, it obviously does not make sense in a nonreligious context. But I do not think it does so in a Christian one either. Christianity is not Platonism. If God created through evolution, he surely designed it and used it properly. As I shall suggest, Bishop Butler, who was no atheist, points us toward a far more coherent view of human wholeness than Descartes. How immortality is to be conceived is certainly a difficult problem, but it is so whatever you do. Descartes' shortcut creates as many problems as it solves about *what* survives. Every religion in fact demands that far more should survive than the Intellect.

But the chief difficulty about accepting continuity between man and other species, or between the human intellect and the rest of man, now comes not from traditional religion, but from those who do amputate the soul. It stems from the deep reverence people now feel for human success, and particularly for success in science. In this area, people often do not realize how many of the difficulties raised by religion they are needlessly keeping while officially jettisoning its metaphysics. They revere what they take to be the highest human capacities, particularly the speculative intellect, so deeply that they are inclined to find natural explanations of them quite as blasphemous as religious people used to find natural explanations of the religious faculties. Reverence for humanity, which at first is a most respectable tendency, often slips across into overtly religious form. Thus

Auguste Comte instituted a regular "worship of humanity" with rituals and a temple in Paris.[1] Thus Nietzsche, after killing off God, came near to worshiping the future of the human race in the form of the Superman. And H. G. Wells called one of his utopian future-fantasies *Men Like Gods*. Wells moreover endued man with so much of the divine prerogative that he called upon him to "bring to trial" every other earthly organism from the rhinoceros to the tubercle bacillus, and alter it to his satisfaction or get rid of it.[2] It is much easier, it seems, to disown a particular God than to get rid of his empty seat and the paranoia that so readily surrounds it. Wells's bold and forceful imagination is very useful to us here, because he made explicit what is often covered up—that the only reason for man's having this status was supposed to be what Wells called his intelligence—by which he meant mere cleverness, calculating power, the sort of thing that can be measured by intelligence tests. The future people in *Men Like Gods* are almost purely intellectual—they have, with a few despised exceptions, got rid of "human weaknesses" such as loving one person better than another. (Significantly, they do not wear clothes.) Wells understood, however, that this meant that any *more* intelligent species, if one appeared, would have the same right to get rid of man. He explained this at the outset of *The War of the Worlds*, where the superintelligent Martians, who are nothing but enormous heads on mechanical trolleys, set out as a matter of course to annihilate the human race without examining it. They are, Wells says, merely exercising the same obvious right we ourselves have always exercised over "the cow and the cucumber."

Much science fiction has followed Wells in this competitive way of reasoning, which has obvious attractions for those who like the popping of ray guns and the sound of titles like *Master of a Thousand Universes*. It is, however, very obscure. What is supposed to be *that* good about cleverness? Being clever is not obviously so much more important than being kind, brave, friendly,

1. I shall come back to the problems about humanism in the concluding sections of this book.
2. In *A Modern Utopia* (1906), the work in which the real genius of the early Wells began to give way to "humanist" paranoia.

patient, and generous that it inevitably confers an instant right
of general massacre. And those qualities cannot be supposed to
follow from cleverness, or be included in it; we know that the
two kinds of thing can be found apart. Modern humanists cannot, of course, fall back on Plato's way of talking and say that the
intellect is man's divinest faculty, his highest dignity, his link with
God, the bridge by which he can approach a reality greater than
himself, a mode of action superior to the grossness of physical
matter, or anything remotely resembling those notions. If they
are good Utilitarians (as Wells was), they should regard it only as
one means among others to securing pleasure. And an impartial
comparison of hedonic level between intellectuals and other
types, or between simple and advanced civilizations, is not likely
to suggest that it is an especially efficient one, at least not so much
as to settle out of hand and with no reference to any other
qualities, the question of who is to exterminate whom. Is there
actually anything more to the position that the intellect is primary than the argument which G. E. Moore noted as being
relied on against the North American Indians (we are more
advanced than they are because we can kill them faster than they
can kill us)?[3] If not, I find the intellectualist fluff in which it is
wrapped up a depressing product after the efforts of the Enlightenment.

What this way of talking relies on, of course, is the immense
respect that both common sense and the philosophic tradition
give to rationality. But rationality is not just cleverness. Even the
word *intelligence* is often used to mean a good deal more than
what Wells meant. And *rationality* always means more. It includes
a definite structure of preferences, a priority system based on
feeling. Now that kind of structure is not peculiar to the human
race, but is also found in the higher animals.

In the philosophic tradition, Reason, though not always
equated with mere intellect, has usually been sharply opposed to
Feeling or Desire. This has determined the attitude of most
respectable philosophers to the related subjects of animals and
human feelings. They have usually just dismissed animal activities from all comparision with human ones, on the general

3. *Principia Ethica*, p. 47.

ground that, in man, decision is a formal, rational process, while animals have only feeling, which is a kind of wholly contingent slop or flow, bare matter without form, so that its analysis cannot concern philosophy. Thus, typically, even Hume, who really did want to show that feeling mattered, went to great trouble to show it simply as an undifferentiated physical force, much like gravitation, moving people in much the same sense in which gravitation moved billiard balls. *Understanding* it, for him, simply meant fitting it into a scheme of mechanics, which should be as economical and simple as possible. (Here the modern Emotivists are his successors, boiling down feeling to the straight dynamic function of being for or against something). Hume wanted to be the Newton of psychology, an ambition that unluckily has survived him.[4] Psychology did not and does not need a Newton. It needed, and still needs, a Darwin—a careful, patient, thorough observer, who would *distinguish* the various forms of motivation, relate and compare them, and eventually work out concepts suitable for classifying and explaining them, rather than imposing slapdash fashion an unsuitable model from an alien science.

Because I need to use the common philosophical language of *form* and *matter,* I must digress here to explain that the traditional use of these terms has been oversimple.

It will not do to analyze motivation once and for all into Thought as Form, and Feeling as blank, contingent, undifferentiated Matter. It will not do because the distinction of form and matter is never final; it is always a repeatable one. All actual matter has a form; all actual forms fit a matter. For instance, when Aristotle gave the name *hylê, wood,* to matter, he was thinking of a carpenter imposing form on wood by making it into a table. But of course, the wood before that was not just neutral stuff. It already had its own form. It was beech or pine, with a definite grain and structure. If further form was to be imposed on it, the wood would have to be chosen and prepared. (You cannot make a table out of neutral stuff, nor from a transverse

4. See *Enquiry Concerning the Principles of Morals,* secs. 163, 192, 227. It was in exactly the same spirit that Moore gave his book the pretentious title *Principia Ethica* and repeatedly claimed in it to be initiating a "scientific" treatment of the subject. See, for example, p. 4 of that work.

slice across a freshly cut pine trunk, nor from chalk or honeycomb either.) And, to look in the other direction, the completed table along with other furniture can be treated as matter, raw material for the art of the moving man, the art historian, or the interior decorator. And so forth. So, though it is quite true that the philosopher's business is with forms, it never follows that he can disregard matter, nor that what is treated as matter for one particular inquiry will not show its formal element in another. It all depends what you are trying to do at the time.

Feeling has its forms, both in man and other species. If it had not, reason could make nothing of it, and rational decision would be impossible. The crude antithesis between feeling and reason, form and matter, is inadequate even to map the human scene—before we start trying to look for some continuity between man and other species, as we must to make evolution intelligible. If you treat morality as entirely a matter of formless feeling (as Hume did) or entirely a formal matter (as Kant did), you oversimplify disastrously. Moreover, bluntly opposing feeling and reason is inclined to lead to personifying them. Hume, who quite rightly said, "we speak not strictly and philosophically when we talk of the combat of passion and of reason," nonetheless fell into this trap when he added that "reason is, and ought only to be, the slave of the passions, and can never pretend to any other office than to serve and obey them." Making these two abstractions into Employer and Employed is no better than setting them to fight it out like a couple of drunks. "Reason" is not the name of a character in a drama. It is a name for organizing oneself. When there is a conflict, one desire *must* be restrained to make way for the other. It is the process of *choosing which* that is rightly called reasoning. But the ill effects of the dramatization constantly appear in Romantic writing, for instance, Blake's *Marriage of Heaven and Hell:*

Those who restrain desire, do so because theirs is weak enough to be restrained; and the restrainer or reason usurps its place and governs the unwilling.
And being restrained, it by degrees become passive, till it is only the shadow of desire.
The history of this is written in *Paradise Lost,* and the Governor or Reason is called Messiah.

Romantics like Blake gave the name Reason to desires they disapproved of—say, caution, or the force of habit, or a mere dreary negativeness—and reserved that of Desire or Passion for the ones they favored. This has become common usage, but it is a mess. Reason and feeling are aspects of all our motives.[5] Feelings themselves have a form, and one that fits the matter. In fact, of course, it can be our duty to *feel* in one way rather than another—something for which the tradition has little room. (Criticism of "the undeveloped heart" is moral criticism.[6]) Practical reasoning would be impossible were not some preferences "more rational" than others. Rationality includes having the right priorities. And deep, lasting preferences linked to character traits are formally a quite different proposition from sharp, isolated impulses.

The higher animals have a structure of deep, lasting preferences too. So in showing the importance of a definite, lasting structure of feeling in human life, we show that we can rightly compare it with the parallel (though distinct) structures found in other species.

We lose nothing by this. It does not infringe on the distinctively human structural properties involved in conceptual thought and language. Acting for the common good deliberately and consciously, with a full understanding that you could do otherwise, and after explicit reflection on the alternatives, is a very different thing from doing it unthinkingly. Backing a principle that you can *state* is a very different thing from just steadily acting on it. All the same—as Kant himself recognized[7]—it is a

5. Reason has moons, but moons not hers
    Lie mirror'd on her sea,
   Confounding her astronomers
      But O! delighting me.   —Ralph Hodgson

6. See an admirable article by Nicholas Dent, "Duty and Inclination," *Mind,* 83 (1974).

7. I cannot do any justice here to the subtlety of Kant's position. Right at the outset of his argument in the *Grundlegung* he allowed that good feeling, like happiness, did have value in itself, though that value was *conditional* on the state of the will—that is, a bad will could negate it. About the talents, and perhaps even happiness, this makes good sense. But it is not so clear that good feeling loses all value if the will is bad—nor, indeed, quite what "the will" is under such conditions.

very narrow notion of value which *confines* it to the rational and deliberate, and does not prize good feeling itself.

Let me try now to explain, however roughly, what I mean by the structure, or constitution of human nature, so as to understand the place of the feelings within it.

I want to get away from the essentially *colonial* picture (used by Blake) in which an imported governor, named Reason, imposes order on a chaotic alien tribe of Passions or Instincts. The colonial picture, which is Plato's, was handed down through the Stoics, Descartes and Spinoza, to Kant.[8] It performed a very good service by honoring Thought. But once doubt arose about how thought could establish values, it ceased to do so. Schopenhauer, Nietzsche and the Existentialists changed the governor's name from Reason to Will. Kant spoke of the will, but he meant by it reason in action—"the Will is nothing but Practical Reason."[9] But the will now stands mainly for arrogance, arbitrariness, and contempt for the natural facts.[10]

Instead of being colonial, I want to look at the continuity—to use Bishop Butler's (and to some extent Aristotle's[11]) picture, to talk of what Butler called "the whole system, as I may speak, of affections, *including rationality*, which constitute the Heart."[12] I

8. For example, *Grundlegung*, end of chap. 1: "Reason, without promising anything to inclination, enjoins its commands relentlessly, and therefore, so to speak, with disregard and neglect of these seemingly equitable claims, which refuse to be suppressed by any command" (Paton tr., p. 70).

9. Ibid., chap. 2, sec. 36 (Paton tr., p. 76).

10. As Iris Murdoch argues in *The Sovereignty of Good*, this seems just as true of the muted, polite, Anglo-Saxon kind of Existentialism found in philosophers such as Stuart Hampshire as in the splashily colored European variety.

11. Aristotle's position too is far too complex to be condensed here. I have called him down once or twice in this book for a kind of Greek intellectualist arrogance which he shared with Plato, but which I do not think was at all central in his thought. (It is what puts off many readers of the *Politics*.) On the positive side, however, he stands as *the* biologist among philosophers—indeed as the inventor of the biological attitude, which takes the world as a continuous organic whole to be studied and accepted on its own terms, not as a tiresome mass of matter tolerable only because it instantiates mathematical laws. This is beyond praise. Moreover, his method in the *Nicomachean Ethics* is exactly the one I am trying to follow here. He understands morality as the expression of natural human needs. This side of his work was largely ignored by the tradition, because biology itself was neglected. Obsession with the mathematical model, predominant in both Plato and Descartes, has left a terrible gap here.

12. Sermon 12, "Upon the Love of our Neighbour," sec. 11.

want to consider reason as growing out of and completing a natural balance of parts. I think we all take for granted that there is such a system, and need the idea for our practical thinking. We know that there have to be some things that are naturally more important, more central to human life, than others, and we have a good general idea which sorts of things they are, and how to compare them. We are not really in the helplessly ignorant situation philosophical discussions often suggest, where the only thing that we could safely call important is survival. Of course important things take different forms in different ages and cultures. Of course we must, as it were, keep learning new languages. But where we know the language (as we do in our own culture) we know how to start distinguishing important things from unimportant, and thereby good from evil. Such distinguishing is very often the theme of serious novels and plays. When we are following them we grasp the process very well. It is odd that people are struck with total ignorance when they turn to moral philosophy. Pretending that we do not have this skill is in fact a form of hypocrisy. The hypocrisy of past ages was usually classical and dogmatic, the hypocrisy of this age is romantic and skeptical. We pretend *not* to know. Instead of trying to see, we shut the curtains and revel in tragic darkness, concentrating carefully on impossible cases and taking the boring possible for granted.

Conflict and Integration

I want to dispense with this hypocrisy in considering briefly how we deal with conflict. It will be helpful to begin by asking a few questions about self-control—about what is controlled, what does the controlling, and what it means to have a controlling center to one's personality. Throughout this section, I am trying to come to grips with the question, what is it, essentially, that we so respect about rationality? What is so good about it? Why, for instance, does Kant sound convincing when he suggests that it is the *only* thing that can command respect?[13] We would not be likely to take this view of mere cleverness. Indeed there is a

---

13. *Grundlegung*, chap. 1, sec. 16, note (Paton tr., p. 66).

sense, though a boring one, in which computers can be clever, but only people very deeply misguided and prone to the pathetic fallacy could respect them.

There are, I think, two distinct elements in rationality: cleverness and integration.[14] By integration I mean having a character, acting as a whole, having a firm and effective priority system. The second is a condition of the first, not the other way round. For the full respect that we give to rationality, we need both. But integration alone is something of enormous value, and respect seems a suitable name for the recognition with which we salute it. And integration is not confined to people.

To illuminate these ideas, let us consider what happens when integration fails, first in some animal cases, then in human ones. It will become clear that the problem and the first stage of the solution are common to both.

In Niko Tinbergen's book, *The Herring Gull's World,* there are two especially instructive illustrations. One (p. 145) shows a gull reposing, eyes closed and wings folded, the picture of fatuous parental contentment, on an empty nest, while its eggs addle in the cold, a foot away. Helpful ethologists have removed the eggs to see which the creature would prefer, and it has settled for the nest. The other (p. 209), still more remarkable, shows an oyster catcher trying to perch on top of a monstrous egg, larger than itself, ignoring its own egg and a rather larger gull's egg that is there for further choice. The large egg, a dummy, has been provided by the ethologists to test the bird's powers of discrimination. These are two of many examples where interference has shown how slight, how easily garbled, are the natural cues creatures act on, even in cases essential to survival. Herring gulls, it seems, care more about nests than eggs; oyster catchers like their eggs substantial. And these preferences do no harm in the normal situation where there are no experimenters around, for normally the eggs stay in the nest, and all available eggs are roughly the same size. So there has been no selection pressure to alert gulls about roving eggs, nor to control the romantic dream,

14. I have borrowed this word from Jung, whose book *The Integration of the Personality* shows, in spite of much characteristic perversity, a real grasp of the problems involved.

which oyster catchers apparently cherish in their hearts, of one day finding an egg really worth sitting on.

Things like outsize eggs are called supernormal stimuli.[15] In these cases, the creature wants what it needs, but wants much *more* of it than it needs—has, in fact, not the slightest idea when to stop. Unlike overeating, which brings on discomfort, or oversleeping, which is broken off naturally, tastes such as outsize-egg-hunger have no built-in corrective. In these situations, tastes depend for their regulation on outside circumstances, which in the course of evolution plainly did not often fail. Their owners simply have no way of knowing when they have had enough of a good thing.

This is sad, we think, and bizarre, but, naturally, nothing to do with *Homo sapiens.*

But isn't it? Might not a species that cannot stop stuffing itself with chocolates, drinking spirits, racing fast cars, gambling, wasting resources, competing, fighting, and watching Miss World on television have something to learn from that unlucky gull and oyster catcher?

Chocolates are in fact an interesting example. A taste for sweetness has some selective values for fruit eaters, because it leads a creature to prefer ripe but not rotten fruit. And of course, in the wild, other sweet things are rare, so no firm safety-stop on sweetness is necessary. This is why, given a supply of sugar, human teeth and human figures are in such danger. The case of Miss World is also instructive. In their strong visual interest, human beings are much nearer to birds than to most animals. In all human cultures, people pay a lot of attention to their own and one another's appearance, and particularly to that of their sexual partners. Cultures differ in what they emphasize, but there is a general tendency to emphasize *something,* to pick out some one set from the repertoire of possible sexual cues and build it up, often beyond what is comfortable, healthy, or (difficult but necessary word) "balanced." Tinbergen mentions lipstick, which seems harmless enough. More alarmingly, some peoples pick on a long slender neck, and produce Giraffe

15. For the term, see *The Herring Gull's World,* pp. 206–208.

Women. The Chinese used to like small feet, and imposed them accordingly. And some African tribes shut up their girls in a fatting house to beautify them before marriage—sometimes só successfully than when the great day comes they are too fat to walk.

Obsessiveness unbalances people's tastes against biological advantage. In no species do instincts form a perfectly balanced, infallible set, a smooth machine, such as human envy supposes animals to have. Miss World adds an extra twist to this unbalance, in that she is, so to speak, purely visual and speculative, possessing no practical or tactile components. She is doubly abstracted. Voyeurism does not lead anywhere. But this is no different, in principle, from the gull's problem.

Male adornment works differently, partly because women's sexual interest is less visual, but to a greater extent because everywhere men's appearance has an imposing and aggressive, not just a seductive meaning. Male dances are typically war dances. Male ceremonial tends to serve another general interest that can also get out of hand—the competitive taste for impressing, terrifying, and outdoing possible rivals. Where this taste takes charge, people may again be caught in an inconvenient and unbalanced pattern of life. Even if they want to resist it, their obsession traps them. (*Obsession* means a siege; you can't get out). They are caught by their own inability to resist a particular type of stimulus. So I think it right to link this kind of situation with supernormal stimuli—although of course there is the very important difference that pugnacious exhibitionism is a *much more general* motive. It covers a whole class of stimuli, not just one, like the outsize egg. It appeals not to a single desire, but to a whole character trait. Certainly if we wanted to atomize we could list suitable stimuli for each martial society—the clash of arms, the shouts of the warriors, the gleam of weapons, the enemy's voices—most of all, perhaps, the accepted words and gestures of insulting challenge. (Or, for Academic Man, a bad book, a detested phrase, a pretentious opponent. . . .) Such lists sound quite behavioristic. But of course we know that we are speaking of a central uniting factor, the character trait to which all these appeal. We know what it is like to be roused. This is what makes it possible to group the stimuli, and to keep the list open for all sorts of further additions—for instance, on particular occasions, a sudden silence or an especially polite mode of address. All appeal to the pugnacious side of human nature.

That side is real and important. But even for the most pugnacious of us, it is only part of the personality, and often conflicts with more central parts. There is therefore, I think, a characteristic feeling of *exasperation* about these partial stimuli—a feeling of being dragged apart. One side of us has been worked on separately and roused to a feeling that excludes the rest. And our nature fits us to operate as a whole.

We may, of course, deal with this conflict by clamping down sharply on the competing interests, or by trying to make one of them prevail. But one way or another we must try to deal with it, because, unlike the gull and the oyster catcher, *we can see what is going on,* though we often find that we cannot do anything about it. The exasperation is even sharper in a way when the stimuli seem petty and isolated, but still irresistible. Recently I read two furious letters to the newspaper from people wanting particular petty stimuli banned—one a smoker objecting to cigarette advertising, the other a supermarket customer objecting to candy piled at the checkout counter. Both writers said quite honestly that it was not just the simple peasantry they wanted to protect, but themselves. And I think what they wanted protection against was *fragmentation,* not just the ill consequences of smoking or eating candy. ("How dare you set me against myself?") Perhaps this is the basic objection to advertising generally, and indeed to the whole overstimulating surface of our cities—"stop setting me in conflict." Perhaps it is a perfectly proper protest against fissiparous forces too strong for the center to cope with. Being torn apart by conflicting motives and unable to hold oneself together can be, as Catullus knew, agonizing:

> Odi at amo; quare id faciam, fortasse requiris.
> Nescio, sed fieri sentio, et excrucior.

> (I hate her and I love her. Perhaps you ask me why I do this? I do not know. I only feel it happen, and I am in torment.)

Trivial cases do not, of course, mean agony, but such internal conflict is always confusing, disquieting, and somehow sinister. We are trapped on one side; we cannot pull free. (Supernormal stimuli are, of course, typically the kind of thing used to *bait traps.)* We feel that our nature demands that we should be able to extricate ourselves, to understand what is going on within us and either endorse or control it. We feel that it demands integration.

Self-control: The Human Solution

Does this feeling make biological sense?

Bishop Butler puts the problem thus:

Suppose a brute creature by any bait to be allured into a snare, by which he is destroyed. He plainly followed the bent of his nature, leading him to gratify his appetite; there is an entire correspondence between his whole nature and such an action; such action therefore is natural. But suppose a man, foreseeing the same danger of certain ruin, should rush into it for the sake of a present gratification; he in this instance would follow his strongest desire, as did the brute creature; but there would be as manifest a disproportion between the nature of man and such an action, as between the meanest work of art and the skill of the greatest master of that art—Which disproportion arises, not from considering the action singly in itself, or in its consequences, but from comparison of it with the nature of the agent. And since such an action is utterly disproportionate to the nature of man, it is in the strictest and most proper sense unnatural.[16]

About people, Butler is surely right. If a person who had his memory and his intelligence did not *mind* traps, if he had no center, no policy, if he drifted from act to act without any attempt at continuity or interest in relating them, people in any culture would say that he had something wrong with him. We ourselves would probably say there was something medically wrong; we might put it that he was *not all there.* And we would certainly be likely to call him irrational. Sophisticated "policies of not having a policy" are no exception. If they have some guiding principle, they are only partial; if they really have none, anything can happen. A policy of being flexible on certain selected issues is still a policy; there must be constants elsewhere to call for it. *Integration of the personality is not just an optional extra.* It is a need. Human beings must have a structure, a policy, a continuity. Each has only one life to live. He cannot split up as a

16. Sermon 2, "Upon Human Nature," sec. 10.

coral colony might, into several batches of polyps, each equipped to go their separate ways. Without a lasting character, he cannot even follow out a train of thought—which is why I say that this is a condition of intelligence, not vice versa. Complete disintegration, then, is hard to imagine. But partial cases are very common. Most of us have personalities fairly well integrated on one side, the side we attend to, but fragmented on others, to which we pay less attention.

Butler's idea is that if we reflect on our own nature, if we attend to our neglected outlying motives and relate them to the center, we shall be able to judge them—because the reflective center of our personality has a natural authority, is in a position to judge. "Had it strength, as it has right, had it force, as it has manifest authority, it would absolutely govern the world." It "demands in all cases to govern such a creature as man."[17]

Butler calls it conscience, not reason, and this has made some people miss his meaning, because they personify Conscience, even more simply and disastrously than Reason, and see it merely as the voice of prejudice, an irresponsible despot. Butler, however, carefully avoids the errors of personifying. He repeatedly explains that he does *not* mean by conscience any unaccountable oracle or intuition, but a reflective faculty at the center of ourselves, by which we can think about our various actions and desires, stamping some with approval and rejecting others. And of course he does not make the mistake of personifying faculties either. For him conscience (or reflection) is simply the man himself in his capacity as decider—each of us, when we think seriously what we are for and against. Just so, Aristotle speaks of the core of the personality as *the man himself,* by contrast to casual impulses, and calls it (or him) *kyrios*—dominant, in charge.[18]

This is the context that justifies Butler's political metaphor of the *authority* of conscience or reflection. What rules us is our own center. It is indeed a "governor," but not an alien, colonial one. It is our own sense of how our nature works. (To be *conscious* in Latin is simply to share an understanding; it is a word used of

17. Sermon 2, sec. 14, and Preface to the *Sermons,* sec. 16.
18. *Ethics* 9.4, 9.8, 10.7, for example.

conspirators, and from thence reflexively, to describe the aspects of the self working together. *Conscience* is originally just being fully and thoughtfully aware of something. It became specialized to the moral case merely because that particularly bothered people.) By reflecting, Butler says, we stumble on the moral law, because that is the law of our own nature. "Your obligation to obey this law is, its being the law of your nature." It is not imposed from without. It is "the most intimate of all obligations; and which a man cannot transgress without being self-condemned, and unless he has corrupted his nature, without real self-dislike." He repeatedly points out that it does not depend on any religious sanctions, because it is more fundamental than they. It is as binding on pagans and unbelievers as it is on Christians. "Man is thus by his very nature a law to himself."[19]

People are alarmed when Butler speaks of the "absolute authority" of conscience or reflection over other motives, because they smell political despotism. Now if Butler had meant by conscience what some people mean by it—prejudice, egoism, or fancy—he would, of course, have been cutting short reflection before it could begin. But he means reflection itself. In a full discussion of self-deception, he makes it clear how wrong it is to distort the term conscience by using it to set up any such private oracle. (The position about the infallibility of conscience is rather like that about the infallibility of reason. If people argue confusedly, we do not say that their reason misled them, but that they did not reason properly. Bad argument is by definition *not* the voice of reason, nor, similarly, is bad morality a manifestation of conscience.) What Butler intends is quite different. He is saying that reflection demands action. To put it philosophically, he is pointing out the peculiar "prescriptive" form in which the conclusions of practical thinking emerge. They are not just theoretical and informative, but imperative and practical as well. If your night's reflection makes clear to you that in your inmost being you loathe and reject the corruption of the city council, then there will follow particular commands—like "refuse that bribe." And this command cannot be treated just as one motive

19. Sermon 3, sec. 5; Preface to the *Sermons,* secs. 28 and 29.

among others, a mere impulse to refusal, competing on even terms with other impulses and winning or losing according to its force at the moment.

Which is to be obeyed, appetite or reflexion? Cannot this question be answered, from the economy and constitution of human nature merely, without saying which is strongest? . . . How often soever [impulse] happens to prevail, it is mere *usurpation*. . . . every instance of such prevalence is an instance of breaking in upon and violating the constitution of man.

All this is no more than the distinction, which everybody is acquainted with, between *mere power* and *authority;* only instead of being intended to express the difference between what is possible and what is lawful in civil government, here it has been shown applicable to the several principles in the mind of man.[20]

To put the point more psychologically, Butler is pointing out the dangers of a confused personality, remarking that the price of ignoring one's center or refusing to reflect properly is disintegration. In his sermon "Upon the Character of Balaam," he looks at the case of a self-deceiving religious obsessive, carefully keeping to the letter of his duty while he violates the spirit of it. This man, he points out, has failed in reflection quite as much as any corrupt contractor. He is deeply disorganized; he is refusing to know what he is about. Butler discusses this phenomenon of self-deception in the next sermon, and finally breaks out: "If people will be wicked, they had better of the two be so from the common vicious passions without such refinements, than from this deep and calm source of delusion, which undermines the whole principle of good; darkens that light, the *candle of the Lord within,* which is to direct our step, and corrupts conscience, which is the guide of life."[21]

The formal, philosophical point about the authority of conscience is the same one Kant later put in terms of the claims of practical reason—that our thinking, if it is thorough, will land us with imperatives we cannot dodge, conclusions about what we must do, as well as with unavoidable conclusions about the facts. The distinctive thing about Butler is his managing to combine

20. Sermon 2, secs. 13–14.
21. Sermon 10, sec. 16.

this formal point with a proper attention to human feeling. He insists that it is our emotional constitution that gives us the material to reflect on. This dependence of thought on feeling is the aspect of the truth which Hume grasped at in saying that "reason is, and ought only to be, the slave of the passions." Butler, however, sharply refuses to take sides here, to oppose reason to feeling. He entirely rejects the idea behind Hume's tendentious question, "concerning the general foundation of Morals, whether they be derived from Reason, or from Sentiment?"[22] Butler saw no reason to set up a dogfight by regarding these obviously complementary elements as alternatives:

There are two ways in which the subject of morals may be treated. One begins by enquiring into the abstract relations of things; the other from a matter of fact, namely what the particular nature of man is. . . . They both lead us to the same thing. . . . The first seems the most direct, formal proof, and in some respects the least liable to cavil or dispute; the latter is in a peculiar manner adapted to satisfy a fair mind . . . and is more easily applicable to the several particular relations and circumstances of life.[23]

This is surely right. Hume's question, indeed, can only appear to make sense by exploiting the extreme looseness of words like *foundation, basis,* and *derive.* It is really no better to ask this than to ask "What are the foundations of physics? Are its truths derived from rational principles, or from the material facts?" The proper answer to such a question is simply "yes," which is the treatment Butler gives it. He again sharply refuses to be drawn into this sort of controversy when considering the various names that might be given to Conscience, refusing to classify it as reason or sentiment. It works, he says, "whether considered as a sentiment of the understanding or a perception of the heart, or, which seems the truth, as including both."[24] With this deliberate

22. *Enquiry Concerning the Principles of Morals,* sec. 134. Hume there takes this question as the theme of his book, welcoming it as one already under discussion. And clearly Butler, from his comments, was already familiar with it. Butler's *Sermons* were published in 1726, Hume's *Enquiry* in 1751. So the dispute takes place in reverse.
23. Preface to the *Sermons,* sec. 12.
24. *Dissertation upon the Nature of Virtue,* sec. 1.

paradox he resists Hume's vicious abstraction. The "force" Hume enquired about certainly has its emotional side. Good moral arguments do indeed express powerful human tastes and preferences. But it has its rational side too. These arguments *relate* those tastes and preferences in the way our nature as a whole demands. The "force" this gives them is the force of our demand for wholeness. The sanction of resisting it is not just logical confusion, but disintegration.

This insistence on the emotional element in goodness makes it possible for Butler to make better sense of wickedness than single-minded rationalists like Kant. Kant, in his discussion of the man naturally short of sympathy and "not exactly framed by nature to be a philanthropist,"[25] seems to suggest that such a man, *whatever* his natural emotional constitution, if he reasons honestly, will see the necessity of virtue, and can act on this insight. But there are intelligent psychopaths. What do we say about them? Rationalists can, I think, fairly point out that we have such difficulty in penetrating their thought that the supposition of its perfect consistency is not a very clear or strong one. Still, the most natural way to describe some psychopathic killers certainly is not in terms of a confusion of thought, but of a *deficiency of feeling.* Other people do not matter to them. They do not care about anybody, they are unable to form personal ties, and so forth. This deficiency deprives them of the premise that Kant rightly thinks essential for rationality—namely, that oneself is not an exception to all rules, that what is sauce for other geese is sauce for this gander. But Butler explicitly recognizes this role of feeling here:

Reason alone, whatever anyone may wish, is not in reality a sufficient motive of virtue in such a creature as man; but this reason joined with those affections which God has impressed upon his heart.... Neither is affection itself at all a weakness; nor does it argue defect, any otherwise than our senses and appetites do.... Both our senses and our passions are a supply to the imperfections of our nature.... But it is not the supply, but the deficiency, as it is not a remedy, but the disease, which is the imperfection.[26]

25. *Grundlegung*, chap. 1, sec. 11 (Paton tr., p. 64).
26. Sermon 5, sec. 3.

Kant takes for granted that his "naturally unsympathetic" man still comes within the range of emotional normality. So he does not see that normal emotions are as necessary for morality as thought is. Butler simply points this out. By doing so, however, he gives us what we certainly need—language to express the fact that psychopaths are not supermen. The murderer (and indeed the solitary, such as Nietzsche himself) does not have to be seen as a hero, strong enough to dispense with supports on which weaker minds rely. To represent him that way is indeed a piece of sentimental bad faith, unless we actually ourselves accept his option. It is every bit as plausible to see him as we normally see psychopaths, as an emotional cripple, stunted and incomplete because he does not have the normal equipment for a full human life. Intensity in the remaining faculties may to some extent compensate for this handicap in particular cases, as can happen with other handicaps. But all the same a handicap, and not an asset, is what such crippling is. And in looking at the matter in this way, Butler and Freud are at one.

The advantage of Butler's method of making self-control intelligible is that it shows controller and controlled as parts of a single whole. By so doing, it gets rid of any arbitrary, despotic, or miraculous element in our notion of rationality, and shows how our development can be continuous. We begin to see how it is not ridiculous to suppose that we evolved as the kind of creatures that we are. In explaining the work of conscience, Butler's argument indeed is throughout thoroughly biological. It rests on *function.* He asks, what *use* is the conscience? He starts from what he calls a fact, namely the human tendency to reflect on our own and each others' conduct, to judge it, to accuse and excuse ourselves and other people, and to feel *shame* when we ourselves fall short. Shame particularly interests him; he asks quite simply, what is its function? And he notes the great force of such functional arguments in general: "A man can as little doubt whether his eyes were given him to see with, as he can doubt the truth of the science of optics, deduced from ocular experiments. And allowing the inward feeling, shame, a man can as little doubt whether it was given him to prevent his doing shameful actions, as he can doubt whether his eyes were given him to guide his steps."[27] The capacity for shame, therefore, is a part of our adaptation as social beings. Putting this question is like asking, why does this creature have legs? If the only intelligible answer is "to get around with," it follows that the creature is *designed, adapted* or *programmed* to get around;[28] that a stationary life will not suit it, indeed will be bad for it, if only by being a waste of this important resource. Just so with the human capacity for shame and also more generally with the power of reflection—their use is practical. They are fairly central parts of us—not a peripheral one like the appendix or the kiwi's wings. So trying to ignore them will be at best wasteful and probably destructive. So they ought to be used. And in the case of conscience or reflection, Butler suggests, the argument is especially strong, because the position it seems designed for is such a central one. Outlying faculties, if neglected, might atrophy quietly, but, as he says, "you cannot form a notion of this faculty, conscience, without taking in judgment, direction, superintendency." Bypassing such a central nexus would be something like deciding to dispense with the central nervous system. Psychosurgery is out of place here.

The Shared Solution

As far as people are concerned, Butler's view of how our nature is integrated seems to me thoroughly sensible and a great improvement on the colonial picture. Where it falls short is where all other accounts fall short—in oversimplifying the position about animals for the sake of the contrast.

In the human case, Butler saw plainly that reflection could not work if there were not, so to speak, some unevenness for it to get a grip on, some preexisting balance and structure among the

27. Sermon 2, sec. 1.
28. See my discussion of these terms, pp. 72–76. As Butler is scrupulously careful never to let his argument depend on the existence of God as designer, but only on the fitness of the thing examined for one purpose rather than another, his remarks make perfectly good sense in a post-Darwinian context. (For his intention to make them independent of any religious belief, see, for example, Preface, secs. 27–28.)

motives, for reflection to discover when it started reflecting. For instance, he thought that both justice and truth-telling were important and valuable elements in human life, quite apart from their tending to make for happiness. It follows that impulses to be fair or truthful have a special value. Reflection recognizes this and does not create it. *Conscience is not a colonial governor imposing alien norms;* it is our nature itself, becoming aware of its own underlying pattern. It does not invent a new set of priorities; it sees those that are called for. It is not free to make up the rules of the value-game. Why, for instance, in Butler's example of entering the snare, is prolonged well-being more important than instant gratification? Because we are "formed such sort of creatures" as to go in for long schemes, for memory, hope and regret, planning and fruition. (We might not have been.) Why is parricide[29] (another of Butler's examples) *unnatural*? Because we are brood-tending creatures, of a sort that forms bonds of affection, gratitude and cooperation in infancy, bonds that can persist and grow through life, making a great part of the creature's concern and structuring its existence.

Creatures capable of such bonds (they include, I think, all the more intelligent mammals) do not make light of them; their *use* lies in their being central to life. They are part of our animal nature, not a colonial imposition. In *On Aggression* Lorenz makes this extremely important point well:

It is a widely held opinion, shared by some contemporary philosophers, that all human behavior patterns which serve the welfare of the community, as opposed to that of the individual, are dictated by specifically human rational thought. Not only is this opinion erroneous, but the very opposite is true. If it were not for a rich endowment of social instincts, man could never have risen above the animal world. All specifically human faculties, the power of speech, cultural tradition, moral responsibility, could have evolved only in a being which, before the very dawn of conceptual thinking, lived in well-organized communities. Our prehuman ancestor was indubitably as true a friend to his friend as a chimpanzee or even a dog, as tender and solicitous to the young of his community and as self-sacrificing in its defense, aeons before he de-

29. Sermon 2, sec. 17. For the related topics of ingratitude and parental care, see Sermon 1, sec. 8. I have already made some remarks on what "unnatural" means in this context (pp. 79–80).

veloped conceptual thought and became aware of the consequence of his actions. [p. 246]

Hume missed this point by a mile because, as usual, he was trying to think like a physicist, not like a biologist. He remarked that parricide was not wrong for trees and would not be so even if they had "choice and will."[30] Therefore, he concluded, its wrongness for men was just a matter of feeling, and therefore contingent. This is an excellent example of how *uncontingent* biological truths really are. They make sense only within their proper context. Items like "choice and will" cannot just be tacked on to the notion of a tree; the phrase "choosing tree" makes no better sense than "liquid tree" or "invisible elephant." If someone wrote a story about one of these, he could of course explain how he conceived it to work—but he would have to have a point in doing so, and until it is done such terms are unintelligible. Nothing, or everything equally, follows from them; they are therefore useless. Until we understand the nature of a given species, we cannot tell (1) what kind of "choice" it might be capable of, (2) what place gratitude and affection, for instance, have in its life, or (3) whether the notion of a *parent* makes for it any beyond genetic sense. Codfish do not, in the social sense, have fathers at all; wolves and beavers do. For bees, the killing of a genetic father (though never of a mother) could be considered a duty as well as a pleasure. And many creatures are quite willing to attack *any* intruding conspecific, and kill it if it cannot escape. But the more intelligent animals—all those for whom the notion of deliberate choice might conceivably make sense—tend strongly to avoid such killing, most particularly in the case of a close friend or relative. And this tendency is not an isolated one, but an integral part of their whole pattern of motives. Social bonds structure their lives. *Communication, and therefore intelligence, develops only where there are these long-standing deep relationships.* It may be possible for it to occur in another context, but if so, nobody knows what it would be like.

Hume, as so often, is bogged by his mysterious ontology by which "all beings in the universe, considered in themselves, ap-

30. *Enquiry Concerning the Principles of Morals*, Appendix 1, sec. 243.

pear entirely loose and independent of each other."[31] Not in this universe they don't. Experience does not work like that; it is not atomic. To experience things at all, we have to perceive them within a familiar frame of reference, and relate them to it. No principle, therefore, could be less empiricist than Hume's.

The reason Butler's contrast between man and animal is too simple is, moreover, that animals have frames of reference as well. They are not just bundles of disconnected perceptions and motives. They have natures of their own, each according to their species. And actions, which can very well take place, can all the same be contrary to those natures.

Butler's example of the snare is not, in fact, especially typical of animal behavior, at least above the insect level. (It is worth noting that both the snare situation and those of the poor deluded gull and oyster catcher result from human interference, not from conditions normal to the species.) Animals that respond to a supernormal stimulus are indeed somewhat passive. But then, so are people who do so. It is the sort of case where it is only a slight exaggeration to say, with Descartes, that the creature concerned, whether human or not, does not *act;* it is acted upon. The single stimulus drives it to a single, easily predicted piece of behavior. If the whole life of other species were like this and human life never was, the contrast would be fair. But it is not. Actually, as pest control people know all too well, animals can very often resist traps. Their natures are quite equal to the effort. Exterminating rats, in particular, is extremely hard, because rats learn so quickly from experience; they will not take a bait their leader refuses, and he is remarkably canny at this bit of induction. Loyalty, Prudence, and a little Intelligence among them beat the supernormal stimulus, for that is the nature of the rat. Human beings, on the other hand, quite often do fall into traps, not only into those laid by other human beings, but even those laid by animals, as for instance when a wounded rhinoceros circles round to lie in wait on its own trail and charge the hunter who is following it, or a man-eating lion ambushes

31. *Treatise of Human Nature,* Bk. 3, pt. 1, sec. 1.

jungle paths. But then here, as usual, theorists are considering animals as they are, and human beings as they should be.[32]

Every species has its own characteristic temperament, of which systematic caution is often a part. Consider, for example, what Richard Carrington says of elephants.

The caution shown by elephants is a characteristic trait. No animal is more wary of unfamiliar objects, nor more quick to take fright for the most unaccountable reasons. . . . Elephants have an instinctive preoccupation with their own safety, which amounts almost to a neurosis. For example, even domesticated elephants who have acquired great confidence in their human masters will often refuse to cross a bridge before they have tested its strength carefully with their fore-feet, or rapped it smartly with the tip of their trunk, rather as a surveyor tests the strength of a plasterboard partition. This is not to say that such behaviour reflects on the elephant's character, and on one view it could be taken as proof of his intelligence. [*Elephants,* p. 76]

As elephants can weigh up to twelve tons, the last remark seems reasonable.

Again, on the equally crucial subject of sex, Carrington writes (p. 52): "Elephants are creatures of affection, and perhaps none of the so-called lower animals enriches the purely mechanical processes of reproduction with a nicer sensibility. . . . I learnt myself in India during the war how elephants often showed an affection and solicitude for their mates that could well be held up as an example to members of our own species."

Elephants, in fact, do *not* simply do the first thing that comes into their heads, even when they are reacting to a strong outside stimulus. They are not mechanical toys. But in any case, much of the time they and other creatures are not reacting to any stimulus at all. A great part of a higher animal's life is spent in positive activity of a kind for which stimulus-response patterns are little help. We could take any stretch of the lively social goings-on watched by Schaller or Jane Goodall. Here each species busies itself according to taste—the quiet, dignified goril-

32. At mating time the hippo's voice
   Betrays inflexions hoarse and odd,
   But every week we hear rejoice
   The Church, at being one with God.   [T. S. Eliot, *The Hippopotamus*]

las foraging and exchanging greetings, the lively volatile, outgoing chimps exploring and holding parties. Each member has complex social ties, and develops them according to its character; the conventions are well understood, and *action contrary to the nature* either of the indiviual or the species can be easily spotted by the experienced observer. It shows up as something *wrong*.[33] The observer then looks for an explanation which is still within the repertory—just as he does in human affairs. (For instance, parricide occurs in humans; it can be explained—but certainly it needs explaining. *The Brothers Karamazov* is quite a long book.) With animals just as with people, the observer can use the individual's character as a guide. He can ask, how natural is it for *this* individual to do *that* surprising thing? and what circumstances might make it natural? But of course, people who do not take a species seriously do not distinguish between individual characters. Just so, Pope wrote,

> Nothing so true as what you once let fall—
> "Most women have no character at all".[34]

Again, consider the well-organized wolves Farley Mowat described in *Never Cry Wolf*. Angeline, the she-wolf, gets tired of playing with her cubs. She calls. Out of the den, yawning, comes a young he-wolf, the lodger, evidently sleepy. However, he proceeds to babysit and to play patiently with the cubs while she has a rest. (There are, by the way, no sexual overtones to this story.) Later, Angeline, wanting her lunch, goes down to the lake shore and lures some ducks to the bank by odd behavior which amounts to cleverly feigning madness. She nearly catches one, but it gets away. So, resigning herself to a sandwich, she finds, skillfully catches, and swallows a couple of dozen mice, then returns to the cubs while the others go out to hunt, and return with meat for the family. At another time, when the cubs are older, the adults stage a training hunt for them, carefully driving a few weaker deer toward the cubs while one older wolf remains with them to encourage them, at a time when they would not

33. For abnormal behavior in chimps, see Goodall, *In the Shadow of Man*, pp. 128–129 and 235–236.

34. *Epistle of the Characters of Women*, 1–2.

normally be hunting at all. Nothing is caught, and the adults show no anxiety to catch anything. And this hunt does not take place until George, the father wolf, has repeatedly nudged Angeline and finally stirred her into undertaking it. (Is this "having an intention"?)

All this behavior is *active;* it is not in the least like getting caught in a snare; it will not break down into passive stimulus-response patterns. It is not mechanical but purposive, and the purpose is linked to lasting character traits expressing priorities. Serious neglect of cubs, or brutal treatment of them, would be thoroughly unnatural among wolves. So would disrespectful or uncooperative behavior to elders. These things sometimes happen. But they are not just unfortunate, they are out of character; they show something *wrong,* something, as Butler said, "disproportionate to their nature as a whole."

Stories of this kind often have as their point disputes about intelligence. What I am talking about is, as I have said, something different and much deeper, which is taken for granted; the characteristic basic patterns of motives.

Cub care is *important* to wolves. So is affection for their friends and companions. (Indeed the two things go together; the gestures by which adults show affection are drawn from cub-rearing.) Affection is a prevailing motive. Powerful general motives like this can easily make them delay gratification of immediate desires like hunger or sleepiness. The whole pack is bound together by affection. But this affection too is not "blind impulse"; it has a *backbone,* a structure that keeps it steady through variations of mood. All wolves have claims, which are generally recognized. And a cross or bored wolf will not just bite another; he quarrels, but he gives warning in a set and intelligible manner. Threats express his irritation; the opponent has time to get out or submit. And submission usually disarms the aggressor. A very interesting thing is that at this point a conflict of motives may be visible; one motive does not necessarily replace another smoothly and unremarked. There is *ambivalence,* conflict behavior. The dominant one refrains from biting, but still growls and snaps over his prostrate enemy, making biting and shaking movements; he won't let the loser get up for a while; when he does get up, he chases him away. Both motives are present together; the wolf is in a way identified with both, yet he must choose one for action. We have all done this. *It is surely the kind of situation out of which a real center to the personality emerges.* The choice we make determines the sort of person we are becoming.

"Now see I well," said Sir Lancelot, "that such a man I might be, I might have peace, and such a man I might be, that there should be war mortal betwixt us. . . ." [Malory, *Le Morte d'Arthur*]

We tend to think of animals as not having this problem. *They do have the problem. What they do not have is our way of solving it by thinking about it. But they still have a way of solving it—namely, by a structure of motives that shapes their lives around a certain preferred kind of solution.* If we did not have that too, thinking would get us nowhere.

My point is not just that intelligence, as it develops, is applied to these emotional conflicts. It develops partly as an adaptation to deal with them, for they are quite as serious a threat to life as hunger is, and more serious than the lack of tools. Emotional stability, a solid, continuous character, is necessary to survival. It is quite as necessary as technology, and indeed technology itself depends on it.

So reason does not develop as a neutral, computerlike, technological device, detached from all aims. Form is not a colonial import, to be stamped on brute matter. The only picture that makes evolutionary sense is the Aristotelian one where matter fits its form[35]—not the Platonic one where matter is bare negation, surd, irrational, resistant, indeed the root of all evil. The structure of feeling demands a corresponding structure of thought to complete it. The reason of a social species is not programmable in just any direction. It arises as an aspect of stability and friendliness. So we are not being silly when we expect it to know which way to look for values, what sort of order to demand. We do attach that expectation to terms like intelligence and common sense. We talk of destructive conduct as *stupid* or *irrational,* and undirected conduct as *silly, unreasonable,*

35. Aristotle regarded matter as potency—the power to become some particular thing—not as a general neutral stuff (*Metaphysics,* 8.7).

or *insane*. When human beings reason practically about what would be best to do, they are wondering what would be best "for such a creature as man." The range and pattern of possible aims is given with the species. So is a character adapted to them. What counts as help or harm is not a contingent matter. Treating it as contingent, as something logically separate from morality, was Kant's mistake. For once the nature of a species (or any other system) is given, there are limits to the ways in which you can hope to make sense of it.

A computer would see no objection to organizing life on the principle of maximizing noise, getting everything as clean as possible, making everybody always tread on the lines between the paving stones,[36] or minimizing emotion. Computers are not rational; they are stupid things. They do not know what *matters;* they are only consistent. The people programming them have to be rational—that is, they must be able to see the priorities among human needs. If the programmer is a simpleminded Utilitarian, he may be hard put to it to see why either justice or art should come into his system. This is because he starts with an artificially simple reduction of human needs to pleasure. *There is absolutely nothing rational about this.* Simple schemes of thought are rational only when they fit the phenomena. Human needs are actually very complex. So any system of thought that is to organize them must admit their complexity.

Yet, having admitted this, it *must* simplify to make choice possible. "It lies in the nature of man that he can do more than he may."[37] And this, of course, is what makes the colonial image so attractive. Contrasting the roaring confusion of human desires with the simple, neat, infallible system of instincts that we wrongly take animals to have, we feel that the Gordian Knot will have to be cut by some alien force named Reason—a *deus ex machina* to save desire from the consequences of its own folly. But unless you have a suggestion about where the *deus ex machina* can come from, the colonial picture makes no sense. It is quite

36. See Philippa Foot, "When Is a Principle a Moral Principle?" *Proceedings of the Aristotelian Society,* Supplementary Vol. 28 (1954).

37. Opening sentence of Wolfgang Wickler's book *The Sexual Code.*

evident that, as Lorenz says in *On Aggression,* that "like power steering in a modern car, responsible morality derives the energy which it needs to control human behavior from the same primal powers which it was created to keep in rein. Man as a purely rational being, divested of his animal heritage of instincts, would certainly not be an angel—quite the opposite." (p. 247). No carpenter shapes trees; it is the life within them that achieves that,[38] balancing a branch here with another there, sacrificing height to strength, and vice versa. The formula is not imposed; it is essential to the creature. Equally there is nothing but the life within each of us that can resolve our conflicts—though certainly, as compared with trees or even most animals, that life has learned a trick or two. Our intelligence is part of the adaptation by which we do it, but only part. Below that lies our rough natural structure of needs. It *is* very rough. It will not work, at the best, without friction and much sacrifice. But it is there.

We want incompatible things, and want them badly. We are fairly aggressive, yet we want company and depend on long-term enterprises. We love those around us and need their love, yet we want independence and need to wander. We are restlessly curious and meddling, yet long for permanence. Unlike many primates, we do have a tendency to pair-formation, but it is an incomplete one, and gives us a lot of trouble. We cannot live without a culture, but it never quite satisfies us. All this is the commonplace of literature. It is also, to a degree, the problem of the other intelligent species too. In each, a group of counteracting needs and tendencies holds life in a rough but tolerable equilibrium. In each there are endemic conflicts. Yet an individual depends for his satisfaction on the repertory of tastes native to his species; he cannot jump off his feet. What is special about people is their power of understanding what is going on, and using that understanding to regulate it. Imagination and conceptual thought intensify all the conflicts by multiplying the

38. Readers frightened of vitalism can, if they wish, substitute "genetic programming" for "life" in this sentence. The reasons I have not written this is that I regard vitalism as a dead duck, while the superstitions that surround "programming" and computers generally are lively and vigorous. So I stick to the vernacular.

options, by letting us form all manner of incompatible schemes and allowing us to know what we are missing, and also by greatly increasing our powers of self-deception. As against that, they can give us self-knowledge, which is our strongest card in the attempt to sort conflicts out. It is to deepen that self-knowledge that I want to use comparison with other species.[39]

39. For further development of the views on thought and feeling expressed in this chapter, see my article "The Objection to Systematic Humbug," *Philosophy* (April 1978).

CHAPTER 12

Why We Need a Culture

Culture Is Natural

Where does culture belong in the cluster of properties that together mark man's nature? It has a slightly different standing from language and rationality, for they are not generally viewed as grievances; most people agree to praise them. But romantic individualism does complain of culture. It can be seen not as a positive achievement characteristic of man, but as something alien inflicted on him.

I have several times mentioned this Libertarian strain of thinking. It is not quite so popular now as it was ten years ago. Nonetheless, reading a large batch of examination papers written in 1977 in answer to a question about the meaning of freedom, I found that most of the students made the same complaint, and often in the same words: "we cannot be free, since we are indoctrinated by society." (Does this agreement indicate indoctrination or not? They should know best.) But the important question is, what notion of freedom does that complaint involve? And if culture is alien to man, where does it come from?

The situation is complicated. As I have suggested,[1] the blank opposition of nature to culture does make sense in talking of an individual, but not of a whole group, much less of the human race.

1. In the third section of Chap. 1.

Culture has to come from somewhere, and there is no super-natural being called Society to impose it. Society is past and present people. And they have to have natural motives for inventing the customs they do invent. Each of us has to accept a great deal that we would not have chosen. But each of us also has a hand in choosing how it shall all grow and in imposing it on those around us. How shall we do justice to these complexities? How, in fact, shall we understand social man?

The trouble with him is, of course, that he comes half-finished. Man is innately programmed in such a way that he needs a culture to complete him. Culture is not an alternative or replacement for instinct, but its outgrowth and supplement. Man is like one of those versatile cake mixes that can be variously prepared to end up as different kinds of cake—but never, it must be noted, as a boiled egg or smoked salmon. From a cake mix you can only get some sort of cake, and from a human baby you can only get an adult with some selection from the emotional repertoire of his own species. But just as a cake has to be baked, so a baby has to be exposed to a specific, already existing, culture. He cannot generate it on his own. And even if he is going to reject it later, he has to absorb it fully first.

There are thus two essential points here, which complete each other, and which it is hard to keep in mind together. (1) Culture is essential to us; we cannot live without it. But (2) it is essential *because* of our innate needs. We cannot help demanding and creating it. It is not the opponent of individual growth, any more than the nest is the opponent of a young bird, but its necessary matrix. And it is quite unlike the traditional writing or print placed on blank paper, because it is a necessary completion of the developing creature itself.

The first point, that culture is essential to our life, seems to be the half of the truth that leads people to the Blank Paper theory. They are, rightly, struck by the teeming variety of cultures, by the importance of all that happens to us after birth, by the immense difference it can make in our characters and physiques as well as our circumstances. And they want to move freely within this range. As reformers, they want to get rid of all those obstacles to change which come of treating certain changes as impossible. If human possessiveness and exclusiveness, for example, are making people mean and intolerant toward one another, they want to feel free to treat these as removable evils.

About the immense power of culture, they are plainly right. But power is not omnipotence. We can recognize the power of one set of causes without pretending that there are no others. As for the wish to take a rosy view of humanity in order not to be discouraged from attempting reform, it is self-defeating. Automatic optimism will never help reform. The more we need change, the more we have to study what makes change so difficult, and what distorts it when it happens. The success of modern medicine is not due to the Christian Science principle of denying the reality of physical evils, but to facing them and understanding their causes. How far possessiveness and exclusiveness have innate, as well as outer, sources is a factual question. If they have, it is clear that these can take different forms; the detailed institutions we use are not innate as a whole. We are free to change things within a certain range. Understanding that range is the first step on our way. By contrast, if it were true that people's emotional needs were entirely acquired, things would be black indeed for the reformer. Oppressors would only need to condition peoples earlier and more thoroughly to enjoy slavery; after that it would be impossible to object to it.

Culture is not opposed to freedom. It makes it possible.

I have said that my present point (the natural necessity of culture), is accepted, though not, I think, properly investigated, by Blank Paper theorists. They know that culture is necessary; they only fail to ask *why*. The people to whom it will probably seem alarming are those I have called Libertarians or Existentialists, people who take freedom to be in some sense the supreme value, who see any interference with it as deplorable, even if sometimes necessary. To them it seems that *any* particularizing—any tying down of us to this rather than that—is a deprivation, a sad infringement on what should have been universal scope. They may consider it inevitable that we should be born into one form of life rather than another, just as we have inevitably somehow to be restrained from harming one another. But they think of both things as unmixed loss. They think of our dependence on continuity—both on our own habits and those of our ancestors—as crippling, and our emotional attachment to continuity as a shameful weakness.

I speak of "they," but in truth this position involves all of us today. *Freedom,* that most general of negative words, looms over us. It no longer means just the absence of a few specified evils—slavery, oppression, error—or the entrance ticket to certain specified goods—attractive political and personal choices. It no longer means freedom *from* or *to do* anything particular. It has spread itself to cover the isolation of the individual from all connection with others, therefore from most of what gives life meaning: tradition, influence, affection, personal and local ties, natural roots and sympathies, Hume's "sentiment of human-ity."[2] Yet it presents itself as an absolute demand, a new but unanswerable moral imperative. And it does so especially to those who claim to disapprove of morality altogether. Thus Nietzsche,[3] and after him many others such as Sartre, urge us to cut the painter to our own culture and *invent* or *create* new values for ourselves, taking up the (now vacant) position of God the Father, so that man "chooses without reference to any pre-established values, but it is unjust to tax him with caprice. Rather let us say that the moral choice is comparable to the construction of a work of art."[4] At this point the notion of freedom seems almost to merge into that very difficult concept, omnipotence.[5]

In some ways, however, this business of treating the taste for continuity (both with the past and with those around us) as a

2. It is interesting how easily the word *free* does become a simple negative, as soon as we weaken the notion of badness in what we are free *from.* Thus the medical phrase "a salt-free diet" sounds odd to those who are used to thinking of salt as quite a *good* thing; we must know what is wrong with salt before these words make sense. But complete negation does not sound so attractive a goal as perfect freedom.

3. For example, *Thus Spake Zarathustra,* Pt. 3, "Of Old and New Tables"—one of many places where he explicitly recommends our taking God's place. The tone of exultant blasphemy echoes sadly now. If we know the house is empty, why ring the bell and run away?

4. Sartre, *Existentialism and Humanism,* p. 54.

5. See an extremely interesting article by Peter Geach on the difficulties of applying this notion effectively even to God: "Omnipotence," *Philosophy,* 48 (1973). Applying it to man is really asking for trouble.

shameful weakness is an odd suggestion today. It contrasts strongly with the current attitude toward other "weaknesses" endemic to the human character, notably toward sex. Anyone who today treated the general need for sexual activity of some kind as a shameful weakness would be resisted (rightly), by being told, first, that this is a basic condition of our nature, second, that it is not so much a weakness as an opportunity, a highroad away from some impossible supposed state of sterile independence to the real vigorous activity of a shared world. Exactly the same is true of the need for continuity. The imagined state of isolation and ceaseless change would be possible only to some kind of solitary pure intellect, uncommitted to action in the world it watched—a machine (say) geared to respond on fresh principles to each change in the objects passing before it. But even as we try to imagine this, we see that the idea is nonsense; the machine itself would have to persist, and so would the procedures programmed into it. This idea is a much wilder abstraction than that of an animal without sex; after all there are some of those:

> Unknown to sex the pregnant oyster swells,
> And coral-insects build their radiate shells—

as Erasmus Darwin pointed out. *But continuity, and habit as a means of preserving it, is an essential aspect of all life right through the animal kingdom.* This is one of the points on which an improved knowledge of animal behavior can now correct mindless traditional ideas of what is natural. It used to be supposed that animals roamed wildly and unpredictably over the earth, and that fixed routine was an artificial interference imposed on man by that unnatural thing, society. Far from which, studies of territorial behavior show that fixed and regular movement patterns are almost universal. Migrant birds, and other long-distance travelers, retrace their journeys exactly, given half a chance, not only to the same shore but the same nesting site; creatures that must travel to feed follow crops or prey in a regular order; ritual and ceremonial clothe the lightest interactions of all social creatures. Greetings, bows, and tactful turnings away are of the first importance; unexpected gestures cause alarm and are signs of some serious disturbance. Happiness centers on habit.[6] In fact, the human commuter on the 8:45, far from being in any way biologically exceptional, is a most natural phenomenon, whereas someone who seriously sought to live without routine would be flying in the face of nature far more radically than the most rigid puritan or Trappist. The normal pattern of development in conduct, as in art, proceeds through modest variations on a theme. The Libertarian way of talking is, however, very deep-rooted today. As I have remarked, we tend to think of ourselves as *prisoners* of our culture, as being *limited* by it, "indoctrinated" or "brainwashed" as people often say, into accepting its values—or again, "conditioned," as though taking in the way of life around us were no more natural than the process undergone by Pavlov's dogs.

But how would we manage without a culture?

Every asset can be viewed in this way as a liability. We can think (and people often have) of sex as a monstrous barrier to independence, a fatal breach in the walls, a wound in our personal identity, an incurable defilement ("Inter urinam et faeces nascimur," groaned Tertullian[7]). *Or* we can think of it as our lifeline, the sacred fire that warms us, our bridge to the world, the remedy for all our loneliness. Again, we can think (and people often have) of sense-perception as a screen or barrier set up between us and the real world, even (again) a prison we cannot break out of. Or (much more naturally) as being itself our window on that world; after all, we do see rivers and trees, not just impenetrable sense-data. In the same way, a skeleton can be seen as nothing but a symbol for death.

> Wanderers eastward, wanderers west
> Know you why you cannot rest?

6. Rousseau (who is certainly the source of the anti-habit drive) showed his usual profound ignorance of children when he advised, "The only habit your child should be allowed to contract is that of having no habits," adding that, if new things were constantly presented, the child would acquire no fear of the unknown (*Emile*, tr. Barbara Foxley, Everyman ed., p. 30). Human babies, like the young of other species, are innately programmed to form habits, and are quite unable to make any progress without doing so. Fear of strangers, and of the unknown generally, is also innate, and appears at a certain stage in each species' development, whatever the previous conditioning.

7. "We are born between the urine and the feces."

'Tis that every mother's son
Travails with a skeleton

wrote A. E. Housman.[8] But suppose we had *no* skeleton? (Even Housman's own famous stiff back and stiff upper lip would then have looked less impressive.) Our whole being depends on this stiff, inflexible, in a way lifeless element in us. We do not carry it as a dead weight. It carries us. And the structure of our life does the same thing. We can think of our culture as a prison or a dead weight—or as our skin, or as the part of the world where we happen to be. Aspiring to be free from any culture is in one way like trying to be skinless. (Our skin does indeed come between us and the world—but it is what makes it possible for us to touch it.) In another way it is like trying to be nowhere. And of course restriction to a single place *is* a restriction; it stops us from being elsewhere. But being in any other particular place would do the same. All elsewheres are potential, which is a miserable shadowy thing to be compared with the splendid nowness of being actually here.

Some people do feel that the proper thing would be to bring children up without a culture till they came to years of discretion, and then let them choose. But children who are held apart from life, or rushed from one set of people to another, do not become exceptionally capable of choosing. You can choose only between given alternatives, and to grasp any alternative you need years of acclimatization and practice in choosing from one particular set, in seeing what choices amount to. And you need to learn to hold on to something. *All this is not a misfortune.* A culture is a way of awakening our faculties. Any culture does this to some extent. People proficient in one culture can usually make some sense of another. There is no prison. We can always walk on if we want to enough. What we cannot do is something which is no loss—namely, be nobody and nowhere.

I do not mean that some people may not be very unlucky in their culture, either because it is generally bad, or because it suits them badly. But this is still nothing to the misfortune of having no culture at all.

Just how hard it is at present to grasp this point comes out in

8. "The Immortal Part," *A Shropshire Lad*, XLIII.

an engaging suggestion of Hans Hass's, quoted by Eibl-Eibesfeldt.

To be fair to children [Hass writes], one should probably ground them, from the age of six onwards, only in those moral concepts which are everywhere the same. They should be warned of the dangers of premature fixation and made to understand that they have an inalienable right to form judgments—a right which they will one day exercise for themselves, perhaps in opposition to their parents and the community. This is a Utopian concept at present, but it is possible that just such a trend is already perceptible in to-day's youth.[9]

But "those moral concepts which are everywhere the same" are *general* ones: kindness, fidelity, courage, good craftsmanship, justice. And in order to ground children in anything whatever, one must be *specific*. Children detest the indeterminate; they rightly see it as evasion. They have to live *now* in a particular culture; they must take some attitude to the nearest things in it right away. Simply because human possibilities are so rich, there has to be some selection. Here, fidelity means drawing the bow and speaking the truth. There, it means lying like a trooper to defend one's friends. Here, it relates one to the church; there, to one's class, clan, trade, political party, one's father, or one's schoolmates. And people must be treated respectfully or rudely *at once*. For a child, the penalty for opting out of this aspect of a culture is so severe that he must be given good reason for any abstention, reason consisting in the culture being actually *wrong*, not just in his own right to freedom. And polite respect draws one into the spirit of a culture—unless one becomes a chronic liar. Moreover, occupations must be taken seriously. In Bali, from your earliest years, you are no one if you do not dance. In Bangkok, most boys sooner or later become monks for a time. And in the West, you cannot become a real mathematician, violinist, or ballet dancer if you do not start as a child. An adult who says to a child, "you need not commit yourself to this; you may decide to leave it later," conveys to him only one message, which is, "I do not take this seriously and nor need you." And "this" will of course include the general norm along with the particular form that expresses it. If, hoping to make things

9. *Love and Hate*, p. 27.

clearer, he says, "but you had better stick with it for the moment" he merely adds what looks like a recommendation to procrastination and dishonesty. The child then has to try and work out why the adult is placing him in this complicated and confusing position. He collects "norms" of timidity, shiftiness, and dilettantism, not no norms at all. And these norms limit his freedom later as much as any others.

These difficulties come of not noticing that there is a proper age for each phase of development, and that things have to be learned in their proper order. That children are docile before they are enterprising results from their innate programming. It is not a quirk induced in them by a particular culture, but a condition of culture. Docility is normal in the young of intelligent species, as much as the gradual development of independence as they grow up. "Being fair to children" cannot be achieved by pretending that they are all born at the age of eighteen. They cannot go beyond an order until they have grown up within it. Nietzsche and Sartre, after all, did not issue their invitation to children.

People just growing into adults often become suddenly independent and rebellious, but then so do animals of many species at the same stage. It is rather common for creatures of many species to leave home at this point; many primates on becoming adults leave their own band, wander, and join another one, though nobody is driving them out. The tendency is an innate one, and has obvious advantages in preventing inbreeding. Man can very well take advantage of it to help bring about necessary changes. But it is idle to expect that this phase can be made to start earlier, or to last forever. Peter Pans of eighteen make no better biological sense than Peter Pans of six. The normal pattern is to move on to something you like better and settle down there. Of course variations are possible, but that is what the basic human programming allows for.

Culture as Language

Ruth Benedict has expressed the point about the value of culture very well. She quotes the remark of a chief of the Californian Digger Indians:

One day, without transition, Ramon broke in upon his descriptions of grinding mesquite and preparing acorn soup. "In the beginning," he said, "God gave to every people a cup, a cup of clay, and from this cup they drank their life.... They all dipped in the water," he continued, "but their cups were different. Our cup is broken now. It has passed away."

Our cup is broken. Those things that have given significance to the life of his people, the domestic rituals of eating, the obligations of the economic system, the succession of ceremonials in the villages, possession in the bear dance, their standards of right and wrong—these were gone, and with them the shape and meaning of life. The old man was still vigorous and a leader in relationships with the whites. He did not mean that there was any question of the extinction of his people. But he had in mind the loss of something that had *value equal to that of life itself*, the whole fabric of his people's standards and beliefs.

How, we wonder, can that really have a value equal to that of life itself? Are there no other standards? Cannot people, as Sartre proposed, just invent some? Ruth Benedict replies:

It is in cultural life as it is in speech; selection is the prime necessity. The numbers of sounds that can be produced by our vocal cords and our oral and nasal cavities are practically unlimited.... But each language must make its selection and abide by it on pain of not being intelligible at all.... In culture too we must imagine a great arc on which are ranged the possible interests provided either by the human age-cycle or by the environment or by man's various activities. A culture that capitalized even a considerable proportion of these would be as unintelligible as a language that used all the clicks, all the glottal stops, all the labials, dentals, sibilants, and gutturals.... Every human society everywhere has made such selection in its cultural institutions.[10]

It is amazing how much easier this point is to take in about other people's cultures than about our own. Nearly all of us, I think, on reading Ramon's remark, will feel that he is right. He is not exaggerating his loss. (Most of us, in fact, will go on to feel personally guilty, as though our own feet had trampled this irreplaceable thing, even though the damage may have been done long before we were born. As a mark of the seriousness of the offense, this has a point.) But when we think of our own culture, we tend to take a quite different view—*this* one, people say, would be no loss, this one is a dud, a culture that is nothing

10. *Patterns of Culture*, pp. 21–22, 24; my italics.

but a hindrance, that makes proper thinking impossible. The grass on the other side of the hedge is always greener; other people's rites and ceremonies, boring and obvious to them, are exotic to us.

If our culture were so null, where would we get the lights to criticize it?

The criticism, of course, is part of the culture. From Socrates and Christ through Rousseau and Marx onward, half the business of Western culture has been self-criticism. In fact it is (as those names make obvious) not a single culture at all, but a debating-ground, not a monolith but a fertile confused jungle of sources—Greek and Roman and Jew, Celt and Viking, Arab and Slav, Indian and American. Within that jungle we have to choose, and hard work it is, which is why we sometimes feel like writing the whole thing off. Nor, of course, are other cultures wholly monolithic and self-complacent. There is some argument, some difference of opinion within even the simplest of them. Once you know something about them, you always find disputes going on, tension, matters of doubt and dissatisfaction, which is why they can all receive some suggestions from the outside. Thus, when Margaret Mead first observed the Manus, their society seemed stable, even stagnant, and the people safe in supposing that they should always maximize the delights of trading, quarreling, and being in the right, and should fear the vengeance of their ancestors for failure in these activities. That was the communal choice. But when Manus life was disturbed by World War II, and change began to seem possible, it turned out that many people had not been satisfied. And, as some of Margaret Mead's informants explained to her, they learned from the American soldiers that people mattered more than property.[11]

Disputes, however, can go on only among people who share some presuppositions. That is another way of stating the need for a culture. Our logical and our biological needs for it are two sides of the same coin. We are deeply disposed for it (biologically) because we are communicative animals. And communica-

11. *New Lives for Old* (New York, 1956), pp. 177–178. For her earlier observations, see *Growing Up in New Guinea* (New York, 1930).

tion without a strong background of shared presuppositions is not just difficult but inconceivable.

The comparison of culture to a language is rather fashionable; I want to point out all the same how completely just and necessary it is. Language is just one case of a set of activities which has meaning. And enriching the meaning is the point of culture. Actions are not just physical jerks, they *signify*, they count as something. But they cannot do so except against a background of expectation, of regular, definite alternatives. An unknown man runs up to you holding out his hand. Does he want to pull you over and rob you, take something from you (if so what?), grasp your hand in friendship, or exchange with you the agreed sign of some secret society? We all know what gulfs of misinterpretation can open here, even on such apparently trivial matters, far more if something more complex than a single gesture is involved. Even when we know roughly what sort of gesture this is meant to be (say, a friendly greeting) we are badly hampered if we know nothing of the culture concerned. Is it the common, regular approach to a stranger? Is it an extraordinary, personal decision? Is it something reserved for special occasions of intimacy or alliance? Does he expect us to answer with some sign that we accept it? And what would that commit us to? Wanting to know these things is *not* a mark of some especially timid or conventional disposition—we may *want* to be committed—but unless we know the possible alternatives we simply cannot commit ourselves properly. We shall respond only to a tiny part of what he is doing. Does marriage—*here*—involve affection without respect, respect without affection, business partnership, ritual quarreling, ritual adultery, and/or some sort of role-playing quite new to us? Without some idea about this, how are we to treat married couples properly? (The difficulties of cross-cultural marriage are well known.) You cannot even be rude or unconventional unless you know *what you are doing,* and that means knowing what things count as. Even in art (in spite of Sartre's suggestion) spontaneity makes sense only against a background of what is expected. Art always requires a tradition. To innovate there is to do the same expected thing in a very different way—but there has to be something for it to be different *from.* Creativity in art is *not* playing God the Father and producing a new world. It is saying something new about the world there already is. And that can be done only by means of an existing language. When the post-impressionist artists, early in this century, took to collecting Benin bronzes and other African works, they thought of them as a quite new beginning, as something coming from outside civilization. But of course these objects are part of a complex and elaborate culture; they could not conceivably have been made by someone who suddenly decided, on his own, to create something new. Similarly, jazz was not just a sudden spontaneous upboiling of the human spirit; it had African roots. And Stravinsky startled people, but he is entirely continuous with the European musical tradition.

This, then, is the situation of man. Lorenz, in *On Aggression,* describes it as follows:

To appreciate how indispensable cultural rites and social norms really are, one must keep in mind that, as Arnold Gehlen has put it, contemporary man is by nature a being of culture. ["Contemporary man" here does not of course just mean twentieth-century man, but man in his present evolutionary form.] In other words, man's whole system of innate activities and reactions is phylogenetically so constructed, so "calculated" by evolution, as to *need* to be complemented by cultural tradition. For instance, all the tremendous neuro-sensory apparatus of human speech is phylogenetically evolved, but so constructed that its function presupposes the existence of a culturally developed language which the infant has to learn. . . . Were it possible to rear a human being of normal genetical constitution under circumstances depriving it of all cultural tradition—which is impossible not only for ethical but also for biological reasons—the subject of the cruel experiment would be very far from representing a reconstruction of a prehuman ancestor, as yet devoid of culture. It would be a poor cripple [pp. 264-265]

The example of speech should by now be clear. But speech is only one of many general potentialities that need to be provided with a specific path. *What* language we talk depends on our society; it is a matter of luck. It comes from outside. But *that* we talk does not; no baby can be stopped from doing that without physical mutilation. And to speak no language before a baby would not be to give him the freedom of all. It would exclude him from any. But every language carries a way of life with it.

(Special confusions dog people who are brought up bilingual.) In the same way, *what* customs we learn depends on chance, but *that* we learn some customs does not. There is variation in manners, in clothes and ornaments, in what is praised and blamed, in sexual customs and moral standards generally, in homes and property, in songs, dances, jokes and stories, in how we mourn our dead, in the way our entry into adult life is marked, in forms of marriage, trading, quarreling, work, and friendship. But *that* all these things are present, and present in some definite accepted form, is something that does not vary, because people always ensure it. Forms and ceremonies are not idle. "Stereotypes," as they are ungratefully called, are utterly necessary. And they are *not,* as people often unthinkingly suppose, merely means to an end, devices that any "intelligent" being would naturally hit on for reaching a few, simple, physical ends like food and shelter. In the first place, half of them are not means at all; they are ends in themselves. The joys of friendship and affection, and also of hatred and revenge, jokes, dancing, stories and the whole business of the arts, games and other play, disinterested curiosity, and the enjoyment of risk are natural *tastes,* things that make life worth living, not things that could possibly have been invented as means to staying alive. In the second, many things that would greatly help survival are *not* done, because people do not naturally take to them—for instance, getting rid of war. In the third, even things which do directly serve survival, which might in principle be invented by "pure intellects" operating freely with only that in view—such as language, justice, and everything to do with forming fixed rules—were not freely invented for that purpose by us, in the sense that we had a set of alternative devices available and decided on balance that these were the most efficient candidates. We have no alternatives. We go for them because of natural dispositions we could not get rid of if we wanted to.

The business of fixed rules itself is perhaps the most instructive example, as well as the one that people at present may be most inclined to try and change. I think there can be no doubt that *rule-formation* is a universal human characteristic. The good reasons for this I have been discussing in this chapter—but of course there are bad ones too; nothing more easily gets out of hand. One of the most striking things we notice when we first become acquainted with "primitive" cultures is the number of rules they contain on matters that would not seem to us to need regulating, rules which do nothing for survival and can endanger it. An obvious example is ritual mutilations, such as violent "female circumcision" and the numerous woundings and tattooings of the face and other prominent parts. These are usually not just ornament, but marks of age and status; their meaning is governed by set rules. And these are only part of a mass of other rules—which are the soil from which, after some hard thinking about priorities, real moral standards arise. In that way rule-formation is good. But even where it is not good but bad, where it degenerates into obsessiveness, it is still a natural tendency. This is why it will not do to reduce justice (which is a set of rules on how to treat people) to expediency, as if the rule business could be dispensed with. Our nature sets limits to Utilitarianism. "Act-Utilitarianism," the totally flexible pursuit of pure expediency, makes no sense for such a creature as man.[12] And for the same reason the more general idea of *getting rid of morality* is a nonsense. We cannot ask whether we will have rules, only which rules we will have. Continuity of style is a natural necessity to us.

There is therefore something radically wrong with the idea that culture is something unreal and superficial, a veil you must tear off if you want to reveal the truth. Colin Turnbull, the anthropologist who observed the Ik, argues in this way. The Ik are a desperately unfortunate tribe whose traditional hunting and gathering grounds have been taken from them by the redrawing of political frontiers. They have for some time been actually starving, and are entirely without hope. In consequence, their traditional culture has broken down completely, and they often behave most brutally to each other, and especially to their children. Turnbull comments, "The Ik teach us that our much

12. A point made admirably clear by Bernard Williams in *Utilitarianism: For and Against*, and in the chapter on Utilitarianism in his little book *Morality* (New York, 1972).

vaunted human values are not inherent at all but are associated only with a particular form of survival called society, and that all, even society itself, are luxuries that can be dispensed with."[13] They do nothing of the kind. What they teach us (if we need to learn it) is that any society of living things can be destroyed if it is hit hard and persistently enough. In the process of destruction its more complex and advanced capacities will probably tend to go to pieces before its simplest and most primitive ones. That will not show that they were not inherent. Nobody doubts that a bee's complex instinctive capacities are inherent. But if bees are systematically deprived and harassed to death they will stop their more complex operations before they stop crawling around and trying to feed and occasionally sting. Certainly human values are "associated" with society. But society is not just "a particular form of survival," if that obscure phrase stands for "a particular means to surviving," any more than a hive is just a particular form of survival for a bee. Social animals cannot live the life they are fitted for at all without their own form of society. The demand for it is as deeply inherent as the demand for one's own future safety. This is evident when we see what extraordinarily rash things people will often do for social reasons, in a hundred situations from gambling to auto racing, quite apart from actual deliberate self-sacrifice. Colin Turnbull found little or no altruism among the Ik, which is not surprising when you consider that they have already been in their present desperate situation for quite long enough to ensure a steady selection of those interested solely in surviving. They are a dying society. But what does it mean to suggest that everything else in their lives was a *luxury?* Is the idea that only extreme situations are real and serious? If so, most of life is unreal; what sort of unreality is this?

Nietzsche's mind degenerated and eventually went to pieces under the stress of disease. Does it follow that he was never really a gifted writer at all, but only a potential victim of locomotor ataxia? Or just that he was never really a nineteenth-century romantic philosopher (since that depended on his culture), but only a potential writer-in-general?

13. *The Mountain People* (London, 1973), p. 294.

Michael Frayn has remarked on the odd effect this way of thinking has had on fiction:

You might think sometimes, looking at novels and plays, that the paradigm of literature was the Consumers' Association test report. Like electric toasters, the characters of fiction are tested, by stress and crisis, until they break down. And the convention is that what emerges at this point is their 'real' nature. . . . It's true that in life people sometimes do surprise us at such moments, by revealing flaws and virtues we had not known about before. Because of our fascination with the hidden and its revelation, we are easily persuaded that what emerges is of general rather than particular significance. At last, we feel—with a kind of satisfaction—the truth is emerging! On the surface he has always appeared to be calm and cheerful. But now, after he has spent three days without food, under heavy bombardment, lost his home, and got both shoes full of water, it turns out that *really*—underneath—he is a rather irritable man who lacks the capacity to get pleasure out of life.[14]

This twist of thought is, I think, a reductive one, an attempt to find one central strain of motivation that will account for everything we do. That is a misplaced and futile sort of economy.

If culture in general is in this sense natural, is there still any proper sense in which particular institutions within it can be called natural or unnatural? People often do call them so. About the institution of marriage, Dr Johnson said, "Sir, it is so far from being natural for a man and woman to live in a state of marriage, that we find all the motives which they have for remaining in that connection, and the restraints which civilized society imposes to prevent separation, are hardly sufficient to keep them together."[15] Is marriage natural? What does this question mean?

There is of course a quite crude and trivial way of settling it. If people simply define *natural* by opposing it to institutional, then no institution can be natural. Johnson avoids this use. And I suggest strongly that it ought to be avoided, since it obscures the fact that culture is natural to man in the sense of being quite as necessary to his appropriate way of life as the satisfaction of his particular impulses. Moreover, any act that people can succeed in performing must have its institutional side. Revolt has to find

14. *Constructions* (London, 1974), sec. 26.
15. Boswell, *Life of Johnson* (Everyman ed.), 1, 241.

recognizable paths as well as conformity, and war is an institution. But it is remarkable how often people overlook these well-known facts and talk as if anything that had been shown to be institutionalized was therefore obviously dispensable or unreal.

What Johnson actually means by *natural* is easy, unforced, problem-free. Marriage is *difficult*. Thus, we might say, joking, swearing, drinking, and gambling are natural, but finishing our enterprises and doing our duty are not.

But is prudence natural? Or the strenuous practice of the arts? These things are sometimes very hard, but they are certainly not just imposed on us by society. Should we still call them natural because though they may not be easy, only the individual himself can enforce them? Is what needs an outside enforcer always unnatural? If so, what about the rigors an athlete puts up with from his trainer, a musician from his teacher, a Zen pupil from his master? Should we say that enforced activities can count as natural provided they are undertaken by consent? But consent is necessary for marriage too.

Perhaps Hume can help us—"In so sagacious an animal," he wrote, "whatever arises from the exertion of his intellectual faculties may justly be esteemed natural."[16]

Something like this will have to be said of marriage, because no *long-term* commitment is ever always easy and unforced. And no commitment involving more than one person ever suits all parties equally. Yet human nature certainly demands long-term enterprises. We are therefore bound to be frustrated if we cannot finish them, so commitment is necessary. It also demands many activities that are social and public and depend on other people's not walking out on them. So we are all bound to be frustrated if we all do walk out. Moreover for a creature with memory and foresight even quite trivial activities usually have some long-term significance. Joking, swearing, and gambling can readily be institutionalized, and are quite enforceable by members of one's circle. Getting drunk may be easy, but it can still sometimes be compulsory. We are—quite naturally—intensely anxious to please and be accepted. That is why social

16. *Enquiry Concerning the Principles of Morals,* sec. 258.

pressures work. But this is not just a conditioning mechanism, a string of abstract "rewards" and "punishments." It is an aspect of the fact that we feel affection. We want deep and lasting relationships. And because these are often difficult, we "bind ourselves" in all sorts of ways to go through with whatever we have started, even when it proves annoying. Marriage is simply one of these arrangements.[17] It is not something peculiar; it is a highly typical and natural human device. Campaigners against it, from Shelley and the Mills on, have been remarkably crass in posing the simple dilemma, "either you want to stay together or you don't—if you do, you need not promise; if you don't, you ought to part." This ignores the chances of inner conflict, and the deep human need for a continuous central life that lasts through genuine, but passing, changes of mood. The need to be able to rely on other people is not some sort of shameful weakness; it is an aspect of the need to be true to oneself.

Speaking of an institution such as marriage as natural is, of course, paying it a compliment, the compliment of saying that it meets a fairly central human need. The fact that it is found in some form in every human society is in a way enough to show this. (One could reverse Johnson's argument and say if it is found everywhere in spite of its well-known difficulties, it must be natural.) But it might be thought that marriage became thus widespread only because it was, like adequate sanitation, a means to an end.[18] This is pretty certainly what Hume thought,

17. No doubt the first with which we become entangled is the playing of children's games. To walk out in the middle makes trouble. To have consented to start means (normally) going through with the game. Other activities take off from there, and institutionalizing only completes the process. See my article, "The Game Game."

18. Toilet training is a good example of that rather rare thing, an activity that human beings really do have to learn simply as a means to an end, without an innate tendency to build on. This is not because we are in general without instincts, but because we are primates. Not being den-dwellers, primates lack this particular innate tendency, which the young of the carnivores, like nestling birds, show very early. This is why a puppy or a kitten can be house-broken in a fraction of the time needed to toilet-train a baby, and why apes and monkeys, in spite of their intelligence, can hardly be house-broken at all. If everything we learned were merely a means to an end like this, we would not get far. (For ape insouciance, see Schaller, *The Year of the Gorilla*, p. 179.)

as evidenced by his very confused contrast of natural with artificial virtues. He regarded human sagacity simply as the power to calculate consequences, and counted chastity and fidelity, with justice, as artificial virtues, devices designed merely to produce safety and promote utility. In a species as emotionally interdependent as man this view of marriage is nonsense. Pair-formation could never have entered anybody's head as a device deliberately designed to promote utility.[19] It is true that it does serve the interests of children, and can be said (once it is there) to *serve that purpose* for the race. But individuals want to live in pairs before they have any children, and continue to do so when their children are gone. Moreover, it is often a source of friction because of jealousy, which has great disutility. It is therefore an autonomous taste. As the social insects show, it is perfectly possible to look after the young adequately in a species with no personal ties at all. Even rats use communal nurseries, and Plato was right to wonder whether this might be a practical arrangement for people. The reason it is not lies in our emotional constitution, not in the institutions to which that gives rise.

The difficulty, in fact, is not that marriage does not serve a natural need, but that that need can conflict with others. In these conflicts we have to determine priorities. And marriage, particularly in some forms, may be held to be not worth its price. This should not, I think, lead us to call it *unnatural* (though we might well call some forms of it so). When worrying about priorities, we often do speak of one thing as *more* natural than another, meaning that it serves more important needs and frustrates less important ones. Far down this scale come things we call downright unnatural, because the bargain they represent is so bad. Thus the life of the African girls confined in the fatting house was an unnatural one in a clear sense, and so was the practice of binding the Chinese girls' feet. This is still proper language even though

19. People who think that our species has no natural pair-forming tendency should look in detail at how life goes on in species that actually do not have it, such as chimps. *No social consequences at all* follow mating; all males present mate any female in season (unless she rejects one or two), and everybody walks off afterward to live just as they did before. People are not like this anywhere, any more than wolves or geese.

the sexual demands for which these institutions catered were real and even fairly normal.

If we call particular institutions natural or unnatural, then, we are not being illogical. We mean that they give us a notably good or bad bargain in the satisfaction of our central needs. And as this goodness or badness has degrees, the naturalness of an institution does too. What we very often mean is that the institution is *more* or *less* natural, that is, satisfying, than likely alternatives. In any case, the fact that a habit is institutionalized does not mean at all that it has no genuine attraction, or is unimportant to individuals. To parody Hume: in so institutional an animal, whatever arises from the exertion of his culture-forming faculties may justly be esteemed natural.

CONFORMITY AND PSEUDO-SPECIATION

That our culture should be so deeply important to us is no accident. It has to be in order to do the evolutionary job that it does do for us, that is, make our species so versatile that it can, in a sense, speed up evolution. This versatility is of course another well-known mark of man. Given favorable conditions we can build cumulatively on the achievements of our fathers, because we learn skills, take them for granted, and do not forget them. We can in principle thus advance immensely faster than species that depend for their adaptation on genetic changes. Given unfavorable ones, we can (again in principle) unlearn much of what we know, and after a period of confusion start on a new tack, with much less trouble than most other species. (A few other natural nonspecialists like rats and sparrows compete with us, but much less ambitiously.) This makes the human race at any time resemble in many ways a group of species rather than a single one. As Lorenz says in *On Aggression:*

Culturally developed social norms and rites are characteristics of smaller and larger human groups much in the same manner as inherited properties evolved in phylogeny are characteristics of subspecies, species, genera, and greater taxonomic units. Their history can be reconstructed by much the same methods of comparative study. Their divergence in historical development erects barriers between cultural units in a similar way as divergent evolution does between species; Erik

Erikson has therefore aptly called this process pseudo-speciation. [p. 80]

As he points out, it can work only if whatever the culture dictates for the moment is taken for granted most of the time as unthinkingly as noncultural activities would be among animals. Constant hesitation and argument would make adaptations ineffective. Accordingly, people everywhere are inclined, until they meet different customs, to assume that their own are universal, and when they do meet them, to suppose that they are not dealing with members of their own species at all, but with some sort of inferior imitation which it is probably all right to massacre. Pseudo-speciation interferes with the "sentiment of humanity" and can lead to intolerance and violence. And this of course is a contributory reason (besides the cult of freedom) for deploring culture altogether and trying to escape it. Could we have a universal culture? There are already a number of Universal Languages—"and who speaks them?" as the sad little joke has it—"Nobody." Ruth Benedict's notion of the immense curve of human capacities is probably right—there are simply far too many possibilities to be included in a single way of life.

The Prehuman Roots of Culture in Habit and Symbolism

How far does culture separate us from the condition of other species?

Again, I am going to look for the rudiments and take for granted the enormous difference of degree in the use made of them. We all know that other creatures do not produce symphonies or sciences, television or nuclear weapons. Still, culture, like language, is not a miracle. It is not an alien force that descends on helpless humanity from outside. We make it. What ancient strengths make this possible?

One source, which I have mentioned already, is the immense dependence of virtually all animals on habit. The other, less widespread but extending to all social animals, is the power to use and interpret symbols. And this is the one which man has developed most surprisingly.

HABIT

It is very common to find animals innately programmed to receive, early in their lives, impressions from the outside world which determine their subsequent conduct.

The best-known example perhaps is imprinting, the process by which newly hatched chicks attach themselves to their mother. If any other creature, such as a human being, comes before them at this point, they will attach themselves to it instead, will follow it and take refuge with it exactly as if it were the mother, and may not be able to mate with members of their own species, because they prefer the foster one. With birds this process is swift, brief, and irreversible. With mammals it is a good deal slower and perhaps less final, but it takes place in the long run no less surely. (It may be that in human beings the nearest parallel to the chick's sudden snapshot-effect or Titania-syndrome is fixating on an item of clothing or some similar object as a sexual fetish.)

Now the word *imprinting,* though suitable enough in emphasizing suddenness, can be misleading because it forcibly suggests the passive Blank Paper model. The mother's image certainly does come from outside and is, so to speak, stamped on the chick. But this image alone cannot determine any behavior. The chick has to have first a whole set of innate dispositions to behave in various ways—following, nestling, seeking out in times of danger and so forth—in which a single blank is left for the figure that is going to elicit them. The general effect is to limit the chick's behavior while it is still young and vulnerable, to bypass the cumbrous and expensive process, posited by Blank Paper theorists, of random behavior gradually improved by reinforcement. That process would give such a high probability of the chick's ending up inside a predator that evolution forbids it.

In imprinting, then, there is a strong, natural, internal tendency to receive from outside an impression of a certain kind, and to *use* it in a particular, predetermined way in one's life from then on. The details of the impression are not predetermined. They must come from outside. But the tendency to form such habits is. It is a complex and positive power.

This is the pattern of open instinct or open programming and it is a common one.[20] Another interesting example is the choice of food. In many species it happens that the young receive their first solid food (as well as their milk) from the mother, either by her gift or by grabbing a little of whatever she is eating. They are then unwilling in later life to eat anything they did not first eat in this way, even when it is otherwise a perfectly suitable food for their species. This, again, is an innate open program with a blank in it. It serves the evolutionary purpose of protecting inquisitive young from poisoning, while leaving a fairly wide range of foods open in principle to the species. (There is some difficulty about combining these two advantages. It may be relevant to the human case, but we will leave it for the moment.)

Another striking case is path-finding. Intelligent species, including man, tend as strongly as less intelligent ones to prefer in general a well-known path to a new one. This tendency, again, has such obvious survival value that we can see easily how individuals who were weak in it would quickly be selected out. The point is not just that the familiar path itself is a safe one, free from unexpected pitfalls, slippery patches, or impassable obstacles. It is that familiarity frees the user's attention to look out for other dangers and other advantages. It is true that familiarity can breed contempt and so become itself a secondary danger. But this is only possible because it is in general such an efficient protection.

Accordingly, creatures are often found sticking to the paths they know with a tenacity that may sometimes seem slavish and deplorable. Lorenz describes his water-shrews constantly returning to their nest-box by jumping first onto the top of it and then slipping in through the door with a half-somersault, because that was how they had happened to do it when they rushed home after their original exploration. More remarkable still, he describes their confusion when a familiar stone was removed from their path. Though not blind, they simply jumped onto the nonexistent stone, landed with a bump, went back and did the same thing again, and only after that started to explore the

20. See the first section of Chap. 3.

changed terrain. Water-shrews are insectivores, which are rather primitive as mammals go, and Lorenz remarks that a rat or mouse would be adaptable enough to avoid jumping onto a nonexistent stone: "The preponderence of motor habit over present perception is a most remarkable peculiarity of the water-shrew. One might say that the animal actually disbelieves its senses if they report a change of environment which necessitates a sudden alteration in its motor habits."[21] All the same, even the most advanced animals, including *Homo sapiens,* act this way sometimes, if their attention is distracted. And the general point I want to make is simply that, without habit, without this power of absorbing a background and taking it for granted, man could never have built up customs with the firmness that is necessary if they are to form a complex culture.

Lorenz cites in *On Aggression* another significant case, that of a tame goose, which had become accustomed to make a particular detour every evening on her way to bed. One evening, being late and hurried, she neglected to do this until she had gone up five steps of the staircase. She then stopped suddenly with every appearance of alarm, went hastily down and retraced her usual course, and climbed up again. "On the fifth step she stopped again, looked round, shook herself and greeted, behavior mechanisms regularly seen in greylags when anxious tension has given place to relief. . . . The habit had become a custom which the goose could not break without being stricken by fear" (p.70).

It is customary at present in the West to deplore unreservedly this kind of conduct in people, discounting entirely the way that a Japanese or an Indian would probably look at it. Nevertheless, at the risk of throwing his readers into the same state as the goose, Lorenz makes a deeper observation, in the same spirit as that which I quoted earlier from Ruth Benedict.

We would be neglecting an essential side of the matter if we only stressed the inhibiting function of the culturally evolved ritual. Though governed and sanctified by the superindividual, tradition-bound and cultural superego, the ritual has retained unaltered the nature of a habit which is precious to us. . . . The austere iconoclast regards the

21. *King Solomon's Ring,* p. 110.

pomp of the ritual as an unessential superficiality which even diverts the mind from a deeper absorption in the spirit of the thing symbolized. I believe that he is entirely wrong.... We love the traditionally transmitted.... It is this feeling of affection that reveals to us the value of our cultural heritage. [pp. 74–75]

C. S. Lewis makes the same point very shrewdly about prayer. His senior devil, Screwtape, is advising a junior tempter on how to make human prayer futile:

This is best done by encouraging him to remember, or think he remembers, the parrot-like nature of his prayers in childhood. In reaction against that, he may be persuaded to aim at something entirely spontaneous, inward, informal and unregularised.... One of their poets, Coleridge, has recorded that he did not pray 'with moving lips and bended knees' but merely, 'composed his soul to love' and indulged 'a sense of supplication'. That is exactly the sort of prayer we want.... At the very least, they can be persuaded that the bodily position makes no difference to their prayers; for they constantly forget, what you and I must always remember, that they are animals, and that whatever their bodies do affects their souls.[22]

In all species, of course, the cautious and conventional power of habit sometimes conflicts with more positive motives. And in the more intelligent, less specialized ones it has to contend particularly with curiosity, with the wish to explore and use unfamiliar things. But only in an extremely secure situation like the one we in the civilized West have for some time enjoyed could the romantic suggestion that it ought never to win have seemed plausible.

Habit is necessary. And it does not just restrict. As Lorenz points out, it has also a positive value, which will become clearer if we now move on to consider symbols. Long familiarity and intense experience of the patterns in our lives are necessary if we are to draw out their full meaning.

THE USE OF SYMBOLS

The power to read expressive movements and gestures is not acquired by conditioning; it is innate. Eibl-Eibesfeldt makes this point in *Love and Hate:*

22. *Screwtape Letters* (London, 1942), pp. 24–25.

Rhesus monkeys isolated from birth prefer pictures of their own species which are projected on the walls of their cage to other pictures. They emit contact sounds, invite them to play, and when the projection is switched off they quickly learn how to project these pictures for themselves by pressing a lever. At the age of two months, these socially inexperienced rhesus monkeys also recognize the expressions of their conspecifics. The picture of a threatening monkey then makes them shrink back and emit sounds of fear, and the rate of approach falls off sharply when they see this picture. [p. 20]

The same sort of thing is clear in the response of a human baby, when only a few weeks old, to a smile, or even to the picture of a smile, and to other facial expressions and tones of voice, including unfamiliar ones.[23] The young of intelligent species such as man do not have merely a few isolated tendencies to react in fixed ways to particular stimuli—a "basic alarm system." They have a versatile power of responding across the whole range of expressions and movements typical of their species. The development of this is delayed somewhat while their senses and their motor coordination are coming into play. This process takes longer in them than in less intelligent creatures; in very advanced species, which are particularly nice to their young, it is not hurried. A small baby can blunder across the path of a crusty elder unrebuked, unconscious as yet of the warning signs a slightly older child would notice and respect. But what makes the change is simply the maturing of the faculties; hard experience is not necessary, and will not work if the baby is not maturing properly.[24] In a normal infant, the power to read expressive movements simply unfolds, not needing conditioning any more than does the power to walk and run in the manner suitable to one's species.

Now these movements do not somehow convey the mover's emotions directly, as a pipe conveys water. They symbolize them. The symbol is a natural one, not arrived at by convention. What it usually is is a kind of movement that is more or less typical of

23. See Morris, *The Naked Ape*, pp. 122-123; Eibl-Eibesfeldt, *Love and Hate*, p. 11.

24. See, for instance, Jane Goodall's interesting account of regression and the loss of this perceptiveness in an ailing young chimpanzee (*In the Shadow of Man*, pp. 226-227).

someone feeling the emotion in question, but stylized or "ritualized" into a fixed form by inheritance, not by culture. Examples are smiling, frowning, laughing and crying, growling, stamping, purring, snorting and spitting. These expressions and expressive noises are more or less standardized. In *Love and Hate,* Eibl-Eibesfeldt writes: "In the process of their differentiation into signals, behaviour patterns undergo a number of typical modifications. They are generally simplified, but at the same time exaggerated in the manner of mime in their execution. Often the movement is rhythmically repeated, as with the drumming of the woodpecker. Expressive movements furthermore frequently take place at a typical degree of intensity, which makes them unmistakable as signals" (p. 50). Thus, for example "When they are slightly embarrassed, people all over the world mask their faces either slightly or completely. This is certainly a ritualized hiding movement. . . . I have even observed a small boy who had been born blind hiding his face with his hands in embarrassment" (p. 49). Many examples of this sort of thing are found in other animals, notably symbolic courtship feeding in birds and even insects, where no real food passes but either uneatable objects are given or the movements of giving are gone through without a gift.[25] Or again a threatened animal shows its submission, not by doing just anything its mood might dictate, but by a regular signal, such as bowing or (in dogs and wolves) lying on the back. Because this is familiar, it gets through to the threatener much more quickly than a less typical gesture would. And, as Eibl-Eibelsfeldt notes, "if it is of advantage to the transmitter of the expression of emotion for another animal to understand him, this expression will progressively become transformed into a signal through the process of natural selection" (p. 46). That is, individuals that are good at getting their point across are better able to promote both their own success and that of their group—so we can expect there to be steady selection for understandable signaling.

25. This succeeds as courtship, of course, not because it *deceives,* but because its point, in its present form, *is* expressing the mood to which it is now connected. A gesture that has quite lost its original point and taken on another—such as the offer of food where no food is present—is said to be "emancipated" from its original purpose. See Eibl-Eibesfeldt, *Love and Hate,* p. 44.

RITUALS

Giving the name "ritualization" to this signaling process upsets some people. What ethologists are doing, however, is merely following the Freudians in making it a slightly more general term than it used to be, using it in such a way that cultural rituals are seen as only one form of a wider genus, the others being inherited ones and those built up by individuals in their lifetime without cultural help—for instance, family rituals, and also private ones like those of washing compulsives. Eibl-Eibesfeldt, while he goes to great trouble to distinguish these different kinds of rituals, also is concerned to account for their likeness by convergence of use. "We should not be surprised at such similarities," he writes, "for the requirements of the receiver of a signal are constant, whether it is a matter of phylogenetic, traditional or ontogenetic ritualization. And the way a signal evolves is dictated by the receiver. The receiver is the one who determines the meaning of a particular behaviour pattern in his partner, and in so doing elevates it to the status of a signal" (p. 50).

This is, I think, another case where looking at other species enables us to put something human in a wider context that explains it. Why do cultural rituals work? Why are they so prevalent? For it is important to remember that human ritual is not confined to organized official uses—say, in religion or government. Official uses are often, in fact, somewhat weak and decaying compared with the unofficial ones surrounding such things as fighting, gambling, drinking, and swearing, or with those of children. (Anyone who is surprised at this suggestion can try the experiment of walking into a bar that has a homogeneous clientele, wearing unexpected clothes, talking in unfamiliar tones, and ordering what is not normally drunk there.) Our need for the rituals of culture seems to be an outgrowth of our need for natural ones. Our power to use the first depends on our power to use the second. We can see this clearly enough in the case of someone who does it badly. People who are crass and insensitive in using and responding to ordinary expressive movements are not going to be suddenly successful as actors or dancers, teachers or priests, however carefully they may be conditioned.

The Place of Conventional Symbols

How great then is the gap between this widespread power to use natural symbols, and the human power to use conventional ones successfully? Is there here, perhaps, a discontinuity in explanation of the kind which Chomsky suggested, comparable to that between breathing and walking?

Even apart from the evidence of chimps using Ameslan, this could not be right. Those who can receive and respond to natural symbols possess the power to *interpret* symbols generally. And that is the real nub of the symbolism business.

It is the receiver who has to have the flexible imagination. He must be able to receive and identify symbols for feelings that he does not at present feel, has never felt yet, and may never feel. But everyone starts as a receiver, since this is the situation of every baby in a social species. And a receiver must not stop at a mere standard passive reaction, such as taking cover. He must become aware of the nature of the feeling being expressed. This is the only way in which he can become educated in the range of response necessary for his species. Moreover, he must not stop at identifying a few standard *kinds* of emotion (anger, affection, fear). He needs to be able to distinguish, right from the start, the various shades and nuances which indicate different moods in different individuals. This ability manifests itself, rather inconveniently, in both babies and domestic animals when they are approached by people who in a general way want to show good will toward them, but who are slightly nervous or aggressive because of unfamiliarity. These people do not themselves respond quite suitably to the child's or animal's own signals. It notices this at once, and will not trust them. It is very quick, too, to pick up and remember every scrap of information, however slight, about what the behavior of those around it means. It notes divergencies and reads them. Imagination is constantly alert in interpreting behavior, and memory in filing it. And those are the powers which make the use of conventional signs possible.

We all know that animals which live among people can rightly interpret a great deal of human behavior, including a number of words, and can, indeed, become remarkably hard to deceive.

This is true of dogs, elephants, horses, and plenty of others as well as of apes. Moreover the young of different species can understand each others' behavior, as is evident when they play together. The innate power to read expressive behavior is therefore highly versatile and open-ended. There is no limit in principle to what behavior can be received and understood as a signal.

When Mike, the ambitious chimpanzee, clattered kerosene cans to impress his colleagues, he was using a new symbol to express not just standard ambition—standard signs would have been good enough for that—but his own personal kind. (It was, Jane Goodall remarks, a striking trait in his character.) When several apes combine in a primitive dance, they do not just make standard movements, they vary their behavior according to mood, character, and occasion. And they can respond suitably to each other's variations. In the same way, a human toddler sizes up variations in the behavior of those around him, and responds in a way that shows his own character. People who think in terms of "association" treat this feat as simple. He has just come to associate particular words and movements with reward and punishment. But if he did not have the power to grasp imaginatively the whole mood involved, he could never make such associations. Particular words and movements hardly ever have regular consequences. Someone who merely associated them externally, without grasping the mood that explains them, would not be equipped for human life at all. Moreover, half the "rewards" and "punishments" themselves consist in aspects of these very moods. All social animals care, quite directly, about being treated with affection and respect rather than ignored, scolded or cursed at, even if nothing else follows. They are therefore particularly on the lookout for anything that symbolizes either kind of treatment, and are quite able to pick up the shade of meaning conveyed by a new sort of symbol.

Because there is no limit in advance on what behavior creatures in social species can view as a symbol, there is none on the general possibility of extending the range of symbols by agreement. The basic conditions for doing it are present. What is needed for actually extending the range is chiefly strong and persistent motivation. Creatures must really want to convey things that their innately supplied range of gestures does not let them convey. And this is as true of the rest of culture as it is of language.

Evidently the chimps who use Ameslan do want this. They are prepared to take trouble, they use it spontaneously. We respect them the more for this, and surely we are right to. But our own prehuman ancestors must have wanted it with an enormously stronger passion, or they could not have met with such success. I do not mean, of course, what Lamarck suggested—that the mere passion for communication and communal effort itself directly develops the powers, as the giraffe's effort to reach upward was supposed to stretch his neck. Things are less direct than that, but just as sure. Every effort made to form a more complex, reflective way of life tends to favor, in the next generation, those naturally gifted enough to cope with it, and disadvantage the slower and stupider.

Our ancestors then wanted intensely to convey something. But *what?* They did not, I have suggested, just want the convenience of shunting information quickly to and fro, of having spears brought and houses built promptly. That would only have produced a "language" like the simplified model Wittgenstein describes in *Philosophical Investigations* §2, where two men are building together and one simply calls to the other the names of the things he wants—"block," "pillar," "beam," "slab" and the like compose the whole language. If talk was thus limited, people's way of life would be a purely technological one. It might have every device and machine for survival, but there would be no other part of culture, no communal activities to make surviving worth while. Wittgenstein's purpose, of course, was deliberately to bring out the strangeness of this idea. He speaks of this single language-pattern as a *language-game,* that is, just one pattern out of the many that can be abstracted from existing language. He is pointing out that neither propositional form nor any other form is *the* pattern of language, that the idea of a single basic pattern is a chimera.

Our ancestors plainly did not have this technological obsession; nor did they want only to assert propositions. They wanted to interact socially in all the innumerable ways that go to make up a culture. They needed language for performance, not just to exchange information. In manners and ceremonies, arts and sports, the performing element is primary, and it is still very important in sexual customs, law and morality, religion and government, even in trade and finance. Our ancestors' needs so shaped language that it will serve for all these things. In this way they succeeded in widening the scope of human capacities to such effect that we now suffer from an embarrassment of riches.

We are capable of far more than we can fit into even the richest individual life-span. We have to choose. It is this enormous enriching of our capacities that gives rise to free will. Since there is much more on the table than we could possibly eat, we have to choose, in a sense in which other species do not. Much of our choosing, however, is communal rather than individual. Some of it has to be done for us by our parents and their generation, before we are in any position to advise them. To look at it another way, we have to choose for our children as well as for ourselves, and also, since we can influence others, in part for those around us too.

Romantic individualism is wrong if it suggests that we can choose alone. To choose at all (rather than just flipping a coin), we need intelligible alternatives. And they can be provided only by a culture, that is, by an unseen host of collaborators. Culture is necessary to make rational choice possible. It is the condition of freedom.

Part Five

THE COMMON HERITAGE

"Look out of the window, James, and see wot'un a night it is." James staggered up, and, after a momentary grope about the room, . . . exclaimed, "Hellish dark, and smells of cheese!"

"Smells of cheese!" repeated Mr Jorrocks, looking round in astonishment; "smells of cheese? Why, man, you've got your nob in the cupboard—this be the window."

—Surtees, *Handley Cross*

CHAPTER 13

The Unity of Life

Our Emotional Constitution

In the last three chapters I have been trying to show how the traditional distinguishing marks of man—speech, rationality, culture—are not something opposed to our nature, but continuous with and growing out of it. Our need for some form of them is natural, not an accidental, external need like the "need for a car," which might as well or better be served by a horse or a helicopter. But this means that facts about our other needs, about our whole system of needs, have to come in to determine what sort of culture, what rational way of life, can suit us. Our full emotional nature determines our aims, as well as the formal, structural characteristics discussed so far.

There are those who think that we cannot compare even our emotional nature with that of other species, and in this chapter I shall examine the validity of this position. The main business of this book is to deal with the initial problem of whether and how we can compare, not with the details of comparison. For this reason I shall be fairly brief and dogmatic here on substantial points about our actual needs.[1] The book will have done its job if

---

1. I cannot talk here as fully about our emotional nature as I would like to. The way Anthony Storr deals with it in *Human Aggression,* using ethological concepts to restate and reorganize psychoanalytic ones, seems to me very sensible. More of the same sort of thing would probably help—though, of course, aggression must not be allowed to take over the whole scene any more than sex.

it convinces its readers *that there are* such particular needs, for our species as for every other, and that they form a system that can guide us. People disagreeing about *what* they are can start a separate argument later.

The specific expressions of our needs vary widely. So does the balance chosen among them. We have great freedom here. But the main structure and the main problems it sets are constant. So there are limits on what can constitute either a culture or a rational system of life—or indeed a language. Let us look at this last case, which, though large enough, is smaller than the others. What must a language be like to suit such a creature as man?

The limits imposed on speech by its uses are evident. Languages serve definite social purposes. They are not calculi, nor mechanical devices for stating propositions. Someone with "nobody to talk to" does not just lack a convenient source of information. Human languages cannot merely be the means of reporting that cats are on mats, or even of "expressing feelings" in the sense of just pouring them out. They exist for, among other things, making *ourselves* understood. That means for creating and strengthening particular social bonds. They are for promising, threatening and offering, for "asking, thanking, cursing, greeting, praying."[2] They therefore contain all manner of forms of address—polite and rude, contemptuous and ribald, suited for endearments and insults, and for addressing old men and young men, kings, lovers, friends, enemies, animals, women, and children. Everywhere it matters enormously *how* you speak, what social approach you use. Language is for a varied life, one where personal relations of many distinct kinds are possible—not for exchanging standard information units among standard users. Languages expand themselves especially in greetings, apologies, forms of address, and similar devices. (Even the abominable Dobu in New Guinea have a formula for thanking people; it goes, "If you should now poison me, how would I repay you?"[3]) The business of greeting also has enormous weight in every other social species—apparently because a new

2. Wittgenstein, *Philosophical Investigations,* sec. 23.
3. Benedict, *Patterns of Culture,* p. 166.

arrival would otherwise be alarming, would constitute a threat, and the threat must be neutralized, a friendly bond forged, as soon as he appears.[4] Otherwise we would all spend our lives having heart attacks every time somebody started to come out of the undergrowth.

> O come ye in peace here, or come ye in war?
> Or to dance at our bridal, young lord Lochinvar?

The question must arise. In other social species, including all the primates, it is taken care of by gestures which (as experiments show) are in part innately determined.[5] In ours, such gestures are still of the first importance, as anyone can see if he tries merely *speaking* his greeting without turning his head, raising his eyebrows, moving his hand and eyes, stopping, or in any other way visibly marking his sense of a new presence. But of course the words are needed too; the opposite experiment (gestures without words), though less disastrous, may still cause confusion.[6]

Thus, though languages differ very much, what they *do*, the social patterns they can express, differs much less. And when it comes to less conscious things, to expressive gestures and common natural symbols, the likeness between people in different cultures is astonishing. And it, too, often extends to other primates. Eibl-Eibesfeldt has illustrated similarities of gesture admirably from photos of people in the most varied cultures in his book, *Love and Hate*. (For instances also involving apes, see especially pp. 18, 29, 119, 133, 176.) As he shrewdly remarks, "In New Guinea alone several hundred dialects are spoken. This is bound up with the tendency of human beings to isolate themselves into small groups, especially by means of customs. . . . But if one finds that in spite of this, in certain situations, such as greeting, or in the behaviour of the mother towards her child, the same behaviour-patterns recur repeatedly and amongst the

---

4. For the great importance of this, see Eibl-Eibesfeldt, *Love and Hate*, index under *Bond-establishing rites, (ii)*; also Lorenz, *On Aggression*, pp. 186–187, and Wickler, *The Sexual Code*, pp. 214–218.

5. See p. 311.

6. See the last section of Chap. 10.

most differing peoples, then it is highly probable that these are innate behaviour patterns" (p. 13). Another fascinating example, not on Eibl-Eibesfeldt's list, is laughter. We all need it, and miss it if it is long absent. ("I haven't had a good laugh like that for a long time.") Details of jokes vary with the culture, but themes and situations recur. Sex jokes, for instance, are widespread, and that no doubt for the reasons Freud suggested in his book on wit—that laughter releases tension, and not even the most prosaic and easy-going societies have been able to take all the tension out of sex. Some cultures, of course, frown upon laughter and try to restrain it. But far from showing that they do not naturally have it, this indicates quite the contrary. They want to subordinate it so some other good. And however solemn the adults, laughter is found in healthy children everywhere.

People do not, I think, always notice what an astonishing coincidence this sort of thing would be if it were not innately determined. They take it as natural that expressive gestures are passed on. But if they are found, virtually identical, in a South American Indian, a Frenchwoman, a Papuan and a Balinese,[7] there can be no cultural link less than many centuries old. What has to be accounted for then is the selective survival of *this* similarity where all other aspects of life have come to vary so much, or the selective adoption of *this* tendency where nothing else is adopted. The parallel of language shows that modes of expression do not just persist through inertia. And many gestures, concerned with less central matters, do in fact vary widely. But in certain central human situations, a fixed repertory of gestures reappears in culture after culture. Were it not innate, this would be absolutely extraordinary.

Faced with this dilemma, people tend to respond by saying, "Oh well, *that*. . . ." Gestures seem trivial. They are the kind of thing we take for granted. How, we are inclined to say, would we express amusement except by laughing? How would mothers or lovers express their affection except by embracing and kissing? But this obviousness is indeed my point. If you have amusement or affection, the laugh or embrace obviously goes with it and vice

7. *Love and Hate*, pp. 14–15.

versa. But how would you explain either connection to a creature that did not have them—to an intelligent crocodile, if there
were one, or (what may be equally unlikely) a rational but nonaf-
fectionate alien being? Why should parent-child exchanges be so
like those between lovers? What could it mean that, if we have no
one to embrace or laugh with, we *miss* something, we are lonely?
To be disposed to make the gestures, you *must* also be capable of
the emotions. The occasional person whose emotions are not
normal finds it impossible to imitate the gestures convincingly:
people see through him at once. Inevitably, therefore, these gestures bring us all back to the same group of behavior patterns
for our deepest exchanges. Anyone who thinks this a boring
restraint should reflect that, without it, we should have no
chance of reciprocation at all. People might learn the gestures,
but how would that ensure the feeling? My instance of the
stranger who runs up holding out his hand is significant here,
for this is in fact (as Eibl-Eibesfeldt shows) an innately established gesture of friendly greeting, a part of the universal species
repertoire, though of course it is not everywhere institutionalized as it is in Europe.[8] It is also done by apes. Here we come
back to the main branch of innate sociability on which cultures
supply the twigs, and to my point that culture is necessary *because it completes* nature. In discussing this example before, I
was concerned to show how much *more* we need on top of these
innate tendencies for a full human life. One could think here of
the difference between the chance handshake of strangers and
the greeting—which might look outwardly very much the
same—between two old friends who meet again after they
thought they had lost each other, after years of difficulties and
estrangements. (Or of "Dr Livingstone, I presume?") What culture, and our personal history within it, adds must not be belit-
tled. But my present point is the other side of the matter, and to
my mind the more neglected—the extraordinariness of the
chance handshake between strangers, the startling fact that encounter works. As Martin Buber expressed it: "The relation to
the *Thou* is direct. No system of ideas, no foreknowledge, and no

8. Ibid., pp. 174–176.

fancy intervene between *I* and *Thou*. The memory itself is transformed, as it plunges out of its isolation into the unity of the whole. No aim, no lust and no anticipation intervene between *I* and *Thou*. . . . Every means is an obstacle. Only when every means has collapsed does the meeting come about."[9] Culture is the cup that saves the water of encounter from being spilled on the sand. But it could not generate it in the first place. Encounter has to be natural.

We take these things for granted just because they *are* constant. And in a way our business is always with the mutable, with what we can change. This makes some people think it a waste of time to attend to innate factors. But not trying to *do* anything about innate factors is a quite different thing from denying that they exist. And in fact, if we want to change anything we obviously must attend to innate factors, since they include the possible mechanism for change. To effect any change, we have to understand the permanent. An obvious instance is the set of currently popular suggestions that marriage, or "the family" in the abstract, is a dispensable institution, a mere passing whim of certain cultures, or that there is really no maternal instinct, just cultural conditioning by the women's magazines. Or that we should behave in exactly the same manner to women and men. Or, of course, that it is only bad education which makes us aggressive. All this, I think, is just spitting against the wind. We can vary enormously the forms these things take and our own individual part in them. We can no more get rid of them than we can grow wings and tusks. Nor is there any good reason why we should want to.

Families and Freedom

In an earlier chapter, I discussed generally the sense in which we can say that marriage is natural. Here I want to look briefly at the currently fashionable idea that it is unnatural because it forces on each individual a role determined merely by gender, instead of leaving each person free to play a role entirely of his own creation.

9. *I and Thou*, pp. 11–12.

I have suggested throughout this book that it is no misfortune to have a specific nature—that freedom, in the sense in which we really value it, does not mean total indeterminacy, still less omnipotence. It means the chance to do *what each of us has it in him to do*—to be oneself, not another person. Though all human ranges overlap, we each have a distinctive range of talents, tastes, and emotional possibilities. The advantage of innate individuality— the positive enjoyment of one's own capacities—more than outweighs the drawbacks of not being infinitely pliable. And belonging to one gender rather than another is just one aspect of this. If we all came as standard models, life would be far poorer and thinner than it is. It is an essential feature of vigorous human life that we are constantly being confronted with people who react to the world so differently from ourselves that they stagger us. The whole range of human possibilities is so much wider than any one of us can encompass that people of the most diverse sorts are needed to cover it. The full human sound goes up only from the whole orchestra. Moreover, each of us has a nature that itself is very complex, and we are constantly being delighted and appalled by discovering more of its elements. Cultures help us to simplify this rich confusion somewhat by providing separate roles for people of obviously different kinds, active and contemplative, old and young, men and women. And this seems absolutely necessary.

Naturally, I am not denying that the *particular* roles provided can be grossly unsuitable. Often they are. And, because men are stronger than women, serious injustice sometimes results. Injustice, however, is also found between parents and children, rich and poor, healthy and sick. But distinctions of role in these cases are still necessary. Injustice is no adequate reason for abolishing a role, though it is a good reason for altering it.

How should we deal with the drastic, sweeping, and usually negative suggestions of those who want to abolish marriage and "the family," and who think that women should altogether be treated in the same way as men? This is a good case of something which people tend to call "unnatural," and which is defended by declaring that concept vacuous. It is not vacuous, but we are dealing with the double sense of *natural* I noted in Chapter 3.

Things that are natural in the minimal sense—widely practiced, emotionally seductive, hard to eradicate—do not have to be so in the strong sense in which we are called upon to approve them. We may admit them as real tendencies, but ones which must be kept down, because if they spread widely they will distort the whole. Instances are cruelty and hypocrisy, and also the excesses that arise from many good qualities if they get out of hand— obsessiveness, sentimentality, fanaticism.

Now it seems to me that those who want to abolish the distinctive female role, or "the family," or the degree of male dominance that usually accompanies it, object to them in this way. They cannot plausibly treat these things as just local institutions, mere cultural aberrations, like astrology or hara-kiri. They are far too widespread, and too important in people's lives. But they can regard them as springing from two well-known human weaknesses—first, the inability to stand alone emotionally, and second, the tendency to abuse power.

First, the matter of independence. There evidently are many people of Existentialist leanings around who think the ability to stand alone is an absolutely central part of human dignity. They value individuality so highly that they want to do away with any institution that tends to entangle us with each other, to make us say "we" rather than "I." Thus they regard family life as self-indulgent and would like to get rid of it.

The first thing to say about this position is that the genuine form of it must be distinguished from a confidence trick often played in its name, whereby people who are *frightened* of human contact, and cannot deal with it, denounce it as self-indulgent and congratulate themselves on their ability to live without it. That said, however, no doubt some real neo-Stoics remain. And their position is this: they are proposing an *ascetic* way of life, a renunciation of things commonly wished for and taken as part of the human bargain. This puts them in the same position as those who, in various cultures, have sternly built institutions to control quarreling, boasting, or cowardice, to maintain virginity, or to train shamans. There is nothing unnatural about such asceticism—nothing we need object to—*provided* that no lies are told about it. The cost must be admitted as a real cost, and nobody should be asked to join in without full and informed understanding of this fact. People preaching against domesticity have to be as honest as monastic institutions on this point. Not everybody shares their tastes, and there is no excuse for missionary intolerance in the matter. To describe people of different tastes from one's own as *unreconstructed* is the language of open tyranny; what could possibly justify it in people championing freedom? It seems often to be supported by an odd assumption that the masses do not know their own minds, and are helpless victims of cultural conditioning, whereas the reconstructors are fully autonomous. This is just one aspect of an intellectual snobbery common to all Existentialist morality, an exaltation of positions that in fact are open only to intellectuals as the only *morally* respectable ones, and an ignoring of the characteristic forms of self-deception which the intellectual life encourages.

The extreme terms in which I have been discussing the problem, and in which it is often posed, are, however, probably misleading. To speak of *marriage* or *the family* in the abstract leads us to ignore the enormous range of forms these things take. What is really needed is piecemeal reform. We could, after all, quite plausibly say that friendship or sport or the arts threatened freedom, because some forms of them certainly do so; this would be a bad reason for abolishing them altogether. Families can be unduly possessive. But then they can also be unduly neglectful. Why is the one danger more important than the other? Finding the right degree of family closeness is not simple. This is clear from the Israeli experience. There the founders started, as usual, with the onesided aim of avoiding the faults of their own upbringing. Reacting against the stifling, overprotective domesticity typical of central Europe, they let fresh air in everywhere, and did all they could to keep family bonds loose and minimal. And things have gone well—but each generation of young parents changes the bargain a little, and so far usually in the direction of reweaving the bonds that were loosened, of demanding more time with their children. Evidently we cannot work with the simple dichotomy of *bond* versus *free*. Most of us are deprived if we are not allowed to forge and maintain certain important bonds in our own way.

What, now, about dominance? Here the problem is a much more general difficulty in modern life, one that has nothing to do with gender. It springs from the intense competitiveness of the Western world. Obsessed with success, with examinations, tests, and record-breaking, with competitive sport, trade, and manufacture, we have drifted into behaving as if life were not worth living except at the top of the dominance hierarchy, as if that place alone marked excellence. This is expressed in extraordinary words like *meritocracy,* which means the rule of those who pass exams, but claims to mean the rule of those with merit.

The natural effect of this state of things is that groups lower down struggle sharply upward, kicking each other in the face as they do so. At the top, however, there are only a limited number of places. Most people, therefore, will still be at the middle or bottom, however hard they kick. And if this is allowed to destroy their self-respect—if they are given reason to think they are being despised for being what they are—they will be miserable, and will make those above them miserable as well.[10]

Against this perspective, the question of whether the few at the top are male or female is one in which I find it hard to take much interest. Most women, as well as most men, would still be in what they regard as outer darkness even if all sex barriers were removed. The only thing that could make the change important would be *if* females at the top, being rather less competitive by nature than males, could do something to bring about a saner climate. To get there and do this, however, they would have to compete without catching the competitive spirit. This is a lot to expect. We cannot hope for it if we treat the matter as a straight conflict of women's interests against men's. Fairness to women is not a partisan, competitive gain. It means a saner life for everybody. We all have strong elements of both sexes in our natures, and restriction to single-sex ideals hurts us all. As for

10. I have already mentioned the mess in which the concept of Freedom currently wallows. Equality is, if anything, in an even worse fix: a hotly competitive society pays lip service to it, producing complete confusion. (See Bernard Williams's admirable paper, "The Idea of Equality," in his collection, *Problems of the Self* [Cambridge, 1972].) Tackling the quite tough problems of women's life with these concepts is like trying to dig a garden with a brush and comb. The tools are totally unsuitable.

our natural interest in dominance, it is not a lust for oppression. It is a taste for order, one that can get out of hand, but does not have to. Based on the relation of child to parent, it is essentially protective, and protection can be mutual. It needs to be supplemented by more equal kinds of fellowship. But it remains one element in our emotional nature.

Understanding the structure of human feeling should help us to determine how far different ways of life are possible. It is not that we have to rule out all suggested changes as soon as we know they may make emotional trouble. But we have to understand their price. The experience of religious and other specialized communities should by now have shown us (what Plato, when he wrote the *Republic,* could not know) the difficulties of a way of life which overrides the natural balance of human feelings. As Freud pointed out, people who despise sex and think themselves above it are liable to be ruled by less attractive forms of it than those to whom they feel superior. As he failed to point out, the same is true of all other major human motives, including aggression. And the structure to be found does *not* consist of a set of converging lines by which all motives can be shown to derive their strength from one central one (sex, power, or any other), or from two (balancing it with self-preservation, hunger, the death-wish, or what not). Freud's, Hobbes's and Nietzsche's patterns were quite unbiological. No species has such a nature. The structure must consist of a number of motives which are genuinely distinct and autonomous, but which are adapted to fit together, in the normal maturing of the individual, into a life that can satisfy him as a whole.

Why Intelligence Does Not Replace Instinct

Behaviorist thinking, however, still tends to regard the idea of such a structure of instincts as unusable for people, suitable only for "animals." People believe, I think, that as animals have grown cleverer, they have become less and less dependent on *instinct*— by which they mean "closed instinct," automatic, fully detailed behavior patterns like the bees' honey dance. Instead of instinct (according to this view), higher animals use intelligence, and man has become so much cleverer than every other animal that he has switched over to intelligence altogether. So he has entirely freed himself from the limitations of an instinctive structure.

This won't do. *Instinct* and *intelligence* are not parallel terms. *Instinct* covers not just knowing how to do things, but knowing what to do. It concerns ends as well as means. It is the term used for innate tastes and desires, without which we would grind to a halt.

With closed instincts, desire and technique go together. A bee cannot just want to dance-in-general; it must dance (and therefore want) only the exact figure that will tell the other bees where it has been. But as you go up the evolutionary scale, much wider possibilities open. The more adaptable a creature is, the more directions it can go in. So it has more, not less, need for definite tastes to guide it. *What replaces closed instincts, therefore, is not just cleverness, but strong, innate, general desires and interests.* It would be useless to replace the hidebound hunting habits of the wasp simply with the greater intelligence of cats and otters. There must be also a strong, general wish to hunt. (And in fact it is just these intelligent carnivores that play-hunt for pleasure, especially the cubs.) The less firmly the next action is settled in advance, the stronger must be the general desire that will lead to discovering it. More obviously still, mammals could not improve on the automatic brood-tending of bees merely by being more intelligent about what benefits infants. They have to *want* to benefit them. And they must want it more, not less, than bees, because they are so much freer, and could easily desert their infants if they had a mind to, which is the sort of thing that could simply never occur to a bee. Mammals, of course, sometimes do desert or neglect their young, and are sometimes stupid in looking after them; sometimes, too, they eat them. But this only shows that their instincts are not mechanically perfect devices—which is exactly my point. Tastes and interests are not the sort of thing that could possibly be mechanically perfect devices. They are indeed "evolutionary devices." But for the individual, they are the sort of thing which determines what devices, mechanical and otherwise, are *for*. They deal in ends, not means.

Just in proportion as automatic skills drop off at the higher levels of evolution, innately determined general desires become more necessary. This transition has always been obscured because the word "instinct" was used for both. That is less odd than it may look, since there really is continuity between them.

It is a continuity typical of organic evolution, which can hardly ever move (as the development of a machine sometimes may), by simply scrapping an unsatisfactory model or feature and starting afresh with something quite different. Birds' wings are adapted forelegs, not a purpose-built new design. Tusks are adapted teeth. And in the same way, the more advanced and subtle parts of our emotional life too are adapted versions of cruder ones, and are often deeply marked by their strange history. How these adaptations work is complicated, as is the evidence for them and the shrewdly designed battery of principles on which ethologists evaluate it. I shall simply point briefly to a few examples.

The first and simplest example is the use of patterns drawn from sexual behavior as appeasing gestures to calm aggression. Unnumbered species do this; it is the simplest way of making possible wider social contacts among creatures that have the primary tendency to drive their fellows away in order to get enough space to live on. Sex is the oldest, original, soft answer; it is rivaled as a conciliator only by its successor, the care of the young. As soon as the latter became current (chiefly among birds and mammals, though teleost fishes and certain reptiles did some of the pioneering), it provided an excellent repertory of gestures that could be used to soothe anger, to beg for help, and in every way to oil the wheels of society. Creatures that have to deal with helpless and demanding young must be capable of genuine kindness and tolerance. This makes it possible for fellow-adults to tap these resources if they behave in a childlike way. Thus, courting birds continually approach each other with gestures typical of nestlings, and inferior creatures do the same to dominant ones. And mutual relations can be formed, in which both parties can, on occasion, play both roles. *It is at this point— long before the emergence of primates—that nature ceases to be Hobbesian.* Friendship becomes possible. And it is on such a foundation (however unsuited to human dignity) that the serious business of social life is actually grounded.

Because these are the roots of society, they still determine its structure. I am not suggesting that the connection is simple, or that the original elements do not change when they are built into a more complex pattern. Indeed this historical method of understanding motives calls for a much less simple basic scheme than those of most kinds of psychology which have attempted the job so far. But this seems to be because the phenomena *are* complicated in the way that calls for such a scheme. We cannot hope to achieve simplicity in the long run unless we invest a little more in concepts when choosing our basic principles.

If we are to think historically in this way, we shall certainly need to compare remote species, to talk of wasps as well as wolves. A useful bit of terminology about the propriety of this is the distinction between *homology* and *analogy*[11]—analogy being used here in a special technical sense, not just for any apparent likeness. (The terms are drawn from bodily evolution.) A homology is a likeness due to kinship, an analogy one due to function. Since all birds are akin, there is a relation of homology among all their wings. It is not altered by the difference in function affecting flightless birds such as kiwis and penguins. Birds and bats, however, are not akin. The likeness between their wings is a functional one, therefore an analogy. It can also be called an example of convergent evolution—that is, the production of a similar device in two quite different creatures by a similarity of need.

Both these kinds of relation are most important for our reasoning, but in quite distinct ways. If one wants to know how a species got to be the way it is, one approach is to study its near relatives, see how far they differ from it, and try to trace the course of evolution. This is following the homologies. But the other method is particularly useful if we are dealing with a species that happens to be short of near kin (like man, the giant panda and the elephant, and unlike Darwin's finches)—or if the function itself is what particularly interests us. Thus, if we were studying the penguin's flippers, we should look at the flippers of seals and whales, the fins of fish, and quite possibly the propel-

11. See Lorenz, *On Aggression*, chaps. 5–7, Eibl-Eibesfeldt, *Love and Hate*, chap. 3, Wickler, *The Sexual Code*, chap. 3.

lers of submarines, as well as the wings of birds. The absence of kinship can be a positive help to our understanding, because it shows that what produces likeness must be the function. Airplane designers have interested themselves a good deal in the flight of birds, seeking light on the functional problem of flight in general. In terms of behavior, if we want to understand what pair-bonding does for a species, we can observe it as a successful arrangement through a great gamut of species, ranging from wolves, gibbons, and lemurs through numerous birds down to less conspicuous quarters such as mites and the painted shrimp. Scientists who look into this (as Lorenz and Wickler are doing) — want to see how the interests served by the arrangement differ with different circumstances, how pair-bonding and non-pair-bonding species differ in a variety of contexts. Some of them hope then to be able to talk more sense about that partially pair-bonding species, man.

If we are to compare the basic elements of human social life with those of any other species, we need to use analogies, because many of the functions these elements serve simply are not served in any other primate species. Primates do not have big cooperative enterprises, nor therefore the loyalty, fidelity, and developed skills that go with them. Nor do they have fixed homes and families. But the hunting carnivores do. And neither apes nor wolves have anything like the human length of life, nor therefore the same chance of accumulating wisdom and of deepening relationships. But elephants do. And no mammal really shares the strong visual interest that is so important both to our social life and to our art, nor perhaps needs to work as hard as we do to rear our young. But birds do. This is why it is vacuous to talk of "the difference between man and animal" without saying *which* animal.

Several groups of animals, *not* closely related, have independently "invented" fairly advanced forms of social life. They are, that is, not "anonymous herds" whose members stay together but take no notice of one another.[12] They can *do* things together, help and look after one another to some extent, and have indi-

---

12. For this interesting variation, which brings out unsuspected points in the meaning of "social," see Lorenz, *On Aggression*, chap. 8.

vidual friendships. Examples are (at their own level) many birds (such as geese and jackdaws), such carnivores as wolves and wild dogs, elephants, many primates, and probably whales and dolphins. (So little is known of these last that I cannot firmly include them in what follows—but what *is* known does not seem to conflict with it.)

Right across this range, social life shows certain common structural features. The first of these, noted by Lorenz, can be crudely summed up by saying that *it rests on peacemaking*—that the positive social bond consists of friendly gestures that arise from the need to counter an existing possibility of aggression. Species incapable of mutual attack do not, apparently, ever find the occasion to become friends.

"The falling out of faithful friends renewing is of love." Animals in an anonymous herd never get to know one another. Real social animals can clash, and sometimes do. But clashes are commonly averted by friendly and appeasing gestures, particularly on arrival, or whenever one member has occasion to impinge on another. Most of these gestures are, as I mentioned, drawn from the repertoire of sexual or infantile behaviour. They are often subtly altered, however, in a way which, along with the context, allows them to express more complex social attitudes. For instance, appeasing quasi-sexual behavior imitates the female invitation to mate (never the male one) but with characteristic alterations. Those to whom the gestures are made respond with others, often drawn from the same repertoires, though also characteristically altered so as to work as signals. Moreover, within a social group there is a dominance hierarchy, in the sense that some members are respected more than others, are deferred to, and tend to decide the movement of the group. This hierarchy is complicated, and I do not want to oversimplify it. Those who come low in it in one context may come high in another. "Mutual respect" is common and important. Rank is by no means a tyranny. Still, it is real. Groups tend to have leaders.

There is usually little or no actual use of force; even threats are often unnecessary. *But rank is very closely linked with the behavior typical of parent and child.* Those of lower rank defer to those they respect in the same way that they did to their own parents, and where a conflict looms, one participant has often only to make infantile gestures to appease the other, who responds with parental ones. These are often symbolic beggings for food and gifts of it. Apart from this imitation of infants, actual infants are often remarkably popular with adults (not only with their parents). They are not only widely tolerated, they are often sought out, helped, and played with. And their mere presence can put a stop to conflicts among adults.[13]

The way in which appeasing gestures are drawn both from the behavior of females and infants tends to approximate these two roles. There are species in which females apparently outrank males (such as beavers) and others in which they come about on a level with them (such as hyenas, which, significantly, *look* almost indistinguishable). Elephants, like some deer, seem to give the higher rank to females, simply because they stay together and preserve the continuity of the group, while males range more widely and are more loosely attached to it. But in most of the species with a well-developed social life the top rank is held by males; females tend to rank lower (though young, unproved males may come lowest of all). But the lot of subordinates is not especially oppressive. Dominant members in general really do protect them by coming forward to help them when danger threatens, whether from outside enemies or from other members of the group. In the latter case an interesting and very common pattern is for low-ranking members to be rescued from middle-ranking ones by those higher still—a situation that clearly holds part of the material for human justice and government. Also, females in particular often *need* rank less than males, since they tend not to be quarreled with so much, and may have a good answer if they are. Gender nearly always *makes a difference*—an experienced observer can tell a creature's gender at once, both from the way it behaves, and from the way others treat it. There is absolutely no need to wait for human culture to bring this about; it is almost universal.

To conclude this highly foreshortened sketch—in all these

13. Eibl-Eibesfeldt, *Love and Hate*, pp. 149–150, 189. Baboons can be seen turning to infants to save themselves in a squabble in one of Jane Goodall's films.

groups, if one asks, what holds this bunch of creatures together? the answer is attachment; a bond of affection constantly fed and maintained by friendly attention. It is not fear. Many of these creatures can survive on their own very well, and sometimes do so when they feel like being solitary. (Elephants and gorillas are impressive examples.) It is not food. Only the hunting carnivores tap the economic advantages of cooperating. They just like each other.[14] And not indiscriminately; they have preferences. To end where we began, they are capable of a quarrel.

My points here are two—*likeness* and *complexity*.

First, it is really remarkable that these very diverse species should have so similar a structure to their social life— *that there should be no equally intelligent species with a quite different one,* for instance, something much less emotional, more egalitarian, efficient, and impersonal, on the model of the social insects. Those who think of *intelligence* as a property on its own, the sole hallmark of a higher development, ought to be puzzled by this. The ants and bees constitute a terminus. Science fiction has many times pushed around the counters to devise successors for them, but to do so it must credit them with aspirations, ambitions to do better, which have no meaning in their life. They lack further *aims*.

Second, though these species are (in this rough sense) alike, what they have in common is not reliance on a single factor, either a single instinct or just "intelligence" itself, whatever that may be. A great web of innate motives is involved, which can be grouped under the main headings of aggression, sex, dominance, and the care of the young if we are thinking of their sources, but which includes numerous independent tastes (for instance, for play among infants and for various sorts of skill, exploration, friendship, and cooperation among adults). It is not necessary or useful to "explain" this web by reducing it to any single basic motive. But people have by now come to expect this, and to expect the motive in question to be exciting and disreputable. They have therefore repeatedly taken ethologists to be putting forward such a motive, let them say what they may.

14. See Schaller, *Year of the Gorilla,* pp. 122, 183.

Thus, Desmond Morris has been widely understood as *merely* advertising sex, and Lorenz aggression, notions that ensure missing the point of their arguments. It is well that Eibl-Eibesfeldt has come along to redress the balance, with a notably quiet, unaggressive approach, a better knowledge of anthropology than some earlier ethologists have, and a balanced insistence on the one main motive that has been underestimated throughout—the care of the young. That is not a cure-all either, but it is the missing piece of the puzzle, overlooked because it was too quiet and obvious.

Eibl-Eibesfeldt agrees with Lorenz that the capacity for aggression is a necessary precondition of positive love and friendship, but not that therefore love is "a child of aggression." Aggression in defense of those to whom one is bound can strengthen the bond—but only, he points out, if it exists in the first place. And such bonds seem to exist almost exclusively among creatures that cherish their young:

> While there is no friendship without aggression, there is also, with few exceptions, no friendship without parental care. . . . Love is not primarily a child of aggression, but has arisen with the evolution of parental care. . . . Among the animals that do not look after their young, we know of no group defence and no fighting partnerships. . . . Brood care, on the other hand, calls very early for individual partnerships and individualized cherishing of the young, and thereby offers the necessary basis for a differentiated social life. . . . Aggression plays only a secondary role in strengthening a bond. . . . The sexual drive, on the other hand, is extremely rarely used as a means of cohesion, although in the case of human beings it plays an important role in this respect . . . . *The roots of love are not in sexuality,* although love makes use of it for the secondary strengthening of the bond.[15]

The point is strangely obvious, once you think of it—and it is really the only way of accounting for the kind of motive love actually is, for the fact that it is *not* just another way of eating people. Caring for the young is the only relation in which such an outgoing motive could have developed. Prolonged, reliable affection, an affection which is *not* a recognition of superiority, nor a lively sense of benefits to come, is absolutely necessary for

15. *Love and Hate,* pp. 123-124, my italics.

it. The brief contact between independent adults necessary for mating does not call for that kind of affection at all. But the young are helpless. Among birds and mammals, they *have* to be helpless, they are warm-blooded, and will eventually develop into rather complex creatures; this takes a long time. (Those such as guinea pigs, which hurry the process, can survive only in favorable conditions, and do not develop highly in the long run). Unlike the social insects, such creatures do not just need to be fed; they need a long and gradual *cherishing* into maturity. So they must be individually known and "personally" cared for. (I think, with Lorenz, that "personal" is a quite proper word here.[16] *Person* did not originally mean a human being, but a character in a play, an unique, irreplaceable individual. It can, after all, be nonhuman, like the Persons of the Trinity, or a Corporate Person. And the point about a personal attachment is that no one else can play just that role.) Only this emotional history could have developed the innate attitudes that give a curious multiple meaning to words like "care." How would you explain to a creature of quite different emotional makeup that *caring for* people means serving their needs as well as wanting to be near them, and the connection of these things with thinking highly of them?[17] Again, what is such a creature to make of the fact that we want children *of our own,* and that to *disown* a child is a terrible injury, though people are not property, and being too *possessive* is a fault? In the cardinal case of parenthood, there is absolutely no substitute for *one's own. Belonging* nowhere is a disaster. And the way in which this set of attitudes carries through into other sorts of affection is quite evident from the use of childish language and diminutives among lovers. I shall come back to this point in a minute.

In this section, I have made only one move toward under-standing the structure of our motives, namely, to suggest how they may be historically connected, how one may have grown out of another. Much more would be needed if we were to analyze what we are doing when *now* we group one under another—

16. *On Aggression,* p. 138.
17. Apparently it needs explaining too to those who have invented that fash-ionable phrase, *the caring professions.*

when we say that a particular act was really just an attempt to dominate, or a piece of showing off, or a sexual approach, or when we make general remarks about what motive is liable to bring in what other. But it should now be plausible, even to people who do not always think historically, to suggest that the historical connection, if present, makes a difference to the meaning of the motives we trace today. For instance, the play of small children, especially boys, involves (quite spontaneously and without tradition) a lot of highly stylized aggression[18]—that is, mild attacks and defenses of a sort are made. But typically, and unless something goes wrong, nobody gets hurt and everybody is squealing with laughter.[19] Exactly the same thing can be seen with puppies, kittens, and many other young creatures. Now *why* should there be this element of aggression at all? If Lorenz is right that it is in some sense the grandfather of all our close personal contact, that the *first* form of notice we became able to take of one another was a rather indifferentiated pushing, it makes sense that this should still be the most natural form in which we can get the feel of other people's presence, or their real solid otherness. And as, obviously, it has been "emancipated" from its original context and lost all real hostility, it is perfectly harmless. (In fact the sort of refined parent who tries to stop it does children great harm.) Ambivalence goes deep; it must be respected and understood.

Eibl-Eibesfeldt in *Love and Hate* notes many other important applications of this kind, from which I can only quote briefly:

From what has been said so far, it should be clear that in point of fact, many behaviour patterns which are regarded as typically sexual, such as kissing and caressing, are in origin actually actions of parental care. We remind the reader of this because Sigmund Freud, in a strikingly topsy-turvy interpretation, once observed that a mother would certainly

18. If anyone doubts this, it is easy to check, since every baby reaches a stage at which it is first introduced to strange babies, and in the case of an eldest child it is easy to exclude example. I never realized, until I watched my own children, how completely they would *know what to do* on these occasions, while behaving in a way unknown among adults, and which they had therefore never seen.

19. See "An Ethological Study of Some Aspects of Social Behaviour in Children in Nursery School," by N. G. Blurton Jones, in *Primate Ethology*, ed. Desmond Morris.

be shocked if she realized how she was lavishing sexual behaviour patterns on her child. In this case Freud has got things back to front. A mother looks after her children with the actions of parental care; these she also uses to woo her husband. . . .

In certain situations the adult behaves as if he were a child, and as we have already mentioned, such regressive manifestations belong to the normal behavioural repertoire of animals. In man it is the same. . . . Regression of this kind is not at all pathological, and this must be emphasized. . . . This is only true of people who cannot find their way back out of the role. [pp. 143–144]

I cannot pursue this fascinating point here further than to say that I prefer to formulate it, as Eric Berne does, by saying that the Child still survives within each of us; that it is not a passing role, but a lasting aspect of our character. "Actually," Berne writes, "the Child is in many ways the most valuable part of the personality, and can contribute to the individual's life exactly what an actual child can contribute to family life; charm, pleasure, and creativity. If the Child in the individual is confused and unhealthy, then the consequences may be unfortunate, but something can and should be done about it."[20] Freud was not strong on this point, and his language of *regression* is too disapproving. But I must leave the matter there and return to the idea of a direct evolutionary source for human emotional patterns.

What could be the alternative to it? Given that the general structure of social life I have just described has many striking parallels with that of man over his various cultures, given that there are also the detailed likenesses in gestures and so on pointed out in the first section of this chapter, what, *other* than inheritance, could have produced this likeness, which is far too strong to be due to chance? In what way could intelligence *replace* instinct, producing such similar results? As I have said, evolution is conservative. Nothing that works at all gets replaced by something else merely because that something else is better. There is no selection pressure to get rid of a device unless it actually fails. Innumerable odd and crude arrangements which we can all see ways of improving persist in nature, simply because they do not prevent survival. So to develop new means of brnging about an

20. *Games People Play* (New York, 1964), pp. 25–26.

unchanged result would call for a drastic two-way movement, first to get rid of the habit entirely, then to acquire it again, by convergent evolution, in a quite different form. Such two-way movements are certainly possible. Snakes, for instance, have got rid of their legs and gone back to creeping, and aquatic mammals have gone back to swimming in the water their ancestors left. But then the *point* of creeping or swimming is obvious in their circumstances; anything living in holes and corners will do well to creep, anything living in the water *must* swim. *What similar pressure of convenience could require that we imitate so closely the emotional structure of mammalian life?* It is impossible to conceive a position from which that question could arise or be answered—because it makes no sense to imagine choosing without already having some emotonal structure. Which brings out how impossible it would be for a creature to survive if it got rid of that structure. The fair analogy is not with taking your legs back into the water, but with giving up locomotion altogether for a few centuries. Having no emotional structure is a far worse form of nakedness than that of a crab without his shell. (It is pretty much the situation in which Existentialists tell us that we are—a position that, I have suggested, makes little sense.)

What people have in mind when they make the implausible suggestion that in man intelligence has replaced instinct is, I think, the real range of cases where, by intelligence, we do things that *in other species* are done by instinct—such as building (a thing for which our primate inheritance has not prepared us), domesticating animals and growing crops (which the social insects do to some extent), and hunting, where we need various devices to do what the carnivores can do on their own. (Even here I think it is clear that we often have a basic instinctive interest to work on. Apes do hunt enthusiastically, though not constantly, and make nests, and we have had time to evolve on our own, converging with the carnivores, and our cousins the gibbons, an instinctive taste for a fixed home.) In any case it is quite impossible to extend the pattern of these cases to get rid of the general structure of our instincts.

Moreover, if instincts *had* ever been got rid of, it is impossible to see why they should have been so closely imitated by the structure that "intelligence" then took it upon itself to impose. An intelligent plan supposedly would provide for safety and social harmony. Why should there still be so much quarreling? Why so much insistence on looking up and looking down? Why do people have the inconvenient tendency to insist on *respect*, to want notice taken of them? And why is it such hard work expanding the bounds of affection—loving one's neighbors and enemies? There does not seem to be any sense of intelligence that could account for these things.

What Is Anthropomorphism?

It is nonsense, I have been suggesting, to suppose that intelligence or rationality could replace instinct. And I have said that the structure of our instincts is inherited from our primate forbears, though of course with many alterations evolved by our own species. People may make a further objection to this idea, saying that the names we use for human feelings and motives—fear, anger, affection—cannot properly be used of animals at all, or that, if used, they do not carry the same sense they do with people. In that case the likenesses I have just been discussing are misleading.

Now people obviously sometimes do attribute to animals feelings or motives that they do not have, treating the animals as if they were people. And this is called *anthropomorphism*. The ordinary use of this term, however, implies that the mistake is one of fact; there are other feelings the animal *does* have, and we can often name them. Thus the sentimental dog owner attributes affection to his pet when bystanders attribute greed. And this (it is important to note) is a difference of opinion that can occur in a human context too—the company president claims that his deputy is devoted to him; others understand the fellow's actions differently.

It is a much more extreme position to say that we would be wrong, not just in attributing affection to *this* dog, but in attributing to any dog any feeling or motive whatever. Students of animal behavior do quite often disclaim any right to talk about the "subjective" feelings of animals. They should consider whether they have any right to talk about the subjective feelings of people either, for the position is very similar. In no case can we *be* anybody but ourselves. We cannot "get inside" someone else— we genuinely do not know what the exact quality of the feeling accompanying his actions is like, and would doubtless be astonished if it could somehow be conveyed to us.

But knowing what somebody's feeling or motive is does not demand this. The word *feeling* is not so hazardous to use. Fear, greed, and the like are *not* just feelings, sensations. They are attitudes. It is possible to have a feeling and be utterly puzzled by it—to be unable to give it a name. What enlightens one may well be observing one's own actions or thoughts. A man is depressed—but does not realize it until he notes with amazement that he has neglected, or simply forgotten, to do something he normally thinks very important. He is frightened—but his fear is so chronic, so familiar that he does not think of it as such, until he finds he cannot face some minor trial. This is very different from having a toothache, which you know about directly. We can make mistakes in identifying other people's feelings. But then we can make mistakes about our own too. Saying that somebody has a feeling is *not* claiming a hot line to his private experience; it is finding a pattern in his life.

Does it involve saying something about his private experience too? I think myself that it does, and that philosophers recently have been too timid about this, too willing to concede a tricky point to the crude behaviorist who used blandly to turn his back on consciousness (and who ought, as has been suggested, to use the greeting, "You're all right; how do I do?"). What seems to be involved if we say that George is frightened or depressed is that we *do* believe not only that he will act in certain ways, but that he is, some of the time at least, having feelings, sensations, which are *like* what we ourselves have on some occasions, which are not only nasty, but nasty in the same general sort of way. We believe this because we are innately framed to do so. George's feelings can be different from ours, to accord with the general peculiarity of George's life—but they have to fall somewhere within limits set by our powers of sympathy. Otherwise, if we find them becoming obscure and unimaginable to us, we shall say, in a quite special way, that we do *not* understand him, can no longer sympathize. And people do say this of feelings they themselves cannot share.

If we did not grasp the general motive uniting apparently diverse actions, it would be impossible to explain behavior in either man or beast. For explaining it *is* bringing it under a general motive. *That* approach was an insult and a demonstration of independence; *this* one, differently carried out, is a friendly greeting and an offer of forgiveness. That prostration is a sign of submission; this one of despair. Both in animal and in human life we constantly need such explanations. And we can safely use them, provided that we have and use the relevant experience of this sort of context. We are not illicitly claiming private access to the exact quality of the subjects' feelings, we are classifying their behavior by the essentially public criteria common to their species. Novelists do it:

Mrs. Ferrars was a little, thin woman, upright, even to formality, in her figure, and serious, even to sourness, in her aspect. Her complexion was sallow, and her features small, without beauty, and naturally without expression; but a lucky contraction of the brow had rescued her countenance from the disgrace of insipidity, by giving it the strong characters of pride and ill-nature. She was not a woman of many words; for, unlike people in general, she proportioned them to the number of her ideas; and of the few syllables that did escape her, not one fell to the share of Miss Dashwood, whom she eyed with the spirited determination of disliking her at all events. [*Sense and Sensibility,* chap. 12]

So do ethologists:

Even in those days Flo looked very old. She appeared frail, with but little flesh on her bones.... We soon found out that her character by no means matched her appearance; she was aggressive, tough as nails, and easily the most dominant of all the females at that time.

Flo's personality will become more vivid if I contrast it with that of another old female, Olly, who also began to visit camp at that time. Olly, with her long face and loose wobbling lips ... was remarkably different. Flo, for the most part, was relaxed in her relations with the adult males; often I saw her grooming in a close group with two or three males out in the forests, and in camp she showed no hesitation in joining David or Goliath to beg for a share of cardboard or bananas. Olly, on the other hand, was tense and nervous in her relations with others of her kind. She was particularly apprehensive when in close proximity to adult males, and her hoarse, frenzied pant-grunts rose to near hysteria if high-ranking Goliath approached her.... For the most part, the relationship between Flo and Olly was peaceful enough, but if there was a single banana lying on the ground between them the relative social status of each was made very clear: Flo had only to put a few of her moth-eaten hairs on end for Olly to retreat, pant-grunting and grinning in submission. [*In the Shadow of Man,* pp. 80–81]

Neither writer claims a private line to anyone's stream of consciousness. The important difference between their methods is not that. Nor is it that the one is describing people and the other chimpanzees, nor that one book will be found in the literature section of the library and the other under zoology. It is simply that Jane Goodall can, if asked, produce detailed statistical documentation for everything she says, and Jane Austen could not. (No doubt she would have been willing to collect it if someone had asked her. ...)

As Ryle pointed out in *The Concept of Mind,* none of us need suspect that (in spite of our constant success) we are constitutionally unable to pronounce on other people's feelings, that we are locked away in a Cartesian solitude. Solipsists apart, most of us would be ready to accept that we can know something about human feelings. Ought we to hesitate about extending this ability to our contacts with animals? Do we really not know what they feel?

We have, it seems, a choice here. As with other skeptical suggestions, we can simply proclaim that *we know nothing*—and then try not to use the powers we have disclaimed. Or we can use them, and see where they take us. As I have suggested (following Ryle) to attribute a feeling or motive to an animal is (among other things) to discern a pattern in its life. If one asks, "is this genuine nest-building or displacement activity?" one is asking about contexts—what else has it been doing, what will it go on to do? And the answer will involve all kinds of details about its behavior and the other contexts in which these same actions have previously appeared. The whole thing can be made to look perfectly external and behavioral. And for those who *are* crude behaviorists—who genuinely believe that nothing more can be known in a human context either—there can be no question in any case of a difference between man and animal. If consciousness is a myth, or is irrelevant to describing behavior, it is so for both equally.

Most of us, however, can see that that will not do. The words by which we describe behavior—seeking, escaping, frowning, attacking, withdrawing, eating, resting—have been built up, so to speak, from the inside as well as the outside. We mean by them something we *do* as well as something we watch—and if we did not do a thing, we would often not have the word at all. (What is "resting well" or resting at all, from the observer's angle?) Two things decide the success with which we use these words of others: our own familiarity (from the inside) with the act or feeling in question, and our familiarity (including attention) with the particular creature—man or beast—being observed. The species barrier is, in itself, irrelevant. Members of one species do in fact often succeed in understanding members of another well enough for both prediction and a personal bond. Nothing more is necessary.

On the first point, our own familiarity with the feeling, Tinbergen, who is officially anxious to disclaim any insight into the subjective moods of animals, gives himself away in *The Herring Gull's World* by an intriguing example: "The period of incubation . . . is a rather monotonous phase in the reproductive cycle, monotonous at least for the observer who, missing any incubation instinct in himself, has some difficulty in understanding the satisfaction which a bird presumably feels when just sitting on eggs" (p. 134). That is to say, incubation is *exceptional* in that it really must be defined from the outside only. If we were dealing with creatures—say, from another planet—all of whose actions had to be so defined, we could not, as he justly says, "understand their satisfactions" at all. And this has to mean, not just expect them, but imagine them, find an analogue to them in our own emotional repertoire.

The second point, familiarity with the creature observed, is the one on which we more often fall short. The best way to misunderstand people's motives is not to pay sufficient attention to them. But even if one is trying to attend, one can still fail to understand because one has not known the person long enough or well enough, or because one is familiar with no other example of the kind. Someone who knows just one woman or one child, one rich man or one Spaniard, is at a disadvantage because he does not know what to expect of them. Now I think that our mistakes about animals are, in fact, usually owing to such a lack of knowledge, and that "anthropomorphism" is simply one form of a more general kind of failure, often found with people as well. We mistake motives because we do not have the necessary background, and because we do not even try to think out what is probable, but simply make them up by projecting our own feelings and setting up whatever drama attracts us at the time. Thus as children, and again as elderly persons, we may misunderstand people in other age-groups by reading their motives as though they were our contemporaries. But nobody has thought it worthwhile to call us paedomorphic or gerontomorphic for doing so. The defect is too general.[21] And people who are really familiar with animals (or any other group), people who take them seriously, can avoid it.

Thus, let us look at a case where people often think Lorenz is anthropomorphic:

A gander may have affairs of long duration, regularly meeting a female other than his wife in a "secret" place and copulating with her. However, she is his partner only in copulation; he never accompanies her when she is walking and he never gives even the slightest hint of a triumph ceremony in her presence. In this respect he remains absolutely faithful to his wife. Nor does he guard the strange female's nest; should she happen to be successful in acquiring a nest site and in rearing a family, she must do so unaided by the gander. He does not love her in the least.[22]

Every term is given its meaning by a full, detailed, and unsentimental knowledge of the species's behavior. The last sentence, which is the one most likely to cause alarm, seems to me perfectly justified. He has explained just what behavior he is referring to. Now suppose we tell a similar story about people—he does absolutely nothing for her; he never wants to see her except in

21. We are andromorphic and gynaecomorphic too—also plutomorphic and pauperomorphic. Any more?
22. *On Aggression*, p. 203.

bed—will there be objections to giving the same summary of the position? If there are, they will probably be of the what-is-love? order—suggesting that we have too narrow a notion of what can possibly be included. But this applies in both cases. I do not think that the species barrier is very important.[23] There are people who understand horses very well, but go all to pieces when they have to deal with people.

In a passage in *King Solomon's Ring* Lorenz gets, I think, to the root of the matter. He has been describing how a low-ranking female jackdaw conducted herself on becoming the mate of the troop leader:

She knew within forty-eight hours exactly what she could allow herself, and I am sorry to say that she made the fullest use of it. . . . She did not stop at gestures of self-importance, as high-rankers of long standing nearly always do. No—she always had an active and malicious plan of attack ready at hand. In short, she conducted herself with the utmost vulgarity.

You think I humanize the animal? . . . What we are wont to call "human weakness" is, in reality, nearly always a pre-human factor and one which we have in common with the higher animals. Believe, me, I am not mistakenly assigning human properties to animals; on the contrary, I am showing you what an enormous animal inheritance remains in man, to this day. [p. 152]

In sum, whether, and how far, interspecies communication works for feelings and motives is an empirical question. On the whole, it does. *That* it does is not surprising given our evolutionary relationship, and the fact that it could often be quite dangerous to misconstrue the behavior of creatures outside one's species, and quite convenient to read it. Threats had to be understood, and useful warnings developed. And there is no special reason why the general nature of feelings, as opposed to their particular forms, should have changed past recognition. Particular forms do vary, which is why you have to know a good deal about a species to read its gestures reliably. But then they vary in human life too; culture does what it can to confuse us. The skills we develop for penetrating the curtain of culture probably help us in dealing with other species also.

To say this is not to deny that animals can have feelings that

23. For the techniques of ethological "motivation analysis," see ibid., p. 97.

are a complete mystery to us. What is it like to be an incubating gull? still more an emperor penguin?[24] What are chimpanzee carnivals? Why do elephants interest themselves deeply in a dead elephant, sometimes take the trouble to bury it, and remove and carry around tusks and bones from a skeleton?[25] Goodness knows. These are real questions. They are real because they all have an answer. Fresh understanding of the context could illuminate them. But they do not erode the central area where we know what is going on. Difficult cases crop up in every area of inquiry; they never give ground for general skepticism. Interspecies sympathy certainly encounters some barriers. So does sympathy between human beings. But the difficulties arising here cannot possibly mean that any attempt to reach out beyond the familiar lit circle of our own lives is doomed, delusive, or sentimental.

The Egoist's Blind Alley

Here we come to an important philosophical point about the otherness of others. Can we be concerned at all with anything which is not fundamentally the same as ourselves? Some philosophers have thought not—indeed, the idea has been latent in a great deal of European thought. Spinoza, for instance, puts the case about animals thus:

It is plain that the law against the slaughtering of animals is founded rather on vain superstition and womanish pity than on sound reason. The rational quest of what is useful to us further teaches us the neces-

24. They spend the Antarctic night standing without food on ice at almost lethal temperatures, nursing an egg. Of course this baffles our imagination. But not in the way that we are baffled when we try to imagine what it is like to be a star or a sewing machine. It is simply a much further-out version of the kind of bafflement we encounter if we try to think what it is like to be Mozart or a newborn baby. The imagination is *meant* for that kind of job.

25. See I. and O. Douglas-Hamilton, *Among the Elephants* (London, 1975), index entries under *Death*. This is perhaps a clearer case of a genuine problem. More information would eventually enable us to find the pattern into which this behavior fits: for instance, whether having known the dead elephant is a condition of it, whether the individuals prone to it are of his group, or have some other uniting property, whether they do it at any special time. Also, it would be useful to have reports of behavior to the dead on the part of other advanced species.

sity of associating ourselves with our fellow-men, but not with beasts, or things, whose nature is different from our own; we have the same rights in respect to them as they have in respect to us. Nay, as everyone's right is defined by his virtue, or power, men have far greater rights over beasts have over men. Still I do not deny that beasts feel; what I deny is, that we may not consult our own advantage and use them as we please, treating them in the way which best suits us; for their nature is not like ours, and their emotions are naturally different from human emotions.[26]

Many people today would, I think, simply echo this, including all the obvious confusions. What principles are involved here?

The foundations of Spinoza's ethics is Egoism. For him, each of us seeks merely his own. Each can only be concerned with what is like himself, and only in so far as it is like himself. This is not Hobbes's crude, political Egoism, which says that I can need others only for my outward advantage.[27] It allows for love of, and identification with, others—but only insofar as they are like oneself, are engaged on the same quest. And the aim of that quest is the intellectual love of God. But then, God too is not a being distinct from me; he is simply Everything. And Everything does indeed concern me; but only in so far as it is like me. This likeness Spinoza finds in the community of reason—in the intelligible order of the universe, which all individual intellects echo.

There are splendid things about Spinoza's morality, but they are not our business here. What is not splendid, what is downright wrong, is his notion about other people. What would a world be like in which we only cared for others in proportion as they were like ourselves, where we never welcomed or delighted in the fact that they were *different?*[28] Still more, what would a world be like where we only admitted that they had any claim on us in proportion to their likeness? Loving none but those who were mirror images of ourselves would be straight narcissism, fully extendible only to identical twins. Spinoza, of course, does

26. *Ethics,* Pt. 4, prop. 37, no. 1.
27. Nor did Hobbes himself confine himself to the crude kind. See p. 8.
28. Individuality is central to love, yet it is really difficult to fit that fact into the great rationalist tradition. See an admirable article by Shirley Robin Letwin, "Romantic Love and Christianity," *Philosophy,* 52 (1977).

not really mean this. What his rationalism demands is one single qualifying likeness, namely, that all parties should have reason. But he is not so unrealistic as to suppose that love is in fact merely a recognition of reason. He knows that we are concerned with other people's emotions. And he is anxious to show that virtue is to our interest, so he wants to claim that, in promoting the welfare of others, we are really promoting our own. So they must be like us emotionally. This is why he rules beasts out of the reckoning, on the ground that "their emotions are naturally different from human emotions." But this is an even less intelligible ground for excluding them from moral consideration than their irrationality is.[29] In what way do they have to be different? Human emotions themselves are not as standardized as tidy rationalists might hope. There is, among other confusing diversities, much natural difference brought about by age, and there is the difference of sex. What charge, for instance, is Spinoza actually making when he says that regard for animals shows a *womanish* pity? This is, I think, a fair example of a line drawn on the basis of a natural difference of emotions. Could there be anything especially rational about taking more notice of the feelings typical of one sex than of those typical of the other? Does intellectualist *machismo* have an intelligible basis?

Sex-linked moralities cannot really be much use. Not only is their potential efficiency halved by the fact that 50 percent of people belong to either sex. More important still, we all have the emotions of both sexes within us—not enough to realize them fully, but enough to need more, enough to make a single-sex world a poor one for anybody. A man without pity is a monster; so is a woman without courage. If there is something specifically wrong with the kind of pity normally felt by women, then it can be stated, and it ought to be, in other ways than just by mentioning the sex involved. Different cannot mean inferior here. Splitting the human race like that is not rational at all. Cultures in which the two sexes do operate separately, having each their own standards, customs, and sometimes even language, waste a great part of human potential. They narrow everyone's life. But

29. Discussed in Chap. 11.

they do it on the best Egoistic principles. People who, on the contrary, are prepared to "associate themselves" with those unlike them, certainly will meet difficulties, pains, and sometimes great dangers. But they stand the chance of growing and learning much more than they could have done had they stayed among their mirror images. Of course, too, even those who are like us are not like us in every way. And the ways in which they are not like us seem every bit as important for love as those in which they are. How can this be?

Kant cracked Spinoza's problem here, and his doing so is surely one of the most important things in his moral philosophy—quite as important as his work on freedom, and connected with it. He said that we value other people *because* they are other. The proper, sane, and rational way to view them, said Kant, is as ends in themselves, not as means to any end of ours, however exalted. The respect we have for them is the "consciousness of a worth which thwarts my self-love,"[30] that is, of something good we did not invent and do not own, something genuinely outside and over against us, capable of opposing our wishes. The economic metaphor of exchange, from which such words as *value, worth, preciousness* are derived, must be broken through here. Kant says that while things have value or price, people have something different, called dignity. The best choice of words, of course, varies with the context. But if we prefer still to talk of value and so on here, we must at least explicitly part company from Hobbes, who says that "the Value or Worth of a man is, as of all other things, his Price, namely, as much as would be given for the use of his Power."[31] Making a sacrifice for a friend is not just shifting an investment, trading for a gain. Our friends are indeed ours, but never in the sense in which property is ours, disposable at our will. A robot world, programmed carefully to one's own specifications, would be a desolation from which each of us would willingly fly even to the company of the usual set of unsatisfactory independent human beings.

The trouble with the Egoist is that he thinks of all our desires as flattened out on the pattern of hunger—tendencies to

30. *Grundlegung*, chap. 1, sec. 16, note (Paton tr., pp. 66–67).
31. *Leviathan*, Pt. 1, chap. 10.

ingest—or at most on that of sleep—tendencies to repeat internally things we have done before. But actually most of them are just as near to the pattern of curiosity—tendencies to find something new and see what unknown thing it involves us in. (Think of the child's progress to full physical activity, its constant attempts to wander.) The lines of life lead *outward.* In a social species, impulses of direct interest in the doings of others have to be very common, and (as Butler pointed out) the deliberate pursuit of our own advantage is a secondary business,[32] a way of partially organizing and using them—but never a possible substitute for them. Someone who *only* wants his own advantage and has no direct interest in anyone else's is a psychopath, and usually a disappointed one. He is in the same position as someone who wants to win a race but does not in the least care for running, sailing, swimming, or any other sport in which races are held. He wants a round trip ticket without knowing where to go.

It is quite true that in our outgoing dealings with others there is a rhythm of return; after going out and finding a new friend or place, we want to relate him or it to our established ideas. We find out how the friend likes our previous activities. But we want, too, to visit *his* previous life with him. We want things to happen which are not yet any part of our life at all. The sense of them revives us like air after a dungeon, lifts off the oppressive lid of the ego, whose weight was stifling us.

"Aha," the Egoist replies (swiftly becoming tautological), "so you like new experience when you find it, do you? Then clearly you undertake it for your own advantage. And this is true of everything, however unexpected and apparently selfless, which you finally choose to do. You need not think you can evade it by becoming a wanderer, an explorer or a martyr."

Now if the Egoist is just extending the notion of advantage to its wide everyday sense again, meaning merely "something we want," this is true enough, but trivial, because we can want things right outside ourselves, for instance, that man should reach the moon. If, however, he means something specific and interesting by it—that what we are trying to bring about is always really

32. Sermon 11, sec. 9. See my earlier discussion in Chap. 6.

some inner state or change in ourselves—he is simply crassly wrong. As Michael Frayn says,

The feeling lingers that it's all some sort of self-gratification, one way or another; that each of us is shut up inside himself, acting merely in order to produce an effect upon his own state of mind.
And sometimes we do behave like this. We know this kind of masturbatory feeling. But we recognize it by contrast with our feelings at other times! We don't start love-affairs to secure the stimulation of our pubic nerve. (That would be an insanely long way round to go, like buying a car to get the use of the cigar-lighter). . . . Our objectives are external to us (even our unworthy ones).

This is clearly right, since people often do things that will not be to either their outward or inward advantage. Indeed, "people cast themselves away like old boots—into intoxication, into addiction to intoxicants, into love, into religious and political irresponsibility. . . . We set events in motion, (some insane, some merely banal) in order to get ourselves caught up in them."[33] People, in fact, are not very prudent, even emotionally. And Egoism is not a report of existing psychological facts, but a reforming doctrine, an attempt to do something about this wasteful habit. Philosophers such as Spinoza want individuals to take themselves more seriously, to *be* themselves, to assert their independence and refuse to be lost or merged into their tribes and families. Western thought has long occupied itself with prising individuals loose from their surroundings in this way, with making them autonomous. Initially the process is enormously liberating. But, carried through systematically, it comes to a point where it means severing all personal bonds. (The Stoics accepted this, and there is much Stoicism in Spinoza.) At this point the program, like all simple moral programs pursued in isolation, becomes crazy, because it takes us into a temperature that will not support human life. It is not moral weakness that makes us need personal bonds, but the nature of our faculties, constantly involving us in enterprises, both practical and emotional, which we cannot complete alone. We must have people *unlike* ourselves. And our relation with them must *not* consist of an uneasy bargain whereby each constantly tries to bend the

33. *Constructions*, secs. 142, 144-147.

other his way and puts up only reluctantly with the intervals when the other prevails. It involves real outgoing sympathy, which is to say, the accepting of ends that are not, at the time, one's own ends at all, though acceptance may make them so. This is not inconsistent with *being oneself*, since oneself is not really designed as an exclusive system. But it *is* inconsistent with drawing a rigid line round those like one as the only beings with whom one should associate.

This, roughly sketched, is the answer to Egoism. It can be formulated either empirically or rationally. Butler put it empirically, by pointing out the facts about our social nature, and this is the side I have been most concerned with in this book. Kant put it rationally, showing how all our moral thinking, even at its crudest, requires such a notion of otherness, and notably how this is involved in the idea of a rational being. A rational being is someone who sees himself as a unit among others, not as the core of the universe. And I have suggested that, even for people dubious about many things in Kant, our ordinary notion of sanity requires this idea.[34]

Living in the Whole World

Kant, however, thought that treating others as ends was necessary or possible only within our own species. He drew a sharp line at the species border. Man, he said, "is certainly titular lord of nature, and, supposing that we regard nature as a teleological system, he is born to be its ultimate end." Or again, "The end is man. We can ask, 'Why do animals exist?' But to ask, 'Why does man exist?' is a meaningless question."[35] What about that? Kant is taking nature as a pyramid, converging towards a single end.

34. It is also involved in the insistence of modern linguistic philosophers on the publicity of language, which is at last getting rid of the solipsistic temptations introduced by Descartes. Certainly I think, therefore I am—But I also speak, therefore *you* are too. Indeed "I" makes no sense without "you." This Kantian point is common to philosophers as diverse as Wittgenstein, Ryle, and Martin Buber.

35. "Duties towards Animals and Spirits," *Lectures on Ethics*, p. 239. Clearly he was thinking of the reason for the animals' existing as provided by their usefulness to man.

This will not do, not only because we are not sure who forms the purpose. It makes no sense to consider the enormous range of animal species as existing as a *means* to anything, let alone us. They are not going in this direction at all. The oddity of suggesting that they are emerges rather pleasingly in an essay by the economist Kenneth E. Boulding.[36] He is explaining that there is no need to study animal behavior, since we have its raison d'être, man himself, the finished product, already before us. He writes, "The critical question is, how much we could learn about the jet plane from studying the wheelbarrow or even from studying the automobile—If the jet plane is man, the automobile perhaps is the mammal, the wheelbarrow the fish." This has to mean that all animals are devices for a single known purpose (apparently something parallel to rapid transport?), devices differing only in the degree of progress they have made toward efficiency. And now that we have Mark 12 before us, Mark 3 and Mark 7 are of interest only to industrial archaeologists.

This sort of thing leaves me speechless. A device can put another out of date only so far as they are means to the *same end*. Does Boulding think it just obvious what the aim of all human life actually is? And, having solved that question, does he think it clear how all other existing species—elephants and albatrosses, whales and tortoises and caribou—are just bungling and inadequate shots at the *same* target? Is there nothing to a giraffe except being a person manqué? And if, as Wells suggested, something more intelligent turned up, would that eliminate us without further question in favor of Mark 13? *Man is not something we have designed at all,* and innumerable things about the way he works are completely mysterious to us. Kant's question "Why does man exist?" is not at all meaningless; it has the perfectly good sense "How can he best live? To what way of life is he best adapted?" To deal with this, we need to understand adaptation. Evidence about it must be found in other species. And the same question, in the same sense, can be asked about them too.

People obsessed with the cost-benefit analysis pattern see no alternative to their own way of thinking, even though often they,

36. In *Man and Aggression*, ed. Ashley Montagu, p. 86.

like the rest of us, have a sense of chill, of oppression, of loneliness, as human life grows steadily narrower. The dungeon encloses us, the lid of the ego presses down. Under what compulsion? Why look at things this way? In *The Sovereignty of Good* Iris Murdoch writes, "I am looking out of my window in an anxious and resentful state of mind, brooding perhaps on some damage done to my prestige. Then suddenly I observe a hovering kestrel. In a moment everything is altered. The brooding self with its hurt vanity has disappeared. There is nothing now but kestrel. And when I return to thinking of the other matter it seems less important" (p. 84). Certainly we *could* (she goes on) think of this as a measure of mental hygiene, regard the kestrel as a device for regaining balance. But there is something perverse about doing so; "More naturally, as well as more properly, we take a self-forgetful pleasure in the sheer, alien pointless independent existence of animals, birds, stones and trees." This has to be right, because the release itself depends on the kestrel's not being such a device. If we found that we were in Disneyland, with plastic kestrels going up at carefully randomized intervals, the entire point would be lost.

What we need here is to get rid of the language of means and ends, and use instead that of part and whole. Man needs to form part of a whole much greater than himself, one in which other members excel him in innumerable ways. He is adapted to live in one. Without it, he feels imprisoned; the lid of the ego presses down on him.

The world in which the kestrel moves, the world that it sees, is, and will always be, entirely beyond us. That there are such worlds all around us is an essential feature of our world. Calling the bird's existence "pointless" means only that it is not a device for any human end. It does not need that external point. It is in some sense—a sense that can certainly do with study—an end in itself.[37]

37. Philosophers often accuse Kant of confusion because he uses this phrase. If they just mean that what he is saying is not wholly clear, they are right; it is rather a difficult thing to express. But often they mean rather that it doesn't make sense in an Egoist framework—that "ends" are, by definition, internal. But Kant is denying this. He really is trying to break out of the Egoist squirrel cage. And common sense is surely with him.

We may throw some light on the difficulties here by looking at the same problem where it crops up at the heart of Kant's aesthetic. Kant was much occupied with the Sublime, which was the (quite convenient) eighteenth-century name for things that impress us, not by being what we already want (like the Beautiful), but by their vastness and total disregard of our needs—in a word, by their absolute Otherness. The sea is sublime; so are mountains and deserts. So even, sometimes, are very small things, if they are exceedingly strange and unaccountable.[38]

Kant's careful analysis of this element in experience, and the seriousness with which he treats it, are admirable. It is plain that he was a man genuinely disposed to be bowled over by such things. But he finds a real difficulty in understanding this concept. *What* is actually sublime? Here the rules of his Rationalist framework hamper him. It can hardly, he says, be the actual sea and mountains, for they are just dead matter, so many tons of basalt or H_2O. How can one revere that? He sees that sheer size is often central to the experience. Yet size impresses us only by contrast to the size of our own body, which seems to him a contingent matter. So he concludes that what is sublime is not the objects themselves, but what they stand for, that is, the vastness of the human task. "The feeling of the Sublime in nature is respect for our own vocation."[39] In part this is right. The vast does stand for the difficult, the not-yet-attempted. But it has to be more than just a symbol. It has to matter in itself, or it cannot symbolize effectively. Powerful symbols are not just dispensable manmade boxes in which we deposit ideas for convenience, retrieving them unchanged when we need them. Kant's point is that mountains and distances constitute difficulties for us, and that difficulties teach us our weakness. But mountains are not *just* examples of difficulties. They are not just wastefully extended treadmills. They tell us not only that we are small, but that they are great. Indeed the first point would have no meaning without the second. If they were merely educational devices to bring home our weakness to us, we could forget about them once we had seen the point. Or, if we decided still to use them as

38. *Critique of Judgement.* See the whole section on The Sublime.
39. Ibid., Meredith tr., p. 106.

a reminder, we should think of them, I suppose, in a resigned sort of way, as we do regard purely educational devices, perhaps rather as we think of our alarm clocks and desk calendars. (Did the Romans regard the skeletons at their feasts in this way?)

The truth is, it is no contingent fact about us that our bodies are the size they are. We—ourselves—are not, as Descartes suggested, purely mental creatures. We are not tentatively considering possible incarnations. We—ourselves—are members of a vulnerable species, easily destroyed in an avalanche, with a place on this particular planet, and none anywhere else.[40] To such beings, there is no way in which x million gallons of H_2O (including saline impurities) does not constitute an enormous and sublime ocean, nor in which whales and albatrosses, capable of dealing with it in any state of agitation, are not sublime creatures. Stunting this response is stunting our highest faculties. For (what is less often mentioned than the vulnerability) we are receptive, imaginative beings, adapted to celebrate and rejoice in the existence, quite independent of ourselves, of the other beings on this planet. Not only does our natural sympathy reach out easily beyond the barrier of species but we rejoice in the mere existence of plants and lifeless bodies—*not* regarding them just as furniture provided to stimulate our pampered imagination.

Literary criticism often does not look at things this way; it tends to an official doctrine that the physical universe matters only insofar as we can make poetry out of it. I think this is cockeyed, and that no poetry of the slightest value could be made on this supposition. The trouble is, however, a discrepancy between theory and practice on the matter, not only (as I have suggested) in Kant himself, but in great writers who have followed him. For instance, Coleridge, explaining his own dejection, his failure to respond to a splendid sunset, wrote

> O Lady, we receive but what we give,
> And in our life alone does Nature live,
> Ours is her wedding garment, ours her shroud.[41]

---

40. As far as I know, the doctrine of the Resurrection of the Body means that this is the proper view in a Christian context as well as in an agnostic one.
41. "Dejection, an Ode."

But this isn't and couldn't be true, and the end of that very poem shows that he didn't believe it. As Iris Murdoch says in *The Sovereignty of Good,* "I do not think that any of the great romantics really believed that we receive but what we give and in our life alone does nature live, although the lesser ones tended to follow Kant's lead and use nature as an occasion for exalted self-feeling. The great romantics, including the one I have just quoted, transcended 'romanticism.' . . . Art, and by art from now on I mean good art, not fantasy art, affords us a pure delight in the independent existence of what is excellent" (p. 85). Man is not adapted to live in a mirror-lined box, generating his own electric light and sending for selected images from outside when he happens to need them. Darkness and a bad smell are all that can come of that. We need the vast world, and it must be a world that does not need us; a world constantly capable of surprising us, a world we did not program, since only such a world is the proper object of wonder. Any kind of Humanism which deprives us of this, which insists on treating the universe as a mere projection screen for showing off human capacities, cripples and curtails humanity. "Humanists" often do this, because where there is wonder they think they smell religion, and they move hastily in to crush that unclean thing.[42] But things much more unclean than traditional religion will follow the death of wonder. In truth, as I have suggested, wonder, the sense of otherness, is one of the sources of religion (not the other way around), but it is also the source of curiosity and every vigorous use of our faculties, and an essential condition of sanity. And there is less difference than some people suppose between its religious and its scientific expression. When the Lord answered Job out of the whirlwind, he only said what any true naturalist may say to himself, whether he believes in any god or not.

---

42. *Ecrasez l'infâme:* Voltaire's remark about the political iniquities of the Roman Church. But there are other things to worry about today. John Passmore in *Man's Responsibility for Nature,* an otherwise excellent book, is constantly brought up short by the fact that what seems like a helpful reaction to ecological crime also seems like a religious one. But the great religions have combined innumerable elements, many of them essential to life. These cannot be abandoned just because of the way people have misused them in the past.

Hast thou entered into the treasures of the snow? or hast thou seen the treasures of the hail? . . .

Who hath divided a watercourse for the overflowing of waters . . .

To cause it to rain on the earth where no man is, on the wilderness, wherein there is no man,

To satisfy the desolate and waste ground, and to cause the bud of the tender herb to spring forth? . . .

Canst thou bind the sweet influences of the Pleiades, or loose the bands of Orion? . . .

Canst thou draw out Leviathan with an hook? . . .

Will he make a covenant with thee? wilt thou take him as a servant for ever? . . .

He esteemeth iron as straw, and brass as rotten wood. . . .

He maketh the deep to boil like a pot, he maketh the sea like a pot of ointment.

He maketh a path to shine after him; one would think the deep to be hoary,

Upon earth there is not his like, who is made without fear.

He beholdeth all high things; he is a king over all the children of pride.[43]

That is the sort of way Charles Darwin looked at the physical universe, and, unless I am much mistaken, Aristotle too.[44] That is the sort of universe in which our nature is adapted to live, not one alien and contemptible to us, from which we must be segregated. As I understand Humanism, this is its message. Humanism cannot only mean destroying God; its chief job is to understand and save man. But man can neither be understood nor saved alone.

43. Job, 38 and 41.

44. See, for instance, *Ethics* 6.7, where he takes it as obvious that man is not the best thing in the world. Recent Humanism tends to be more arrogant. Thus Keynes, speaking for Moore's circle, remarks, "We lacked reverence, as Lawrence observed and as Ludwig Wittgenstein also used to say—for everything and everyone" (*Two Memoirs*, p. 99). But contemplation *without* reverence is a very odd thing.

Bibliography

Alpers, Antony. *A Book of Dolphins.* London: John Murray, 1965.

Anscombe, G. E. M. "Brute Facts." *Analysis,* 19 (1958).

———. *Intention.* Oxford: Blackwell; Ithaca: Cornell University Press, 1957.

Ardrey, Robert. *The Territorial Imperative.* New York: Atheneum, 1966. London: Collins, 1967.

Austin, J. L. *How to Do Things with Words.* Oxford: Oxford University Press; Cambridge, Mass.: Harvard University Press, 1962.

———. *Philosophical Papers.* Oxford: Oxford University Press, 1970.

Benedict, Ruth. *Patterns of Culture.* Boston: Houghton Mifflin, 1934. London: Routledge & Kegan Paul, 1935.

Blurton Jones, N. G. "An Ethological Study of Some Aspects of Social Behaviour of Children in Nursery School." In *Primate Ethology,* ed. Desmond Morris.

Buber, Martin. *I and Thou.* New York: Scribner's, 1958.

Bueler, Lois E. *Wild Dogs of the World.* New York: Stein & Day, 1973. London: Constable, 1974.

Butler, Bishop Joseph. *Sermons* (1726). Ed. W. R. Matthews. London: Bell, 1969.

Carrington, Richard. *Elephants.* London: Chatto & Windus, 1958.

Carthy, J. D., and F. J. Ebling. *The Natural History of Aggression.* London and New York: Academic Press, 1964.

Chomsky, Noam. *Language and Mind.* New York: Harcourt, Brace & World, 1968.

Clark, Stephen. *The Moral Status of Animals.* Oxford: Clarendon Press, 1977.

Darwin, Charles. *The Expression of the Emotions in Man and Animals* (1872). Chicago: University of Chicago Press, 1965.

Dent, Nicholas. "Duty and Inclination." *Mind,* 83 (1974).

Descartes. *Philosophical Writings.* Tr. P. T. Geach and G. E. M. Anscombe. London: Nelson's University Paperbacks, 1954. Indianapolis: Bobbs-Merrill, 1971.

Dobzhansky, Theodosius. *Mankind Evolving.* New Haven: Yale University Press, 1962.

Douglas-Hamilton, I., and O. Douglas-Hamilton. *Among the Elephants.* London: Collins; New York: Viking, 1975.

Eibl-Eibesfeldt, Irenäus. *Love and Hate.* Tr. Geoffrey Strachan. London: Methuen, 1971. New York: Holt, Rinehart, & Winston, 1972.

Foot, Philippa R. "Moral Arguments." *Mind,* 67 (1968).

——. "Moral Beliefs." *Proceedings of the Aristotelian Society,* 59 (1958–9). Reprinted in *Theories of Ethics,* ed. P. Foot.

——. "When Is a Principle a Moral Principle?" *Proceedings of the Aristotelian Society,* Supplementary Vol. 28 (1954).

——, ed. *Theories of Ethics.* Oxford: Oxford University Press, 1967.

Ford, E. B. *Ecological Genetics.* London: Methuen, 1964.

Frayn, Michael. *Constructions.* London: Wildwood House, 1974.

Friedrich, Heinz, ed. *Man and Animal.* London: Paladin, 1972.

Frisch, Karl von. *Bees: Their Vision, Chemical Senses, and Language.* Rev. ed. Ithaca: Cornell University Press, 1971.

Geach, Peter. "Good and Evil." *Analysis,* 17 (1956). Reprinted in *Theories of Ethics,* ed. Philippa Foot.

——. "Omnipotence." *Philosophy,* 48 (1973).

Geist, Valerius. *Mountain Sheep and Man in the Northern Wilds.* Ithaca: Cornell University Press, 1975.

Goodall, Jane van Lawick. *In the Shadow of Man.* Boston: Houghton Mifflin; London: Collins, 1971.

——. *The Innocent Killers.* New York: Ballantine, 1970. London: Collins, 1974.

——. "Mother-Offspring Relations in Free-Ranging Chimpanzees." In *Primate Ethology,* ed. Desmond Morris.

Harrisson, Barbara. *Orang-utan.* London: Collins, 1962.

Hinde, R. A. *Animal Behavior.* New York: McGraw-Hill, 1966.

——. "Ethological Models and the Concept of Drive." *British Journal for the Philosophy of Science,* 6 (1956).

——. "Some Recent Trends in Ethology." In *Psychology: A Study of a Science,* Vol. 2, ed. Sigmund Koch. New York: McGraw-Hill, 1959.

Hooff, J. A. R. A. M. van, "The Facial Displays of the Catarrhine Monkeys and Apes." In *Primate Ethology,* ed. Desmond Morris.

Huizinga, J. *Homo Ludens* (1938). New York: Harper & Row; London: Paladin, 1970.

Huxley, Julian. *The Courtship Habits of the Great Crested Grebe* (1914). London: Cape, 1968.

Kant, Immanuel. *Critique of Judgement.* Tr. J. C. Meredith. Oxford: Oxford University Press, 1952.

———. *Grundlegung zur Metaphysik der Sitten.* Tr. H. J. Paton, with title *The Moral Law.* London: Hutchinson University Library, 1948. Tr. Lewis W. Beck, with title *Foundations of the Metaphysic of Morals.* Indianapolis: Bobbs-Merrill, 1959.

———. *Lectures on Ethics.* Tr. Louis Infield. London: Methuen, 1930.

Keynes, John Maynard. *Two Memoirs.* London: Hart Davis; New York: Kelley, 1949.

Köhler, Wolfgang. *The Mentality of Apes* (1925). Harmondsworth: Pelican, 1957.

Kovesi, Julius. *Moral Notions.* London: Routledge & Kegan Paul; New York: Humanities Press, 1967.

Linden, Eugene. *Apes, Men and Language.* New York: Saturday Review Press, 1974. Harmondsworth: Penguin, 1976.

Lockley, R. M. *The Private Life of the Rabbit.* London: Corgi, 1954.

Loizos, Caroline. "Play Behaviour in Higher Primates: A Review." In *Primate Ethology,* ed. Desmond Morris.

Lorenz, Konrad. *Civilized Man's Eight Deadly Sins.* Tr. M. K. Wilson. London: Methuen, 1973. New York: Harcourt Brace Jovanovich, 1974.

———. *Evolution and Modification of Behavior.* Chicago: University of Chicago Press, 1965. London: Methuen, 1966.

———. *King Solomon's Ring.* Tr. M. K. Wilson. New York: Crowell; London: Methuen, 1952.

———. *Man Meets Dog.* Tr. M. K. Wilson. Boston: Houghton Mifflin, 1955. London: Methuen, 1964.

———. *On Aggression.* Tr. M. K. Wilson. New York: Harcourt, Brace & World, 1963. London: Methuen, 1966.

Marais, Eugene. *My Friends the Baboons.* London: Methuen, 1939.

Mayr, Ernst. "Behavior Programs and Evolutionary Strategies." *American Scientist,* 62 (1974).

Mead, Margaret. *Growing Up in New Guinea.* New York: Morrow; Harmondsworth: Penguin, 1930.

———. *New Lives for Old.* New York: Morrow; London: Gollancz, 1956.

Midgley, M. "The Game Game." *Philosophy,* 49 (1974).

———. "Is Moral a Dirty Word?" *Philosophy,* 47 (1972).

———. "The Neutrality of the Moral Philosopher." *Proceedings of the Aristotelian Society,* Supplementary Vol. 48 (1974).

Montagu, Ashley. *Man in Process.* New York: Mentor, 1961.

———, ed. *Man and Aggression.* Cleveland: World, 1961. Oxford: Oxford University Press, 1968.

Moore, G. E. *Principia Ethica.* Cambridge: Cambridge University Press, 1948.

Morgan, Elaine. *The Descent of Woman.* New York: Stein & Day, 1972.

Morris, Desmond, *The Biology of Art.* New York: Knopf; London: Methuen, 1962.

——. *The Naked Ape.* New York: McGraw-Hill; London: Cape, 1967.

——, ed. *Primate Ethology.* London: Weidenfeld & Nicolson, 1967.

Morris, Ramona, and Desmond Morris. *Men and Apes.* London: Hutchinson, 1966.

——, and Desmond Morris. *Men and Pandas.* London: Hutchinson, 1966. New York: McGraw-Hill, 1967.

——, and Desmond Morris. *Men and Snakes.* London: Hutchinson, 1965.

Mowat, Farley. *Never Cry Wolf.* Boston: Little, Brown; London: Ballantine, 1963.

Murdoch, Iris. *The Sovereignty of Good.* London: Routledge & Kegan Paul, 1970.

Passmore, John. *Man's Responsibility for Nature.* London: Duckworth, 1971. New York: Scribner's, 1974.

Peters, R. S., ed. *Nature and Conduct.* Royal Institute of Philosophy Lectures, Vol. 8. London: Macmillan; New York: St. Martin's, 1975.

Quinton, Antony. "Has Man an Essence?" In *Nature and Conduct,* ed. R. S. Peters.

Ryle, Gilbert. *The Concept of Mind.* London: Hutchinson, 1949.

——. *Dilemmas.* Cambridge: Cambridge University Press, 1964.

Sanderson, Ivan. *The Dynasty of Abu.* London: Cassell, 1960. New York: Knopf, 1962.

Sartre, J-P. *Existentialism and Humanism.* Tr. Philip Mairet. London: Eyre Methuen, 1958.

Schaller, George. *The Year of the Gorilla.* Chicago: University of Chicago Press; London: Collins, 1964.

Schneirla, T. C. "Some Conceptual Trends in Comparative Psychology." *Psychological Bulletin,* Nov. 1952.

Simpson, George Gaylord. *The Major Features of Evolution.* New York: Columbia University Press, 1953.

Singer, Peter. *Animal Liberation.* London: Cape, 1976.

——, ed. *Animal Rights and Human Obligations.* Englewood Cliffs, N. J.: Prentice-Hall, 1976.

Skinner, B. F. *The Behavior of Organisms.* New York: Appleton-Century, 1938.

——. *Beyond Freedom and Dignity.* New York: Knopf, 1971. London: Cape, 1972.

——. *Science and Human Behavior.* New York: Macmillan, 1953.

Smart, J. J. C., and Bernard Williams. *Utilitarianism: For and Against.* Cambridge: Cambridge University Press, 1973.

Stevenson, D. L. *Ethics and Language.* New Haven: Yale University Press, 1945.

——. *Facts and Values.* New Haven: Yale University Press, 1963.

Storr, Anthony. *Human Aggression.* New York: Atheneum; Harmondsworth: Penguin, 1968.

Tinbergen, Niko. *Curious Naturalists.* New York: Anchor Books, 1968. Harmondsworth: Penguin Education, 1974.

———. *The Herring Gull's World.* London: Collins, 1953. New York: Basic, 1961.

———. *Social Behavior in Animals.* London: Methuen, 1953.

———. *The Study of Instinct.* Oxford: Oxford University Press, 1951.

Warnock, Geoffrey. *Contemporary Moral Philosophy.* London: Macmillan; New York: St. Martin's, 1967.

Wickler, W. *The Sexual Code.* London: Weidenfeld & Nicolson, 1969. New York: Doubleday, 1972.

Williams, Bernard. *Morality.* Harmondsworth: Pelican; New York: Harper & Row, 1972.

———. *Problems of the Self.* Cambridge: Cambridge University Press, 1972.

Williams, George C. *Adaptation and Natural Selection.* Princeton: Princeton University Press, 1966.

Wilson, Edward O. *Sociobiology: The New Synthesis.* Cambridge, Mass.: Harvard University Press, 1975.

Wilsson, Lars. *My Beaver Colony.* New York: Doubleday; London: Souvenir, 1968.

Index

About the Author

MARY MIDGLEY is a Senior Lecturer in Philosophy at the University of Newcastle upon Tyne, England, where she has been teaching since 1963. The author holds a degree from Somerville, College, Oxford, and has contributed to the *New Statesman*, the BBC, *Twentieth Century* and *Philosophy*.